CAMDEN
A POLITICAL HISTORY

Piers Wauchope

▲SHAW BOOKS▲

First published in Great Britain in 2010 by
Shaw Books
11A Upper Grosvenor Road,
Tunbridge Wells
TN1 2DU

A CIP Catalogue of this book is available from
the British Library

ISBN: 978-0-9565206-0-9

Cover designed by Sarah Sherrington

Typeset by www.chandlerbookdesign.co.uk

Printed in Great Britain by
Ashford Colour Press Ltd.

This book is dedicated to all
Camden's councillors

– past, present and future.

Unnumber'd suppliants croud Preferment's gate,
A thirst for wealth, and burning to be great;
Delusive Fortune hears th'incessant call,
They mount, they shine, evaporate, and fall.

The Vanity of Human Wishes, by Samuel Johnson, written in 1748
"in the course of one morning in that small house beyond
the church at Hampstead".

CONTENTS

5

1978-1982
Roy Shaw: the battle with the Left

Ken Livingstone and the housing committee; Frank Dobson selected to replace Jeger; the NUPE strike, the "Winter of Discontent" and the Camden supplement; rate increases; the May1979 general election; the "Right to Buy"; rents up by £1; rates up 31%; housing subsidy and rate support grant cut; Shaw's "U Turn"; attack by director of housing; Neil Fletcher's leadership challenge; supplementary rate; rate rebellion and the 42% increase; Nuclear Free Zone and police harassment of minorities; Anne Sofer defects to SDP; another supplementary rate; the St Pancras North GLC by election; threat from the SDP; the 1982 borough election.

6

1982-1986
Phil Turner: the Left triumphant

The Falklands War; the police committee, Kate Allen and the Women's Committee; an Asian coup at the CCCR; the race committee; the new Tories; Marx's centenary; George Shire; Mandela Street; the 1983 general election; Labour splits over rents; the abolition of the GLC; the Rates Act; Decentralisation; Kodikara appointed director of social services; the Brighton bombing and Camden's response; Homeless Persons Unit strike; Homeless Bengalis occupy the Town Hall; Latham, Kirk and Sumray held by protestors; Turner weeps, Livingstone acts (as Santa); Rate capping; refusal to set a rate; again and again and again; Labour group splits; rate set on fifth attempt; Lesbians; the 1986 council elections; Labour triumphant.

7

1986-1990
Tony Dykes: Left and Far Left

Conservative collapse; first Liberal SDP Alliance councillors; Dykes replaces Turner; rate capping defeated by the Banque Paribas Loan; future Labour government to bail out Camden; the Sinn Fein address; the Roundhouse Black Arts Centre; Gay & Lesbian unit; Police Consultative Group riots; Labour splits; £56m budget deficit; 1987 general election; more Labour splits; Dykes sacks the left wingers; cuts in grants to voluntary groups; no surcharge for the rates rebels; Dykes sacks the right wingers; Roy Shaw and "The 1990 Campaign Group"; Anti-Poll Tax Campaign; failure of the Direct Services Department; Camden sets the Poll Tax.

2006
Raj Chada: the bitter end

The election issues; Labour Party selection; infighting in the
Conservative Party; The LibDems target Camden; Crime and
policing; parking; Miliband, Tony Blair and the ALMO; the Kentish
Town Baths; the Greens and Respect; The New Journal does its
bit; Chada in Gospel Oak; the Campaign across the borough;
high turnout; no overall majority; the LibDem offer of coalition;
a pact to exclude Labour.

Appendices

Index

GLOSSARY OF ABBREVIATIONS

ALMO	Arms Length Management Organisation
CCCR	Camden Committee for Community Relations
CCT	Compulsory Competitive Tendering
CND	Campaign for Nuclear Disarmament
CPO	Compulsory Purchase Order
CPZ	Controlled Parking Zone
DCH	Defend Council Housing
DoE	Department of the Environment
DSD	Direct Services Department
GLC	Greater London Council
IDeA	Improvement and Development Agency for Local Government
ILEA	Inner London Education Authority (abolished 1990)
LCC	London County Council
MTC	Migrant Training Company
NALGO	National Association of Local Government Officers
NUPE	National Union of Public Employees
Ofsted	Office for Standards in Education

PHAG	Primrose Hill Action Group
PFI	Private Finance Initiative
PLUG	Public Libraries Users' Group
SDP	Social Democratic Party
SOLACE	Society of Local Authority Chief Executives
SSA	Standard Spending Assessment
UCLAF	Unité de Coordination de la Lutte Anti-Fraude
UTA	The St Pancras United Tenants Association

Preface

A political history of this kind, of a single local authority, has not been attempted before. It is not a conventional history. There is no attempt to catalogue and analyse the provision of services or the management of finances. It is a record of what seemed to be important at the time, and an illustration of the fact that it is in the nature of politics to give importance to matters that often do not actually matter at all.

I had intended to write this for some time, and spoke to Roy Shaw about it, but it was not until after he descended into his final unhappy illness that it struck me that I must write an account, not so much of my time on the council, but of the council over the years. The catalyst was a conversation I had with a new (2006) councillor who told me of an impending by election in Haverstock. "That old Labour bloke", said the new councillor, "what's his name –he's standing down through ill health".

By "what's his name", he meant Roy Shaw, the man who had dominated Camden politics for over a decade, who had led the council during the most difficult of times, and who had continued to affect the running of the council long after his political obituary had been written. He was a man who had devoted his life to local government in general and to Camden in particular. He had been on the winning side in fifteen consecutive council elections and had been a councillor continuously from 1956 to 2007. Although greatly respected, his life of service left him with nothing other than an OBE and the many friendships he had made over the years. Unmarried, he was, before his final removal to a nursing home, alone in a one bedroom council flat. It seemed to me that his immediate successors would not even learn his name, let alone have any idea of what he did. The same goes for so many councillors of the past: men and women who gave up great parts of their lives to the better administration of Camden and its political struggles, and whose final reward is to be forgotten.

In order not to be seen to be trying to influence any future elections, I have covered the period only up to the council elections of 2006. I am very grateful to all the council officers and councillors, past and present, of all parties who have helped me in writing this book. Nevertheless, all the mistakes that may be found in what follows are entirely the result of my own ignorance and prejudice.

Why those knowledgeable and erudite newspaper editors, the twin colossi of Camden's press, Gerry Isaaman, formerly of the *Ham & High,* and Eric Gordon of the *New Journal,* have not written an account of Camden, I cannot tell. I hope they will, and that my effort may one day be seen as a stop-gap for the greater work yet to come.

Piers Wauchope
5 Pump Court
The Temple
January 2010

Acknowledgements

Almost all the *Ham & High* photographs for the 1980s were donated to the Camden Local Studies and Archives Centre above Holborn Library on Theobalds Road, and I am indebted to Nigel Sutton —for so many years the photographer for the *Ham & High*- for his permission to reproduce many of his photographs in this book. I am likewise indebted to Chris Taylor, then and now a freelance photographer, who has also been kind enough to let me use his work.

The earlier photographs generally come from the Harvey Johns collection donated to the Local Studies Centre on the final closure of the studios, and many of the formal portraits are old Camden press office photographs held by the Local Studies and Archives Centre. I am especially grateful to the staff at the centre, especially Aidan Flood, Tudor Allen and Richard Knight, for their courteous assistance in guiding me through the centre's collection of photographs and newspapers.

The last four photographs have been released to me by the *Camden New Journal*, for which I am very grateful.

The central section of photographs is taken from *Camden Life*, with kind permission of the London Borough of Camden.

I have also copied a few photographs from private collections, and in some cases I have been unable to establish ownership of the copyright for which, given the nature of this book, I hope that I may be forgiven.

I am also most grateful to Richad Lefley of Camden's democratic services for digging up old election records without which the appendices would have been a difficult task.

Before Camden, Hampstead, Holborn and St Pancras

Camden Town, is the western outpost of the East End of London, and does not exist officially. No authority recognises it. All that can be said about its boundaries —for it is real enough- is that they run somewhere between the Euston Road and the black, rat ridden Grand Union Canal, the Nash terraces in Regent's Park and the great railway jungle of King's Cross, Euston and St Pancras. It is impossible to be more definite, for there is no Camden Town except insofar as people say they live there, and not, say, in Kentish Town or King's Cross or Chalk Farm....There is nothing monumental or historic about Camden Town. Its great buildings are the pseudo-Egyptian Black Cat Cigarette factory, the baroque music hall, and the austere red brick baronial of the Rowton House lodgings for single working men. It is Victorian, except for the south west, now blitzed and slum-cleared, and the beautiful grey, black and yellow Mornington Crescent. The Irish with their nose for Georgian architecture, have settled there, and the coloured seamen drink in the pub at the corner, where they can see the statue of Richard Cobden, the only man in Camden Town with a monument. What gives Camden Town its special air is simply the fact that its ordinariness is slightly démodé. Somehow it has stuck fast in the period when Sickert painted it, and Bernard Shaw campaigned to get it to elect him to the LCC.

Eric Hobsbawn, *Lilliput, April 1947*

I n Harold MacMillan's last year as prime minister, the Local Government Act 1963 was steered through parliament. It abolished the London County Council (LCC) and the twenty eight London metropolitan boroughs. London's boundaries were pushed deep into the Home Counties annexing great swathes of Kent, Surrey and Essex. Middlesex was wiped from the map and Barnet was plucked from Hertfordshire. The Greater London Council (GLC) was formed to govern the new Greater London which had a population over twice that of the old London County and which covered an area five times bigger. The new municipality was divided into thirty two London boroughs, the inner twelve of which were formed by amalgamating the old metropolitan boroughs. It had to happen: larger municipal units were expected to rationalise services, provide greater efficiencies, and enjoy significant economies of scale which would keep the rate bills down. Elections for the new councils were set for May 1964, and after a year of coexistence with the old Metropolitan boroughs, the new London boroughs would assume their powers on 1 April 1965.

Parliament was faced with a difficult decision concerning which metropolitan boroughs should be joined together to form each of the new inner London boroughs. Some boroughs, even though geographically adjacent, appeared culturally to be miles apart. "The most extraordinary amalgamation," Lord (Herbert) Morrison told the House of Lords, is "between the respectable Conservative borough of Hampstead and the former red flag borough of St Pancras. It is an extraordinary marriage. If it does not lead to divorce I shall be very surprised". The marriage was not exactly popular on either side. The Labour majority in St Pancras wanted to merge with (Labour) Islington or (Labour) Finsbury. Hampstead Conservatives wanted to join (Conservative) Marylebone or, failing that, (Conservative) Hendon. Neither got their way, and marriage it was to be, although the addition of (Conservative) Holborn, the smallest borough in London, into the ménage took some of the sting out of the proposals as far as the Tories were concerned. The population of the two Tory boroughs of Hampstead (99,000 inhabitants) and Holborn (22,000) together all but matched Labour St Pancras (125,000). At the time of the amalgamation, St Pancras had an overwhelming majority of Labour councillors, but it also had had the least stable political history, whereas both Hampstead and Holborn had been run by the Conservatives since the 1940s[1]. The boundaries of the new borough also coincided with three parliamentary constituencies: the solidly Labour St Pancras North; the staunchly Conservative Hampstead; and the volatile Holborn & St Pancras South.

Hampstead, once the village of Keats and Constable on the heights overlooking London Town, had enjoyed a quiet political history as a metropolitan borough on the northern flank of the County of London. Ever since the political parties had imposed themselves on municipal

---

[1] Although Labour had taken control of Holborn for one term just after the war.

BEFORE CAMDEN, HAMPSTEAD,
HOLBORN AND ST PANCRAS

politics, it had been dominated by the Conservative Party. Although the parties greatly differed on subjects such as the need for a direct labour force and the level of council house building, it was an inclusive domination and generally polite enough. There was even talk of making the leader of the Labour group (Florence Cayford) mayor, and when the new Swiss Cottage library was opened in 1963, every member of the libraries committee, of all parties, was included in the line up to greet the queen. To the rest of the country (or at least to *Daily Telegraph* readers) Hampstead was typified by that wealthy socialist, "the Hampstead thinker" (so famously caricatured in Peter Simple's *Way of the World* column, in which the moneyed, uncompromising Communist snob, Anna Dutt-Pauker lives in her luxurious Hampstead mansion, Marxmount). Accepting the reality of liberal Hampstead, the conservatism of Hampstead Tories was often of a type barely recognisable outside its own boundaries. It was what the Thatcherites would come to describe as "wet".[2]

By the early 1960s, the Conservative domination of the borough was under threat. The Labour Party had a stronghold in the working class Kilburn ward and had managed to double their number of councillors in the 1962 election by also taking all six seats in the adjoining Priory ward. But the Labour vote was negligible in the rest of the borough, and the Tories faced a growing challenge from the Liberal Party. The Liberal campaign in the 1962 elections had pressed the Conservatives hard. In every ward that they contested the Liberals got over a thousand votes and they came close seconds in every ward that the Conservatives won. For the first time the Liberals took three of the six seats in Hampstead Town. Their councillors were in electoral terms attractive: Archie MacDonald, who had been briefly the assiduous MP for Selkirk and Roxburgh in 1950-51, and the two prolific novelists, Ernest Raymond and Pamela Frankau. Miss Frankau had topped the poll with 1503 votes,

2   On the subject of wet: 1961 was the year of the Hampstead swimming baths regulations debate. Enid Wistrich, who was elected to the council in the following year, was told that she could not wear her two piece swimming costume in the baths. Under the 1937 regulations, women were to wear costumes "approved by the superintendent" that were "of one piece devoid of openwork". Promising that "this is no socialist intrigue", her husband, Ernest Wistrich, a Labour councillor, forced a debate on the issue to amend the regulations. "It is time", said Victor Lyon, "that he bought his wife a new bathing costume". The chairman of the baths and washhouses committee, Norman Oatway (yet to be Camden's first Conservative mayor), argued that two piece costumes were unsuitable for indoor swimming as the tops could come off causing embarrassment all round. The motion was passed unanimously. "A great step forward", said Councillor Wistrich.

which was all the more impressive as she overturned a Tory majority of twelve hundred. The council in 1962 comprised 32 Conservatives, 12 Labour and three Liberals.

The borough of Holborn bridged the City of London and the West End, an area which commercial estate agents have since designated Midtown. It was the smallest of the twenty eight metropolitan boroughs, both in area (407 acres or 1·6km²) and in population. Importantly, as a commercial district Holborn brought in more in commercial rates than did the other two boroughs put together. The ruling Conservative group on Holborn council relied heavily on the support of the business vote, cast by those electors who did not live in the borough but who paid business rates there. In one way the amalgamation hit Holborn harder than the other two boroughs: the 42 Holborn councillors elected in 1962 were to be replaced by six councillors representing only two wards in the new Camden.

The largest of the three metropolitan boroughs was St Pancras, and politically it was the most influential. It joined the new borough with an overwhelming Labour majority, whereas both the other boroughs joined with Conservative majorities. For the first forty four years of Camden's existence, all but three of the early years (1968-71) saw the borough ruled by a Labour group, and in the early years that Labour group was dominated by former St Pancras councillors. While the Conservatives generally had their political roots in Hampstead, the new ruling class in Camden was formed of the political successors to St Pancras. As if this point needed emphasis, the new Camden councillors took their seats in St Pancras Town Hall which they then renamed Camden Town Hall.

Cosmopolitan St Pancras had long had Irish, Jewish and Italian councillors, including John Sperni, mayor in 1932 who as a serving councillor was interned during the war for "fascist sympathies".[3] Nevertheless, according to the Labour councillor Peggy Duff, the borough's politics had "been abysmally dull. Since the end of the war the council had swung with each election, first Labour, then Tory, then Labour again, and there was not all that much difference between them. Certainly there was much more cooperation between the very orthodox Labour leader, Fred Powe, and the Tories, than between Fred and his backbenchers. Council meetings were brief. Occasionally we

---

3   The Metropolitan Borough of St Pancras was formed in 1900. One of the founding members was George Bernard Shaw who at the end of his single term let it be known that "I am convinced that the borough councils should be abolished".

BEFORE CAMDEN, HAMPSTEAD,
HOLBORN AND ST PANCRAS

were treated to a measured speech, usually on libraries, and, once a year, on the rate. Backbenchers slept on the backbenches".[4]

The quiet times did not last. The Labour group, led by three intelligent, influential Labour councillors embarked on a collision course with both the Conservative government and the national Labour Party. David Goldhill, Hilda Lane and the remarkable John Lawrence, all members of the Holborn & St Pancras South Labour Party, were linked by a Trotskyist past in the Revolutionary Communist Party. In 1956 they brought about a shift in the political make up of the Labour group by having two sitting councillors deselected and replaced with their supporters. Following the Labour victory at the 1956 St Pancras borough elections, Fred Powe was again elected unchallenged as leader by the Labour group. He then announced that he had entered into a gentleman's agreement with the Tories that the aldermanic seats should be allocated proportionately on the basis of the seats each party held on the council. The Conservatives were to be allowed to nominate five aldermen. John Lawrence objected and Powe, unwilling to go back on his word, threatened to resign if the Labour group passed Lawrence's motion to allocate all the seats to Labour members. The motion was passed, Powe resigned and Lawrence was elected leader in his place.

Lawrence made his presence felt straight away, not only in the belligerent way in which he scrapped the gentleman's agreement, but in a number of high profile, publicity seeking stunts that drew national attention to St Pancras. Peggy Duff, a fellow St Pancras councillor and, more often than not, an ally of Lawrence, described him in this way: "John was really a rather old fashioned type of agitator. He was born too late. In the nineteenth century, or even in the twenties or thirties, he might have been a great national leader. But he tried to preach revolution, a rather simple, naïve type of revolution, in very non-revolutionary times, and on a small borough council hardly ripe for radical change and with none of the powers required for it. It was his personality which won him friends and followers. His excesses had a charm of their own, a sort of slap happy, up and punch 'em approach which enlivened the council chamber and even delighted the Tories. When he got up to speak, they would settle down in their seats to enjoy the show. He would call the ladies 'gals' and oddly enough they liked it. They enjoyed the excitement and the way in which

---

4   Almost: Labour won the post war elections in 1947, 53, 56 and 62, and the
     Conservatives won in 1950 and 59.

St Pancras was getting the headlines. It was never boring"[5].

Headlines mattered to Lawrence. Against bitter Tory opposition, he introduced a closed shop to St Pancras so that only fully paid up members of a union could draw council salaries. He also cut the mayoral allowance from £1799 a year to £300, and took the mayor's chauffeur driven car away. Alfred Hurst, the mayor, argued that he still needed the car even if it was only for going to school parties. "What's wrong", asked Lawrence, "with the mayor going to a schoolchildren's party on a number 68 bus?" The Holborn & St Pancras Trades Council, dominated by Lawrence's supporters, turned down the TUC's appeal for Hungarian refugees who had fled the Soviet suppression of the uprising in 1956. Communists in England eyed the refugees with suspicion, not least because so many of them were anti-Communist. "There are many families in England living in shocking housing conditions", said Hilda Lane. "Some of them are living in one room, yet houses can be offered to these Hungarians as soon as they arrive". The TUC responded by suspending the trades council. [6]

Lawrence refused to implement the Civil Defence Programme whereby the council was duty bound to set up an organisation that would operate in a national emergency, and would in the meantime run courses in emergency procedures and first aid. There had been widespread dissent in the Labour Party about the Civil Defence Programme on the grounds that it was both a waste of money and it served to lull people into the belief that the effects of a nuclear strike could in some way be handled by a Civil Defence Corps. Coventry City Council had refused to implement civil defence in 1954, but had backed down once the government threatened to surcharge the councillors for the cost of administering the scheme from London. On 4 June 1957, John Lawrence handcuffed himself to the gates of the Civil Defence Headquarters on Camden High Street[7], while Peggy Duff hurriedly phoned the press with news of what the council leader was up to. "We want these premises for housing, not for useless civil defence purposes!" Lawrence shouted to the gathering crowd as he was being cut free by

---

5 In her highly readable book *Left, Left, Left. A personal account of six protest campaigns 1945-65*, 1971

6 Hilda Lane was described by George Wagner, another Labour councillor, as "the brain power" behind the Lawrence group. "A very well read Marxist of the Trotskyite variety, with absolutely no sense of humour. Whenever you looked she always had the corners of her mouth firmly tucked under her armpits".

7 Now occupied by the Argos showrooms.

BEFORE CAMDEN, HAMPSTEAD,
HOLBORN AND ST PANCRAS

the police. "There is no defence against the H-Bomb. There are six thousand people on our housing list and we want to provide homes for four families to live here!" He was taken away in a police car onto the back of which someone had jammed a Ban the Bomb placard.

More importantly, the Lawrence group campaigned on rents. Lawrence had inherited a differential rent scheme (introduced by Fred Powe and the Labour old guard in 1953) whereby rent went up by two shillings a floor. The higher the flat, the higher the rent, so that in an eleven storied block the tenants on the top floor would pay a pound more than those on the ground floor. Lawrence had the scheme scrapped. "Probably", boasted Peggy Duff, the housing chairman, "the last time a council in Britain actually *lowered* rents". The Conservatives' response was to call in the district auditor who refused to intervene, although his presence was to be felt again and again in the last years of St Pancras. The difficulty was that under the new rent scheme, the housing revenue account deficit began to rise substantially for the first time. In order to keep the deficit low, the rents had to be subsidised by the rate payers, but the involvement of the district auditor made this difficult. The borough was left with an increasing deficit and increasing interest charges which made future action the more painful the longer it was put off.

Lawrence's influence within the party grew as he led national resistance to the 1957 Rent Act which affected rents in the private sector. He launched the Holborn & St Pancras Workers' and Tenants' Defence Committee and an advice centre was opened at the Holborn & St Pancras South Labour Party headquarters on Hampstead Road. At the Labour Party conference in 1957 he proposed that the future Labour government would put all rents back to their 1956 levels.

Lawrence gained national notoriety on 24 February 1958 when the Holborn & St Pancras South Conservative Association arranged a public meeting in Holborn Town Hall for Henry Brooke, minister of Housing and Local Government (and MP for Hampstead), to explain the benefits of the new Rent Act. Five hundred attended, mostly hostile to Mr Brooke. Many in the audience were Labour Party supporters, but there were also substantial numbers of Communists and supporters of Oswald Moseley's Union Movement. After twenty minutes of barracking, Brooke gave up and retired to a back room leaving the platform to be fought over by the Moseleyites and the Socialists. Bottles and fists were thrown, chairs were brandished, and Lawrence mounted the stage to announce triumphantly that "The Tory meeting is over!" before being bundled off by three policemen who had belatedly made it from the police station across the road. Curiously, no one was arrested. Brooke was eventually escorted by the police through a side door to his car. "This shows", he said, "the depths of what would happen if Communists ever came to control in this country".

The resultant national press coverage caused the Labour Party great embarrassment. Lena Jeger, the MP for Holborn & St Pancras South and a bitter opponent of the Rent Act, felt it necessary to apologise to Brooke in the House of Commons. The arguments against the legislation, she said, did not need "organised hooliganism and personal exhibitionism". In the eyes of the Labour Party, Lawrence had committed a further crime after breaking up Brooke's meeting. He went with some of the protestors to the nearby Bourne estate and addressed the tenants' committee on a platform which he shared with Jock Nicolson, the Communist candidate in the approaching LCC elections.

The final straw was Lawrence's plans for May Day 1958. He announced that the council's 1,300 employees were to get the day off, and that the red flag would fly over St Pancras town hall for the day. The Tories acted with predictable horror which was reflected in their campaigning[8]. "The St Pancras Socialists are doing the Russians' work for them" read one of their leaflets. Nevertheless, the Labour Party won all the St Pancras seats in the April 1958 LCC election[9]. Lawrence thought himself unstoppable, and he allowed himself to be interviewed at length by the *Sunday Times*. "We were elected to do socialist things", he was reported as saying. "We intend to use the council to inspire in ordinary people the hatred and contempt for capitalist society we feel ourselves. I think, with Marx, that you need a revolution to get rid of the privileged classes and the muck of ages in men's minds". Such a revolution had made Russia "the number one country today". If he lived in France or Italy, he said, he would join the Communist Party, but he had no intention of doing so in Britain: "Why should I leave a big party to join a small party?"

As May Day approached, Lawrence decided to liven things up

---

8   The Reverend Hector Morgan, vicar of St Luke's & St Paul's, expressed his horror in this way: "To some of us who have seen men die for the Union Jack and all that it stands for, it is a sacrilegious insult....it may be a good thing if every loyal subject of the British crown in St Pancras puts out the Union Jack on May Day just to show what a minority follow the blood soaked banner of the neo-communists".

9   Although, to put the St Pancras results in context, Labour took 27 seats off the Conservatives across London, giving them a 74 seat majority on the LCC, the widest margin in 24 years.

BEFORE CAMDEN, HAMPSTEAD,
HOLBORN AND ST PANCRAS

by concentrating on what the Union Movement might do. His press statement read as an invitation to a punch up. "In view of the open threats made by Fascists to tear down the Red Flag and create public disorder, the Labour Group asks Socialists and trade unionists in the London area to come to St Pancras Trades Council's May Day Rally opposite the town hall on Thursday at any time between midday and dusk to prevent Fascist interference with Labour's traditional May Day celebrations".

On 30th April, the Conservatives presented the council meeting with a petition opposed to flying the red flag. They arrived to find that vandals had daubed in red paint twenty hammer and sickles, each three foot high, on the white stone walls of the town hall. Lawrence happily confirmed the accuracy of his remarks as reported in the *Sunday Times* and expanded on them. Tim Donovan, the Conservative leader, said that if Lawrence "felt that Russia was such a great and glorious power, he hoped he would not hesitate to go there". Tony Prior, the opposition whip, called Lawrence "an avowed and committed Communist". Lawrence was undeterred: "The red flag will still fly over the town hall and, for my money, over Buckingham Palace as well!"

As dawn broke over the borough on May Day 1958, fifty newsreel, newspaper and television cameramen were setting up their apparatus on the steps leading down from St Pancras station, from where they had a clear view of the town hall. Just before half past seven, Lawrence led a small group to the roof, raised the red flag, waved cheerily to those below him, and went back inside. All was quiet until midday when the Union Movement set up a platform and two union jacks in Ossulton Street, three yards away from the platform to be used by the Holborn & St Pancras Trades Council for their lunch time rally. Lorry loads of police were set down in the St Pancras goods yard and mounted police patrolled Euston Road. A crowd gathered, and speakers from the two platforms angrily denounced each other. Sensing that a major public disorder was about to erupt, the police ordered both meetings to stop. As they had achieved what they had set out to do, the disruption of the Trades Council meeting, the outnumbered Union Movement men complied. The Trades Council people were less willing.

John Lawrence, wearing his trademark red tie, sprang onto the platform and asked the crowd whether the meeting should stop. The crowd shouted for more and Lawrence launched into his prepared speech. The police pulled him from the platform and then arrested anyone else who took his place. According to the *North London Press*, "It took six policemen to hold Councillor Lawrence, who struggled the whole of the

BEFORE CAMDEN, HAMPSTEAD,
HOLBORN AND ST PANCRAS

150 yards to the waiting Black Maria. It took many more police to drag struggling Councillor David Goldhill, Bernie Holland and other speakers to the Black Maria as well....mounted police rode out into Ossulton Square and lined the pavements in readiness for any further trouble". Only the MP Lena Jeger was allowed to speak, and she was drowned out by the Union Movement men chanting "The reds, the reds, we're going to get rid of the reds!" There were scuffles between the two groups. The police made ten arrests, including five Labour councillors, and charged them with obstruction. "May Day 1958", reported the somewhat breathless St Pancras Chronicle, "will long be remembered as one of the most exciting days in the borough's history".

The five guineas that John Lawrence was fined by the magistrate proved to be the least of his worries. The Holborn & St Pancras South Labour Party ("the South Party") was dominated by left wingers who, through a system of affiliations to left wing trade unions, had a clear majority whenever it came to a vote. They drew attention to themselves by demanding that one of their members, Woodrow Wyatt, be removed from the list of approved Labour parliamentary candidates. Wyatt, a former MP working for the BBC's Panorama programme, had exposed vote rigging and Communist infiltration in the Electrical Trades Union.[10]

The National Executive Committee (NEC) responded by ordering an investigation into both the South Party and the Labour group on St Pancras. The first consequence of this was that twenty one left wing trade unionist delegates were excluded from the South Party because they did not live in the constituency, and Lawrence found himself politically exposed. On 15 May 1958 the constituency's general management committee narrowly rejected (by 35 votes to 33) a motion to expel him for discrediting the Labour Party.

Two days later, twenty seven members of the South Party wrote to the NEC asking it to overturn the decision not to expel Lawrence. Active inside the local party, they wrote, is "an organised group strongly believed to have links with organisations outside the Labour Party", who had "forced the Party into actions and decisions of which a large part of the membership disapproves", bringing "discredit on the party locally and nationally". This cry for help was exactly what the NEC wanted to hear. John Lawrence and the whole of the South Party were suspended

---

10 Woodrow Wyatt (1918-97) had been a Labour MP from 1945 to 1955, initially as an outspoken left winger. He returned to parliament from 1959 until 1970. A newspaper columnist of trenchant views, he was given a life peerage in 1987 where he sat on the cross benches as a cheerleader for Mrs Thatcher's government.

BEFORE CAMDEN, HAMPSTEAD,
HOLBORN AND ST PANCRAS

from membership of the Labour Party.

The Labour group met on the same day of the NEC's announcement, voted to keep Lawrence as their leader and demanded that the NEC specify the charges against Lawrence. The NEC refused, but it was clear to everyone that the national leadership of the Labour Party wanted Lawrence out. His fate was settled by a special meeting of the Labour group on 28 May 1958. His chief whip, Jock Stallard, proposed a motion that the group "should reaffirm John Lawrence as the leader of a united Labour group until such time as the NEC can convince us that his views and activities –which the majority of us have supported- are incompatible with membership of the Labour Party". The fear of suspension, especially among those councillors from the St Pancras North Labour Party, decided the matter. The motion was voted down by 23 votes to 15, and Charlie Ratchford was elected leader in Lawrence's place. The Lawrence loyalists then walked out of the meeting in protest at this betrayal. A statement was issued by Lawrence, Dave Goldhill and Jock Stallard saying that "We are not an independent group. We are a Labour group fighting for socialist policies and against dictatorial interference by the NEC. We shall do this as a test of the socialist character of the Labour Party".

The NEC in the meantime set about reorganising the Holborn & St Pancras South Party. The officers were immediately readmitted and told to filter out the communists. Special ward meetings were held without notifying Lawrence supporters. Although not invited, David Goldhill turned up to his own ward meeting and refused to leave. The official from Transport House abandoned the meeting and arranged for it to be held again in secret so that a ward association could be formed of those already vetted. All the readmitted members had to sign a pledge accepting the NEC's reorganisation of the party. This was, said the *Tribune*, "the language of McCarthyism".

John Lawrence was expelled from the Labour Party in June 1958 together with all the members of the Socialist Labour group who supported him and fifteen or so other party members from the South Party, in all about 30 members. The decision was taken in Lawrence's absence. The NEC ruled that as he had not specifically asked for an interview, he should not be offered one. "If this had happened on the other side of the Iron Curtain", said Lawrence, "Mr Gaitskell would have organised a meeting to protest".

Lawrence played his last card at the Labour Party conference at Scarborough, where he hoped to have the NEC's purge overturned.

Every delegate was given a copy of a 24 page pamphlet, *The St Pancras Story*, illustrated with a picture of the red flag flying over the town hall. It was written in uncompromising terms. "The NEC says that our views and activities are indistinguishable from those of known communists. We deny it, but we could reply with far more justification that the views and activities of many prominent party members are indistinguishable from those of known Tories.......by going along with this anti-communist crusade we become the bugle boys of imperialism instead of its grave diggers.....we are not ashamed of what we have done and we don't regret it. Now the NEC –overriding all protests from the local labour movement– has cast us out. You, the rank and file delegates to the great conference have the power to put us back".

Lawrence, Hilda Lane and David Goldhill did not get inside the hall, nor did Jock Stallard even though he was a delegate of the Amalgamated Engineering Union. On behalf of St Pancras North, Peggy Duff moved the suspension of standing orders to allow John Lawrence to speak in his defence, but the main unions had their instructions and the suggestion was rejected by four million votes to two and a half million. When the debate moved on to the expulsions the South Party's delegate, Tom McKitterick, launched a scathing attack on Lawrence and his group. The conference approved the purge by six million votes to half a million.

It was the end for John Lawrence as far as the Labour Party was concerned. Within a fortnight of the Labour Party conference, he together with Hilda Lane, David Goldhill and eight others applied to join the Communist Party[11]. He was still a councillor and still led his fourteen strong Socialist Labour group on St Pancras. There followed a split between those members of his group who came out as Communists, and those, including Jock Stallard, who remained as Socialist Labour members. The official Labour group kept control, but somewhat uncomfortably, and suffered several defeats when the disaffected Labour councillors voted with the Tories.

With the district auditor breathing down its neck, the council cautiously raised rents. It was not by enough, and when the Conservatives proposed a differential rent scheme to produce "really low rents in cases of genuine need whilst charging no tenant more than he can reasonably afford", they were defeated by the votes of both the Labour

---

11 So twitchy was the Communist Party about "Trotskyist entrists", that it conducted two enquiries and did not accept the applications for over a month for fear that the Lawrence group were joining to disrupt it from within.

BEFORE CAMDEN, HAMPSTEAD,
HOLBORN AND ST PANCRAS

groups and Lawrence's Communists. There followed another complaint to the district auditor. He declined to intervene over the rent levels overall, but did intervene on the level of rents raised on the borough's derequisitioned houses.[12] Despite warnings from the council officers, the housing committee decided to subsidise all the derequisitioned rents from the housing revenue account. The district auditor surcharged each of the councillors who had voted for the subsidy £200, and in the following year surcharged them a further £1400 each[13].

As if to make the point that John Lawrence was bad for business, the borough elections on 8 May 1959 brought the Conservatives back, albeit by the narrowest of margins. The Conservative campaign leaflets had again featured the Red Flag over the town hall. The headline on the *North London Press* read: "Council Rents Up. Red Flag Down. Closed Shop Out". There was a swing against Labour in London (they also lost Lewisham), and in St Pancras the Labour Party was also up against Socialist Labour candidates and former Labour councillors standing as Communists. John Lawrence and Hilda Lane both stood as Communist Party candidates, and both lost their seats with embarrassingly low votes. The simple fact was that Lawrence and his friends had damaged the Labour Party, and this was shown with great emphasis in the October 1959 general election when the sitting MP for Holborn & St Pancras South, Lena Jeger, lost her seat to the Conservative, the BBC presenter Geoffrey Johnson Smith.

The May 1959 borough elections themselves had almost, but not quite, given power to the Tories. It needed one more push as, having been beaten at the polls, the Labour Party made a last ditch attempt to

12 Properties that had been requisitioned for housing during the war and were now to be handed back to their owners together with the tenants who were themselves to lose their tenancies after a set period of time. The council had a duty to collect the rent and pass it on to the landlords. The landlords were entitled to rents set at the levels allowed for by the 1957 Rent Act, rents that were far higher than those allowed for those in council properties. The council chose to subsidise the tenants by collecting the old council rents from them which they paid to the landlords together with the balance from the housing revenue account.

13 Of the 23 councillors who were surcharged £200, four did not appeal the decision. Thirteen others (including Peggy Duff, Peter Jonas and Charlie Ratchford) appealed successfully to the Minister for Housing and Local Government, Henry Brooke, who felt that as they had not intentionally acted unlawfully they need not pay. Lawrence and five other councillors (including Lane, Goldhill and Stallard) rather than throw themselves at the mercy of a Conservative minister, appealed instead to the High Court where the Lord Chief Justice ruled against them. "Have councils any powers whatever", asked Lawrence, "other than administering the siting of public lavatories?" There were no appeals against the surcharge of £1400 for the following year.

BEFORE CAMDEN, HAMPSTEAD,
HOLBORN AND ST PANCRAS

keep control of the council through the mayor's casting vote and the appointment of five Labour aldermen. They lost by a single vote. Martin Morton, then one of the newly elected Tory councillors, describes the drama of 25 May 1959 in this way:

> "The May 1959 election left the Town Hall with 33 Conservative and 22 Labour councillors, plus ten Labour aldermen, giving them 32 votes. However, the retiring deputy mayor, Councillor Mrs Hilda Lane, who had not been re-elected, remained a member of the council until after the election of the new mayor, as did the retiring five senior aldermen. All six were able to vote in the mayoral election, giving Labour a potentially equal vote of 33. In the event of a tie in the mayoral election, Councillor Tom Barker, the outgoing Labour mayor, was to use his casting vote for the Labour candidate. Unfortunately for Labour, one of their councillors, Jim Rackham, a dedicated member of the Co-operative Party, had been so mesmerised by Hugh Gaitskell at a TU conference on the south coast, that he missed his train - and the vote. The first item of business was the election of a new mayor. As was allowed in those days, each party chose a candidate who was not a councillor, and the voting was 33 for the Conservative nominee, Harold Percival Doughty Bastie (a name I shall recall and recite to my dying day) and 32 votes for Labour's Hilda Chandler. Once the mayor had been chosen, the retiring deputy mayor stood down as did the five senior aldermen, and the Conservatives then took the five replacement aldermanic seats by 33 votes to 27 – (that is the 22 Labour Councillors plus their five remaining aldermen). All 33 of us had been closeted in a committee room to be carefully drilled on procedure by whips Roland Walker and Clare Mansel. On the mayoral ballot form we had to state the full name, place of residence, and description of the person for whom we voted. Any mistake, spelling or otherwise, if challenged, could invalidate that ballot".[14]

After the meeting, the council was formed of 39 Conservatives (33 councillors, five aldermen and the mayor) and 27 Labour (22 councillors and five aldermen).

In July 1959, the council approved the Conservatives' new rent scheme at a council meeting which lasted over nine hours, ending at 4.20 am. The new scheme aimed at reducing the deficit on the housing revenue account by introducing a system of maximum and minimum rents based on rateable value. Some people would pay less, but (as

---

14 "Half minute means different mayor" was the headline over the report in the *Times* which ended: "The missing Labour councillor, Mr J.H.Packham [sic], who arrived in the council chamber just as the Town Clerk was announcing the result, said that he was at a conference of the National Union of Furniture Trade Operatives in Eastbourne and was unable to get away until Mr Gaitskell had finished speaking".

BEFORE CAMDEN, HAMPSTEAD,
HOLBORN AND ST PANCRAS

the deficit was so big) most council tenants would pay more with over half paying the new maximum rents. Many tenants on the pre-war estates had their rent trebled, and rents on the post war estates were doubled. Tenants associations sprang up everywhere, and the St Pancras United Tenants Association (UTA) was set up by Don Cook, a 38 year old Communist shop steward at the Handley Page aircraft company in Cricklewood and a former member of the Parachute Regiment, who lived in a council flat in Kennistoun House in Kentish Town. UTA called for a borough wide rent strike. Many tenants refused to pay the increases and some even withheld all their rent. In all cases notices, warning letters, threats of eviction and notices to quit followed. The strike faltered as isolated tenants paid up rather than face being made homeless. The UTA decided to fight two evictions: those of Don Cook and Arthur Rowe, a 59 year old waiter who lived in a flat in Silverdale on Hampstead Road on the Regent's Park estate. The county court issued eviction notices in June and thereafter the two men lived in a state of siege. The door on Rowe's flat was removed and replaced with six inch thick steel plates buttressed with timber beams. His windows were barred with thick planks. Don Cook was barricaded in his top floor flat behind barbed wire, twelve pianos and wooden doors over the windows. Night and day their supporters kept guard to warn of the approach of the bailiffs.

On the evening of 21 September 1960, five hundred protestors gathered outside the town hall to picket the housing committee. John Lawrence was in the thick of it. Denied entry, he led a sit down demonstration which was cleared with the help of mounted police. Fighting broke out as Lawrence led a group of fifty men in an attempt to force their way into the Town Hall, shouting "We won't move until we get hold of Prior" (the council leader), and "Let's tie the bastard up to a lamp post". On being told to desist by a police superintendant, Lawrence beat him to the ground with his fists and, before he could be arrested, punched a constable in the face.

Shortly after 5am the following morning, 22 September 1960, hundreds of police blocked off the roads around the two flats with cordons three deep and mounted police. Heavily escorted bailiffs then made their way into position at 5.45am. Don Cook set off a signal flare to alert his supporters who came running to his aid. Many were clothed in their dressing gowns and pyjamas, but once the police were in position, it was too late. Although equipped with hacksaws, crowbars and pick axes, the bailiffs soon gave up on Arthur Rowe's door and instead took the easier option of smashing their way through the wall.

BEFORE CAMDEN, HAMPSTEAD,
HOLBORN AND ST PANCRAS

It took them an hour. Don Cook held out for two hours. On the stairs the bailiffs were pelted with bricks and bottles and were soused in engine oil, but they eventually got in by smashing through the slates on the roof and dropping through the ceiling.

John Lawrence, bailed by the magistrate in the morning, marched at the head of hundreds of railwaymen from the Camden Goods Yards and building workers from the Shell site at Waterloo to demonstrate at Kennistoun, which was still cordoned off by police. Fighting broke out again on Leighton Road. Crowds gathered as Don Cook and Arthur Rowe made speeches urging tenants not to pay their rent. According to the *Times*, "the crowd cheered as speakers made abusive remarks about the town council, the police and the press". In the evening they moved off to demonstrate outside the town hall. Mainly good natured (only a few broken bus windows), a few thousand protestors marched down Kentish Town Road. Things turned ugly when they reached the police cordon on Euston Road. The evening erupted into the worst violence yet. "Hundreds of police", reported the *Daily Express*, "have just charged the crowd in Euston Road and are locked face to face in the most vicious fighting I have yet seen. I heard dozens of women screaming...It was a nightmare of confusion of flying fists and boots...unconscious men, blood streaming from their faces, were dragged across the streets".[15]

The next day, the home secretary, Rab Butler, invoked the Public Order Act 1936 (introduced to stop Blackshirt marches) to ban all demonstrations in St Pancras for three months. The Holborn & St Pancras South Labour Party issued a statement to say that its members

15 Tony Prior the leader of the council, lived on the Holly Lodge estate in Highgate. Another Highgate man, Roland Walker, who was also the chief whip, remembers the events well. "There had been a build up in feeling for several months before the evictions of Cook and Rowe and for security reasons no one was told when they would take place. On 21st September there was a full meeting of the council and during one of the breaks in business the deputy town clerk, Don Whitlum, took me aside and told me to look after Tony Prior. I took this to mean that the evictions were imminent. Sure enough, the next morning we woke to hear on the national news that the evictions had taken place. I drove Tony Prior to the City that morning and as we passed the top of Leighton Road we could see one of the blocks of flats surrounded by a sea of blue helmets. We heard later that the operation involved the whole of the Metropolitan Police force as every area had provided officers to cover the two evictions. Both Tony and I had meetings at the Town Hall that same evening where we heard that the rioters were planning to march on the Town Hall with "lighted tapers". This later proved to be false and they did all their damage in the centre of the borough. However the threat to Tony was taken very seriously and it was not safe for him to return home. We gave him a drink and stayed with him until news came that his wife and small children had been evacuated to his parents' flat near the Town Hall where he joined them. We found that the Holly Lodge estate was sealed off by the police and Tony's house had a policeman on duty outside for several months afterwards"

BEFORE CAMDEN, HAMPSTEAD,
HOLBORN AND ST PANCRAS

were "appalled at the undemocratic actions of the home secretary". "It's martial law", said UTA. A month later, October 1960, Lawrence and others faced trial at Clerkenwell Magistrates' Court. Lawrence called five witnesses to allege that the superintendant had pointed him out with the words: "There he is! Get him!", and that three or four constables then dragged him away, flung him in a police van, beat him up and had him charged with assault. The stipendiary magistrate found otherwise: it was a great affront, he said, for a senior police officer charged with keeping public order to be knocked to the ground in front of a hostile and hysterical crowd. He sent Lawrence to prison for three months[16].

Labour's manifesto for the 1962 borough elections concentrated on the resentment that had built up following the rent strike. The message was clear: the Conservatives will put up the rents and Labour will bring them down and get rid of the hated differential rent scheme. Charlie Ratchford led Labour to the biggest swing in the country, taking nineteen seats from the Conservatives. The new St Pancras council was formed of 48 Labour to 20 Conservatives and two others.

The Labour victory was swiftly followed by the realisation that they could not get rid of the differential rent scheme unless the standard rents were fixed so high that only a small proportion of tenants could pay them. Any overall reduction in the council's rental income would have the immediate effect of increasing the housing revenue account deficit and the certainty of all the councillors who voted for such a scheme getting surcharged. The rents stayed up and Labour stayed in power.[17]

*　*　*

16　Lawrence was initially bailed after the trial pending an appeal, but he abandoned the appeal and served his sentence in Brixton Prison. His interest in St Pancras declined after this. He concentrated on journalism and continued to be active in the print unions. Just as the Labour Party had tired of his brand of uncompromising, confrontational politics, so did the union leadership. During a Fleet Street strike in 1972, he was sacked by the Press Association for being "a professional activist" and the union settled the strike without demanding his reinstatement. In 1973 he left London for Shoreham in West Sussex where he wound down his political activities. He died in 2002.

17　"The district auditor, in fact, dictated the level of council rents, not the councillors, nor the citizens who elected them. Later on we got to the point where the district auditor informed us at the end of the financial year how large a deficit on the housing revenue account he was prepared to accept....This meant that the citizens of a borough were free to vote, as they had, to get rid of a scheme, but the council had no power to carry out their wishes, except at the risk, indeed the certainty, of surcharge. Government by district auditor, an official appointed by the ministry, unelected, unmoved by local opinion." Peggy Duff, *Left, Left, Left.* p96.

BEFORE CAMDEN, HAMPSTEAD,
HOLBORN AND ST PANCRAS

The naming of Camden was not straightforward. A joint committee of representatives from the three boroughs was set up to make recommendations concerning the coming amalgamation. Charlie Ratchford wanted the new borough to be called St Pancras, or, if forced to compromise, Greater St Pancras. It was not to be a merger so much as a takeover. Leslie Room, the Conservative leader on Hampstead council liked the idea of naming the new borough Camden, as Camden Town was in the centre of the new boundaries. Neither got any support from the Hampstead librarian, William Maidment, who advised against Camden because it is not a local name, but an area named after the eighteenth century politician and landowner, Lord Camden (who, Peggy Duff remarked, was "another bloody Tory"). Nor did he like St Pancras, which was named after a teenager martyred in fourth century Rome. Maidment's suggestion was that the new borough should be called Fleet, because the River Fleet flowed through all three boroughs, or that it should be called Fleethurst or Fleetside in recognition of this. Brian Wilson, the Hampstead town clerk, agreed and thought Fleethurst the best name. Geoffrey Finsberg, one of the Hampstead councillors, also liked the suggestion, but preferred Fleetheath because Hampstead Heath would also form an important part of the new borough. But the River Fleet, historically a muddy stream flowing into the Thames, but now a subterranean sewer that no one had seen, drew little real enthusiasm[18]. In July 1963, after some debate, the joint committee agreed on Camden. The St Pancras people liked it because Camden Town was after all part of the old borough of St Pancras, and the Hampstead and Holborn people liked it because it was not St Pancras, and so when Leslie Room proposed the name, he was seconded by Paddy O'Connor, one of the St Pancras councillors.

On Friday, 13 September 1963, Sir Keith Joseph, the minister for housing and local government, announced his approval of the name Camden. So it was that "London Borough N° 2", yet to become politically the most interesting of all the London boroughs, came to be named after that unfashionable area north of the city where once Charles Dickens spent the most miserable part of his childhood (and where he described Bob Cratchit living in four rooms with his wife and four children); to where generations of teenaged Londoners would flock to the Camden Lock

---

18 The public were asked for ideas for a name and soon suggestions flooded in of every conceivable compromise: Panhamborn, St Hamborn, St Bornham, Bornhamcras, Hohampan, St Panholmstead, and so on.

BEFORE CAMDEN, HAMPSTEAD,
HOLBORN AND ST PANCRAS

Market and the old Camden Theatre (in its various guises through the years as the Music Machine, the Camden Palace and now KoKo, "London's premier live music venue"); outside which, at the more depressed end of the High Street, stands the marble statue of the radical MP Richard Cobden; and where Cobden's son in law, Walter Sickert, the founder and driving force behind the Camden Town Group of artists, painted his depictions of the Camden Town murder, the throttling of a prostitute in a terraced house on what is now the Agar estate.[19]

---

19 The formation and early years of Camden is covered in great detail in Enid Wistrich's *Local Government Reorganisation: the first years of Camden* (1972), a fascinating book to which I am much indebted. Its somewhat unattractive title is explained by the fact that it was written for the benefit of those councils outside London facing merger. The book was commissioned and published by Camden, and written during the years that the author, like so many of her Labour contemporaries, was off the council between 1968 and 1971. Other publications concerning the last years of the Metropolitan Borough of St Pancras are: Peggy Duff, *Left, Left, Left* (1971); Dave Burn, *Rent Strike: St Pancras 1960* (Pluto Press, 1972), Bob Pitt's article 'Red Flag over St Pancras' in the journal *What Next?, No 14 (1999)*, and John McIlroy's article in the same journal, (*No 26* and 27) 'The Revolutionary Odyssey of John Lawrence'. The last three of these are available in full online.

BEFORE CAMDEN, HAMPSTEAD,
HOLBORN AND ST PANCRAS

21

Charlie Ratchford
and the first four years

1964 was an election year at all levels in London. Five years had passed since Macmillan's victory in 1959, and following the shake-up in local government there were elections for both the new Greater London Council (GLC) in succession to the London County Council (LCC) and for the thirty two new amalgamated boroughs across London.

The Conservatives held two of the three parliamentary seats in the new borough of Camden. St Pancras North was considered a safe Labour seat, and Hampstead was a safe Conservative one. Of greater interest was Holborn & St Pancras South where in the 1959 election the Conservatives had fielded the dashing 35 year old BBC television newsreader Geoffrey Johnson Smith and had managed to ease out the sitting Labour MP Lena Jeger by 656 votes. Mrs Jeger, whose husband had been MP for the constituency before her, had promised on the night of her election defeat that Johnson Smith was only "borrowing" the seat from her and that she would have it back at the next election. She had been working hard to make that happen.

The newly constituted Camden incorporated the three old metropolitan boroughs of St Pancras, which was overwhelmingly Labour; Hampstead, which was overwhelmingly Conservative; and Holborn, the smallest of the three, which was solidly Conservative if only because of the strong business vote. The problem for the Conservatives was that the differences in population sizes meant that St Pancras would be allocated half the sixty seats on the new council, Hampstead would get twenty four and Holborn only six. It was going to be very close, and the stakes were high. "In the borough of Camden it will mean everything we have cherished in Hampstead life will be in dire jeopardy," Neil Shields, the chairman of the Hampstead Conservative Party, told a party meeting in February 1964. "The effects on the rates can easily be imagined."

The first GLC elections took place in April 1964, a month before the first Camden elections. The new three member constituency used the same boundaries as the new Camden borough. Labour's three candidates topped the poll with just over 50% of the vote, leaving the Conservatives with 39%, the Liberals with 6%, and Jock Nicholson, the sole communist, with 4%.

The Camden poll in May 1964 found the Tories on the back foot. Labour and the Conservatives were the only parties to contest all the seats in the borough. Labour campaigned on "fairness and equality for all", promised 100% mortgages to council tenants and adopted the St Pancras council policies for housing and funding for the arts. The Conservatives pledged to maintain "all that tradition of progressive administration for which Hampstead has so high a reputation" and promised 100% mortgages to council tenants. They also, and there was much talk of it at the time, launched advertisements in the local press promising not to let the red flag fly over the town hall as had notoriously happened when Labour had control of St Pancras in 1958 and 59. The Liberals promised fair play for tenants, to fight Rachmanism and overcrowding and to improve welfare provision. Everyone knew what it all meant: Labour would spend more and would cost more, the Tories would spend less and would cost less, and whatever the Liberal position was, they would not win in any event.

The poll was close, but crucially Labour took seven seats in Hampstead (in Kilburn and Priory wards). Although the Conservatives won all six seats in Holborn, they were all but wiped out in St Pancras where they managed to win only three. Labour took the council by 34 seats to 26. "We in Hampstead pulled our weight", said a disappointed Neil Shields, "but we were swamped by St Pancras". Nevertheless, he was pleased with the red flag advertisement which he had copied from the St Pancras Conservative leaflets in the successful 1959 borough election. "It brought our supporters out and it certainly put the kybosh on the Liberals." [1] The former Liberal MP, Archie Macdonald, who came eighth out of the nine candidates in Town ward, was furious with Shields's campaigning. "The Tories had to resort to fear and smear tactics. When Liberal councillors

---

1   The 45 year old Neil Shields, MC (he had "a good war" with an anti-tank battery in Northern Europe) was knighted in the Birthday Honours List the following month "for political and public services to London and Hampstead".

were elected in Hampstead in 1962, Mr Shields said he would move heaven and earth to get us out. Now we know what he meant." [2]

It had been a two horse race. The Liberals stood in Highgate ward and all the wards in the old Hampstead borough, where they came third behind the Labour and Conservative candidates, and in Camden Town ward where they came fourth behind the Communist candidate- the only ward in which the Communists did not come last.

The new leader of the council was the 63 year old Charlie Ratchford, a British Railways clerk at Euston station who had served on St Pancras borough since he had been co-opted in 1940. He romped home in Grafton ward with a massive 2,777 votes. Within a week of being elected leader of Camden, he was also made the last mayor of St Pancras.

The first meeting of the Labour group after the election discussed the thorny issue of aldermen [3]. Ten aldermen, with the same voting rights as councillors, were to be appointed by the council. The group decided to appoint ten Labour aldermen so that the party's strength on the council would be increased to 44 votes against the Tories' 26. Unluckily for those who wanted to take all the spoils, the *Ham & High* managed to get wind of what was going on and splashed it over the front page. The leader of the Conservative group, 64 year old Hampstead councillor Leslie Room, had been around as long as Ratchford, having been first elected to Belsize during the war. A man with an enviable grasp of local finance, he was nevertheless (said the *Ham & High*) "unimaginative, dull and ponderous". He was furious at the news. Here, he said, is what we meant by the "red flag threat" from St Pancras. The Conservatives had hoped to be allocated four of the ten alderman posts. Charlie Ratchford refused to comment on the issue, but by the time the Labour group next met they were aware of local disquiet and had considered a letter from Leslie Room. The Conservatives were allowed to nominate two of the aldermen. It was not much, but "wiser counsels have prevailed", said the *Ham & High*.

On Tuesday 26th May 1964, Camden held its inaugural council meeting. There was to be no mayor for the first year, but Sammy Fisher, a 60 year old St Pancras councillor was elected chairman of the council. Fisher had been born in Stepney, the son of immigrants from Russia, and had left school at fifteen. He pursued a career as a Hatton Garden diamond trader and became the secretary and vice-president of the

27

2   Archie MacDonald had been briefly the MP for Roxburgh & Selkirk in 1950-51.

3   Aldermen were abolished by the 1972 Local Government Act.

London Diamond Bourse. He had also served as the mayor of Stoke Newington. Although a man of great charm, he was also notably thin skinned, and was painfully conscious of his lack of height, having taken to backing himself against the wall in formal photographs so that he could better balance on tip toe. [4]

At that first meeting, Charlie Ratchford outlined his programme for the next four years. The council's priorities would be planning, housing (there were 10,000 on the waiting list), the welfare services which had been inherited from the LCC, and a programme of improvement of the libraries and funding of the arts. It was a cautious start. For the first year the new borough ran in tandem with the three old boroughs which were not formally wound up until May 1965, and during that year only the three old councils had the power to collect rates.

Hampstead was a much studied constituency in the October 1964 general election as its sitting MP, Henry Brooke, was the home secretary. As the last months of the Douglas Home administration drew to an unpopular end, he was forced to start his campaign early. Elections should not be held in bitter hostility, he said, somewhat hopefully, but he was dogged and abused by his Labour opponent who went for the jugular. Jack Cooper was a goatee bearded, forty three year old wartime RAF Regiment officer and father of four. He had come into the public eye in 1960 by proposing a motion at that year's Labour conference calling for Hugh Gaitskell's resignation. Now a *Times* journalist, an amateur painter and a Camden councillor, he looked upon Brooke not only with a lack of deference, but with unusual contempt. Brooke was "a laughing stock" and "the fall guy" responsible for the 1957 Rent Act because he did not have the imagination to see what the consequences would be.

Also much in the limelight was Holborn & St Pancras South where Geoffrey Johnson Smith was defending his 656 majority where the electorate was over 5,000 down on 1959 because of, said Lena Jeger, "excessive office development". Housing was seen by both sides as the main issue, and Johnson Smith was somewhat hampered

---

4   For the first year, the new London boroughs were to have chairmen rather than mayors, so as to avoid confusion with the mayors of the constituent metropolitan boroughs. Sammy Fisher was elected Camden's first mayor in 1965 and was knighted in 1967 "for services to local government in the Inner London area". Although he stayed on the council as an alderman, he did not stand for re-election in 1968. He went on to become the president of the Board of Deputies of British Jews in 1973, a life peer in 1974 (Baron Fisher of Camden) and then the chairman of the Governing Board of the World Jewish Congress. He died in 1979.

by the government's approval of plans for the new National Library in Bloomsbury south of the British Museum, which would displace a thousand residents. Just as the nominations deadline closed, a Pakistani barrister, Ali Mohamed Abbas, entered as an independent candidate hoping to get some commonwealth representation in parliament. Rumours immediately spread, fuelled by the *North London Press* (under a pretence of putting the rumours to sleep) that Mr Abbas was funded by "hidden and unknown sources" in a "right wing plot" to lure black and Asian voters away from Labour.

The election of 15 October 1964 was close, but amid scenes of great relief and, as always, the singing of the *Red Flag*, Lena Jeger won her seat back. "Thousands of voters stayed away", was the understated headline of the *Camden & St Pancras Chronicle* ("the ONLY local paper in St Pancras"), noting that on a reduced turnout Mrs Jeger had received fewer votes than she had when she lost in 1959.[5]

The greater shock came in Hampstead. Brooke's majority in 1959 had been in the region of 12,000 votes, but that had been over the novelty Labour candidate Dr David Pitt, a West Indian much interested in matters of immigration and race. Brooke's majority was slashed by ten thousand. He beat off his challenger by fewer than two thousand votes. The swing of 10½% against Brooke was, said Ernest Wistrich, "the largest in any election this century until then". Nor had the Liberals done well. Their candidate, Renee Soskin[6], a 57 year old widow and mother of six, had the best Liberal result in London, but it was still 700 votes down on 1959.

Only in St Pancras North did things go as expected where Kenneth Robinson easily beat his challengers, the Conservative Kenneth Warren[7] and the resident Communist candidate, Jock Nicolson "a tall rangy Scotsman", said the *North London Press*, and "a railway goods checker".[8]

An important early action (and one important to this narrative) was taken by the council in April 1965: the purchase of Branch Hill Lodge and eleven acres adjoining Hampstead Heath for £460,000 from

29

---

5   Geoffrey Johnson Smith returned to parliament in the East Grinstead by election in 1965 and remained there until, following a knighthood, he retired as MP for Wealden in 2001.

6   The sister of Lord (Max) Beloff and the formidable *Observer* journalist, Nora Beloff (or, as *Private Eye* called her, Nora Ballsoff).

7   Kenneth Warren became the MP for Hastings (and then Hastings & Rye) from 1970 until he retired in 1992.

8   According to Martin Morton: "For a communist, he was a nice chap".

Lord Glendyne, an 87 year old stockbroker. Charlie Ratchford was delighted. The old house was to be transformed into an old people's home and the outbuildings could be converted into a children's home. There could be no council estate there, let alone "a sky scraper block of flats" as suggested by the *Ham & High* because, as Charlie Ratchford explained in a press release, "the remainder of the site will be kept as an open space and it is on this understanding that Lord Glendyne has agreed to sell the property to the council".

Camden set its first rate in March 1965. It was, as the Conservatives had predicted, a high one. "Rates up all round", declared the *Ham & High*, pointing out that the rate of 9s. 4d. in the pound meant an increase for ratepayers in all three boroughs. "Ninety per cent of the increase is because of Tory political manipulation and ambitions which went wrong", said John Diamond, the chairman of Camden's finance committee, referring to the very creation of Camden and its having to set up new departments which used to be run by the LCC. "Now the public have to pay for it". Henry Brooke, who had gone from home secretary to the back benches with no place in Heath's shadow cabinet, was of the other view: "The moment I saw Labour had control of the GLC and Camden I knew spending would be extravagant and that rates would go up more than they need".

At the same meeting that set the rate, the council adopted the Camden symbol of eight linked hands, designed by Messrs Main Wolff & Partners to suggest "voting, giving, receiving and unity". Geoffrey Finsberg, the punchiest of the Tory councillors, did not like it: "It's a monstrosity. We are proud of this borough but we can't be proud of a symbol like this". Madeleine du Mont agreed: "If this is the best our Camden artists can do, we'd be better off without one." [9] Theirs was a minority view. "It's almost a replica of a Polynesian fertility symbol", said Jack Cooper soothingly, and Labour's literary man, Johnny St John, went further: "It reminded me of something from oriental mythology – Ying and Yang, the life force between man and woman" [10]. Or "an elephant's foot", suggested Ernest Wistrich.

---

9   When the Conservatives took power in 1968, they wanted to use the borough's new coat of arms (which Brian Wilson had hidden in the town hall safe throughout the Labour administration) but as so much money had already been spent on putting the symbol on, for instance, council vehicles and stationery they felt obliged to compromise. "We don't particularly like the symbol, to be honest", said Cllr Sydney Jaque, "but as it is well known we have decided to keep it".

10 St John had served in the Royal Marines with Evelyn Waugh (an account of which he wrote in *To the War with Waugh*), and later joined the Communist Party from which he resigned in 1956. He died in 1988.

The council also voted to impose a closed shop for its employees as had been the case in St Pancras but not in the other two boroughs. The proposal had been made by the chairman of the staff committee, Luke "Paddy" O'Connor, who had tried to slip it through in a staffing committee report. It was spotted by the young Victor Lyon who expressed irritation that O'Connor had not had the guts to come clean about what he was proposing. O'Connor was furious and gave the Conservatives a taste of St Pancras style debating by calling Lyon a "puppy" and Julian Tobin a "nit" before having the proposal approved.[11] Without consulting anyone, Finsberg gave a "firm and unequivocal pledge this decision will be immediately reversed when we come to power".

The Labour government's 1965 White Paper, outlining its plans to restrict immigration, hit a nerve in Camden. In the summer the Hampstead Labour Party attacked the proposals as "economically unjustifiable and morally indefensible" and prepared an emergency resolution for the Blackpool conference calling for the white paper to be scrapped. Jack Cooper described it as "a complete sell out to the back-street black-haters". Holborn & St Pancras South also tabled a motion attacking the white paper, expressing "disgust with the government's appalling acceptance of racialism as the basis of its policy in dealing with Commonwealth immigration". Roger Robinson, the chairman of St Pancras North, announced that he was "very disturbed" by the White Paper. "I know that many people in this area which has a large immigrant population feel the same". The MP for St Pancras North, Kenneth Robinson (no relation), was now the minister of health: "As a cabinet minister I support government policy", he told the press.

Camden's "immigration committee" held its first meeting and adopted the new name of the Camden Committee for Community Relations. Ernest Wistrich, who had come to England from Poland as a boy in 1937, was elected chairman. He announced that the CCCR was looking for a full time liaison officer at an annual salary of £1,750. Brian Jones, a 34 year old youth employment officer and a Labour councillor in Hammersmith took the job.

As the conference drew near, Hampstead Labour Party organised a special meeting on the white paper. It was attended by a hundred and fifty members from thirteen constituencies who agreed not to assist

---

11   Victor Lyon stood down from Camden in 1971. He was a councillor on the London
     Borough of Barnet from 1978-2006, during which time he was the mayor in 1993-94,
     and the leader of the council from 2002 -2005.

any Labour MPs who supported the immigration policy. "This could be the forerunner of a national movement against the white paper", said Phil Turner, the eager young public relations officer for the constituency Labour Party. It was to be a rocky ride: at Blackpool the emergency resolution to overturn the white paper was defeated by the unions casting a block vote of over four million. Undaunted, Camden council passed a resolution condemning the white paper (with two Labour councillors, Peter Best and Tim Skinner, abstaining). The white paper was, said Peggy Duff, "fertiliser to racial intolerance".

Things were very different then. At the beginning of 1966 a joint campaign by activists in the Labour and Liberal parties in Hampstead visited scores of shops and estates agents where signs had been placed marking properties to let with the caveat: "No Coloureds" or "Europeans only". All but one refused to take the offending signs down. "We are considering a boycott", said John Keohane, secretary of the Hampstead Labour Party, "and we may also picket the shops with placards to point out their racial bias". One West Hampstead estate agent was commended for a sign which read "Coloureds Welcome". The CCCR set out its plans to set up "inter-racial hostels". Roger Robinson, the chair of their housing sub-committee said: "We want to set up hostels where students of all colours and creeds will mix". He also wanted to set up a conciliation service where "a rota of qualified volunteers" will sort out racial disputes between landlords and tenants. Kenneth Archer of the Camden Committee for International Cooperation observed without criticism that the coloured influx could cause race riots in Camden as had happened in Notting Hill. After the *Ham & High* used a headline "The Furtive Jamaican", the editor of the CCCR's Bulletin, Paul Foot, criticised the paper for referring to racial and national origins of people in its reports. "Arrant nonsense", replied the *Ham & High*.

The Belsize Village Residents Association was formed to voice local complaints concerning two noisy late night coffee bars on Belsize Lane in Hampstead. "These young beatniks congregate in large numbers and when you try to walk past them you are jostled", one resident told the *Ham & High*. In January Henry Brooke, now with time on his hands, announced that he was sponsoring a private members bill to limit the opening hours of such premises.

Housing was more to the fore in the minds of politicians locally, and the Labour Party was keen to keep down council rents. The new Rent Act came into force in 1966 introducing the principle of a "fair rent". Camden had adopted differing rent schemes from the three

32

old boroughs and the new act threatened to force a rise in rents in St Pancras. Fearing the tenants' reaction, the council announced that it was going to instruct the London University Centre for Urban Studies to prepare a report on how the schemes could be standardised in order to delay the decision for a year. Richard Crossman, the minister for housing and local government, made a speech in March tailored for a Camden audience: Tory plans to cut aid for local housing programmes would increase rent by ten shillings in every council house in the borough.

Crossman also announced his determination "to build 500,000 homes a year between now and 1970" and in London started an "all out drive" to build homes. "We're rearing to go", enthused Peter Jonas, the chairman of the housing committee. "In Camden no amount of private development will be able to offer a solution to the problem". He announced that the minister had approved the council's plans to build 4,250 homes by 1968. [12] The council had £9m to buy property and to cut slums in the coming financial year, twice the figure for 65/66. "We are definitely not going to slow down our programme", said Peggy Duff. The only obstacle was the manpower shortage. Camden took on 250 manual workers in the direct works department in the first year, and was still 150 short of its thousand man target.

But the credit was there and the length of the housing list pushed the council's appetite for property. These were, as the Ham & High was later to acknowledge, "the heady days of Charlie Ratchford and Paddy O'Connor who, wanting to municipalise the whole borough, bought literally thousands of houses, often without a survey, and then found themselves with crumbling, squatted properties unfit for anyone". The Tories could see that the spending was often poorly considered and quoted examples. Their housing spokesman, Julian Tobin, remarked: "We have felt disquiet for some time. If you become known as a willing buyer people will take advantage and drive a hard bargain". Any criticism was met with anger. "You have only one object in mind: that we should have a lower deficit and lower rates", said Peter Jonas. "What Mr Tobin has said", said Victor Bonafont, "is to the devil with the housing list and people living in rotten, horrible conditions". The rate went up by another shilling to 10s 6d. "There is", said the Conservative Luigi Denza, "nothing easier than spending other people's money".

Over half of Camden's building target involved the redevelopment

33

---

12 An increase of 181% over the 1570 new homes built by the three old boroughs in the preceding four years.

of Gospel Oak, one of the oldest parts of the borough, where 150 houses were to be subject to a compulsory purchase order, demolished and replaced with 2,500 new homes. "Whole streets will be wiped off the map", noted the *Ham & High*. "Gospel Oak will have one of London's first communities in a traffic free shopping centre. Walkways at first and second floor levels will link shops at Lismore Circus with hundreds of new flats, houses and maisonettes." It was not easy going. Peggy Duff, who chaired the planning committee, was shouted down at a meeting of 400 residents. "We want to redevelop Gospel Oak because most of the housing in this area is not fit to live in" she said, to cries of "Who says so?" and "This is not a slum area – you don't know what you're talking about!" Oak Village, a double row of early nineteenth century artisans' houses which had been bought and gentrified by the middle classes, was also to be included in the CPO. Unmoved by the furore, Peggy Duff announced that "we don't want a middle class ghetto in the middle of this magnificent housing scheme". When questioned by the press about the protestors, she was optimistic: "I thought they were all on our side. I think they want this development as much as we do."

Despite his great success in all but demolishing Henry Brooke's majority in Hampstead, in March 1964 Jack Cooper decided not to stand again. He was now 44 and reasoned, somewhat presciently, that even if he won he would risk having to find himself a new career should the political wind change after a single term. Within a few months, Hampstead Labour Party had found themselves a very different candidate in the 29 year old barrister Ben Whitaker. He was not a councillor (although had joined "Willesden's race relations organisation") was educated at Eton and Oxford, had served in the Guards, and was a son of Major General Sir Charles Whitaker, Bt. Whitaker soon proved himself to be every bit as abrasive as Cooper, and the papers delighted in reporting his utterances on all subjects: Edward Heath, he declared, "is not fit to run a boy scout troop", Henry Brooke was "out of touch" and he called for a ban on all price increases "except those in the national interest".

Of all the other declared candidates hoping for an election, his activity was matched only by another young barrister, Lord Julian Byng, the Conservative candidate in Holborn & St Pancras South, who caused a stir by telling a meeting of the Hampstead Young Conservatives that "Tories are innately superior to Socialists" because of their sense of service. Socialists, on the other hand, "are nasty little men on the make". He was, explained the *Ham & High*, a younger son of the Earl of Strafford.

When Harold Wilson called a general election for March 1966,

34

Ladbrookes gave odds of 2-1 on for Brooke to hold onto Hampstead. Whitaker was quoted at 6-4 against (and the Liberal Renee Soskin at 200-1). In the following month the polls improved for Labour nationally, and there was an additional interest in the young Hampstead candidate. Educated, articulate and confident, he was young, good looking and a very interesting man. He had been sent by Amnesty International to visit prisoners of conscience in Rhodesia. He had visited the former prime minister of that colony, Garfield Todd, and had even got Todd's daughter, Judy, to campaign for him in Hampstead. He had written a book on the police (entitled "The Police") which was, said the *Ham & High*, "Excellent". His wife was glamorous and they were having their first child. Even the fact that he lived in Pimlico rather than Hampstead seemed in itself somewhat risqué and attractive. His campaign was also exciting and glamorous: he had a series of big names from the cabinet visiting the constituency. The *Ham & High* printed a large photograph of Whitaker looking thoughtful while clutching a telephone to his ear. The caption read: "Whitaker: communicating".

Henry Brooke on the other hand seemed very much yesterday's man. His time as Home Secretary had not been a happy one. He had been ridiculed in the press generally and quite mercilessly in *Private Eye* and *That Was The Week That Was*. Locally, he had never recovered from his rough handling at the polls from Jack Cooper two years before. Edward Heath had no job for him in the shadow cabinet and, as he had been Alec Douglas-Home's home secretary up to the fall of the Conservatives in 1964, he seemed somehow to smell of defeat. Just as he had been too polite to respond to Cooper's attacks in the last election, he was too polite to deal with the barrage of cutting remarks from Whitaker. He would not invite any names from the shadow cabinet to come and help his campaign because, he said, they would be too busy helping "genuinely marginal seats".

Whitaker won by 2253 votes. A week after the result the *Ham & High* headline read: "Rhodesia –new MP acts" above a rather lame report that, following his victory, Whitaker had met other Labour MPs interested in African matters and was "considering sending a delegation to Mr Wilson". The turnout had been higher (72.4%) than in 1964 (67.6%), and Henry Brooke's vote had gone up by over eight hundred votes, but the Liberal vote had fallen from 8019 to 5182 and their candidate, Renee Soskin, had lost her deposit. She described Whitaker's campaign as "underhanded" for adopting so many Liberal policies. Brooke, on the other hand, took it on the chin. "I have enjoyed this election more

35

than any other I have fought", he said, "I was very pleased that my vote increased". He declined the opportunity to complain of the personal attacks made on him by Whitaker. "It was very fair", he said, adding only: "I am sure that after a few years of Labour government, Hampstead will be won by the Conservatives again". He was elevated to the peerage in the dissolution honours list a month later. The *Ham & High* congratulated him and wished him luck: "There is no doubt", read the editorial, somewhat guiltily perhaps, "that Henry Brooke was the most unjustly maligned politician of the post war years."[13]

The results in Camden's other two constituencies were as expected. Kenneth Robinson increased his majority in St Pancras North and Helen Jeger increased her majority in Holborn & St Pancras South[14]. All the people of Camden were now represented by Labour politicians in Parliament and on the GLC, and enjoyed a Labour run borough council.

Paddy O'Connor, a 49 year old ticket inspector on the buses was named as Camden's new mayor. Born a Dubliner, he had been in England since he was a teenager and had served in the RAF during the war. "It is appropriate that I should be chosen as Camden's next mayor", he said, to the bafflement of those listening, "as 1966 marks the fiftieth anniversary of the Irish rebellion which gave Ireland her freedom". Charlie Ratchford continued as leader with Jock Stallard, now back in the fold, as his deputy and Roy Shaw as the Labour Party whip.

The leader of the Conservative group, Leslie Room, now 65, had stood down a few months earlier "for personal and family reasons". He was replaced by the 39 year old Geoffrey Finsberg who had been a Hampstead councillor since 1949 and was now the national chairman of the Young Conservatives. The first change he brought about was in his title. He insisted on being referred to in all council communications as "the leader of the opposition", rather than "the leader of the minority party" as had been the case with Leslie Room.

In the summer the Labour leadership announced the formation of a fifteen member "cabinet" or "a special advisory committee" made up of Ratchford, his deputy, the Labour whip and all the chairmen of the

---

13 Following his sometimes unhappy career in the Commons, Brooke became a regular front bench spokesman in the House of Lords where, according to his 1984 obituary in *The Times*, "he was very much at ease and his great experience and conscientious accuracy of mind earned him great respect".

14 Ernest Wistrich, the most deserving of Labour candidates, who had been quoted by Ladbrookes odds of 4-7 on to overturn the Tory majority in Hendon South, failed by 600 votes.

main committees. There would be no representation by members of the opposition. Finsberg was furious and compared it to the Star Chamber. He was ignored, but made much of it in the press. "It is only advisory", said Sammy Fisher, "I can't understand this simulated indignation".

Finsberg had plenty of incentive to be indignant as often and as publicly as possible. Even before his elevation to the peerage, Henry Brooke had made it clear that he would not be contesting the seat again, and the rush to succeed him was on. Had he stood down after his drubbing by Jack Cooper and not contested the 1966 election, his successor would have undoubtedly been Neil Sheilds. But things had moved on and the Hampstead Conservative Association found itself hosting a battle for succession. The final shortlist included the 27 year old Leon Brittan, Neil Shields, and Geoffrey Finsberg. Finsberg won, edging Shields in to second place. Had Shields not decided to retire from Hampstead council and take himself out of the limelight rather than transfer to Camden council as Finsberg had done, things may have been very different. "I have known Neil for twenty years and hope that we will remain friends", said Finsberg, but Shields had had enough. Let down by the association he had served and run for twenty years, he resigned as association treasurer in a huff and faded into the Hampstead sunset.[15]

In the Labour Party, Phil Turner resigned as Ben Whitaker's agent because, he said, he disagreed with the government's policies on "the wages and prices freeze, Rhodesia, immigration and Vietnam".

In early September the University of London's Centre for Urban studies at last released an interim report setting out how the council could consolidate the three different rent regimes inherited from the three old councils. "Put them all up", was the unsurprising burden of its recommendations. Still the housing committee hesitated, fearful of what the reaction among the old St Pancras tenants would be. The delay prompted a letter from the district auditor, Samuel Evans, who warned Camden that they were failing to stem the growing council housing deficit. In 64/65 it had been £645m, it was now running at over £1m and next year was expected to exceed £2m. As soon as the district auditor's letter was made public, the St Pancras United Tenants Association (UTA) began organising a mass demonstration against any rent rises at the October council meeting. The council proposed that the

37

---

15 No longer distracted by the banalities of local politics, Shields pursued a business career which left him very wealthy. He also served as the highly successful chairman of the Commission for New Towns 1982-1995. He died in 2002.

maximum rents should be doubled by 7s 6d to 15s a week[16] in order to claw back the deficit and then adjourned any decision until a deputation had met Anthony Greenwood, the local government minister.

It was all grist to the mill for Finsberg. "You are paying in rates this year £1,700,000 to cover the housing deficit because the Labour council hasn't the guts to raise council rents. The poorer people in Camden are subsidising richer council tenants",[17] he told his supporters. "One by one inexorable moves are being made by the socialist majority on Camden designed to make the council conform to the straightjacket of socialist dogma", and then listed as examples the May Day holiday for council workers, compulsory union membership, in house catering without tendering, and the "cowardly delay" in implementing a fair rents policy.

The minister had not been able to help, and at the November council meeting, councillors were greeted by a line of protestors led by the gaunt, donkey jacketed and gauntleted figure of Ken Gillen, UTA's secretary, clutching a placard which read, somewhat tamely: "DO YOU WANT 12/- MORE ON YOUR RENT?" The new rents were approved. It was a difficult meeting attended by a noisily packed public gallery. The chairman of housing, Peter Jonas, emphasised that the district auditor had compelled the council to raise rents. If the rises were not approved, he pleaded, councillors will risk being surcharged or even disqualified. Amid shouts of "traitors" and "Judas Jonas" and the throwing of bundles of leaflets from the gallery, the Labour group split. (Mayor O'Connor rose to the occasion by bellowing back: "Wrap up!", "Belt up!" and "You're not even a council tenant!") Jock Stallard, the deputy leader of the council, and the former UTA leader Dick Collins led an internal revolt. The Tories wanted the rents to be increased by more but eventually voted with the majority party for the rises. There were twelve Labour votes against[18]. It was a taste of things to come. Afterwards the chief rebel, Jock Stallard, told the press that despite being deputy leader of the Labour group, he had no intention of resigning. "My job is to stay on the council and

16   "Rents Shocker" was the headline in the *North London Press*.

17   Finsberg's sentiments were fed to John Boyd Carpenter MP who used them in the House of Commons debate on the Housing Bill in December. Camden should be excluded from the provisions of the legislation and be forced to hold elections in 1967 rather than 68 because, he said, it was in danger of becoming a dictatorship. Lena Jeger loyally declared that "the borough is the most splendid in London".

18   They were Aldermen James MacGibbon, Frank Bennett, George King and Ivy Tate, and councillors Stallard, Collins, Charles Tate, James Buckland, Tom Barker, Roger Robinson, Jim Greenwood and Arthur Graves.

fight these rent increases from the inside", he said. Nor was there any question of expulsions. "Least said, soonest mended", said the whip, Roy Shaw. The *Ham & High*'s editorial column was blunt: "The time has now come for all council tenants to appreciate that they can't have their cake and eat it". In January 1967 UTA went on the offensive and distributed thousand of leaflets urging non payment, but to no effect. "Week one of the Rent Strike and it's a flop", moaned the *North London Press*, deprived of a good story.

Housing was still the headline catcher. Jill Craigie's film "Who are the vandals?" was released to show the miserable housing conditions on the council's Regents Park Estate. It was, said Peggy Duff, "unfair, facile, immature and ill informed." Having adopted Hampstead council's housing development plans in Swiss Cottage, the council began demolishing the Chalcots Estate where nineteenth century housing was to be replaced by four 22 storey blocks of council flats separated by rows of town houses for private buyers. The council also announced its new plans to compulsorily purchase the terribly run down New Town area of Highgate for housing development.

Branch Hill raised its head again at the beginning of 1967. In January Lord Glendyne died, and a fortnight later Camden revealed its plans to use the site for housing. "Branch Hill Shock", read the *Ham & High* headline. Although there had been no restrictive covenant in the contract of sale, there had been a clear understanding that had been outlined to the press on several occasions by Charlie Ratchford. Now that answers were needed, Charlie Ratchford went to ground and Brian Wilson, the town clerk was uncommunicative. "I have no comment to make", he told the papers. Peggy Duff, the planning chief, was left to field the questions: "I know of no gentlemen's agreement", she said. "I was not involved in the negotiations", and "I did not know that Lord Glendyne had just died". Within a month Ben Whitaker and Paddy O'Connor were expressing support for the New Hampstead Society's plan for "a village within a village" at Branch Hill. Ratchford should resign, said Finsberg, for reneging on his agreement with Glendyne.

The second GLC elections were held in the spring of 1967. The Labour Party, who held all three seats in Camden, were defending a 6,000 lead over the Conservatives who needed a 5% swing. The council did its bit by freezing the rate at 10s 4d in the pound[19]. Labour's new

---

19 The London rate equalisation scheme had again favoured the council but, warned the finance chairman, John Diamond, "this is the last time it will operate in its present form".

candidate, Paddy O'Connor, was confident that Labour would win again. "There is no possible shade or shadow of doubt about it," he said. He was wrong. The Tory swing was 9.8% leaving them with a 4,000 majority. ("Four thousand nails in Labour's coffin" ran the *Ham & High* headline.) O'Connor's confidence had been shared by others and scuffles broke out when the results were announced in Camden Town Hall. The lead Tory candidate, Richard "Dickie" Butterfield, a 41 year old Camden councillor and former Grenadier Guards officer was heckled and spat at as he tried to make his speech. The other two Tory winners, Clare Mansel and Lena Townsend fared little better. "Until next year's borough elections the Socialists in Camden are living on borrowed time", predicted Alderman Townsend to boos from the hall. Labour across London had collapsed. The economy was in a mess and Wilson's government was at its most unpopular. The turnout had dropped from 45% to 41%, and with it the Labour share of the vote[20]. Paddy O'Connor made another prediction in his speech after the result. "Around this time next year there will be another Labour council in Camden", he said, and then set off with Mrs O'Connor on his ten day trip to the Soviet Union, taking with him two bottles of "Irish brewed vodka" as gifts[21].

At the Labour group meeting in April 1967, Charlie Ratchford remained as leader, but his deputy, Jock Stallard stood down to be replaced by Paddy O'Connor. Peter Jonas stood down from housing. The convention of the deputy mayor succeeding the mayor was not yet established and so the deputy, Tim Skinner, who had been leader of the opposition on Hampstead council, had to seek election from within the Labour group. He failed, and Camden's new mayor was the 44 year old Labour group chairman and former social worker, Millie Miller. Forceful and determined under her dyed auburn hair, she possessed the brisk movements of a fighter, and was also the only person on the council shorter than Sammy Fisher. Like Sammy Fisher, she had served as mayor of Stoke Newington in the 1950s, and like him had moved to Camden shortly before the 1964 borough elections. Her husband, Monty, who

20 The Conservatives each got about 32,000 votes, the Labour candidates 28,000 each, the Liberals 4,000 and the solitary Communist, 2,000. Cllr Butterfield had also managed to take £2,000 off the bookies by betting on himself and that the Conservatives would win the GLC with a majority of over 25. (In 1967 a "luxury two bedroom flat" in Hampstead could be bought for £8,000.)

21 He was back in early May weighted down with tins of caviar and crab meat, a pedal car for his grandson and a proposal that the borough should be twinned with Zhdanovsky, a "Camden sized" suburb of Moscow.

had a chemical factory in Islington, was her mayoress, as he had been in Stoke Newington.

On 21 April 1967, the Greek colonels took power in Athens in a coup, locked up the Communists and banned miniskirts. Peggy Duff was finding the planning meetings increasingly distracting from her main interest in the International Confederation for Disarmament and Peace. She was already disenchanted with the Labour Party. It was bad enough that Harold Wilson had maintained a cosy relationship with President Johnson notwithstanding the bombing of North Vietnam, but Wilson's failure to sort out the Greeks was just too much. She resigned from the party (and the planning committee), but remained on the council as an independent socialist.

Millie Miller's mayor making ceremony was somewhat marred by the outgoing mayor, Paddy O'Connor, agreeing to let Ernest Wistrich table a political motion deploring the suppression of democracy in Greece following the recent coup by the Greek colonels. It gave Finsberg another headline grabbing opportunity. He and the whole Conservative group walked out of the chamber declaring the motion irrelevant to the work of the borough, although "as individuals we all wish a swift return to full constitutional government in Greece or Nigeria or Sierra Leone". "I'm sorry to say that the walk out reminded me of Munich" said Ernest Wistrich afterwards, assuming the guise of injured innocence. "So many people said that Czechoslovakia was a far away country that did not concern them. This lack of concern has often led to the death of democracy elsewhere."

Charlie Ratchford came under fire at the July council meeting over the council's announcement to develop Branch Hill for housing. The Tories pointed out the obvious: Ratchford had himself given assurances that there would be no development of the land beyond the simple and worthy objectives of homes for old people and children. He had agreed that at County Hall, and the minutes showed just that. Leslie Room had been with him at the same meeting and had left knowing full well what the understanding was. The proposal to build maisonettes at the density of 38 people per acre was "a breach of our word to the vendor, who could have got a considerably higher figure if he knew the site was to be used for housing". Finsberg said: "A bargain was made and we believe bargains are made to be kept". Ratchford denied having made any such assurances. "If this took place while I was there I'm prepared to resign", he said, and then mysteriously: "This is diabolical. I am flabbergasted. It is scandalous".

41

When the *Ham & High* repeated his earlier assurances, he denied them. "I never met Lord Glendyne" he said. "I never did. The poor chap's gone. So I can't have made an agreement with him". Never mind that he had never corrected the *Ham & High*'s coverage of two years ago, he demanded that whoever had reported his comments should check his notes and confirm that he had never said any such thing. Paddy O'Connor did his best to help. If it were left up to him he would develop the area not for 38 people an acre but for 138. "The Tories", he shouted across the chamber where the Tories were facing both him and Charlie Ratchford, "are trying to stab Mr Ratchford in the back". They only wanted to preserve property prices by not having a council estate in Hampstead.

Although Paddy O'Connor remained loyal, Ratchford's performance impressed no one inside or outside his party. The assurances he had given in 1965 had not been incorrectly noted by some careless junior reporter. They had been issued in a press statement signed by Charlie Ratchford and sent to the local papers. "It won't wash, Charlie, really it won't" read the *Ham & High* editorial. "You have put your head on the block. Don't blame us if someone chops it off".

In the next issue the paper printed in full a long rambling explanation from Ratchford. He had been distracted in the council debate and had not heard what Finsberg had said and so had not made himself clear in his response. Importantly, when in 1965 he had said that "the remainder of the site" would not be developed, "I had meant to say the remainder *after the use of it for a variety of purposes* but on reflection I agree it could have been better worded". It was something of a relief to him that the council meeting was then severely disrupted by members of the St Pancras United Tenants Association who burst into a chant of "No rent increases" and had to be cleared from the public gallery by the police.

Feelings about Charlie Ratchford were somewhat different after this. Geoffrey Finsberg announced to the press that very week that "we'll win the 1968 borough elections hands down". When Branch Hill raised its ugly head again at the next council meeting, Charlie Ratchford issued another denial that he had said the site would not be used for housing. Finsberg suggested that if the *Ham & High* had got it so wrong, he should make a formal complaint to the Press Council. The *Ham & High* noted, with some satisfaction, that Ratchford made no reply.

The Liberals also got involved in the dispute, hoping to capitalise on Hampstead's bookishness and polite reservation towards council housing. "Scrap the plan for council housing on Branch Hill", said Fred Cook, chairman of the Hampstead Liberal Party, "and build the British National Library there instead so that council homes could be built next to the British Museum in Bloomsbury".

In the middle of this, the council leadership chose to make the first of its international gestures or distractions, and began a tradition that lasted as long as the Labour Party found itself in control of the council. On 6 August 1967, the twenty second anniversary of the dropping of an atom bomb on Hiroshima, the mayor, Millie Miller, a committed unilateralist, planted a tree in Tavistock Square "in memory of the victims". The tree chosen was a cherry, a tree whose blossom does not "wither on the tree, but scatters in full bloom" and which had been, incidentally, the emblem of the kamikaze pilots.

In September 1967 the district auditor, Samuel Evans, issued his interim report into the council's direct labour building force. "Inefficiency and fiddle", ran the headline on the *Ham & High* above a report on widespread fiddling of bonus claim forms by the 530 employees, and how the department had frequently put in low tenders to secure work and then gone spectacularly over budget without anyone being penalised. Albert Ullmer, the building department's manager, was pushed forward to answer for the council. He put it down to human error rather than fraud. Many council employees, he explained, "found handling a pencil and paper more difficult than handling tools". The council's name had been tarnished, said Finsberg. The report showed inefficiency and ignorance in the building department and "the utter incompetence of the people running the council." Dick Collins, the chairman of the housing committee should resign, and so should Ratchford, "a tired man who tends to be rather accident prone". "I take no notice of what Mr Finsberg says", said Charlie Ratchford wearily. "He is only out to make political capital".

The *Ham & High* agreed with the district auditor's comments and noted that no one was to be sacked or disciplined and that no one was going to resign. The problem was a symptom of a greater malaise: "What worries us more is the frightening lack of brains and talent even in a go ahead authority such as Camden. Both the major parties carry too much dead wood. And Labour, particularly, faces a leadership crisis that must be resolved". The local government reforms that had created Camden were expected to attract people of higher calibre onto the council. "As yet we have the same old faces that served on the old authorities. We certainly hope things will change".

43

Housing dominated Labour thinking. When the British Railways Board announced that St Pancras Station was to be closed to make King's Cross "the major terminus of the 1970s", Roy Shaw, the chairman of the planning and development committee, was quick to announce that the council's aim was to have St Pancras station demolished so that new homes could be built as soon as possible on the forty five acres that would be freed up[22]. In November, the minister for housing, Anthony Greenwood, who lived in Hampstead and was a former Hampstead councillor, opened the new Curnock Street housing estate of 213 homes which had been put up by the direct labour department in under two years. Camden was putting up houses faster than any other borough and that, said Ratchford, was because of in-house labour. "We are proud", he said, "of the profitability of the department". "And", added the bullish Victor Bonafont, laying down the gauntlet for the coming election, "there will be no sale of council houses in Camden. We are proud of the 1500 families we re-housed this year".

1967 also saw the strange case of a London Borough of Croydon Labour councillor whose day job was that of Camden council's "children's officer". Kenneth Urwin had a house in South Norwood which he needed to sell in order to move to Highgate where he could be closer to his work. He put the house on the market and accepted an offer from "a Jamaican postman". His neighbours in South Norwood were upset at this, and urged him to reconsider, eventually clubbing together and coming up with the asking price. Mr Urwin then tore up his agreement with the postman and sold to his neighbours who in turn found another buyer. When the story hit the national press, Camden found itself somewhat embarrassed. "The real tragedy of this situation", said Bob Humphreys, the (Labour) chairman of the children's committee, finding a positive spin, "is that Mr Urwin went ahead with the sale to a coloured man without it occurring to him that his neighbours might not regard the colour of the new resident as irrelevant as he did". He referred to the great pressure that had been placed upon Mr Urwin and his family: "None of us can say with absolute certainty we would have been able to act differently. He retains my full confidence". Ernest Wistrich, speaking as chairman of the CCCR, was mildly censorious: "While we appreciate all the personal pressures put on Mr Urwin, we feel that we must express our regret that he changed his mind. We don't agree with what he did".

---

22   As a sop to the conservation lobby, he added that he was in favour of retaining St Pancras Chambers "provided a suitable use can be found".

He then announced that the CCCR was planning to offer advice "to help those in Camden wanting to sell to coloured people".

Of greater irritation to the Labour leadership was the behaviour of one of their Chalk Farm councillors, Hilda Chandler, a former mayor of St Pancras. The council had slapped a compulsory purchase order on the five bedroom house on Kingstown Street off Regents Park where she lived with her husband and an adult son. She was entitled to be rehoused by the council, but not in anything bigger than a two bedroom flat. Mrs Chandler felt that she had been let down personally by Charlie Ratchford who had, she said, made certain representations to her. She resigned and a by election was set for 14 December 1967.

The stock of the Labour Party was low when the by election was called, and then plummeted after the 14.3% devaluation of the pound that took place on 15 November.[23] The *Ham & High*, despite its strong misgivings about Charlie Ratchford, nevertheless felt that Labour deserved to win because the council had opposed the Motorway Box Scheme around London which was supported by the Conservative GLC. It urged local people to "vote on local issues and for once divorce local government from the broken promises of Wilson and Whitehall." Such pleas fell on deaf ears, not least because Chalk Farm lies somewhat on the fringe of the usual distribution area of the *Ham & High*. The Conservative candidate, Peter Moloney, romped home on a 12% swing. "A magnificent victory!" enthused Finsberg. "It can be silly to prophesy, but it looks almost certain that there will be a Conservative council next year".

As the election drew closer the battle lines were drawn over council rents. The London University's Centre for Urban Studies, who had been commissioned (for £60,000) in 1966 to find a way through the tangle of Camden's inheritance of different rent regimes, eventually produced their final report in a weighty document that provided more than one solution to the problem. Part of the report, prepared by Professor Marian Bowley, advised that in order to wipe out the council's housing account deficit of £2¼m, maximum rents would need to be raised by an average of £2.10s. The Labour group seized instead on a passage in the main part of the report drafted by Professor Ruth Glass which helpfully suggested that social housing could not be looked at merely in financial terms. Labour immediately pledged that council

---

23 Not improved locally by Whitaker's support for the devaluation: "I wish we'd done it earlier", he said.

rents would be frozen in the event of a Labour victory, and at the same time warned of massive rent increases should the Conservatives win. In order to avoid having to quantify high rent rises, the Conservatives simply rejected the report in its entirety. Their housing spokesman, Julian Tobin, instead promised somewhat coyly that the Conservatives would take six months or so to work out a new rent system "to protect those who need protection".

But it was not as simple as that. Professor Glass's report also pointed out 62% of privately owned homes in Camden were overcrowded and lacked essential facilities in that the occupants had to share with other households a WC, sink or cooker. 42,000 people were living in substandard accommodation in the borough and thirty thousand new homes were needed in Camden to rectify the situation. Both sides pledged to keep building. "The waiting list in Camden stays just about the same every year. I cannot see how there can be any let up in council building", said Alan Greengross, the Conservative planning spokesman. The difficulty was that the finances for the housing programme would be affected by the money raised through rent. The Tories were concerned about "the privileged bunch": those lucky enough to get council housing who were now being promised rent freezes by Labour.[24]

The run up to the election saw the most extraordinary internal fights within the constituency Labour parties. In St Pancras North the management committee was so upset by the reintroduction of prescription fees and the increased dental charges that in January they demanded that their MP Kenneth Robinson, the minister for health, resign from the government.[25] Robinson refused. In February, Millie Miller, the mayor of Camden, was deselected from her Euston seat and not picked for any other except Highgate where the chances of re-election were poor[26]. She was only saved by the Labour group who, when Alderman James MacGibbon resigned the following week, elected

---

24 A sentiment echoed thirty years later by John Macdonald, then the Labour chief whip: "I hate council tenants. I call them lucky bastards."

25 "I note that the St Pancras North Labour Party have reacted to my statement last week by insisting that Mr Robinson resign from the government", read a press release from James Moorhouse, the Conservative prospective parliamentary candidate for St Pancras North.

26 As will be seen below, her deselection from Euston saved her political career.

her as an alderman in his place so that she would not need to stand.

Also in February the Hampstead Labour Party fought off an attempt by local left wingers to disaffiliate the local party from the national Labour Party because of the government's policy towards Vietnam. Wilson had not only failed to oppose the Americans, but had allowed them troop training facilities in Malaysia. Whitaker survived this embarrassment and prevented any other criticism from the left by his outspoken stance on the Commonwealth Immigrants Bill designed to curb immigration by Kenyan Asians. It was, he said, "a miserable measure which could be better called the Alf Garnett Appeasement Bill", written not by Labour policymakers but by Enoch Powell. Whitaker and Lena Jeger were among the 35 Labour MPs who voted against the bill. Kenneth Robinson narrowly survived a second attempt to deselect him (by 20 votes to 17) because he did not vote at all. The CCCR struck him (and Henry Brooke) off their list of vice presidents for this crime "We have", explained Alderman Wistrich, the chairman of the CCCR, "to make a stand on this issue".

In the final run up to the borough elections, immigration became an issue following Enoch Powell's speech in Birmingham on 20 April 1968. Powell opposed the government's Race Relations Bill and, he said, trouble lay ahead if mass immigration was not curbed. "Like the Roman I seem to see the River Tiber foaming with much blood." Powell, a former cabinet minister and the shadow spokesman on defence, was sacked by Edward Heath the next day, but polls showed that his popularity was great. The newspapers were keen to learn the views of the Tory candidates. Ken Graham, a 24 year old post office clerk, chairman of the Hampstead Young Conservatives and candidate in Kilburn, told the *Ham & High* unequivocally "Powell was right". Others thought otherwise, notably Peter Hilton and Pip Raymond-Cox, both standing in Priory ward. Powell, said Mrs Raymond-Cox, was "unwise, misguided and wrong". "But", reported the paper, "many Conservatives were reluctant to say they disagreed with the substance of Mr Powell's remarks". Finsberg would not be drawn, but said that he was also against the Race Relations Bill. "Legislation is not the answer. I do not believe you can make people good by law", he said, and added: "I am certain that the Conservative Party is right to say that immigration should be stringently restricted".

Finsberg's main assault on the Labour council was its inefficiency and its spending. There were going to be savings. "Nothing is sacrosanct", he promised. Hector Dimmock, chairman of the Camden branch of

47

NALGO complained that staff were upset at being "kicked around like a football" by the Conservatives in their campaign. Finsberg assured Camden staff they were "first rate", but that there would be changes. And there was to be an end to Socialist posturing: the staff holiday on May Day was going to be scrapped.

A month before the election, Finsberg made his point on rents. It was the fault of the Labour government. "There will no rent increases," he promised, "if Mr Anthony Greenwood, the minister of housing, meets our deficit". Or to put it another way: "Council rents will not be frozen unless we are given a substantial subsidy from the Exchequer. I do not see why ratepayers should meet this continuing burden. We do not intend to get rid of the total rent deficit, but we have said that the rent deficit must be reduced, and reduced it will be".

At the last council meeting on 24 April 1968 both parties voted to abolish minimum rents for council tenants as had been recommended in Professor Glass's report at the cost of £10,000 a year. The only dissenting voice was that of Peggy Duff, now sitting as an independent socialist and not seeking re-election, who said that the main issue was not rents at all, but the squalid accommodation used to house tenants in the private sector. Police then had to be called to clear the gallery of members of the St Pancras United Tenants Association. "Leaflets cascaded from the gallery", reported the *Ham & High*, "as tenants shouted 'You're a shower, the whole lot of you' and chanted 'Labour-Tory, Tory-Labour, all the same'".

The *Ham & High* reported that there were several council candidates with well known associations. Mrs (Janet) Whitaker was standing (somewhat hopelessly) in Adelaide ward for Labour, and 34 year old Peter Brooke, the son of Henry Brooke, was standing for the Tories in Tory held Highgate. The Liberals were fielding Alison Snow, the wife of "TV newscaster Peter Snow"; the former MP Archie MacDonald (again); and the mountaineer Margaret Darvall "who took part in the disastrous all women expedition to climb the Himalayan peak of Cho Oyu" in 1959[27].

In the week before the election, the confidence of the Conservatives was, to the dismay of *The North London Press*, all too apparent. "What is disturbing is that reports indicate that in places like Camden —where Labour at present forms a strong and on the whole capable majority group —the anti Labour swing may well reduce the party's representation

---

27 Four dead

to vestigial proportions". "If we are to be judged purely on our merits as a council", said Roy Shaw, "We would get back".

The Conservatives won. Charlie Ratchford attended the count in a sports jacket of a check so loud as to drown out his red rosette, and shook Finsberg's hand once it was all over. "It was a fair fight", he conceded, "We'll be back in three years". The new council had 42 Tory members and 18 Labour. The Conservatives had taken fifteen seats from Labour, including all the seats in Euston, King's Cross (by 500 votes), Regents Park, and Priory. They mopped up the last remaining Labour seat in Chalk Farm and even managed to take one of the seats in both Camden and Gospel Oak wards. Charlie Ratchford's own vote was down by nine hundred. "Labour lost control", said the *Ham & High* editorial, "not because of mismanagement in the council, but through disaffection with the government". The Liberal vote had collapsed, leaving them third everywhere, even in Hampstead Town. "It seems" said their leader, Fred Cook, "voters have chosen two evils and ignored the good".

Of the 57,000 who voted throughout the borough, 30,000 voted Conservative, 21,000 Labour, 3,000 Liberal and 2,000 for the other candidates. The swing was 12.8% against Labour, somewhat short of Finsberg's predictions that the Conservatives would get 52 seats. Against the GLC elections the Tory vote was down 2,000 and the Labour vote was down by 6,500. The collapse of Labour had been far worse in neighbouring boroughs: thirty three Labour councillors had lost their seats in Haringey and all fifty Labour councillors had been voted out in Islington. The Conservatives now held 28 of the 32 London boroughs. Finsberg felt robbed. The Labour Party had saved itself from all but total destruction by using "lies and scare tactics" about rents to alarm council tenants. But, he said, "Camden will now have an opportunity of three years of good honest government". "The wind of change did not blow anywhere near as hard in Camden", said the *Ham & High*. "There are two reasons: it is a more politically conscious borough and it had a Labour council that gained a reputation for progressive policies".[28]

49

28 To put the Camden result in context, in London in 1964 the Conservatives had 668 seats and Labour 1112. (There were also 63 independents, 13 Liberals and three Communists.) After the 1968 election the Conservatives held 1434 seats and Labour 351. (There were 65 Independents, ten Liberals and still the three Communists.) Or in percentage terms: in 1964 Labour held 60% of the council seats in London against the 36% held by the Conservatives. In 1968, the Conservatives held 77% of the seats and Labour only 19%.

3 |

Geoffrey Finsberg and Martin Morton: a Conservative council

O n 17 May 1968, a week after the election and five days before the first council meeting, Alderman Millie Miller, now a Labour mayor of a Conservative controlled borough, performed the last of her mayoral duties. She accompanied the prime minister to Tavistock Square Gardens for the unveiling of a statue of Ghandi[1]. The mayor and Harold Wilson stood uncomfortably while the Indian High Commissioner, Shanti Dhavan, read out his speech calling for peace and understanding between nations. His words were drowned out not so much by the roar of traffic, but by the hundreds of students chanting "Wilson Out!"

The statutory council meeting was altogether a more peaceful event. Norman Oatway was elected mayor. "Camden's first Tory mayor will be", moaned the St Pancras based *North London Press*, "a Hampstead man". The five aldermanic vacancies were taken by the Conservatives because, it was explained, the five existing aldermen were all Labour. Geoffrey Finsberg then announced the end of hostilities by offering the position of mayor to the Labour Party for the next year, 1969. There were, he pointed out, twenty six new councillors untarnished by the enmity that had existed between Tory Hampstead and Labour St Pancras, and both Charlie Ratchford and Leslie Room had worked hard to help consolidate the new borough. The idea of Finsberg (of all people) being nice to him wrong footed Charlie Ratchford. He told the press that he would have to go to the Labour group but that they would probably reject it. "They've been elected", he said rather sulkily,

---

1   Sculpted by the Polish born Belsize Park artist, Freida Brilliant.

"it's their job to provide a mayor". His chief whip, Roy Shaw, did not like the idea either and, as he told the *North London Press*, he could not work out what Finsberg's motive was. Anyway, he said, remembering a former Labour group leader on Hampstead council, the Conservatives cannot be trusted as they did not keep their promise to make Dame Florence Cayford mayor of Hampstead. He was to regret mentioning that name. Finsberg remembered the case well and resolved that if he could not get a sitting Labour councillor to be mayor, he could perhaps make his peace with Dame Flo.

The *Ham & High* liked the idea of a Labour nominated mayor very much and, in an uncharacteristic flight of whimsy, enthused: "There is still an outside chance that Labour will accept –and nominate a leading member of the community, perhaps a coloured man, as mayor". [2]

The first full council meeting of the new administration lasted sixteen and a half hours, from 7pm on Wednesday 17 July until 11.28am the next morning. It was, said the *North London Press*, "the longest and bitterest meeting of Camden council". St Pancras United Tenants Association and their supporters picketed the town hall to protest at the plans to put up rents. Councillors of a nervous disposition were escorted into the building by police who promised substantial reinforcements (sitting in a Black Maria around the corner) on a thirty second stand by. The Labour tactic was to swamp the majority party with a long list of amendments challenging every aspect of the new agenda. There were 27 divisions, each preceded by lengthy (and often theatrical) contributions by the experienced Labour rump, to be replied to briefly by the few Conservative old handers while the new councillors sat and watched. "The Tories appear to have followed Brer Rabbit and decided to lie low and say nuffin", reported the *Ham & High*. "The new opposition –and it is a far better one than the Tories ever produced –wanted to make itself felt in no uncertain manner". [3]

Heckling from the crowded public gallery descended into "moments of wild disorder" through the rents debate. The new housing chairman, Martin Morton, [4] proposed putting up council rents by an average of 7s 6d a week on the ground that the council had to choose

---

2   Not until the 1972 Local Government Act were London boroughs restricted to choosing a councillor as mayor.

3   A view endorsed by Martin Morton: "They were a far better opposition than we had been".

4   In Australia at the time of the 1968 election, Morton had remained on the council by becoming an alderman.

GEOFFREY FINSBERG AND MARTIN MORTON:
A CONSERVATIVE COUNCIL

between putting a stop to the building programme or putting up the rents. If rents were frozen, the housing deficit would be £2.7m by the end of 1969. In any event, those most in need would be protected by the differential rents system that linked rents to income. "I speak for very many workers in Camden", said Jock Stallard, with passion, anticipating what many Conservatives would say in years to come, "who refuse to submit themselves or their families to a means test. I know this pride is causing them hardship. I know many of them are extremely worried, even to the point of breakdown". Millie Miller pledged herself to getting the minister to intervene on the grounds that "new tenants won't be able to pay the rents". Four hours and ten futile divisions later, at two in the morning, the council finally agreed Morton's proposals. Rents were going up. The immediate battle over, the St Pancras UTA demonstrators filed out noisily promising a rent strike, leaving only eight people in the gallery[5].

The new Conservative plans for the council committees, approved in general terms by all parties when outlined by the town clerk before the election, were now seen as something of a Tory plot. The old all-Labour "advisory" committee or cabinet was discarded in place of new Policy and Resources Committee which had so much power, argued Sammy Fisher, that the council "will become nothing more than a cipher". The existing committees were to be made smaller and two of them were to be abolished. "Some new members may not get the chance to sit on two committees", complained Millie Miller. "A typical piece of Finsbuggery", said Corin Hughes-Stanton.

In the early hours, the council moved on to the agenda items concerning the Conservative plans for redevelopment in which they set out their plans that every new large estate should be made up of at least 40% private housing. It was an attempt, before its time, to prevent the development of sink estates and to ensure neighbourhoods were mixed. Roy Shaw was having none of it: "This is one of the most disgraceful items on the agenda. Hidden in it are the real intentions of the Tories. They have not the guts to state openly what they mean, but wrap it up in verbiage and downright lies. Their main concern is to help their middle class friends and the property owners and sell off the council's assets. If this policy is pursued those who suffer will be the lower paid

---

5   Seven of whom the papers identified as Ray Benad, the vice chairman of the St Pancras North Liberal Party; four Young Conservatives; and two men who were asleep. Of the latter, one was Dickie Butterfield, the Conservative GLC member whose snores interrupted the council meeting until he was shaken awake.

workers living in poor conditions. This brands the Tories as a class party which says to hell with the people!" 40% of houses for private buyers meant 40% fewer houses for those most in need.

The council moved on to the council's decision to delay spending the £1½m required to start urgent improvements on four run down pre-war housing estates.[6] The plans for modernisation needed to be reviewed, said Martin Morton, for two reasons. First, it may prove to be cheaper to rebuild them, and secondly a new and more advantageous subsidy scheme was expected in 1969 and the council was going to take advantage of the new government money. Labour cries of outrage were led by Roger Robinson who spoke with passion of the deplorable conditions and poor wiring that "could easily cause death, disaster or fire". "When Cllr Bonafont was the housing committee chairman", he said, harking back to a golden age that had been interrupted only two months before, "he put repairs to these estates to the top of the list!" But it was no good, and his arguments were rather flattened by another Labour councillor, Bill Oakshott, who, rather missing the point, told the chamber that he had lived in Somers Town for sixty five years and had only seen one improvement in the last forty.[7]

Conservative plans to sell council houses to its tenants were also attacked. The flats do not belong to the tenants, they belong to the ratepayers as a whole, said Ratchford[8]. "It is a wicked decision", agreed Alderman Mrs Ruth Howe. "Another piece of doctrinaire Toryism", said Millie Miller. "Scandalous!" said Roger Robinson. "It's not your job to sell homes, but to provide homes for those in need".

And the Conservatives voted to kill off the quarterly council newspaper. "We put our faith in the local press", declared Alderman Edward Bowman, somewhat hopefully.

As the agenda ground to its conclusion, Paddy O'Connor rose to propose a motion of thanks and congratulations to the mayor for not losing his temper. "I would've blown up", he said, quite truthfully. The council finally rose at 11.28 am. Norman Oatway quickly changed into a spare suit and shirt that had been brought to the Town Hall by his wife, and then disappeared to carry out his mayoral duties.

54

---

6   Montague Tibbles House, Kennistoun House, Denyer House and the Somers Town Estate.

7   Bill Oakshott, says Roger Robinson, was remarkable for his similarity in appearance to Albert Steptoe, the character played by Wilfred Brambell in the television BBC series *Steptoe & Son*.

8   Now, since the Queen's Birthday Honours List, Charlie Ratchford, CBE.

1. The leader and the chairman of the council, and the leader of the minority party in 1964; Charlie Ratchford, Sammy Fisher and Leslie Room. *(Camden)*

2. The full council at Sammy Fisher's mayor making in 1965. Note the three maces from the old metropolitan boroughs of Hampstead, Holborn and St Pancras.

3. The Labour benches in 1965.

Front row: *Victor Bonafont, John Diamond, Peggy Duff, Charlie Ratchford, Paddy O'Connor;*
Second row: *Millie Miller, Ernest Wistrich, Roy Shaw, Peter Best, Jack Cooper (and a guest);*
Back row: *James MacGibbon, Enid Wistrich and Ruth Howe.*

4. Paddy O'Connor. *(Camden)*

5. Dame Flo and Martin Morton.

6. 1970: Geoffrey Finsberg and the last Tory mayor
for thirty seven years, Harold Gould.

7. Millie Miller

8. Frank Dobson following behind Jock Stallard. *(Nigel Sutton)*

9. Roy Shaw *(Camden)*

10. Alan Greengross *(Nigel Sutton)*

11. Julian Tobin *(Nigel Sutton)*

12. May 1981: Charlie Rossi, re-elected to the GLC congratulates Barbara Hughes on winning the St Pancras by election *(Nigel Sutton)*

13. 1982: Annoying the Lefties. Brian Rathbone, Bill Trite, David Neil Smith and Tony Kerpel greet Private Rose on the steps of the town hall. *(Nigel Sutton)*

14. 1983: Annoying the Tories. Tom Devine, Charlie Taylor and Phil Turner raise the red flag over the town hall to commemorate Karl Marx. *(Nigel Sutton)*

At the end of the year, the council planned an exhibition with backing from the Arts Council and the East German Academy of Art of the works of the "photomontage" artist John Heartfield at the Camden Art Centre on Arkwright Road. There was a local connection in that Heartfield, a well known Communist propagandist in pre-war Berlin, fled from his native Germany in 1938 and lived in Hampstead for twelve years. He returned to what had become East Germany in 1950, and died there in April 1968.

On 20 August 1968, Soviet troops, backed by their allies including the East Germans, entered Czechoslovakia to put an end to Alexander Dubcek's liberalising government. The world was horrified. Twelve years after the savage crushing of the Hungarian uprising, public opinion was greatly moved. Pleas were sent out round the word for a boycott of the Soviets and those of their allies complicit in the act. Genuinely disgusted, but with a politician's instinct for a seizing a headline, and without consulting the Arts Council, Finsberg announced in an arbitrary fashion that Camden was cancelling the Heartfield exhibition. The Arts Council had in the meantime also moved in a quick and arbitrary way and, without consulting Camden, had withdrawn its support and cancelled the event. Finsberg's gesture was both late and empty. It was a minor matter and was soon forgotten, but it would return to haunt the Tories. Without meaning to, Finsberg had tasted the fruit so carelessly nurtured by Ernest Wistrich's Greek debate and Millie Miller's Hiroshima tree.

There was more embarrassment for Finsberg over the future of Hampstead Heath which was then GLC land. The Conservative run GLC wanted to relinquish its interest and wanted to get Camden to take over the burden. Finsberg, who was both the leader of the council and Camden's representative on the London Boroughs Association, rather liked the idea and said so publicly. It was another arbitrary decision taken without consulting his colleagues. Twenty of them were against the move, as were all three Conservative GLC members for Camden, and, embarrassingly, the Hampstead Heath & Old Hampstead Protection Society was aggressively hostile to any such move. Their Chairman, the formidable Peggy Jay, led a delegation to Anthony Greenwood, the minister for housing and local government and a Hampstead resident. The idea had no backers, apart from Finsberg who soon wished he had kept quiet on the subject. "An idea is not necessarily wrong because it is dreamed up by Finsberg" drawled Whitaker, "but this piece of imperialism seems short sighted and impractical".

GEOFFREY FINSBERG AND MARTIN MORTON:
A CONSERVATIVE COUNCIL

Within a few days the GLC and the London Boroughs Association issued a joint statement to the effect that the Heath would stay with the GLC "for the time being". For no good reason other than to embarrass Finsberg further, the Labour group backed a motion at the next council meeting to the effect that the Heath should remain with the GLC "forever". The *Ham & High*'s excitement at the prospect of Finsberg being humiliated by his own party, turned to petulance when the Tories gathered round him and voted the motion down. They had put on, fumed the editorial, "a pathetic front of unity and played the tiresome game of follow-the-leader".

On a matter connected to Hampstead Heath, at least geographically, the Conservatives were still in a quandary over what to do with Branch Hill. Building council houses on it would be prohibitively expensive and local groups such as the Hampstead Heath & Old Hampstead Protection Society were against any form of development. The planning committee approved plans for turning the land into a park which was, after all, what the then leader of the council had said it would be for. The Labour Party launched a campaign to force the council to use the land for council housing which was they said the real (if hidden) reason for buying the land in the first place. In any event, there was no call for a new park in the north of the borough alongside Hampstead Heath. "The Tories have listened to their selfish miserable friends in Redington Road and Templewood Avenue. They have virtually told the people of Camden: to hell with you, we don't want your kind in Hampstead!" diagnosed Roy Shaw. "My heart bleeds for the people of Templewood Avenue if they get a few bob knocked off the price of their homes".

The Conservatives were soon in difficulty in their much heralded pledge to sell off council houses. No sooner had they won the election than the minister for housing, Anthony Greenwood, announced that Camden was not to sell off more than one in 400 of its housing stock, a restriction that meant that Camden would be allowed to sell off no more than about fifty homes a year. In October the council voted to sell council houses not only to those living in them, but to sell vacant homes to both council tenants who were already living elsewhere in council property, and to those on the housing waiting list. "We believe in the right of everyone to own their own home", said Finsberg. Somewhat imaginatively, Peter Best led the objections from the Labour Party: "Those with money will be able to buy precedence over those who may be in greater need... Tenants are being offered the opportunity to become minor Rachmans".

GEOFFREY FINSBERG AND MARTIN MORTON:
A CONSERVATIVE COUNCIL

In November 1968 the council sold its first council house to a council tenant. Graham Anthony, who lived with his wife in a council flat on Haverstock Hill, paid £4,000 for 5 Modbury Gardens, a rundown house in Chalk Farm. The house needed a lot of work doing on it. It had been empty for some time and had no bathroom or kitchen. The sale was an important step that had excited no interest in the press and would not have done had it not been for Peter Best's flamboyant behaviour at the November council meeting. "This house is being sold at a price lower than they paid for it", he shouted with some confidence, pointing at the Tories. "This house is being sold to a friend of the party opposite, not to a person on the housing list. This is a crooked deal that is typical of everything they represent. You are a gang of crooks only interested in money!"

Finsberg was livid. It was "a complete fabrication". He demanded that Best withdraw his "lies and innuendo". The housing chairman was also shocked. "I hope that no member of the council would imagine that the allegation could be true", said Martin Morton, before detailing the facts that the house had been bought for £2,900, it was in disrepair and had been left empty, and the cost of repairs would add another £13 a week to the housing deficit. By selling the house the council would not only make a profit but would also get back Mr Anthony's council flat on Haverstock Hill. Best withdrew the allegation. "I just took a chance that I might be right", he winked at the press afterwards.[9]

In October Edwin "Johnnie" Johnson, one of the recently elected Kilburn councillors, died aged only 47. The by election presented the Tories with another opportunity to bite into the Labour rump. The *Ham & High* was not alone in its anxiety to assist David Offenbach, the Labour candidate, a 25 year old solicitor. The actor Peter O'Toole, who was then filming *Goodbye Mr Chips,* also offered his help. O'Toole had canvassed for Whitaker in the general election, feeling himself "well placed to talk to Irish voters".

Finsberg took the opportunity of announcing a fortnight before polling day that he had invited the 71 year old Dame Florence Cayford to be next year's mayor. [10] She was not a councillor, but was an excellent candidate. A long time member of the Labour Party, she had served

---

9   Forty years on, Mrs Anthony still lives in the same house on Modbury Gardens.

10   At the same council meeting, and in the same spirit, Finsberg announced that the Conservatives were co-opting Fred Cook, now the chairman of the St Pancras North Liberal Party, onto the children's committee.

for many years on Hampstead council were she had been the leader of the opposition and eventually the deputy mayor in 1964. She had also chaired the London County Council, and had been the first woman chairman of the Metropolitan Water Board. Ratchford was furious. The Tories had sounded him out months ago about a Labour mayor and had even suggested that he would make the best candidate. He had turned down the offer after taking advice from his colleagues. The offer to Dame Flo had not been made in consultation with the Labour Party and was "a political gimmick" announced just before the Kilburn by election because Dame Flo lived in Kilburn, a ward she had represented for years as a Hampstead councillor. Dame Flo had done more for the Labour Party and for Camden than any of the present Labour councillors, said Finsberg, accusing his critics of small mindedness. Dame Flo accepted. It had nothing to do with any by election, she said, as she had been approached months before, and in any event, she added, quite correctly, it would have no effect on the by election.

The Kilburn by election came and went. Despite the intervention of Peter O'Toole, the turnout was only 23%. The voters, no longer distracted by the presence of a Communist candidate, gave Labour a 200 vote margin over the Tories. A week before polling day, the *Ham & High* had carried an anxious editorial predicting a Conservative win. After the result it printed another editorial celebrating the Labour victory.

The new year brought more difficult decisions. In January Finsberg was predicting "the biggest rate increases in Camden's history" of between 9d and 2s. "The responsibility lies entirely with this Socialist government and their inept mismanagement of the nation's economy" which had brought higher interest rates and had lumbered local authorities with extra responsibilities that were not matched by government funding. "None of the rises is the result of anything done by Camden council", said Finsberg. This sounded somewhat rich as he had described the raising of the rate by the Labour council by a mere 4d in the previous year as "setting the seal on three years of financial mismanagement".

Having said enough to worry the ratepayers, the Conservatives managed to upset the other end of the spectrum by announcing plans to increase the cost of meals at the council's luncheon clubs for old people from ten pence to a shilling. The *Ham & High* did not like it either and pointed out that the tuppence rise was no more than a "spit in the ocean" against the savings needed. This gave the Labour councillors a real opportunity to find their form in the three hour debate at the nine hour (7pm to 4am) council meeting in February 1969. It was a "quite despicable" move which filled me "with shame and contempt" (Alderman Cliff Tucker[11]). "A spit in the face to any decent man. If there is a man or a woman with the soul the size of a silver three penny bit they will reject these iniquitous proposals" (Paddy O'Connor); "Like pinching a crutch from a lame man" (Ivor Walker); and "The meanest, unfairest and most unnecessary set of proposals we have had before us in the history of Camden" (Corin Hughes-Stanton). Ratchford kept rather quiet throughout all this, for reasons which came clear when it was pointed out that he had proposed just such a rise to a shilling a meal in 1965.

In February 1969, Charlie Ratchford announced his intention to resign as leader at the end of the municipal year. He said that his health was failing and that he wanted "a younger man to gain experience as Labour leader before the next council elections in two years time". He had been a councillor for 29 years and had now retired from his day job on the railways. Although he rented a room in Kentish Town, he and his wife now lived in Ruislip, a choice he had taken because he did not want to either pay a high Camden rent or submit to a means test under the differential rent scheme. Three candidates put themselves forward, Paddy O'Connor, who promptly withdrew; Jock Stallard, the former St Pancras rent rebel who was, like Ratchford, a railwayman; and Millie Miller, who won by fourteen votes to nine. "I hope it will mean conducting a team rather than being leader", she said, somewhat hopefully. Peter Best was elected as her deputy.

The row at the March 1969 council meeting was expected, but somewhat overshadowed by the "barrage of left wing slogans and bundles of council agendas" hurled from the gallery by protestors from St Pancras UTA complaining about housing conditions and rents. After being shouted down, Norman Oatway, the mayor, had the chamber cleared and the lights turned out, and when the protestors still refused to leave, the public gallery was cleared by the police.

When things had settled down, Finsberg proposed the biggest rate increase in the borough's history, a rise of 1s 1d to take the domestic rate up to 11s 9d. "The reason is simple", he said, "a socialist inheritance

---

11   Cliff Tucker had been the deputy chairman of the council (when Sammy Fisher was the chairman) in the 1964-5 transitional year. He lived in Hampstead with the literary critic Anthony Dyson, the founder of the Homosexual Law Reform Society. He came off the council in 1971, and died in 1993 bequeathing his property on Dyson's death to the University of Wales, Lampeter where there is now a Cliff Tucker Theatre.

GEOFFREY FINSBERG AND MARTIN MORTON:
A CONSERVATIVE COUNCIL

at the Town Hall and continued socialism at Westminster. We have had four years of a spendthrift Labour council and we now need to get back to a prudent figure. And since 1964 a Labour government has cost us over three million pounds in increased interest charges and other items". In opposition, the Labour Party transformed itself into the spokesman for the hard pressed rate payer. "We hope to get an honest deal for the rate payers", said Sir Sammy Fisher, and proposed that as the government had raised Camden's rate support grant by five pence in the pound, the rate should be reduced by five pence in the pound. Millie Miller agreed. The five pence "had been filched by the council –this is the swindle the council is perpetrating!" It was, said Paddy O'Connor, "a typical piece of Tory incompetence".

"What incenses us", fumed the *Ham & High* editorial, "is that by salting [away] the balances now the Tories ought to be able to keep the rate steady if not reduce it in the next following two years –in which, coincidentally, local elections will be held. It's an old trick. We've seen it before. What's more it works. But what a pathetic way to run a council."

The last council meeting of the municipal year, 30 April 1969, was again targeted by St Pancras UTA. They were joined by the homeless families, some clutching children, who had been housed by Camden in a block in Ralaena Road in Poplar (next to the Blackwall Tunnel) and who were complaining about the poor conditions there. After a barrage of stink bombs and leaflets were thrown from the public gallery, the meeting was suspended for forty minutes while the police cleared the gallery. During the fracas, a policeman's helmet was tossed into the chamber. The protestors were removed singing, somewhat poignantly, "We shall not be moved". Council officers sprayed the chamber with air fresheners before the meeting could restart. Labour councillors were inclined to side with the protestors and forced an assurance from Julian Tobin, the deputy leader of the council, that he would visit Poplar to report on conditions. They then criticised the mayor for clearing the gallery and having the door locked so that the public could not re-enter. So incensed was Paddy O'Connor on this last matter that he stormed out of the chamber. With a sigh, Norman Oatway ordered the door to be unlocked. "Later the mayor looked up but made no comment when he saw Cllr O'Connor sitting alone in silent protest in the gallery". Ignored and bored, O'Connor came back down again.

The mayor making council meeting in May fared little better. "Uproar as Dame Flo becomes mayor", reported the *Ham & High*. The usual squad from the St Pancras UTA took their places in the gallery

GEOFFREY FINSBERG AND MARTIN MORTON:
A CONSERVATIVE COUNCIL

and were on their best behaviour for the first part of the meeting while Finsberg proposed Dame Flo Cayford as the new mayor. The benches were emptier than usual for such an event as half the Labour members, eleven out of twenty three, had stayed away not so much in protest against Dame Flo, who was unanimously respected and liked in the chamber, but more in a sulk following Finsberg's cheeky and successful initiative in getting her to accept the post. As soon as the new mayor took her place, the St Pancras UTA people subjected the chamber to "a torrent of shouts and abuse". She took the oath "as the hubbub raged". Her first act as the fifth mayor of Camden was to order that the gallery be cleared. The meeting was suspended for twenty minutes[12].

Julian Tobin had by this time paid his visit to Raleana Road in the East End and presented his report: "The majority of the families visited had little of which they wished to complain and many of the flats are bright, airy and well maintained". Although they had no bathrooms or hot water "these flats are not bad for people who are genuinely in need of a home".

The Labour Party kept up the pressure on Branch Hill and to guarantee coverage in the local papers arranged a one day token occupation of the site in June. Press releases beforehand promised a demonstration of a thousand people eager for council housing in the heart of Hampstead. The reality was a hundred and fifty at a meeting at the Whitestone Pond overlooking the Heath and then a short walk down to Branch Hill to stage an "occupation" by sitting around on the grass, playing football and listening to the occasional speech until after dark[13]. "Protest Picnic", reported the *Ham & High*: "It is an admirable play and picnic area". Whitaker and a dozen Labour councillors were at the fore, including Roger Robinson in "a coronet of grass and daisies", but no homeless families. Impressed by the example set, of families enjoying the sunshine in a small patch of old Middlesex countryside, Julian Tobin announced that the land would be used as a public open space until a proper use could be found for the land. This was, purred the *Ham & High* editorial, "at the *Ham & High*'s suggestion".

Nevertheless, the serious problem as to what to do with Branch Hill remained. The Policy & Resources Committee considered three

---

12 Dame Florence was to be the only non-councillor to hold the position of mayor. She died in 1987, aged 89.

13 Branch Hill Lodge itself was fenced off for building work to turn it into an old people's home.

alternatives. First the land, minus the Lodge which was being converted into an old people's home, should be offered to the GLC for £163,000 as an addition to the Heath. Alternatively, it should be offered for the same amount back to the Glendyne estate who may then sell it on for low level luxury development, or thirdly the land could be sold on the open market for development restricted to thirty people per acre. As a special council meeting had been called for the end of August to discuss whether a GLC rate rise of 1½d could be absorbed or added to the rate, it was decided to add the Branch Hill decision onto the agenda.

This was, said Millie Miller, "a quite diabolical attempt" to push the decision through in the summer recess. She was, she said, going to get an injunction against the council and stormed off to seek counsel's advice. Finsberg knew that he had slipped up. "In an amazing political somersault"(said the *Ham & High*), he agreed to have the Branch Hill decision put off until October, and left the argument to simmer in the letters pages until then. When he wrote a letter to the press putting his side, the *Ham & High* printed it under the headline: "Branch Hill: Mr Finsberg's Facts". Peter Smith had more success: in making the ruinously expensive move of buying Branch Hill for £460,000 Ratchford had committed the council to paying interest charges to build expensive housing rather than using the money elsewhere to spend on house building and repairs. "We are not prepared to be stamped into what would undoubtedly be a very costly exercise, because the Labour Party, for purely doctrinaire reasons, wish to pursue their egalitarian principles which most certainly would not be in the interests of those they purport to serve".

To the Labour Party it was a great campaigning issue: the Tories did not think working class people should live in exclusive Hampstead, but the Labour Party thought that they should. In September the Camden Trades Council passed a motion that Camden's building workers should black work on any private development on Branch Hill. A thirty car "Branch Hill motorcade protest" drove through Camden in early October. The following weekend, Millie Miller and Ben Whitaker led a march from Camden Town to Branch Hill –all of it uphill save the last few hundred yards- providing a photo opportunity for Mrs Whitaker to hold a "Council Houses for Branch Hill" placard in one hand and to push a pram with the other, a pose she did not hold for long[14]. Others

---

14   Thirty years on, in 1999, Janet Whitaker was created a Labour life peer. She is vice chair of the Parliamentary Labour Party International Development Committee, and vice president of the British Humanist Association and the All Party Groups on Overseas Development, Ethiopia and the UN.

were sent off to picket Finsberg's house, to find that he was away at the party conference, and Martin Morton's house. Morton liked that sort of thing and appeared in his shirtsleeves to hold a debate with the protestors for an hour on his doorstep, pointing out that the rateable value of council housing on Branch Hill would be something like £4 a week and unaffordable for most council tenants. "They went away", he said, rather pleased with himself, "thinking the situation was more complex than they originally thought".

The October council meeting included a three hour debate "punctuated by hysterical interventions from the gallery" on Branch Hill. The Conservatives backed their own plans, but saw the whole issue as something of a bore. When the vote came, two of them (Peter Hilton and Mrs Raymond Cox) abstained, Alan Greengross (who chaired the planning committee) was absent and Morton (who chaired the housing committee) had already gone home[15]. Millie Miller promised to ask the minister for a public enquiry if Camden attempted to transfer the land, although the star of the minister for housing, Anthony Greenwood, was falling somewhat as in the previous week he had been shuffled out of the cabinet[16].

The council's flagship policy of offering to sell homes to council tenants met a hearty response. All the borough's tenants were sent forms asking if they were interested. Over two thousand replied that they were, which proved something of a problem as, under the minister's new rules, the council was restricted to selling fifty properties a year. Finsberg turned this to his advantage in that the council elected to choose the lucky few by lottery, and Finsberg posed for the press drawing one of the names from a large revolving drum. One of the winning families was the Maynards who lived in a flat in Harrison Street in Kings Cross and who were hoping to be able to buy a house with a garden. "This is the best thing that has happened to us in eighteen years of marriage", said Mrs Doris Maynard, photographed with their three adolescent children.

63

---

15 Morton had left quite deliberately to avoid the debate, self consciously trying to disguise the fact that he had his briefcase with him as he slipped out of the chamber.

16 Greenwood, who lived in Hampstead, was the president of the Hampstead Labour Party. He remained as minister for housing, having fared better in Harold Wilson's reshuffle than had Kenneth Robinson, who after four years as minister for health, had been sacked.

GEOFFREY FINSBERG AND MARTIN MORTON:
A CONSERVATIVE COUNCIL

1968 - 1971

The December 1969 Highgate by election, called after the resignation of Peter Brooke[17] who was off to work in New York, was hard fought and was won by the Tories who again took 56% of the vote. Labour saw it as something of a good result as they could claim a 20% swing, but in reality this was simply because they took votes from the Communists, whose vote collapsed, and the Liberals, who did not stand. The winner, 25 year old Harriet Greenaway, posed in thick winter mittens and a short skirted tweed suit with her legs dangling over the ballot box[18].

With council rent rises on the agenda, the January 1970 council meeting proved to be the most violent yet. The usual suspects from St Pancras UTA packed the gallery and, once the meeting was under way, unfurled a banner over the balustrade and started chanting at the councillors below: "Not a penny on the rent". Dame Flo ordered the gallery to be cleared. The protestors noisily stood firm. The police arrived and with a certain amount of enthusiasm dragged the protestors out. "It was sickening" said Millie Miller. Her colleague, Alderman Mrs Lyndal Evans, "was quite appalled at the police behaviour".[19] The papers carried descriptions of the doors of a Black Maria flying open as police reinforcements with truncheons drawn ran from the street into the town hall, of policemen being spat at and kicked, and protestors being whacked with truncheons and roughly dragged down the stairs. Seven UTA people were arrested. When the meeting resumed, Millie Miller demanded a "special committee" to enquire into the unpleasant events of the evening. When she did not get it she marched out of the chamber and took the entire Labour group with her, leaving the Tories with empty opposition benches and an empty gallery to vote unanimously for rent rises of between 6s 6d and 8s 6d a week.

It was Finsberg's last council meeting as council leader. "With the prospect of a general election this year, Finsberg throws down the

---

17 Peter Brooke, MP for City of London & Westminster 1977–2001, was the hapless Northern Ireland Secretary who was coaxed into singing *My Darling Clementine* by Gay Byrne on Irish television on the same day in 1992 that seven construction workers had been killed by an IRA bomb. He has been a life peer since 2001.

18 Now Mrs Harriet Croft, she became the opposition whip before standing down in 1974. She later joined the SDP.

19 Lyndal Evans was by marriage Mrs Kraft, but used only her maiden name. Her mother was the leading suffragette Dorothy Evans, who also used only her maiden name. Lyndal was named after the heroine in Olive Schreiner's *African Farm*. These being pre-"Ms" days, the papers always referred to Lyndal as "Mrs" rather than "Miss" Evans. An obituary was published in the *New Journal* on 4th February 2005.

GEOFFREY FINSBERG AND MARTIN MORTON:
A CONSERVATIVE COUNCIL

gauntlet", read the *Ham & High*. He wanted it to be known that he was confident enough of victory to give up the leadership, and resigned. He also told the papers that he intended to stay on the council for the rest of his term so that he could complete his quarter century in local government. The decision was not altogether voluntary as the Hampstead Conservative Association were insisting that he stand down to concentrate on beating Whitaker, but the announcement came as a surprise outside the inner circle of the Tory group. There were two contenders for his crown: his deputy leader, Julian Tobin, a forty two year old solicitor, and Martin Morton, the housing chairman, a thirty eight year old industrial relations specialist at the CBI. It was close, but Morton won by 23 to 18 votes (with six abstentions). "There's no purpose in crying about this: the better man won", said Tobin, who stayed on as deputy leader.[20] Morton (Ampleforth, Irish Guards, Oxford) was chalk to Finsberg's cheese, too much a gentleman, and too self deprecating to be the politician that Finsberg undoubtedly was. Morton's national service as a subaltern in the guards had left with him with the confidence that, in Roy Shaw's opinion, made him the best orator ever to sit on Camden council.

The Town Hall Seven were tried before the Clerkenwell stipendiary magistrate, David Wacher, who presided over a two day hearing. The protestors were represented by Benedict Birnberg who had made something of a reputation for himself in police bashing cases. The police had, he suggested, behaved with excessive force. The police gave evidence of the protestors' misbehaviour, and the protestors and Millie Miller and Lyndal Evans gave evidence of police misbehaviour. Mr Wacher preferred the police evidence and fined all seven of the protestors[21].

It was not just the rents that were going up. In the March 1970 council meeting, Luigi Denza announced that the council was to put up the rate by a further 1s 4d, a bigger increase than the record breaking increase of the year before. Interest rates had reached, he said, "unheard

---

20 Julian Tobin was bitterly disappointed, especially as he had always shown great loyalty to Finsberg (and continued to do so) and yet Finsberg had declined to endorse him thinking it best not to get involved in the succession. Finsberg's support, thought Tobin, would have made the difference.

21 The Town Hall Seven were: Ellen Luby, 46, a cleaner (fined £10 for spitting at a constable and £25 for using threatening words); Jennifer Chaston, 30, "an optician and college lecturer" (fined £35); Roy Taylor, a printer, of Bracknell in Berkshire (£25); and housewife Iona Dixon, 20; her husband, Philip Dixon, 24, a wages clerk, both from Holloway; Kevin Whitson, 21, a teacher, and Michael Faulkner, 22, a tree pruner (fined £5 each).

of levels of over 10%", the GLC was demanding another 4½d, the building programme was bigger than ever and an increased road provision was necessary because of "the ever increasing amount of traffic on urban roads". Sammy Fisher, having rehearsed his speech the year before, gave it again: "I accuse the Conservatives of deliberately forcing up the rate so they can cut it at the next election. It is a swindle on the ratepayers which in normal commercial life would have brought the perpetrators into court for cooking the books."

By the spring of 1970, the GLC, the new Lord Glendyne and (despite Millie Miller's efforts) even the Land Commission had refused to take Branch Hill off Camden's hands. In May the Policy & Resources Committee agreed to call for a feasibility study to determine whether seven acres of the site could be used for council housing. "Tories think again", said the *Ham & High*, portraying this tentative decision as the first major change in policy since Martin Morton took over from Finsberg. Nevertheless, the expense of building there was daunting and the annual interest charges on the purchase of the land had reached £52,600. "That's two years lost", said Ernest Wistrich "entirely due to former leader Geoffrey Finsberg and the sheep that followed him". If Branch Hill is sold off, said Paddy O'Connor, on whose authority no one ever discovered, the next Labour council would reclaim the land by compulsory purchase. Under this shadow, Branch Hill House was officially opened as an Old People's Home later that month by Lord Balniel, the shadow health minister.[22]

1970 saw three elections of interest, a council by-election, the GLC elections and the general election. The first of these was of interest only in that the ending of the business vote showed the shape of things to come in commercial districts. The Holborn by-election was caused by Alan Greengross becoming an alderman and resigning his seat in a ward which had returned three Conservatives in 1968.[23] In March 1970, the Labour candidate, Betty Grass, won with a 14% swing on a dismal 29% turnout. It is impossible to talk of swings, said Morton, as this is the first election since the business vote was abolished. He was right. Holborn was now a different country. The business voters, those electors who

22 Ben Whitaker accepted his invitation to attend the ceremony, but had been snubbed, said Millie Miller, because he was not asked to sit on the platform.

23 So that Alan Greengross would not have to fight his now highly risky seat in Holborn without the business vote, he took the place of Alderman Ken Furness who had moved to Birminghham and resigned.

GEOFFREY FINSBERG AND MARTIN MORTON:
A CONSERVATIVE COUNCIL

paid rates both in Holborn where they worked and also at home, often in the Home Counties, no longer appeared on the electoral roll.

The effects of this were perhaps felt again in the GLC elections in April. 'Perhaps' because the Conservative run GLC had done little to endear itself to voters in the north of the borough. The problem was the North Cross Route that would connect to the proposed M1 motorway extension. A new road network was planned from West End Lane across to the Finchley Road, Swiss Cottage and down Adelaide Road to Chalk Farm before veering off to Hackney along the North London Line to Leytonstone. In the month before the election, the leader of the GLC, Desmond Plummer, told the Hampstead Conservatives that he was still undecided, not as to whether the North Cross Route would go ahead, but whether or not the new motorway through Hampstead should be in a tunnel or a cutting. The papers gave much publicity to the newly formed party, Housing Before Roads, who were going to put up candidates against the Tories. The best the Conservatives could do was to point out, as Julian Tobin did, that the GLC would happily abandon the North Cross Route if only the government stopped its plans to extending the M1 motorway along the Finchley Road.

Two of the three Conservatives, Lena Townsend and Clare Mansel, were standing again but, for reasons not then explained, the flamboyant Dickie Butterfield was not. He was replaced in the line up by James Lemkin, a lawyer and former member of Hampstead council. Labour chose, again, Paddy O'Connor, now promoted to "senior instructor" on the buses, along with Dick Collins, an electrician and tenants leader on the Regents Park estate, and a smart barrister from Kensington, Alec Kazantzis[24].

Labour won all three GLC seats, but again it indicated little. The turnout was just under a third and the 4.8% swing to Labour concealed the fact that although the Conservative vote was down 8,000 on 1967, the Labour vote was down by 2,000. The Liberal vote had halved. "We're back! Now we'll take Camden!" shouted Paddy O'Connor, giving a thumbs-up for the photographers. The *Ham & High* was less excited: "This month's GLC elections," began its editorial, "provided further proof, if any were needed, that only a minority are interested in local government".

The GLC remained Tory run, but with a reduced majority, although the ILEA was taken narrowly by Labour. Lena Townsend, who had been

67

---

24 Who had married one of Lord Longford's daughters, Lady Judith Pakenham.

the ILEA chairman, stayed on the GLC as an alderman. It had been a great blow to the Tories where they had fought on one front, education, and Labour had fought on another, the North Cross Route. As James Lemkin told the Hampstead Party AGM the following week, absent supporters had put roads before education. "Do they realise that the motorway, if approved, won't come before 1990 while the grammar schools may well be abolished in 1971 if the Tories do not win the general election?"[25] Finsberg was bullish and pledged to fight for the reintroduction of the business vote. "The abolition of the business vote by the government accounts for the loss of Holborn ward at the recent by-election and contributed to the loss of Camden at the GLC election. In effect, Mr Wilson rigged the election".

The reason why Dickie Butterfield did not stand in the GLC election became clear in July when he appeared in the bankruptcy court. He admitted debts of £19,210 and assets of £20.[26] The forty five year old bachelor was now living with his parents in Huntingdonshire, having lost his mother's house in Church Row, Hampstead when she had unhappily allowed him to use it as security for one of his bank loans. Since 1964, he said, apart from the pittance of councillor's expenses, the only income he had received was the £3,010 he had won by betting on elections.

At the end of April 1970 Kenneth Robinson announced that after twenty years he was going to stand down as MP for St Pancras North to become the director of social policy for the British Steel Corporation. There was a flurry of excitement within the constituency Labour Party as some fifty hopefuls (including Roger Robinson and Paddy O'Connor) put their names forward for what was expected to be a safe Labour seat. A shortlist of six was chosen only after the election had already been called for 18 June. From the council were Millie Miller, Roy Shaw, and Jock Stallard. The others were the constituency party's former chairman, Ed Rhodes; Anthony Lester, a barrister; and Jo Richardson, a seasoned campaigner and the secretary

---

25   Lemkin was later elected to represent Uxbridge on the GLC in 1973 and in the final years of that body was the Conservative whip. His family owned the Fred Perry sportswear company. A founding member of the Bow Group, he had become advisor to the Zambian government after independence and in protest at Conservative Party policies on Africa had joined the Liberals and stood for them unsuccessfully in Cheltenham in 1964. He rejoined the Tories and after the GLC served as High Sheriff of Greater London 1992-3 and was made CBE in 1986. His *Times* obituary in 2008 described him as a "political thinker of a radical conservative hue".

26   In 1970, £20,000 would buy a Queen Anne house in Hampstead, with four bedrooms, two reception rooms and a garden.

of the Tribune group of left wing Labour MPs.

Forty eight year old Jock Stallard had moved to St Pancras from Lanarkshire during the war and was now a technical training officer at the engineering apprentice school at Heathrow. Married with two children, he lived in a council flat in Leybourne Street in Chalk Farm. As a St Pancras councillor, he had been surcharged for his part in opposing rents on decommissioned properties. Now both a Camden councillor and an active trade unionist (he had been awarded the AUEW's "Order of Merit"), he relied on the trade unionist vote (or, as the papers liked to call it, "grass roots support"). Still smarting from his failure to get the Labour leadership on Camden, he prepared his ground and won on the fourth ballot, beating Ed Rhodes by a single vote.

Just before the general election was called, Ben Whitaker issued his "May Day message" in which he claimed that "Britain is in better shape than at any time for years". Labour had built two million new homes in five years compared to a mere 1.6 million new homes in the last five years of Tory rule, the £800m balance of payments deficit of 1964 now stood at a healthy £500m surplus and spending on social services, health and education had risen by 70%. And defence expenditure had been "drastically reformed" to save £3,000m on the inherited Tory expenditure programme .

It was a good start and the election campaign proper began with Finsberg attacking the local press for not printing his reply to Whitaker, in which he had pointed out the dire increase in the cost of living since Labour came to power. Rather than apologise, the *Ham & High* responded by printing a letter from Jane Brown of Tanza Road under the heading "Who does Mr Finsberg think he is?"

The Labour Party let the press know that there was to be a star studded fund raising event in the town hall on the 28th June. It was to be called *Oh! Hampstead!* The date had been set when it was supposed that there was to be a general election in October, but the timing had wrong footed them. "If Labour wins, Harold Wilson will attend," said an insider. "But if we lose it'll be just awful".[27] As the election drew near, Harold Wilson fell out with the Left. The usual suspects (such as Peggy Duff) urged people not to vote Labour, and even the Luvvie vote went soft. Marty Feldman went so far as to place (at great expense) a

69

---

27   The promised line up included Marty Feldman, Janet Suzman, Roy Kinnear, Harry H Corbett, Kenny Lynch, Larry Adler, John Dankworth, Cleo Lane and Susan Hampshire. Wilson did not attend, but sent a letter.

quarter page advertisement in the *Ham & High* to say that he intended to abstain from voting because of his "absolute repugnance" of the Labour government's foreign policy in general and "specifically their hypocrisy over Vietnam".

Whitaker distributed 25,000 copies of a newsletter which credited him with "solving 12,000 problems, making Hampstead a better place to live, giving Hampstead a voice in world parliaments, obtaining the first cross borough bus, campaigning successfully to keep the Broad Street line open, producing a plan to answer local transport and road problems and extolling radical new policies". When challenged by the *Ham & High*, Whitaker claimed not to have seen the draft before it was printed, agreed he had not figured in the Broad Street campaign until the trains had been saved, did not understand what "a voice in world parliaments" meant, and when asked about having made life better in Hampstead, he rather limply replied that "that was what some people were saying".

The battle was on for press photos. Harold Wilson, George Brown and Roy Jenkins toured the constituency for Labour. Finsberg got Ted Heath, Tony Barber and John Boyd-Carpenter. The Conservatives also managed to get an old milk float which they drove around Hampstead, decorated with posters and three jolly girls in floral mini-dresses. The press took delight in Finsberg's rough ride at his biggest meeting in Hampstead town hall when he was ambushed by Labour supporters and asked if he wanted Enoch Powell to be re-elected. He disagreed, he said, with Powell on immigration and in any event it was a matter for the voters of Wolverhampton, prompting hostile shouts of "You're dodging the issue!", "Yes or No?" and "Answer the question you bloody hypocrite!"[28]

Jock Stallard and Lena Jeger looked safe in St Pancras North and Holborn & St Pancras South, but Ben Whitaker was in trouble. "Will Hampstead Swing?" asked the *Ham & High*. It did, but only just, by 2.6% on a 63% turnout. Finsberg won by 474 votes[29]. "Hampstead has swung", he said, "because the country is swinging and Hampstead voters, perhaps more sophisticated than some, have seen through Labour's lies".

---

28 It was not a happy event. Local exhibitionist Bernard Kelly began playing a flute during Finsberg's address and then demanded an answer to the question: "Would a Conservative government insist on prayers before intercourse?" When Finsberg failed to answer, Kelly produced a rattle to drown out further debate until dragged from the hall by Young Conservatives in "I Trust Ted" badges.

29 He promptly had a new number plate put on his car to incorporate the number 474.

GEOFFREY FINSBERG AND MARTIN MORTON:
A CONSERVATIVE COUNCIL

Harold Wilson's government fell. Ted Heath's Conservatives won with an overall majority of thirty one. In St Pancras North, the combative James Moorhouse had made little headway for the Tories where his vote went up by only 200 and Stallard won by 4,500. In Holborn & St Pancras South the Labour vote went down by 4,000, but the Conservative vote also declined (by 800) leaving Lena Jeger with a narrow 2,323 majority on a miserable turnout of only 54% (where the average turnout nationally was 72%). The Liberals did not stand in the St Pancras seats, and lost their deposit in Hampstead.

The *Ham & High*'s political obituary of Whitaker was generous, even mournful. He had been "an outstanding local MP, a man of compassion and principle, devoted to Hampstead, its people and problems." Finsberg on the other hand was "a sincere middle of the road Conservative". Oh dear, the electorate had rejected youth, wit and glamour and chosen the bloke in elastic sided shoes from the accounts department.[30]

Finsberg and Stallard were not the only two Camden councillors to be elected to parliament in the 1970 general election. The remarkable Elaine Kellett, a Conservative backbencher since 1968, won in Lancaster, a Labour marginal seat. Then a forty four year old mother of four, she had been widowed in a car crash in 1959 which had left her with terrible facial injuries. This was her sixth attempt at Parliament[31].

The bitterest of debates flared up in the summer of 1970 concerning the ward boundaries. The Tories had been stung badly by the scrapping of the business vote. It had greatly affected their electoral chances in the business quarter of the old Holborn borough and to a lesser degree in the adjacent wards. The other effect was that the Holborn wards now had markedly fewer voters than they had before the government reforms. The Camden Conservative Committee made

---

30 The easing out of Ben Whitaker was not the only disappointment to the *Ham & High* on a night of disappointments. The paper had taken a special interest in the career of the Labour candidate in Hampstead in the 1959 general election:"West Indian Mr David Pitt now seems finally to become the first Negro to be elected to the British Parliament", the paper had enthused just before the election. It was not to be: Pitt managed to transform the 4,176 Labour majority in Clapham to a 3,120 Conservative one.

31 She held Lancaster until her retirement in 1997. Appointed DBE in 1988, she also served as the MEP for Cumbria & Lancashire North from 1975 to 1984. She remarried in 1971 a fellow Conservative councillor on Camden, Edward Bowman, on which they both took the surname Kellett-Bowman. Edward Kellett-Bowman served as an MEP from 1979-1984 and from 1988 to 1999.

up from representatives from all three constituencies had discussed the matter as early as a year before and had worked in the meantime on recommendations for ward changes. The recommendations were for fewer seats in the south of the borough, and for more seats for the north where the Conservatives were stronger. When the topic was brought up at the Finance & General Purposes Committee in June, the Labour councillors were caught by surprise. Not having been stung by the changes, they had done nothing. Suddenly they feared that "in the summer recess" (as Millie Miller put it) the Tories intended to pull a fast one and push through boundary changes.

In fact, the Conservative plans were modest. They felt it too sensitive to deal with themselves and they trusted Millie Miller and her colleagues no more than she and they trusted them. They proposed instead to get the Home Office to effect the most equitable changes. This meant, of course, going to the Conservative Home Secretary, Reggie Maudling. The Labour group was furious. The chairman of the Finance & General Purposes Committee, Julian Harrison, had got Brian Wilson, the town clerk to draw up a paper on the effects of the removal of the business vote in each of the wards. His report made interesting reading. Of the 19 wards in the borough, eleven varied from the average elector/member ratio by more than 10%. Generally, the wards in the south of the borough had too few electors and the wards in the old Hampstead had too many. The worst examples were Holborn ward which now had 27% fewer electors than average, and Hampstead West End ward which had 27% too many. Something had to be done.

When this report and Harrison's suggestion reached the Finance & General Purposes Committee in September, little Sammy Fisher was puce with rage: "In all my years in local government I have never seen an exhibition of this kind by anybody with which I have been concerned", he shouted. "Your conduct has been improper, biased, partial and unethical!" He then proposed a motion of censure against Harrison, which was so unexpected that Harrison had to use his casting vote to defeat it.

It was not that the Labour members denied that there was a problem, but they feared the solution, and particularly resented the fact the fact the Conservatives had prepared themselves to make representations about the new ward boundaries while they had not. The Home Secretary ordered a public enquiry and appointed Edward Lewer, a barrister, to conduct it. In December, the Conservatives made their proposals for fewer seats in the south of the borough and more seats in Hampstead. Sparks flew. Peter Best was on histrionic form:

GEOFFREY FINSBERG AND MARTIN MORTON:
A CONSERVATIVE COUNCIL

"The whole purpose (of the enquiry) is to give some sort of political advantage to the party that sprang this upon us" His colleagues, he said, were agreed that "the Tory scheme would make it impossible for Labour to win control of Camden!"

Edward Lewer's report was presented to the Home Secretary in February before the election and was given immediate effect. It abolished Euston ward and created a new ward in Swiss Cottage. The effect was that the old Hampstead borough was represented by two more seats. 420 voters on Parkhill Road were shaved off the Hampstead constituency, "wiping out", the *Ham & High* noted hopefully, Finsberg's slim majority. Ken Avery, whose Camden Conservative Committee working party had set the ball rolling, described the result as "extremely fair". "It is a serious blow to democratic representation", said Barry Peskin, the chairman of Camden Labour Party's Local Government Committee. "The changes have been rushed through to assist the Tories' chances of retaining control of the council which their record would otherwise certainly deny them".

In his first foray into foreign policy since becoming a MP, Finsberg backed the government's policy on continuing arms sales to South Africa. Exports meant jobs, he said, and the policy had the backing of "genuine and patriotic working members of the Labour Party" whereas opposition to the policy came from "long haired intellectuals". The response from the Labour Party was anticipated, but he was also challenged from within his own party by Peter Smith, who had already announced that he was not going to stand again in the council elections. "In the absence of any comment by any politician in Hampstead on the question of arms to South Africa", he told the press, he felt that he needed to comment as the policy was regarded by some as "a symbol of complicity with apartheid which would encourage increased communist influence in black Africa which would be directly contrary to British interests". Peter Moloney also announced that he was not going to stand again. "I am very unimpressed by the performance of the local Tory party", he told the *Ham & High*. "I haven't seen a true blue Conservative policy emerging where reason prevails over emotion".

Branch Hill lay like a submerged log just below the political surface. The council published a new plan to approach adjoining property holders to waive restrictive covenants to allow the council to build sixty four semi detached houses. There was little enthusiasm within the party to build the most expensive council houses in the country, not least because it was a mess they had inherited from Labour. "I doubt",

73

said Peter Hilton, the new housing chairman, "whether people who are used to having schools, shops and public transport close by will want to live at Branch Hill". Later in the year a fresh plan was announced for fifty houses and a low rise four storey block covering four acres. Martin Morton, too frank for his own political good, could not bring himself to sell the new plan to the press. Although the proposals were now being put forward by the council which he led, he described them as being "not very beneficial", and wearily acknowledged that the council was bending to public pressure.

The election year of 1971 started well for the Tories in Camden. After years of debate and preparation, the first of Camden's new parking controlled zones, which the council hoped would soon include the whole borough, came into operation. Residents were charged a pound for a weekly parking permit while 700 ticket machines and parking meters were installed in Somers Town and Camden Town where sixteen traffic wardens based on Camden High Street were to enforce the new restrictions. Better still, following government approval that council rents could be linked to incomes, rents were reduced in two thousand council properties in February 1971 at the cost to the council of £60,000 a year. "No family living in council accommodation will pay more than a quarter of gross income in rent and rates", was the council's boast, which Millie Miller was forced to agree with through gritted teeth: "This is the kind of reform we've been seeking for ages", she said.

The Tories were also keen to let it be known that they had made the council more efficient. They had set up an all party Policy & Resources Committee, and introduced a system of rate planning under which ceilings would be set for annual expenditure. They had reorganised the departments in an attempt to eliminate waste, set up a scrutiny panel to act as a watchdog on expenditure, pledged to press on with building work for the town hall extension along the Euston Road to Argyle Street and set up area management committees so that council tenants would have a direct role in the many spending decisions.

Less helpfully, the sale of council houses to council tenants had been something of a damp squib after the fanfare orchestrated by Finsberg. The total number of sales in 1969 had been a mere thirteen, not least because the sales were restricted to houses as there was then no legislation to allow the sale of leasehold flats (without which there were too many practical difficulties, especially over service charges, to make flat sales possible). The government lifted its restrictions on house sales in the summer of 1970, and to encourage sales the council offered a

GEOFFREY FINSBERG AND MARTIN MORTON:
A CONSERVATIVE COUNCIL

20% discount on any council house sold to a council tenant. In February 1971 the council sold twenty seven newly built four bedroom houses on Garlinge Road in Kilburn to council tenants. It has, said Peter Hilton, the effect of reducing the housing list by freeing up the houses the tenants vacate. The Labour response was predictable: it is, said Peter Best, "a complete disgrace". "Are these homes too good for the people we are trying to house?" asked Paddy O'Connor.

Against these successes, the biggest disappointment to Martin Morton and his Conservative colleagues was an inability to bring down or even significantly rein in the rates. Even by the end of 1970 it was clear that the rate was to go up by over ten pence in the pound, and would for the third successive year be the highest increase yet. Morton blamed "the collapse of any sort of incomes policy and increased interest rates". It got no better. In February the GLC announced a 27% increase in its precept. "We are victims of higher costs", said Horace Cutler, the chairman of the GLC policy and resources committee. Worse still, the ILEA precept went up by another 11p and the police rate went up by 4p. These last two rises were unexpected and, Morton thought, would have the effect of pushing up the rate by over 16p in the pound. "The rates system is getting beyond a joke", he said.

Millie Miller could not disguise her glee: "The Tories' attempt to put something away so that they would not have to raise the rates in election year", she gloated, "has been completely defeated by inflation". She was right: when the rates were set, the Tories had tightened the belt as much as they could. The best that Labour could propose by way of an alternative budget was to cut the increase by a new penny as the rates went up by 2/8d to 15/4d (77p) in the pound. Morton accepted that "most people would feel as unhappy and impoverished as himself when they heard about the new rate". To the electorate it was the fault of a Tory government, a Tory GLC and a Tory council. Morton had one last card up his sleeve. He drafted a letter to go out with the rate demands. As the *Ham & High* noted: "Tory controlled Camden council at least ought to be congratulated for sending out an explanatory letter with the current increased rate demand, which to our surprise, the Labour opposition has not yet realised is an admirable piece of electioneering".

But the careful and accurate explanations were not enough. The one thing in a changing world that the Tories had hoped they could rely on, the one effective piece of Tory electioneering, their ability to cut the rate, had been denied them. There were other things in their favour, but they were nothing to that part of the electorate who doggedly vote in local elections. As the *Ham & High* read it:"With unemployment rising, cost of living spiralling and the government's unjust cuts in social services beginning to be felt, there must obviously be a swing against the Tories", but in Camden it would be close because "the Camden Tories have a progressive front and are way to the left of their party".

On top of this, the Conservative run GLC released plans for the new Camden Town Interchange. A six lane motorway, carried on a flyover 45 feet above the ground, would sweep through Camden Town passing within a few feet of the Round House. Fresh impetus was injected into the campaign against the scheme.[32]

The local papers carried few reports of the campaigning in the run up to the 1971 election, and they were low key. In the week before the poll, the *Journal* and the *Chronicle* were far more concerned with the great news story of the day: Ray Kennedy's header against Spurs had clinched the football league championship for Arsenal. Football aside, the *Journal*'s front page on the week before polling day was helpfully dominated by a story about a rat infestation in council properties on Retcar and Balmore Streets in Highgate New Town. "Tenants move as rats take over", read the headline, echoed in the *Ham & High* by "Rat invasion in decaying New Town" where "the few remaining families are surrounded by a sea of corrugated iron hoardings, broken windows, peeling paintwork and plump healthy rats". All the tenants were due to be moved out by July, muttered Morton, and the delay has been the Labour government's slowness in confirming the compulsory purchase orders.

The *Journal* also carried a report of the last council meeting which had received a deputation from forty mothers whose children were at Rhyl primary school to complain about the withdrawal of free school milk. In a smart and quite blatant piece of electioneering, the Labour Party thoughtfully laid on a bus to bring them to the town hall. Unhelpfully, Peter Smith, the housing chairman was reported as goading the delegation with the words:"My heart bleeds".

The Tories had prepared a comparatively limp election stunt for the council meeting. To show that they were soft Camden Tories and not harsh Midland Powellites, they proposed a motion censuring the Conservative government for its Immigration Bill (later the Immigration

---

32 To show their disapproval of the Tory GLC plans, Julian Tobin and Brenda Hennessey, appeared on the ballot paper in Adelaide ward through which the motorway would run as "Conservative Anti Motorway candidates."

Act 1971). Of the Conservatives who spoke, Pip Raymond-Cox (who now chaired the CCCR) pointed out that more than a quarter of Camden residents were born outside the country; Peter Smith described the bill as "racialist", and Peter Hilton, the licensing chairman, entered into the spirit of things by saying that "rivers of blood could flow if the bill went through". Finsberg left the chamber before the debate got going so that the motion could be passed unanimously.

Out on the streets, the Conservative and Labour parties contested all twenty wards. The Communists also put up eight candidates, promising greater expenditure on housing and everything else, and an end to the rats in Highgate New Town. The Liberals fought only the seven wards within the old Hampstead borough boundary. Being rather at sea with municipal finances they sidestepped the issue of whether they would need to increase the rates by promising instead to press the government for "site value rating". "This is a Liberal proposal," the *Camden Journal* dutifully reported, "to replace rates by a tax on the development value of all property. This, they say, would encourage the full use of land, release money for building, and bring down the rates". Which would, of course, be abolished only should a Liberal government be elected. The Liberals were in any event much weakened since the last election. The 66 year old Archie MacDonald, their chief spokesman and former MP had not only joined the Conservatives in time to canvass for Finsberg in the general election, but was a Conservative candidate in Town ward. The chairman of the Hampstead Liberals, Philip Vince, morosely observed: "As men get older, they tend to become more conservative in outlook".[33]

All the parties were against the proposed extension of the M1 motorway into the borough and the North Cross Route, and all were keen that surplus land owned by British Rail should be released to the borough for housing development. The Labour Party declared that its main priorities were to increase the supply of council housing and to reverse the welfare cuts such as the free school milk which had been withdrawn by the education minister, Margaret Thatcher, the year before. Although there was an expectation that the Conservative majority would be at least significantly reduced, the local press felt that the election was going to be close. They were very wrong.

*   *   *

33 Archie Macdonald spent one quiet term on the council. He died in 1983.

1968 - 1971

A LANDSLIDE VICTORY FOR LABOUR ran the headline on the *Camden & St Pancras Chronicle*. The election of 13 May 1971, as the *Camden Journal* put it, was not so much a Labour victory as a rout. The Conservatives crashed from 42 seats to 11. Labour went up from 18 to 49. The only wards won by the Conservatives outright were Adelaide and Hampstead Town. They were lucky to stay in double figures: four votes stopped Labour taking a second seat in Highgate, and Finsberg, who had taken a great risk in standing, managed to stay top of the poll in West End, a ward he now shared with three Labour councillors. At 37.6% the turnout was low, but Labour's 36,003 votes were 58½% of the votes cast. The Conservatives had only managed 22,128, or just over 36% of those who voted. The Liberals and Communists gathered the remaining 5% between them.

Millie Miller, at the age of forty eight, was now the first woman leader of a London borough. In her own ward, Grafton, she had polled a remarkable 2,923 votes. She addressed those still standing after the result in Highgate was declared at 2am after three recounts. "We won on national and local issues. Every ward had its own issues. Labour won a fair and square campaign. People have suffered by rents going up and the welfare cuts and this is what they voted against. The results show that the people of Camden, who have suffered for the last three years under the Tories, have had enough", she said before being drowned out by the singing of "She's a jolly good fellow". Martin Morton was polite to the end: "Quoting an eminent socialist last June, I say, we lend you Camden. In three years time we'll take it back". It was a poor prediction.

The Conservatives were in shock. Their handling of the council had been at least fair and none of them had anticipated the magnitude of the swing against them. They had been overwhelmed by national issues. "I am sure we lost control because of government issues such as rising prices, unemployment and so on", said Morton. "It is particularly irritating that the election has been won by a party that has absolutely no policies". The Labour agent for St Pancras was more explicit: "The electorate are angry with the government and are hitting back. There are now half a million school children in the country who have to go without their school meals. Everything is going up, including rates and rents and people are very angry about it".[34]

---

34   In 1968, after four years of Labour government (and within a month of Enoch Powell's speech on immigration) the Conservatives had control of twenty eight London boroughs leaving Labour with only four. The 1971 election, after a year of Conservative government, the Conservatives were left with nine boroughs and Labour with twenty two (leaving only Harrow in no overall control).

GEOFFREY FINSBERG AND MARTIN MORTON:
A CONSERVATIVE COUNCIL

4 |

Millie Miller, Frank Dobson and Roy Shaw

ousing was Millie Miller's priority. "We are going to start to find suitable homes to house all families who are desperately in need in Camden." She was going to press for the release of railway lands for housing development. There was no time to waste in demolishing the first stage of the Highgate New Town area and preparing Branch Hill for house building. "If I had to choose between [avoiding] higher rates and housing –I'd choose housing every time." And predictably: "Labour will stop all sales of council houses at once. Those offered to tenants by the previous Tory council will be stopped no matter how far the sale has gone if the sale would cause a break in the continuity of an estate or a block of property." She also announced the revival of the council newsletter that the Tories had stopped on taking office in 1968. "It will go into every home in the borough so everyone will know what is going on".

With its large new intake of left wingers, the Labour group was politically mixed but united in its hostility to the Conservative government and its "Fair Rents" policy as set out in the Housing Finance Bill. In Camden, this was expected to result in council rents being pushed up by some 50p a week, the cost then, for instance, of four pints of bitter. This was too much for some of the left wingers who, determined to make a stand, came up with a cunning plan. The legislation allowed for any rent increases to "fair" levels after 1 October 1971 to be counted as rises in the 1972/3 financial year. If a council raised rent on, say 2 October 1971, it could not, they reasoned, be forced to raise rent again for at least another two years. And so if the council now, immediately, cut all council rents by £1 and backdated the cuts to cover the month of September 1971, they could then raise rents by £1 next month back to the current levels. Under the rules, they reasoned, the government would have to accept that additional £1 as a rise in rents and so could not insist on any further increase and Camden would have cleverly protected its tenants by freezing rents for two years.

The logic was so good that when the new, overwhelmingly inexperienced, housing committee was ambushed by this proposal in September, it was approved. But the conspirators had needed secrecy in the planning of the ambush and had not sounded out Brian Wilson, the town clerk. When he found out he was less than supportive. It was, he said, simply against the law. The council would certainly suffer the costs of being challenged and defeated in the High Court. The Labour leadership was left with no option but to call an extraordinary meeting of the council on 30 September so that the council as a whole could overturn the decision of the housing committee.

The meeting was something of an embarrassment. The Labour group was jeered by the opposition. It was, said Martin Morton, now the leader of the opposition, "a case of the tail wagging the dog". All the Conservatives made a great show of walking out "in disgust" at the shambles the council was now in and left the Labour group to vote within itself. The decision was taken to accept the town clerk's advice and the cunning plan was ditched but, even then, not yet five months into the new administration, six of the left wingers made their point by refusing to vote.

"Fair Rents" dominated the Labour group's deliberations throughout 1972. In February Millie Miller issued "strenuous denials" that the Labour group was split on the issue. She was correct in that the group was united in its hostility to government policy on rents, but was less willing to admit the important truth: that the group was hopelessly divided over what action the council should take.

In the February 1972 council meeting, with Fair Rents on the agenda, the councillors sat through sixteen divisions until 1.30 in the morning. Mrs Miller asked: "What is the point of people electing us to represent them when the government now takes away our freedom in an area of vital concern?" According to the housing committee chairman, now the tight suited, befringed Corin Hughes-Stanton, the bill was "a body blow to anything we have achieved in Camden". Dick Collins was more forceful. "The Housing Finance Bill is the greatest challenge to democracy that I have seen. I will not implement the bill. If we all stand firm no government can exist!" The glamorous, big-haired Jennie Horne, easily the most eye-catching councillor in the chamber, told the

MILLIE MILLER, FRANK DOBSON
AND ROY SHAW

papers that "it will lead to the destruction of Camden as we know it".

The Labour Party issued a leaflet, much derided by the Tories, which was distributed on the housing estates to point out how the rent rises would bite. The Conservatives had selected as their candidate for St Pancras South a tall, bespectacled, side burned, young Lambeth councillor, John Major. He was keen to join the fray. The scare stories being spread by Labour in Camden, he said, were "cruel and shameful". He had "utter contempt" for the Labour councillors who were "callously and needlessly frightening the borough's elderly and most vulnerable tenants by misrepresenting the bill". The Labour leaflet stated that the new weekly rents would be £15.38, whereas "the true figure for a working man with a wife and two children would after the rebate be £4.95".

He was rewarded with a tortuously long reply from Millie Miller in the *Journal*, the burden of which was that he had omitted to mention "the most obnoxious provision in the act: the final decision on rents would be made by a Rent Scrutiny Board appointed by the government". She then sidestepped the main thrust of his complaint by stating that "the Housing Finance Act does nothing to add one single brick to a new home" and that "if we have the misfortune of continuing Tory government in the coming years the true effects of the 1972 Housing Finance Act will become even more disastrous than its notorious predecessor, the 1957 Housing Act".

Unlike the rate increases under the Conservative run council, the rates increase in 1972 was moderate because one of the effects of the Housing Finance Act was the generation of a £1m subsidy. But it was rents, not rates, that excited the new councillors. The Labour group met on St Patrick's day to debate their response to the new legislation and voted overwhelmingly to break the law if necessary. Only six voted against. Council officers, it was decided, were to be directed not to raise rents as required by the bill, even if this resulted in councillors being fined the maximum £400 each.

The only distraction from council rents in the summer of 1972 was provided by the Gospel Oak by election following the death of John Keohane. A safe Labour ward, it was the first Camden election contested by the National Front who, although their candidate managed less than 3% of the vote, caused something of a stir by issuing a leaflet claiming that immigration spread both venereal disease and drug use. Ed Rhodes, the Labour winner, said that he had sent the offending document "to a lawyer for an opinion" as to its illegality.

81

MILLIE MILLER, FRANK DOBSON
AND ROY SHAW

At the July council meeting councillors found themselves picking their way into the town hall through demonstrators waving placards reading DON'T OPERATE THE RENT BILL and TORIES ARE BENT ON ROBBING YOUR RENT. The council meeting included no items on housing finance that night, but Huntly Spence, a new Conservative councillor, proposed a motion that the council would not encourage anyone to break the law. Mrs Miller was furious: it was an attempt "to trick the council" into debating the Housing Finance Act. Granada Television's *World in Action* had turned up, clearly hoping the trick would give them some footage, but, observed the *Journal*, "apart from Cllr Spence's speech the debate was rather unexciting".

Part of Millie Miller's irritation had simply been that she needed time to work out a strategy. She had already arranged a special council meeting in August, a month usually clear of council business, for a final debate on Fair Rents. That meeting all but tore the Labour group apart. She wanted the council to call the government's bluff by refusing to implement the act. With so many of her group so vehemently against the act, it was a popular line to take. The government's expected reaction would be to suspend the council's housing committee and replace it with a government appointed housing commissioner, and that could prove a massive propaganda coup against the government. Labour councillors now had to consider whether the tenants they represented would be better served by the housing committee being swept aside. The chief whip was busy. John Mills and Phil Turner were congratulated for flying back from holidays abroad "to put their heads on the block with their party".

The open opposition to Mille Miller now came from the inside, from Ernest Wistrich. He proposed an amendment to the Labour group motion agreeing that while the council should condemn the Housing Act, its provisions should nevertheless be implemented in Camden rather than leave the tenants "to the tender mercies of a housing commissioner". He was backed by the housing chairman, Corin Hughes-Stanton. "This is a black and tragic day", he said. Those who spoke for the motion were drowned out by shouts from the gallery of "Sit down!" and "Sell out!" Others supporting his motion pointed out the great risk they faced of being surcharged by a vengeful government (to cries from the gallery of "Are you frightened?" and "No guts!"). Geoffrey Bindman set out the majority view and put his finger on the reason why the government had not acted. He was not in favour of breaking the law, he said: "We are passing the buck back to

MILLIE MILLER, FRANK DOBSON
AND ROY SHAW

the government and telling them to get on with their own dirty work in accordance with the procedure laid down under the act". When the anti-Fair Rents campaigners began yelling down at the Labour group as a whole, Millie Miller addressed them directly: "I want to make it clear", she said, "that the views expressed [by the movers of the amendment] are not those expressed by the majority of this side of the chamber". When the vote came, Wistrich and twelve others voted for the amendment. All thirteen Conservatives abstained.

Martin Morton then proposed an amendment on behalf of the Conservative group, in effect saying the same but without the criticism of the government or the act. Their amendment was voted down by 32 votes to 16. Eight Labour councillors abstained and three voted with the Tories. Only three of the Conservative councillors spoke that evening, and after the defeat of their motion, they were not in it at all. They sat back as cheerful spectators while the Labour members attacked each other to the alternate applause and jeers of a packed gallery. In summing up, Millie Miller told the chamber: "The idea that we should implement this act is totally abhorrent to the vast majority of members on this side", and then for effect, although not exactly on the point, she quoted Pitt the Younger: "Necessity is the plea for every infringement of human freedom. It is the argument of tyrants, it is the creed of slaves". The Labour group's motion not to implement the act was passed, but only narrowly by 30 votes to 26. Those against were the thirteen Tories and thirteen Labour councillors. After the council meeting, Corin Hughes Stanton refused to speak to the press and went on holiday. He returned to find a letter from Mille Miller demanding his resignation as housing chairman. He resigned.[1]

Later in the month the thirty Labour members who had voted for the motion each received a letter from the ministry warning of the plans of a writ of mandamus in the High Court to implement the law or else face contempt proceedings and gaol. "It is pompous and threatening" said Joe Jacobs, "and totally vindictive". But it was hardly a surprise. "It doesn't add much", Roy Shaw, the chief whip, told the press. "It's nothing new".

Camden was not the only council threatening to be difficult, and

83

---

[1]   Corin Hughes Stanton was re-elected in 1974, but rather lost interest in the council after losing an industrial tribunal case after being sacked as editor of *Design* magazine in October of that year. The *Journal* gleefully reported that the tribunal accepted evidence that he was a bully, that he overspent his budget and that his three secretaries spent a quarter of their time on Camden business.

the government, embarrassed by the fuss, offered concessions to avoid a confrontation. There would be lower minimum rents and 5p in the pound off the general rent increase. The council still would not budge. No letters were sent out by the council informing tenants of any coming rent increases. In the November council meeting, the leadership held out by 28 votes to 20. To roars from the Labour benches, Martin Morton told the council that he had advised the government not to appoint a commissioner, but to simply withhold all subsidies. "A plain daft" suggestion said Peter Best, but the government did not think so. Within a fortnight the council announced that rates were to go up by 25% following the government's withholding of the next instalment of housing subsidy.

The December council meeting followed a government ultimatum to serve the rent increase notices within a fortnight. The town clerk, Brian Wilson, issued advice that even the abstainers could be held responsible for yet another decision to defy the act. Phil Turner, the housing deputy chairman, suggested a borough referendum "to defeat the government's action". It will cost too much, said the town clerk. The council voted on another Fair Rents motion to consider the government concessions and threats. Again the Labour leadership won its motion by four votes, this time by 28 to 24. There was another standing ovation from the public gallery.

Millie Miller told the *Ham & High* that she was consulting lawyers about a High Court challenge. "The government is acting unreasonably" read the editorial, "in not appointing a commissioner". The government response, a week before the Christmas break, came in yet another letter. No mention was made of a commissioner, just news that the government was now intending to hold back the whole £8.5m housing subsidy unless Camden complied.

For many Labour councillors, the first Sunday of 1973 was occupied with a demonstration organised by the new Camden Action Committee Against the Act and its chairman, Phil Turner. Nearly 3,000 people marched from the town hall to South End Green chanting "Fair Rent is Robbery". They were addressed by Paddy O'Connor, who referred them back to the 1960 rent strike in St Pancras: "It is in your hands as tenants to refuse to pay the rents! Camden should not retreat! They can stuff their subsidies! We should stand solid!" (The *Journal* agreed: "What if the tenants did refuse to pay?") But to those in the know, the writing was on the wall. Before the march set off, Millie Miller had briefed the *Journal*: the government threats were getting "bigger and bigger", she said, and Camden may not be able to hold out.

MILLIE MILLER, FRANK DOBSON
AND ROY SHAW

On the day after the march, Monday 8 January 1973, the Labour group met to discuss its response to the government's pre-Christmas letter. Although there were those still for No Surrender, for most there was a sombre realisation that this was the end. The council could not afford to run its housing without subsidy unless it radically pushed up the rates, and that could not happen against the background of the council acting illegally. The group voted by 32 to 17 to implement the act.

The council sat two days after the Labour group meeting. There was a four hour debate "remarkable", said the *Journal*, "for its air of resignation". Millie Miller explained that the loss of government subsidy would bring an end to the council's house building programme at a time when there where 12,000 people on the waiting list for council homes, and it would impact on social services for the most needy. Her new deputy leader, Frank Dobson, who had taken over from Peter Best, said that he could "not countenance a massive increase in the rates". But the bitter-enders did not make it easy and the public gallery was packed. Every Labour "implementer", including Millie Miller, was heckled mercilessly. Paddy O'Connor behaved true to form. To cheers from his supporters he shouted: "It is a shame and a disgrace! Down with the law! Break the law because it is a bad law! Tenants ought to stop paying rents completely!" Drowned out by boos and jeers from the gallery, the council voted to implement the Housing Finance Act by 46 votes to 15.

Within a month the council was issuing leaflets to its tenants inviting them to apply for cash payments from the council under the new rent allowance scheme. "Can you please tell me, Mrs Miller, at what point did the notorious Fair Rents Act become known as the (undoubtedly generous) Camden Rent Allowance Scheme?" asked the young thruster, John Major, in the *Journal*. "There has been no transformation to equal this since St Paul journeyed to Damascus".

The *Journal* saw hopeful indications that there would be a rent strike, especially after rents were put up by 85 pence a week in March, but nothing happened. The paper moved on to exposing the thousand empty council properties in Camden at a time when the waiting list stood at 12,000, and fell out, terminally, with Millie Miller. "Spreading distortions", she said, "does nothing to improve the image of the capitalist press".

Instead of returning three members in one constituency as before, the boundaries for the GLC elections of April 1973 were changed so that each parliamentary constituency returned a single member to the GLC. The Conservatives had high hopes of taking the Hampstead seat, but were disappointed by Enid Wistrich, who was also a Camden councillor,

MILLIE MILLER, FRANK DOBSON
AND ROY SHAW

who won for Labour with a majority of over two thousand. The other two seats were walkovers for Labour: the only sitting GLC member to stand again was Alex Kazantzis who won in Holborn & St Pancras South, and St Pancras North returned Rose Hacker.[2]

The statutory council meeting in May 1973 saw many changes. Mille Miller, who had been selected as Labour's parliamentary candidate for the marginal Tory seat of Ilford North, stood down as leader to concentrate on the coming campaign. She was replaced by her deputy, 33 year old Frank Dobson, a stocky Yorkshireman with an impressive set of untidy sideburns. The new deputy was the Cambridge educated 40 year old Geoffrey Bindman, a solicitor and legal advisor to the Race Relations Board[3]. The new mayor, who had given every impression of being a die hard Fair Rents rebel, but who had since relented, was 64 year old Dick Collins, once one of the leaders of the 1960 St Pancras Rent Strike. Unsurprisingly perhaps, he was seen by the remaining diehards as something of a Judas. When his appointment was formally announced, his erstwhile comrades in the St Pancras UTA hurled a plastic bucket and handfuls of leaflets from the public gallery, chanting "Housing for people –not for profits!" Scuffles broke out between the friends of the new mayor and the protestors. A placard waving Ellen Luby shouted down at an obviously shaken Dick Collins: "You're not fit to be a toilet keeper!"[4]

The Fair Rents issue raised its head one last time that year. In August, for the second year running, a special council meeting was called to enforce the Fair Rents provisions and to raise council rents by a further fifty pence (on top of the 85p rise in March). Martin Morton bemoaned the fact that "Camden always delays until the last moment". The protests were over. The public gallery was far from full. Opposition to Fair Rents

---

2   Rose Hacker became something of a late life celebrity in 2006 when at the age of 100 she began writing regular columns for the New Journal. She died in 2008, a month short of her 102nd birthday.

3   Bindman – educated, urbane and comfortably off, had his children educated at private schools. "He married", said the Conservative councillor Julian Tobin, "into the rich side of my family".

4   Mrs Luby, a war widow, had already established herself as something of a firebrand. Having been fined for assaulting a policeman in a council meeting in 1970, she had four months before the mayor making received another conviction at Clerkenwell Magistrates' Court for causing a disturbance at the all night refreshment bar at Euston Station ("having consumed nothing stronger than British Rail tea"). Now in her eighties, she has continued to contribute to council meetings over the intervening years, shouting down to the Labour councillors that "you lot" are "acting worse than Tories" (or "like Nazis" or "like Hitler").

MILLIE MILLER, FRANK DOBSON
AND ROY SHAW

in the council had been replaced by a sense of resignation. Little was said against the proposed rise, and the line was now that the government had reneged on its promises under the Housing Act. The opposition blamed the council for another administrative mess. "The socialists are running propaganda to cover up the generosity of the rebates", said Christopher Fenwick. Only four Labour councillors voted against.

In the early 1970s much attention was drawn to what Camden's politicians saw as the Centre Point scandal. The property developer Harry Hyams, the publicity shy son of a North London bookie, was then one of the richest men in the country with a personal fortune assessed as being between £30m and £50m. He was the chairman of Oldhams Estates Limited in which he and George Wimpey each had 40% of the shares and the Cooperative Insurance Society (CIS) some 10%. He and Wimpey had conceived and built Centre Point which was in part financed by the CIS.

The old London County Council (LCC) had needed the plot for its traffic scheme for St Giles's Circus, but could not buy it because the rules only allowed it to pay pre-war compensation. Hyams seized his opportunity. He bought the plot and struck a deal with the LCC whereby he released to them the land on which part of the road system now stands, and in return kept a 150 year lease (at £18,500 p.a. with no revision clause) together with planning permission to put up a 385ft (117m) building, twice the permitted height.[5] This was in the face of the opposition from the Royal Fine Art Commission, which found that it could not act unless it received a formal reference from the LCC, a reference which never came.

The building was completed in the winter of 1966/67, but by 1972 was still unoccupied. The explanation given was that Hyams wanted a single tenant to occupy the whole site, but his decision not to let was encouraged, in a time of housing shortage, by George Brown's ban on office development in Central London. The undesired effect was that office rents were pushed up and landlords were left with the correct impression that the longer they delayed in letting their buildings, the more they would get for them. With eight million square feet of office space being deliberately held empty during a housing shortage, Centre Point was the focus of demonstrations throughout the late 1960s.

---

5   There was a certain irony in the fact that when the building was almost completed
     in 1964 the Minister of Transport changed the whole road system so that the traffic
     roundabout became wholly unnecessary.

MILLIE MILLER, FRANK DOBSON
AND ROY SHAW

1971 - 1978

In June 1972 the Camden's housing committee agreed to apply to the government for a compulsory purchase order (CPO) on the 36 two bedroom maisonettes which are between the third and eighth floors of the Earnshaw block attached to, but behind, the main tower. This was at a time when the asking price would be about £50,000 a maisonette which would demand an economic rent of some £5,000 a year. Millie Miller agreed that the plan was politically motivated "but we would dearly love to get our hands on the maisonettes. We have 11,300 families on our housing list of whom 60% are top priority. Of course it will be expensive but that ought not to deter us from dealing with the problem. And if the Housing Finance Bill goes through there will be substantial rebates available. Ideally we would like the maisonettes to go to people who needed them, but if the owners sell them off individually, then at least they will be occupied"

Everyone saw Hyams's handling of Centre Point as a scandal. "As a matter of principle, property should not be allowed to stay empty for this length of time," said Alderman Morton. "Insofar as the move is a gesture to prod the owners into doing something about it, we are totally in favour of it. But we believe the council would be financially embarrassed if the CPO was granted. The money could be used to purchase much more accommodation in other parts of the borough." An editorial in the *Times* agreed but argued that the council should buy the flats under a CPO and then to avoid any loss to the ratepayers should sell them on to the open market. The secretary of state for the environment, Peter Walker, was also sympathetic and threatened legislation to stop these unacceptable practices. (The building, he told the Commons, had been empty for eight years, "six under a Labour government, and two under ours".)

In the meantime, the Labour group began talking of a CPO not just for the flats but for the whole development. The deputy leader, Peter Best, announced that the council intended to apply for a CPO at original cost (of £5m), but failing that the council will raise £40m market value and immediately let the building out to companies willing to occupy it in part. He accepted that Camden did not have £40m to spend and that existing legislation prevented the council from borrowing it, but it was "an incredible scandal". Even his colleagues were whispering to the press the words "Pie in the sky". But he pressed on and after a televised council meeting the CPO for the whole of Centre Point was approved in the early hours with Labour members suggesting it could be used as a national library or as "a London university". (Or, Alderman Morton suggested with unusual sarcasm, "an extension for the town hall".)

MILLIE MILLER, FRANK DOBSON
AND ROY SHAW

Hoping that the government would step into the council's shoes, the council then did nothing but await national developments. They did not come, and in May 73 Peter Walker's successor at the Department of the Environment, Geoffrey Rippon, announced that the government was not going to get involved. A public enquiry was ordered so as to inform the department on whether nor not a CPO should be approved.

The head leaseholder, Oldham Estates Ltd had already sub-let the building to a subsidiary company, Sovmots Investments Ltd, and to complicate matters further, two months after the government fixed the date for the public enquiry, Sovmots sublet the flats to Brompton Securities Ltd.

The year 1974 began with news of a meeting of shareholders of Oldham Estates on Monday 31 December at which Harry Hyams ("suntanned, bearded and ebullient" noted the *Times*) had responded to a question on Centre Point: "There is an awful lot I can say on the mythology and unacceptable face of ignorance surrounding the property, but there is going to be a public enquiry and it would be discourteous if I were to discuss the property today".

Frank Dobson, called a press conference to put the council's position. "I admit to be a representative of those who are totally ignorant of the wilder regions of developers' finance and morality, but I am not ignorant of the squalor and overcrowding in which many of Camden's people have lived for the past decade. I wish him and all his like in whatever hell the worshippers of Mammon believe in".

The Conservative group leader, Alderman Morton told the press that it was all the fault of the Labour Party. The flats were too expensive (at £30,000 each) and the council could not afford to buy them. "The young militants among Camden's socialists are now prepared to pay Harry Hyams one million pounds in hard cash which the open market has apparently refused him". The old Labour run LCC was also to blame as it had "traded a road which has never been used for thirty six unsuitable flats. The present unhappy situation is a monument to the political and practical ineptitude of the former LCC" ("How's that for exploiting the issue?" asked the *Ham & High*'s editorial column.)

The public enquiry began on 15 January 1974. David Widdicombe QC opened for the council. Government backing for the compulsory purchase order, he said, "would convince the public of its seriousness in correcting the unacceptable face of capitalism". "Moral and common sense" was offended by flats having remained empty since the block was built nine and a half years ago. The fact that the flats had now

MILLIE MILLER, FRANK DOBSON
AND ROY SHAW

been sublet to Brompton Securities was, he suggested, a transparent attempt to thwart compulsory purchase so that the lease could later be surrendered back to Sovmots. "Not even a crocodile would shed a single tear for Brompton Securities if this CPO was granted"

Edward Tietjen, architect for Sovmots, presented the inquiry with four reasons why the government should not back the CPO. The flats would be worth between £60 and £80 a week (as opposed to the £11 a week Camden was hoping to charge its tenants) and were unsuitable for families; the layout of the flats was unsuitable for council tenants and did not comply with the Parker-Morris standards mandatory for all new council housing; the block would become a thieves' paradise in that burglars let in by tenants would raid the offices on the lower floors; and, finally, council tenants would create refuse problems by living in their flats seven days a week and eating in, while the richer type of tenants for whom the flats were designed would live there for four or five days a week and often eat out.

Widdicombe countered by pointing out that the richer type of tenant would also entertain there and so there were likely to be piles of champagne bottles to get rid of. "I have friends who are council tenants and they have parties," replied Tietjen, somewhat defensively. "They may not have champagne bottles, but they do have beer cans." Camden's Chief valuer and assistant treasurer pointed out that rents would be £11 a week and that the flats would cost about £25k each, as opposed to figures of between "24k and £32k elsewhere in the borough".

The enquiry ended on 8 February 1974: further light relief having been provided on 18 January when a hundred demonstrators occupied the block after two of them had infiltrated Burns Security, the company responsible for guarding the building, and let them in through a back door. Throughout the summer, while the council waited for the report to be released, Brompton let out the flats to tourists for £15 a day.

Throughout the Centre Point hearings, the parties had been campaigning hard for the February 1974 general election which saw the fall of the Heath government. The Labour Party chose as their candidate a Camden councillor, Tony Clarke, a 42 year old former postman who was now a full time official in the post workers' union[6]. Much attention was focussed on Hampstead, where Geoffrey Finsberg held the most marginal seat

---

6   Since 1998, Baron Clarke of Hampstead.

MILLIE MILLER, FRANK DOBSON
AND ROY SHAW

in the capital. The big guns were in evidence: Ted Heath came to rally the troops in Hampstead and Harold Wilson came to shake hands with Tony Clarke.[7] The two Labour MPs in Camden, Jock Stallard and Lena Jeger both won comfortably but, against the trend, Finsberg increased his majority in Hampstead to 2257. In Ilford North Millie Miller lost by 285 votes to Tom Iremonger, the sitting Conservative MP. (And in Fareham Jennie Horne came third.)

In March, Martin Morton launched the 1974 Conservative Party manifesto for the borough elections, attacking high rates and in particular the 25% rise approved by the council that month. The Conservatives would return the council to its sensible 1971 policy of selling off council houses to tenants and would put an end to the scandal of empty desks at the town hall. They would also put an end to "the indiscriminate purchase of housing". The Labour manifesto concentrated again on housing. Frank Dobson promised to provide more homes, to expand the housing programme and to build on Branch Hill. Knowing it would provoke the Conservatives, the council issued a compulsory purchase order for the whole of Mornington Crescent. "It is a small scale experiment", said the housing chairman, John Mills.

As the electioneering got under way in earnest, NALGO, the union to which most Camden employees belonged, called a strike against the poor London weighting they were receiving. Morton saw it as a joke. The union had prepared the strike months ago to embarrass the Heath government, and now it was too late for them to stop even though the government had changed. The town clerk, Brian Wilson, announced that the elections themselves were under threat because of the NALGO action, and then all parties turned on them. The strike fizzled out.

The last council meeting, held only eight days before the election held on 2 May 1974, concentrated on housing, Labour's headline policies. The full council agreed to sign the contract to build 42 new homes on the Branch Hill site. The Conservatives voted against on grounds of expense and uncertainty. The council, said Huntly Spence, should not be signing a contract based on estimates. Labour got the headlines: "There has been a twenty year campaign for housing on Branch Hill", said Tony Clarke, the once and future Labour candidate for Hampstead, "and it ill

---

7   Frustrated that his efforts against Jock Stallard were being ignored, John Major attacked the local press as being biased. "If I make an extreme comment", he told his supporters, "it is far more likely to be printed than a moderate statement".

MILLIE MILLER, FRANK DOBSON
AND ROY SHAW

behoves the Conservatives to now start talking about minor technical points when in their hearts this is a class issue. They don't want council housing on Branch Hill".

The 1974 borough elections delivered another bashing for the Tories. Rather than return to power, or at least to a better situation than before, they managed to win four new seats, but lost three including Martin Morton who lost by eleven votes on the fourth count in his home ward of Highgate. Labour won by 48 seats to 12. The election victory, announced Dobson, was "a great mandate for a socialist council to carry out socialist policies". As an afterthought he added: "and one of those socialist policies is the building of council homes at Branch Hill". The *Ham & High* considered Branch Hill to be Morton's albatross. One of the first acts he carried out as leader of the council in 1970 was to stop the sale of the site to developers, and his last act as leader of the opposition was a half hearted attempt to stop the building of council houses on it.

Many of the old guard on the council had stood down at the election: after two general election wins Geoffrey Finsberg decided to concentrate on parliament and resign from the council, as did the last Tory mayor of Hampstead, Luigi Denza. Of the Labour group, Millie Miller, Geoffrey Bindman, Peter Best, Enid Wistrich and Jennie Horne did not stand. Significantly, for each other at least, Tessa Jowell was elected councillor for Gospel Oak, and David Mills for Belsize. Frank Dobson was re-elected as leader of the council with Roy Shaw as his deputy and the South African Roger Jowell as chief whip[8]. Alan Greengross was leader of the opposition with Julian Tobin as his deputy.

There were ten aldermanic seats on the council, five of which (all held by Conservatives) had become vacant. The figures on the council overall had led the Conservatives to expect two of the appointments, but feelings still ran high. "Everyone in the Labour Party", said Dobson, "has done his damnest in the last few weeks to reduce to a minimum Conservative representation and I don't see why we should give charity now". The five new aldermen were all given to Labour Party members so that all ten aldermen were, for the first time ever, Labour. Dobson's

---

8   Jowell had been the president of the students union at the University of Cape Town. He came to England in 1964 having been, he said, "heavily involved in student politics and anti-apartheid activities". He succeeded Phil Turner as Ben Whitaker's agent after the 1966 general election. Married to Tessa Jowell, he had recently set up what was later to become the National Centre for Social Research. Now a professor at the City University, he was knighted in 2008.

MILLIE MILLER, FRANK DOBSON
AND ROY SHAW

subsequent majority of forty six was the largest ever held by one party on Camden council.[9]

Millie Miller was an obvious candidate as she was no longer a councillor and having narrowly failed to get into parliament by way of Ilford, she had time on her hands. She put her name forward for selection, but was rejected, a casualty of the Fair Rents debates. She had bruised the right wing of the group when she stood with the left, and she had bruised the left when she stood with the right. No one forgot their wounds and both sides saw her as an opportunist. Never mind how obscure or lacklustre other applicants were, they did not have her baggage. An internal ballot instead selected the three Labour candidates who had managed to lose Swiss Cottage to the Conservatives: Bill Budd, Arthur Souter, and Gurmukh Singh, the deputy chairman of the CCCR who had expected to be Camden's first Asian councillor. They also appointed two former councillors, George Trevellyn, who had just stood down from the council, and "old time socialist" Bill Oakshott, a former councillor who had just been deselected.

The general election of 10 October 1974, in which Harold Wilson's Labour government won an overall majority of four, brought more frantic campaigning in Camden, but no change. Finsberg's majority was eaten into by Tony Clarke on a reduced turnout, but not by much. Jock Stallard increased his majority over the ardent John Major and Lena Jeger increased hers. Released from her Camden duties, on the second time of trying, Millie Miller beat Tom Iremonger in Ilford North.

Early in the new year of 1975, Camden's housing acquisition programme took a severe knock when Reg Freeson, the minister for housing and construction, halved Camden's budget. The Labour Party, said Alan Greengross, would now have to follow the sensible Conservative policy of acquiring houses that were vacant, in severe disrepair or in order to protect otherwise vulnerable tenants. Not so, said Phil Turner: "Labour's policy of blanket municipalisation remained alive in Camden, but had been temporarily halted by the cuts".

Early success over Centre Point also turned to disappointment. Peter Boydell QC, the enquiry inspector, had presented his report to Tony Crosland the new secretary of state in August 1974. Boydell emphasised that housing was in short supply, the flats had been empty

93

---

9   Outside London, the system of appointing aldermen to councils had been abolished in England and Wales in 1974 (by the Local Government Act 1972). The system was abolished in London boroughs in 1978.

for nearly ten years and that he could find no legal reason to withhold confirmation of the CPO. In September 1974 Crosland confirmed the CPO, and Oldham Estates announced that the company would appeal the decision. In December 1974, hopes were raised when the Co-operative Insurance Society increased its share of Oldham Estates to 50% and one share, although they kept Harry Hyams on as managing director. Frank Dobson appealed to the CIS to review the company's decision to appeal the CPO. He offered to rethink the price, so that the CPO would remain, but the CIS would get more. No deal was struck, and Camden's plans suffered a setback in the High Court in July 1975 when the CPO was quashed. Camden appealed.[10]

Importantly for the left wingers, the government had forced through the Commons the eagerly awaited Housing Finance Special Provisions Bill which lifted the threats of surcharge and disqualification against the thirty Labour councillors who had voted to refuse to implement the fair rents legislation. The Conservatives were furious, especially as no opportunity had been given for the council to debate the issue. "The bill", said Alan Greengross, "established a tendency in the Labour Party that those who break the law should not suffer the consequences, provided they break the law in the interests of the Labour Party". Dobson had gagged the Labour group, he said, from speaking on the matter, and when challenged, John Mills, the housing committee chairman, had avoided discussion by "simpering". "The future of our society", added his deputy, Julian Tobin, comparing the Labour councillors to soccer hooligans, "depends on upholding the law". To Frank Dobson the matter was beyond debate: "The Labour Party", he said, "had fought two general elections on a promise to rescind the penalties".

Frank Dobson, who outside the council described himself as "an administration assistant" working for the General Electric Generating Board, accepted an offer as an assistant commissioner in the Local Government Ombudsman's Office. There would be a conflict of interest

---

10 Mr Justice Forbes ruled that there was a power to issue a CPO for part only of a block so that the local authority could acquire a flying freehold. However, where the block had never been occupied, it would be necessary for its reasonable enjoyment to acquire certain rights over the rest of the block: rights concerning water, gas and electricity supplies; of the use of soil pipes; and the use of the service lift and fire escape. Without these rights, the flats could not be used. Where those rights did not already exist because the building had never been occupied, words adequate to cover them must be included in the order. As the CPO did not include any such provision, it could not stand and so was quashed.

if he remained leader of the council, and so he sent in a resignation letter in early August 1975 and, before anyone could question him on the subject, fled on holiday to the socialist paradise of Yugoslavia. He left his deputy Roy Shaw to take over until an election could be held at the Labour group meeting in September.

There were three candidates to succeed Dobson. The left wanted Alan Evans and the right wanted John Mills. The man in the middle, now in his twentieth year as a councillor, was "quiet, self effacing, but determined" Roy Shaw. Brought up in West Hampstead, Shaw was old enough to have caught the end of the war as a tank driver from Normandy to the Rhine, and had left the army as a sergeant in the Intelligence Corps. After a career in publishing and then advertising, he had recently been made redundant and was existing on his councillor's allowances (of £5 a short meeting and £10 for a long one). It gave him plenty of time to consolidate his position. First Evans and then Mills stood aside leaving Shaw's leadership bid unchallenged.

It was an auspicious start, but his time at the helm was to be characterised by an unmitigated struggle with the left wing of his own group. In October 1975, the first council meeting after his coronation, the council voted to cut £½m from Camden's in-house repairs and maintenance service. Fourteen Labour councillors led by Phil Turner and Richard Arthur voted against the whip. The following week Brian Loughran, the old hard left Irish die hard, announced that he was going to resign[11] from the council, and by the end of the year Richard Arthur had accepted a job in Singapore and was set either to resign or to be given a leave of absence whereby he could stay away for a year without forcing a by election. In the event, he resigned.

At the beginning of 1976 the Camden Trades Council's Campaign Against the Cuts held a meeting in the old Hampstead Town Hall. Camden council, announced Phil Turner, has been "deafeningly silent" about the Labour government's cuts in public spending. "We might expect Camden to be at the forefront of protests. Instead, some Labour councillors seem to see the cuts as a heaven sent opportunity for introducing what they call greater efficiency in council services."

The by-elections to replace two of Turner's allies, Richard Arthur and Brian Loughran, were held at the end of March 1976 and the balance

11 In June 1975, in order to keep up with inflation then estimated at 30% p.a., the council voted to raise council rents by another 36%, which worked out at £1.81 per week. Tenants were better off under the Tory Fair Rent regime, Loughran pointed out, where rises were restricted to £1 a year.

MILLIE MILLER, FRANK DOBSON
AND ROY SHAW

of the Labour group improved for Shaw. On a reduced majority the voters of Gospel Oak returned the old Etonian Richard Turner[12] for Labour, and in Belsize, by a massive 2169 votes to Labour's 1455, Martin Morton was back.[13]

"Race debate dominates" read the headline in the *Ham & High* on 30 April 1976; "Secret race files move starts row" echoed the *Journal*. The big story was the council debate following the recommendation by the Camden Committee for Community Relations that all housing applicants be asked to fill in a form stating their ethnic origins. This would assist council officers in preventing the formation of ghettos. Roy Shaw agreed: "Coloured applicants fare less well than whites and are becoming concentrated in poor quality inner area estates. Immigrants were just not getting the things they were entitled to, said Alderman Singh.

Old traditional Labour, still the party of the white urban working class, was not ready for all this race business. The Camden Federation of Tenants and Residents Associations ("the Camden Fed") saw the plans as an abuse of the system which would make no contribution to eradicating racial discrimination. What if the records fell into the hands of the wrong people? The Camden Communist Party put it bluntly: "It will provide fodder for fascist individuals and organisations". Alan Greengross shared their view: "This debate is not about opposing discrimination, or about whether discrimination exists in Camden —of course it exists, we can't pretend that everything is OK. The debate is: is this the way to combat the evil of discrimination?" The keeping of such records were "totally evil". "The risks were too high a price to pay and would strengthen the very divisions you are trying to eliminate." It would result in engineered dispersals, quotas and misuse of information. Frank Dobson agreed: it would be bad for race relations, he said.

Roger Jowell, a former chairman of the CCCR, told them it straight with the confidence that South Africans have on such matters: "The ethnic minority groups are for it and it is arrogant for councillors to think they know better". Roy Shaw felt it better to bend with the wind. The proposal was passed by 31 votes to 15, with the details to be sorted out in the housing committee. In his first meeting back on the council,

---

12 The son of Sir Mark Turner, chairman of Rio Tinto Zinc plc.

13 Brian Manning, a local pharmacist, put his name forward as an independent in the Gospel Oak by election and then announced that he was withdrawing a fortnight before the poll. His four votes were and are the fewest number ever received by a candidate in a Camden election.

MILLIE MILLER, FRANK DOBSON
AND ROY SHAW

Martin Morton was the only Tory to vote with the majority. Later in the year, the housing committee decided that the applicants were to be classified into eight categories[14]. If someone refused or forgot to classify him or herself, the housing officer would make a guess on the applicant's behalf. In an unsuccessful attempt to mollify the two Jewish members of the opposition, Alan Greengross and Julian Tobin, the category "Jewish" was deleted. It would, said John Lipetz, who also chaired the CCCR, cause confusion being "both a religion and a race", but "justice must be seen to be done".

These were lively times. In his July newsletter the archbishop of Canterbury, Donald Coggan (whose father had been mayor of St Pancras), called for better race relations and added that "there must be a clearly defined limit" on the number of immigrants allowed into the country. The CCCR helpfully called an emergency meeting in the old Hampstead town hall. The chief speaker was the Liberal peer Lord Avebury who was of the opinion that the archbishop's remarks had "given aid and comfort to the racialists". Twenty five members of the National Front disrupted his speech by chanting "Rule Britannia" and shouting at him: "Get back to Israel, you poof"[15]. The police were called and, when they arrived twenty minutes later, were directed by Lord Avebury to "get the scum out of the hall".

Following pressure from Alan Evans, the chairman of the staff committee, Camden introduced a closed shop agreement so that all white collar workers were obliged to join NALGO from 1 July 1976. More importantly, July 1976 was also the month in which the Hampstead Labour Party revealed its choice of "self confessed Marxist Ken Livingstone, the 33 year old son of a South London window cleaner" as their parliamentary candidate. The selection was the culmination of a successful campaign by left wingers in the constituency. In the final vote Livingstone beat Vince Cable, a 32 year old diplomat with a special interest in the plight of the Kenyan Asians. "It was the activists who mattered" wrote Cable in his autobiography, "and the activists were now firmly on the hard left".[16] Ken Livingstone got stuck straight into council

---

14 The categories were: African, Asian, Caribbean, Chinese, Cypriot, Irish, "UK" and "Others".

15 Eric Lubbock famously won the Orpington by election for the Liberals in 1962. He served as Jo Grimond's whip until he lost the seat in 1970 and the next year succeeded to the title as the fourth baron Lubbock. Twice married, he has four children and professes to be a Buddhist.

16 Vince Cable, *Free Radical* (2009)

MILLIE MILLER, FRANK DOBSON
AND ROY SHAW

business, accused the government of blackmail over council rents and called on council tenants to lobby the next meeting of the Labour group in August to lobby the councillors to freeze rents.[17]

Two years into a Labour government, rent increases and fears of future increases still haunted the council. In August 1976 the housing committee unanimously set an increase of 44p a week, which reanimated the left wing of the party. Phil Turner countered with a motion opposing the rent rises. He was backed by the Tories who felt that the rent rises were not high enough, and by Dick Collins who felt that ratepayers should pay for council house repairs. The majority voted with John Mills, the voice of the establishment. "The cost of housing", he said, quite accurately, "is unlikely ever to be cheaper".

At the end of the summer, the council released the report of its Housing Review Panel that had been set up by Dobson before his resignation. The panel, chaired by Tony Clarke, had taken a year to write the report to conclude that little was wrong with Camden's building department. The *Journal* was not impressed: "It is a wishy washy document that says very little and takes a long time in saying it." It was a "whitewash" said the Conservatives, who then issued their own highly critical report pointing out that decorating a flat costs up to 66% more if done by direct labour, and on top of that, Camden's building department charges were 50% higher than Hackney's and 20% higher than the GLC's. Their modest conclusion was that the building department should not be allowed to keep its monopoly of repairs and building work on the borough's estates.

The Housing Finance (Special Provisions) Act 1975 had been rushed through parliament to save the "Fair Rent rebels" from the fate suffered by the Clay Cross councillors[18]. The effect was a great relief for the thirty Labour councillors who with Millie Miller had voted not to implement Fair Rents in Camden. The loss to the council, by the time they caved in, was £150,000 in lost rent. If the councillors were not going to pay the sum themselves, the question still remained as to where the

17   1976 was also the year in which the mayor, Bernard Taylor, posed naked with his wife for photographs to celebrate the new mixed sex sauna at the Oasis Baths in Holborn. The sauna closed within the year.

18   Clay Cross Urban District Council in Derbyshire had led the opposition to the Housing Act and had refused to implement it. Eleven Labour councillors were surcharged and barred from public office for five years. Their High Court appeal failed in 1975 and they were made bankrupt. The Labour government's attempt to overturn the disqualifications was defeated in the House of Commons on 4 August 1975.

MILLIE MILLER, FRANK DOBSON
AND ROY SHAW

money was to come from. The Labour group agreed that the lost rent would be paid by the general rate payer rather than by claiming back rent from the council tenants.

When this was announced at a special council meeting in October 1976, the Conservatives were furious. The Labour members had gained support on the estates by defying the act, and were now shying away from allowing the tenants to feel the cost of their political posturing. The Labour position was one of hypocrisy, said Alan Greengross. They had opposed an 85p increase three years ago but now, under a Labour government, were committed to annual rent increases. The fair rent rebels should pay the shortfall themselves. They were "cowards", running away from paying the bills they had run up. "Put your money where your mouths are", he said. "You defied the law, you should pay the bill," said the Julian Tobin. "I broke the law!" shouted back Paddy O'Connor, "and I'm proud of it!" Huntly Spence put it more colourfully: the Labour group were "a gang of armchair guerrillas with Walter Mitty dreams of the barricades". The motion was passed by 36 votes to 13 (with two Labour abstentions).

The Branch Hill scheme lumbered on, in that its cost had rocketed from an estimated £33,000 per dwelling in 1972 to £67,000 in 1975. In May 1976 under the headline "Stunning Subsidy", the *Ham & High* worked out that the government would be subsidising each of the forty two new households in Branch Hill at the rate of £58 a week. On top of that there would be a further subsidy of £75 per tenant paid by the ratepayers in order to keep the rents down to an affordable level. "We hoped for a rather better subsidy payment", said the somewhat sheepish Neil McIntosh, the new housing chairman[19]. Roy Shaw was rather more bullish. Had the Tory council gone ahead with building council homes in 1968, or had the Conservative government given funding in 1972, the building costs would have been lower and the council would not be paying so much in interest.

It was not long before the district auditor became involved. The complainant was Basil Rodrigues, a 53 year old ex-artillery officer and retired business man (or "wealthy Hampstead property man" as the *Journal* preferred) who was paying even then £1100 a year in rates on his Rosecroft Avenue house. "I'm paying out so that some council tenants

---

19   The Department of the Environment had pledged £643k contribution on the original tender sum of £1346k, and stuck to that original contribution even when overall cost estimates rose to £2135k.

MILLIE MILLER, FRANK DOBSON
AND ROY SHAW

can live in a home I can't afford to live in myself. Why should I pay out £20 a week rates just so the council can let some bloody fellow who does nothing live in a £67,500 home in Branch Hill?"

Branch Hill was the least of Roy Shaw's worries. By January 1977 Camden was facing the biggest financial crisis in its history. An 18% rate increase was on the cards and even then there would be cut backs in expenditure on services: "This year", Roy Shaw warned the Labour group, "there will be no sacred cows". The package prepared by council officers was laid before them: the libraries would all have to close one day a week and High Holborn library would close altogether. The arts centre at Burgh House would close as would the Flask Walk baths. The grants to the Camden music festival and the Arkwright Arts Trust would be cut. Meals on wheels would go up by 3p. The house building programme would be reduced from the target of 1,400 homes to a mere 600. Council rents would go up by 88p a week and the heating charge by 24%.

There were two by elections in February, neither of which went well for the Labour leadership in that Dobson's supposedly safe seat in Holborn ward was taken by Ken Avery, a 34 year old marketing executive and a retread from the great Tory intake of '68. On the same night the vacant seat in St Pancras was won by Labour's Tom Devine, an Irishman "proud of St Pancras's radical left tradition" and something of a loud voice locally in COHSE, the health service union.

In the April GLC elections, things looked even worse for Labour. Enid Wistrich lost her seat to Alan Greengross in Hampstead and the comfortable Labour majorities in the St Pancras constituencies were slashed (in Holborn & St Pancras South from four thousand to 122).

In April 1977 Camden's compulsory purchase order on the Centre Point flats finally hit the buffers. The council had successfully overturned the High Court decision in the Court of Appeal in July 1976, but as there was an "interesting point of law", Sovmots was granted leave to appeal to the House of Lords.[20] The decision came as something of a

---

20   The Court of Appeal disagreed with Mr Justice Forbes on a narrow ground. Although it was desirable that the authority set out in the order the rights or easements that it required, they did not need to be itemised in the order, because they were "necessary" to enable the maisonettes to be used as dwellings and so could be implied. Unfortunately for Camden, it was an interesting point of law, and the court gave Sovmots leave to appeal.

MILLIE MILLER, FRANK DOBSON
AND ROY SHAW

surprise to Sovmots lawyers and rather than face another appeal, they entered into negotiations with Camden. They offered the Centre Point flats to the borough for £700,000, which was not far away from the anticipated CPO valuation. Camden turned it down. "It was a pity", Julian Tobin told the policy committee after the event, "that we turned our backs on dealing with this in another way, thus throwing away £40,000 of ratepayers' money [on legal costs]". Andrew Bethell, who chaired the committee, thought otherwise. "The deal", he said with some emphasis, "was turned down because it was rushed through and the Cooperative Insurance Society had the same advice as us: that it would not win the appeal".

They were wrong. In April 1977, the House of Lords overturned the Court of Appeal's decision.[21] The bill to the ratepayers for Sovmot's costs were £25,000[22] alone and the council had to pay its own costs on top of that, a total bill of some £40,000. It was seized upon as another example of Labour's waste. Roy Shaw told the press that the council was "absolutely justified" in pursuing the case to the House of Lords. "They rejected our appeal on a technicality which no one who supported our original decision could have foreseen". In truth, it was a decision that had been impossible to anticipate. Of the nine senior judges who had considered the case, five of them (four in the House of Lords and Mr Justice Forbes) had ruled against the council, and four (three in the court of Appeal and one in the House of Lords) had ruled for it. "Technicalities" said Millie Miller, "always win against the needs of the people".

The following council meeting in May 1977 was a difficult one. The Playscheme budget was to be cut by £54,000 and councillors had to enter the Town Hall past a gauntlet of three hundred protestors made up of the usual suspects joined by banner waving parents, children and playgroup leaders, backed by members of the Covent Garden Association hoping against hope to save High Holborn library. The rates were put

---

21 Lord Wilberforce gave the leading judgment in which he said, in effect, that the council had no powers to create rights that did not exist over land that was not subject to the CPO. It was not a question of whether the CPO was inadequate in its wording. The CPO was inadequate in that it could not secure rights on adjoining land even if those rights were necessary for the maisonettes to be used as homes.

22 At a time when a skilled secretary would expect to earn £2,500 p.a. and £25,000 could buy the freehold of a four bedroomed house in Belsize Park.

MILLIE MILLER, FRANK DOBSON
AND ROY SHAW

up by 15½%. The public gallery noisily protested against the cuts, and the Conservatives noisily railed against inefficiency. "What sort of lunatic priority left new social services buildings closed [in West Hampstead] while Camden pressed on with the Swiss Cottage housing scheme which no one wants?" asked Alan Greengross before pointing out that in 1971 the council had debts of £91m and was paying debt charges of £9m a year, and "this year it's £300m with interest charges of £32m". Nicholas Bosanquet, the social services chairman, felt that the best thing had been done in near impossible circumstances: "We are proud that at a time of stringency we have not made mechanical cuts across the board –we have not wallowed in self pity". "It's not a disaster" said John Mills, the deputy leader, "when we have a rate increase in line with inflation". Fed up with the lefties in his own party, Tim Skinner, a former mayor, voted against the budget.

The district auditor's report on the complaint on the expenditure on Branch Hill came out in the summer. He held back from actually censuring the council, but seriously questioned the cost when the weekly rent subsidy was going to be £170 for each dwelling on the estate. Julian Tobin accused Roy Shaw of shedding "crocodile tears". The council adopted wastefully expensive projects such as Branch Hill when "the Socialists are frequently heard complaining that they haven't enough money to do the things we want". Branch Hill, said Greengross, is "a symbol of useless dogma". No, said Tony Clarke, it is "an act of political faith". Roy Shaw was fed up with the criticism. "Everybody knew damn well from the start it would be an expensive site", he said.

The National Front stood again in the October 1977 by election at Swiss Cottage (where Ronnie Raymond Cox had stood down), and again drew great attention with everyone except the voters (they got 2% of the vote). The other three candidates issued a joint statement asking that "all anti-racists should work together against all forms of racist ideology". At the same time the Camden Anti Nazi Campaign was launched. The Left was very much in evidence. At the height of the national Silver Jubilee celebrations, the leading article in the *Hampstead Labour Party News* read "This month her Majesty Queen Elizabeth II by the grace of God the Queen of all Britain, Defender of the Faith, celebrates twenty five years in Britain's best paid job while there are one and a half million unemployed". The celebrations were "a brashly tasteless example of conspicuous consumption". There was criticism from within the council on spending public money on the celebrations. "Surely we've got better things to spend our money on", Phil Turner told the *Journal*.

MILLIE MILLER, FRANK DOBSON
AND ROY SHAW

It was goodbye in 1977 to Brian Wilson, who had been Camden's town clerk since the borough's formation in 1964. He retired in June. And at the end of October, after a long illness, Millie Miller died. She was only 54.

Considerations of race, the new interest of the new left, were never far below the surface. In January 1978 Camden adopted a policy document in which it pledged itself to adopt a "positive discrimination" employment policy. The council was not employing enough (in the words of the day) "coloured" people and was determined to alter the imbalance. All but a small minority of the council's 7,000 employees were white. "The council now recognises that a passive policy of non-discrimination in itself will not be sufficient to break the cycle of deprivation and so guarantee equal opportunities for members of ethnic minority groups". Coloured people had difficulty being employed because often they were poorly educated and could not speak English. Through in-house training the council would put this right. They would then be interviewed by council staff "trained to bring out the capabilities of any coloured applicant". Job advertisements were to be placed in the West Indian World.

The council would also implement what was then a revolutionary new policy of monitoring its success in this field. A record would now be kept of the ethnic origins of all members of staff. This, now adopted everywhere, seemed at the time quite shocking. The chairman of the staff and management committee, Alan Evans, was given the task of fielding questions from the press. He did not mince his words: "If two different people of equal ability but of different colour apply for a job, we will pick the coloured person". And if the policy did not increase the number of coloured employees, said Evans, further steps would have to be taken to accomplish that end.

"Camden Steps Out Too Far" thundered the editorial in the Times. "One way of reducing the proportion of black unemployed (and increasing the proportion of white unemployed) would be to grant systematic preference to black applicants for vacancies....The policy statement as a whole is confused and ambiguous in intent, crossing and re-crossing the all important line between the removal of all traces of discrimination against ethnic minorities and the practice of counter-discrimination in their favour". Opposition came also from the Runnymede Trust who described the move as "a systematic policy of discrimination against whites" which "would provoke resentment and would be counterproductive". The proposals had not been tested outside the left wing hot house of Camden where they were adopted with little comment. The first difficulty was that the Race Relations Act 1976 would not allow positive discrimination. Not that Alan Evans was deterred by that: "If the Act does not allow the full promotion of equal opportunities for minority groups, it must be challenged in the courts or amended in parliament", he said. Others went further. "Positive discrimination means getting the balance right because we have a dearth of black staff", said Roger Jowell. John Lipetz agreed: "We are merely redressing the balance in saying that ethnic origins are now to be regarded as part of the qualifications for a job."

The back pedalling began immediately: Roy Shaw was forced to issue a joint statement with Alan Evans: the new policy would definitely not amount to discrimination against whites. The council simply wanted to ensure equal opportunities, and as some coloured people were disadvantaged in applying for jobs, the council would help them. Coloured people could make some special contribution towards certain jobs, "such as social workers, housing liaison officers, interviewers, estate managers and librarians". Many of Camden's clients are coloured "and would be helped by having someone of their own language and culture to consult".

The spotlight shone bright on Alan Evans, the 38 year old son of a Welsh steelworker. He had read economics at the LSE, been vice president of the NUS, had taught briefly in Nottingham, became personal assistant to the general secretary of the teachers union and was now the head of the education department at the National Union of Teachers. He was, he said, "surprised and depressed" by all the fuss, but pleased that the issue was out in the open. All he wanted was the removal of those obstacles that prevent members of minority groups getting jobs. There could be no discrimination against whites except in the rarest of circumstances when two people of equal ability applied, one of whom was from a minority group, and when the council was deficient in staff from that group. He made a point of not repeating his pledge to take further steps if more coloured people were not employed. Race, he thought, would be an important issue in the coming general election.[23]

The National Front tried to cash in. Their porcine leader, Martin Webster, arranged a meeting in the Enterprise pub on Chalk Farm Road,

---

23 Although perhaps not in Pembroke where he came second to the Conservative candidate.

but the brewery backed down after being contacted by the CCCR. The closest to Camden that the National Front could get was the George & Dragon in Islington, where Webster promised to field nine candidates in the borough elections in Camden. "If you people cannot get in some pretty terrific votes in Camden, then there must be something wrong", he told his supporters.

Eighteen months late and now at an estimated cost of over £100,000 each, the first tenants at last moved into the Branch Hill estate, said to be "the most expensive council homes yet". Among that first intake was Mrs Jean Harding who expressed her gratitude through the *Ham & High*: "The lounge and dining room and roof garden compensate for the absolutely minute bedrooms", she said, before expressing satisfaction with her rent rebate: "If I had to pay the full rent, I don't suppose it would be worth the money".

The 1978 borough election campaign began, as always, with the budget. The Labour group imposed a 2% rate rise, the lowest rise in the history of the borough. It was a desperate measure, but was desperately needed. In Camden the Conservatives had their tails up and were threatening to surge back. The reason in part was their "Value for Money" manifesto, but chiefly they received great assistance from Jim Callaghan's Labour government which had been busy encouraging the electorate to forgive the Conservatives for the Heath years.

It was a close run thing, but Labour held onto the four seats that would have made a difference and won by 33 seats to 26. Two wards were split and there was even a recount in Kings Cross. Labour won narrowly in Kilburn where two ex Labour councillors, Frank Rochford and Tim Skinner, stood as members of the "Independent Labour Party" against the official Labour candidates in protest against the lurch to the left that the party had taken. They each polled over 400 votes. The winners in Kilburn, ominously for the leadership, were all left wingers: Pat Driscoll, Ken Livingstone, the Hampstead prospective parliamentary candidate, and Neil Fletcher who, more than anyone else, had been responsible for Livingstone's selection for Hampstead. It was not just Roy Shaw who was going to have his work cut out, guessed the *Journal* somewhat hopefully, as Alan Greengross was unlikely to survive the new intake of Thatcherites.

The Liberals put up a token campaign only in the old Hampstead borough wards where in every case they ended up behind both the

MILLIE MILLER, FRANK DOBSON
AND ROY SHAW

main parties. They managed a mere 4,423 votes, 3.24% of the total. The National Front's dozen candidates made no impact other than provoking the *Journal* to run an editorial to tell people not to vote for them, and managing to get more votes than a couple of Communist and Workers Revolutionary Party candidates. In Fitzjohns ward the Indian born John Athisayam became, as the *Journal* put it, "the first black Tory councillor". [24]

The total votes cast for the two main parties were 65,328 for Labour against the Conservatives' 63,670, a margin of 1,658, less than 1% of the adult population of Camden. Alan Greengross, the Conservative leader who had been closer than any other to breaking what would prove to be the thirty five years of Labour rule, summed up his feelings after the votes were counted: "One thing is certain: having scraped into power by a total of some 180 votes in a borough of 180,000 people, the Socialists no longer have a mandate for the lunacies of the past"[25].

If he thought that would stop them, he was very wrong. The real fun was yet to begin.

24 He was Camden's first elected Asian councillor, although the failed Labour Party council candidate Gurmukh Singh had become the first Asian member of the council in 1974 by being made an alderman.

25 He referred to the small number of votes by which the Tories failed to take those crucial four extra seats in Bloomsbury, Kings Cross and West End (although, as anoraks were to point out, the Tories needed 30 votes to take the second Bloombury seat, 28 to take the second West End seat and 146 votes to take both Kings Cross seats: a total of 204 extra votes needed –or alternatively, 102 Labour votes switching.)

MILLIE MILLER, FRANK DOBSON
AND ROY SHAW

5|

Roy Shaw: the battle
with the Left

aving won the election, albeit by the narrowest of margins, Roy Shaw was re-elected unopposed as leader by the Labour group. Others had to fight harder, and the divisions in the group were clear from the start. John Mills secured the deputy leadership by defeating the left winger Phil Turner by only 18 votes to 14, and Andrew Bethell saw off the new comer Ken Livingstone by 20 votes to 12 to become chief whip.

But Livingstone did manage to get the chairmanship of the housing committee. He made his mark at the first committee meeting by announcing (without consulting the Labour Group) that council rents would not go up, that the council would not demand rent if intrusive repairs had to be carried out and that there would be a referendum amongst tenants to see if they supported the Tory GLC's plan to hand over its housing to Camden. Members of the public in the committee room noisily applauded his announcements and he made a point of inviting "the people" to speak in preference to councillors. "His presidential style handling of the meeting underscored his reputation as an uncompromising left winger", noted the *Ham & High*. Roy Shaw was less impressed: "He played to the gallery –the left wing gallery, the trades union gallery, whatever gallery would help him at any particular moment. His ploy was to put forward an outrageous proposition, knowing full well that it would not be accepted –not really believing it himself. It would be defeated in the Labour group. He would then turn round and say it's all the fault of those right wing bastards".[1]

---

1   As quoted in *Citizen Ken* by John Carvel. "He was a lousy chairman of housing", said Shaw.

1978 - 1982

Shortly after the council elections, Lena Jeger, who had been first elected MP for Holborn & St Pancras South in 1953[2], announced that she did not intend to stand at the next election. The resultant scramble for selection as the parliamentary candidate in July 1978 was termed by the *Journal* "The Siege of Bayham Street", the constituency Labour Party's headquarters. Disgruntled Labour Party members, led by "mature student" Gloria Lazenby[3] and "bearded cabbie" Mick Morrissey, formed a picket line outside the building to urge delegates to stay away. From behind her "Democracy –Yes, Rigging – No" placard and her Anti Nazi League sticker, the formidable Mrs Lazenby shouted out her disgust at the executive committee for drawing up a shortlist without the favoured left wing candidate, journalist and Birmingham Six campaigner, Chris Mullin.

Although it took three ballots, Frank Dobson, as the *Journal* put it, "walked it". Forty delegates made it in to vote: Patricia Hewitt, the chairman of the National Council for Civil Liberties was one of the two to fall at the first round. (She got three votes.) The closest the left got was in the challenge of a former Camden councillor, David Offenbach, who got ten votes to Dobson's twenty three. John Mills, Camden's deputy leader, represented the pragmatic wing of the local party. After being grilled about his defence of the rent increases three years before, he managed eight votes. "I sensed defeat", he said, "the moment I stepped into the room".

The members of the Central Camden Tenants and Residents Association voted not to campaign for Dobson because they had only been prepared to work for John Mills, and the St Pancras branch voted not to support Dobson but to work for the nearest left wing parliamentary candidate, who happened to be Ken Livingstone in Hampstead.

The November 1978 council meeting was petitioned by King's Cross residents demanding a police crackdown on prostitution in the area. The petitioners were treated unsympathetically. John Thane harangued them to the effect that there were more serious crimes than prostitution, and in any event, he said, the police suffered from an "organised refusal to

---

2   In succession to her husband, Dr Santo Jeger, who held the seat from 1945 until his death in 1953. She narrowly lost the 1959 election to Geoffrey Johnson Smith, but got her seat back in 1964. She was made a life peer in 1979, and chaired the Labour Party conference in 1980. She died in 2007, aged 91.

3   Gloria Lazenby, the former chairman of the Holborn & St Pancras South Labour Party. She had caused a stir two years before by suing her employer, the trade union ASTMS, for unlawful dismissal and threatening to subpoena as a witness Clive Jenkins, the union's general secretary. Her husband was his driver. She received three months pay. She later served as a Camden councillor from 1986 until 2002.

do their duties". This prompted Mick Morrissey to spring to his feet and denounce the police as "a political force" in the pockets of "the ruling class." Police were not available to protect ordinary people, did nothing about prostitutes but were "able to turn out in force on Remembrance Day to protect a gang of Nazis taking part in the Cenotaph parade[4], just as thousands had been marshalled at Grunwick".

Knowing that the Labour government's five year term would come to end in 1979 and that there would have to be a general election by October, NUPE felt it a good time to get concessions from a government that would not want to lose its core support from council workers. They demanded a flat £60 for a 35 hour week. The government, facing high inflation, had imposed a pay limit and demanded that all pay demands be negotiated nationally. Employers such as Camden were placed in a difficult position. They would face the backlash for any strike action and could not settle without permission from central government who could not afford to give permission for fear of opening the inflationary floodgates.

On 6 February 1979 the National Union of Public Employees (NUPE) held a strike meeting of the council's manual workers. Of their 2,500 members, only 1,000 turned up, but after a stormy debate a strike was approved by 113 votes. Rubbish collections stopped, as did road maintenance, meals on wheels and burials. The *Journal* supported the strike: its front page headline shouted: "It's the only way!" and included inside a full page spread entitled "It's a fight for a living wage." The council announced the setting up of public dumps around the borough and Tessa Jowell, the new chairman of the staff committee helpfully said that although Camden could not give in, the council supported NUPE's action. "We don't want public services dependent on high levels of overtime to provide decent rates of pay. This dispute will remind people that NUPE members provide essential services".

As the piles of rubbish grew, so did the pressure on the Labour members. In the group meeting on 16 February 1979 Roy Shaw asked that they stand firm and rely on the national negotiations. His proposal was defeated by 14 – 13, and a new motion proposed by Ken Livingstone

---

4   Two and a half thousand National Front supporters had been allowed to lay a wreath at the Cenotaph under a police escort to prevent a clash with Anti Nazi League demonstrators. Until July 1978, the Grunwick Film Processing works had been heavily picketed in a dispute concerning union recognition.

was approved instead. It was decided to pay £60 for a 35 hour week and that the reduction in working hours from 37 hours would be met by employing more staff rather than by paying overtime.

The success of the motion had taken everyone by surprise, including Livingstone. It still did not bring about the quick result that had been intended as the details had not been thought through. NUPE still refused to go back to work because the motion did not appear to apply to those already above the £44.20 a week basic (with £6.67 London weighting). Phil Turner, now the chairman of the works committee announced that the £60 basic was not to be calculated to include any bonuses. Everyone was to get £60 plus their bonuses. This was too much for the leadership who then proposed £60 basic to include the bonuses. Even that was going to cost the council £2.5m. Roy Shaw forced his compromise through the Labour Group by 21 votes to nine. Livingstone made a public show of his disappointment and NUPE accused the council of reneging on its original offer.

Even though the strike was not over, the *Journal* sensed that great things had occurred. The front page bellowed THE VICTORS over a picture of celebrating council workers. The editorial column ("We say") made the point:

> *The Labour group wrestled with its political soul on Tuesday. To say "Yes" to the NUPE claim could prove unpopular with an electorate expected to pick up most of the bill. To say "No" meant hypocritically turning their backs on all their declarations of support for the underpaid public workers.*
>
> *It was a courageous decision reminiscent of the daring St Pancras council of years ago. It was a victory for what politics should be all about.*

It was a bitterly cold snow laden month and, once the concession had been made, the steam had gone out of the strike. It was not worth holding out for the small print in Camden's offer. On 23rd February the NUPE leadership accepted the council's offer unconditionally and their members went back to work. The manual workers, happy that their pay had been put up by some £17 to give them £60 a week plus their London weighting, set about clearing up the 2,000 tons of rubbish left at the official dumping sites and the 1,500 tons of rubbish now left on the streets. It took them a fortnight.

Roy Shaw found himself having to defend the payment of the "Camden supplement", as it became known: "We had rubbish piling up in the streets and mortuaries were overflowing because no one would bury the dead". Ken Livingstone, was delighted. "The union has acted with incredible responsibility in not insisting on what it wanted but getting something for the lowest paid. I can't think of many unions that have made so many concessions. There has been a redistribution of wealth to the lowest paid". Five days later the council put the domestic rates up by 17.7% (to 85.8p in the pound).[5] The pay settlement with NUPE had not significantly added to the increase, said the leadership, not altogether convincingly, because £1.5m had already been set aside for wages and £1m savings had been found.

Less happy were the Tories. To Hampstead's MP, Geoffrey Finsberg, the deal with NUPE was "totally irresponsible". "When the long suffering rate payers of Camden come to foot the bill –for it will not be the smug self satisfied Socialist councillors who pay up –let them remember, whether they be pensioners, council tenants, one parent families or anyone else, that what the Socialists have done is put their sticky hands into other people's pockets". On the council, Alan Greengross's view was that there was trouble ahead now that wage differentials had been eroded and manual workers were being paid more than white collar workers. "How much longer" he asked, "are we content to go on with the Labour Party's new slogan of Jam Yesterday, Jam Tomorrow and one Hell of a Jam Today?"

The Labour GLC member for Holborn & St Pancras South, Dick Collins, the former United Tenants Association leader, Camden councillor and mayor, died at the beginning of the year. A by election was called for early March where Labour defended a slim 122 vote majority over the Tories. The new Labour candidate was a council pest controller, Charlie Rossi, of whom the *Journal* greatly approved. "Rat Catcher Rossi: The People's Choice", ran their headline in the week before the poll. He won, and with a majority only nine fewer than Collins's.[6]

One of the consequences of the pay settlement was that both sides were already fired up when the general election was called for May

---

5   With accurate cynicism, the *Ham & High* had predicted in January that after the previous year's pre-election budget which imposed the "lowest rise in the borough's history" the council would need to put up the domestic rate by 18% in 1979.

6   The front page of the Journal in March also carried a photograph of a happy couple following their marriage at Camden Town Hall. Both recently divorced, they were David Mills, a father of three and the former councillor for Belsize, and Tessa Jowell, now a councillor for Gospel Oak.

1979. Finsberg kicked off his campaign by claiming that Camden was run by "mad Marxists". Hampstead's Labour candidate, Ken Livingstone, responded by calling on Finsberg to "get out of the gutter and discuss the real issues" which he listed as being "import controls on inessential goods and export controls on capital which should be redirected into industry". He also wanted compulsory planning agreements to make industry more competitive, an increase in public spending, more aid to the third world to promote world trade and the implementation of firm price controls. As housing chairman, Livingstone took it upon himself to announce that the council planned to issue compulsory purchase orders on 2,000 properties in the borough over the next four years. His purpose was to stop "get-rich-quick property tycoons planning to slaughter the tenants and turn Camden into another Chelsea or Pimlico. No speculator's going to come down here winkling out local people and destroying the community!" When Finsberg described the Anti-Nazi League as "thugs in action, and not different from National Front thugs", Livingstone attacked Finsberg's "shameful" record on race relations and called for the disbanding of the Metropolitan Police's Special Patrol Group for their rough handling of anti-NF demonstrators in Southall. "This is the dirtiest campaign ever in Hampstead", said Finsberg.

The bad feeling lasted up to the count. Finsberg won with an increased majority and, on a higher turnout, both Ken Livingstone and David Radford, the Liberal candidate, managed an extra couple of hundred votes each.[7] The three mainstream party candidates had agreed beforehand that only the winner would make a speech, as if the others also spoke then the National Front candidate would also get a platform –albeit late at night in front of an audience of committed party workers and council employees. Finsberg, relying on this, made a speech in which he thanked the returning officer and the police and then pointedly thanked David Radford for the clean campaign he had fought. This was too much for Livingstone who snatched the mike from him as he finished and treated the audience to what the *Ham & High* called "a fiery political rant". (He had been provoked, he said afterwards, by the "fulsome praise" that Finsberg had lavished on the police who had only that day subjected one of his party activists to a body search.) "It's appalling" said Radford, "that an agreement was

---

7   When it became clear that he had not won, Livingstone turned to Neil Fletcher and said: "Oh well, it'll have to be the GLC then".

made and he was unable to keep it". [8]

Nationally, the election result was the most significant in modern years. Mrs Thatcher led the Conservative Party to a landslide victory. The election in Camden's two Labour seats had been quieter than in Hampstead as no one saw Labour losing, especially in St Pancras North, Jock Stallard's safe seat, but it was uncomfortably close in Holborn & St Pancras South where Frank Dobson was standing for the first time. He was elected but with only half the majority left him by Lena Jeger. The Conservative candidate, Robert Key was only 2,323 votes behind him. [9]

With the election result in mind, the St Pancras Labour Party raised £420 to pay off Mick Morrissey's rent arrears. He had been suspended as a councillor while he faced eviction from his council flat in Gordon Mansions in Torrington Place. £420 to prevent a by election in the current political climate was a good deal, and the *Journal* was right behind him: "Recently the *Journal* discovered that hard working Mick had never claimed expenses for his council duties. Inevitably his earnings as a taxi driver had suffered because of his council commitments." (This, immediately above a short article beginning: "A Tory bid for massive rent increases for Camden council has been rejected by the town hall's ruling Labour group...") [10]

Michael Heseltine became the Secretary of State for the Environment with a brief to curb spending. In Camden, there was trouble ahead. In July the council was presented with an unhappy paper bearing the signatures of the chief executive, Frank Nickson, and the director of finance, Frank Budd, pointing out that Camden faced a "bleak future". Inflation and government cuts to the rate support grant were predicted to force a 30% rate increase (another 32p in the pound) at the current rate of spending and even then Camden was heading for an unprecedented £700k deficit. The only alternative that faced the council was to fix rate increases at the annual rate of inflation (then 16%) and make cuts accordingly. Having digested the figures over the summer, Roy Shaw announced that Camden would follow a "no cuts" policy which he estimated would require a 40% rate

113

---

8 Not that it really mattered: no newspaper printed anything of the National Front candidate's address. The Labour party activist, who had been whisked away to Paddington Green Police Station for a body search (and then released without charge), was Maggie Fletcher, Neil's wife.

9 The son of Bishop Key, Robert Key was elected to parliament in 1983 in Salisbury, and has remained there since. He was minister for Roads and Traffic in 1993.

10 Mick Morrissey nevertheless stood down from the council in the following year.

rise. He was supported by Frank Dobson who claimed that £2 had been put on the rates "thanks to government spending cuts" and his views were in turn trumpeted by the *Journal* ("Tory Blitz on London" being one of their more colourful headlines).

Locally, the Conservatives were unrepentant and used Shaw's predictions to ram home their points about waste and over expenditure. If the council did not cut its workforce, they predicted, rates would need to be doubled in two years. The *Journal* began to change tack and forecast 3,000 redundancies, half the total workforce. "Labour's dogmatic refusal to find savings in its wages bill", said Alan Greengross, "will lead the borough to financial ruin". Roy Shaw's plan to push up the rates by 40% was one of "unmitigated hypocrisy". "Labour bemoan the plight of the poor people of Camden yet at a time when we all have problems, how does Camden take care of its poor? Its rates go up". The new generation of Tories were less forgiving. The Belsize councillor Tony Kerpel wrote to the *Ham & High* in November 1979: "By its own deliberate profligacy, Camden has fouled the nest of every inner city borough in London and will now reap the consequences of its own making". Michael Heseltine threatened to "seek powers" to penalise councils who put up the rates to avoid cost cutting.

By the end of the year, the *Journal* had turned on Shaw. Under a headline "Camden Horror Show", it analysed his master plan. Unable to control his left wing, he intended to make ratepayers pay for the government cuts in the hope that the Tory government fell and that a new Labour government would reverse the policy. But in the meantime further government cuts would require further rate rises: "Another 50, 60, 70, 90 per cent?" asked the paper before concluding that "there is little doubt there is much waste in the Town Hall".[11]

The squeeze on council spending hit hardest at the council's ambitious policy of municipalisation –the housing in council owned stock of as much of the population as they could. The new environment secretary, Michael Heseltine, announced in August 1979 drastic cuts in local authority spending on housing development, rehabilitation and acquisition. He began that month by (against the advice of his own inspectors) rejecting Camden's compulsory purchase orders on derelict properties. His behaviour was "blatantly political", said Shaw. "The Tories are bashing Camden" agreed Dobson. As if to confirm the

---

11   1979 brought about great changes to the mayor's transport. Camden's 1934 Rolls Royce
was changed for a Ford Grosvenor VI.

point, Heseltine then announced (in a press release rather than by a letter) that he was putting a stop to four of Camden's housing schemes (including that for 93 new homes on the Elm Village site in St Pancras) on the ground that the cost of £35,900 per home was "substantially in excess of what normally would be considered acceptable". Camden's ambitious plans "to build 522 new homes a year" were torn up. Housing associations, the government announced, were to be given land and property to ease the council's burden.

That summer also saw change in the leadership of the Conservative group. Alan Greengross resigned as leader as he had become the chairman of the planning committee on the GLC, and was replaced by "bearded solicitor" Julian Tobin who beat Martin Morton by 15 votes to 10 (the same margin by which Morton had beaten him for the leadership after Finsberg's resignation in 1970). Derek Spencer, a barrister who had only been elected to the council in 1978 beat Morton to be deputy group leader by fourteen votes to nine. "I have," said Morton, "been underexposed in the group over the last few months".

In September 1979 the housing committee approved an eviction order against the eleven gypsy families who were occupying a vacant site at the junction of Parkhill Road and Haverstock Hill. They had annoyed the locals with their makeshift latrines, piles of rubbish and barking dogs. The gypsies should be moved to another part of the borough, said Ron King, the Conservative group whip and a former Royal Navy commander, but was unable to specify where, other than "somewhere where they are nowhere near any other housing". The committee chairman, Ken Livingstone, agreed. "Gypsies are no longer what they were", he said. "If we had a happy group of rural gypsies sitting around making clothes pegs then the committee might've been minded to leave them there, but the place is more like a breaker's yard. They have become urban junk men". To John Lipetz, it was a race issue: "There is a lot of prejudice against Gypsies because their lifestyle and ethnic background is different".

In November, Chairman Hua Guofeng, the president of the People's Republic of China, made a state visit to Britain and visited Karl Marx's grave in Highgate Cemetery in the north east of the borough. He was accompanied on his pilgrimage by the mayor of Camden, Sally Peltier, who had made an impromptu arrangement for him to meet John Suddaby,

115

the wispy bearded, long haired, militant secretary of Camden NUPE who had arranged the manual workers' strike in February. Not especially interested in industrial practices or human rights abuses in China, or the Chinese colonial policy in Tibet, Mr Suddaby begged Chairman Hua not to be friendly to Maggie Thatcher. His placard read: "Remember Karl Marx! Break links with the Tories!" Through the Chinese interpreter he told Hua: "He is supporting a government which is making a savage attack on working people in this country". Hua looked at him vacantly and went on his way to pose for the photographers with a wreath in front of Marx's memorial.

November also saw the first consultation on the government's plans to allow council tenants the "right to buy" their council homes. Labour councillors were against the plans and Conservatives were for them and caricatured the Socialists as people who were opposed to any form of private ownership. The consultation was a "double mockery" said Roy Shaw as local authorities were to be given only twenty nine days to respond. "Let's nail now this lie that we're opposed to home ownership –but at the same time we have a duty to protect our housing stock". The Tories loved it: "The Socialists are right to fear this as the Sale of the Century", their deputy leader Derek Spencer said cheerfully, "because that's exactly what it is!" Tony Kerpel compared Labour councillors to "feudal barons watching in terror as their rottenly treated serfs are set free", and even the usually careful opposition leader Julian Tobin got carried away in the general sense of euphoria: "It is a fundamental right", he said, "of people to buy their own homes". Hyperbole to the right and hyperbole to the left: Joan Hymans described the plans as "a crime which will cost Camden dear" and Ken Livingstone bemoaned the 50% rise in home ownership in Camden since 1974 which had led to the situation where "the only way ordinary people could afford to live in the borough was by getting a council home". To Tory jeers, the council passed a motion calling on the government to shelve its plans.

Before Roy Shaw faced the battle to put up the rates by his predicted 40%, he had to face the wrath of the left over rent rises for council tenants. In January 1980 the Labour group voted to freeze council rents for the third year running. In order to achieve this, a cross subsidy was needed from the ratepayers. It soon became clear that as the rate increase was likely to be the greatest in the borough's history, such a move could invite legal challenge. Roy Shaw managed to persuade the February Labour group meeting to agree to put up council rents by a modest £1 a week. The *Journal* was quick to see the enemy within. Roy Shaw's U turn had come about because "the district auditor, armed with heavy surcharges and disqualifications, and kept informed by hostile local Tories, was seen lurking down the road."[12] Shaw's task was made slightly harder by the fact that the Community Planning and Resources Committee had only the week before been caught in a Tory ambush[13] and had passed a proposal that rents be increased by £1.66 a week. The left were furious. "The one pound increase", said Livingstone, "will mean hardship for ordinary families for the sake of saving the ratepayers ten and a half pence a week". To show how upset he was, he immediately issued a leadership challenge, which Shaw easily survived (by 21 votes to 10).

The rent increase was voted through in the February council meeting.[14] Tom Devine railed against the result which had, he said, been carried "by well heeled lawyers and professionals" in the Labour group. The *Journal* agreed and pointed out that of the 32 Labour councillors only eight were council tenants. It went on to expose the wealth of some of those who had voted for the rise. "Cllr Jonathan Sofer is rich, powerful and happily married to a titled lady" and "lives in a beautiful house in Primrose Hill". His father in law is Lord Crowther, chairman of the Trust House Forte Group. Sofer had committed the additional crime of saying that "it's humbug to think of all council tenants as poor". The paper also selected for special treatment Tessa Jowell "a top employee of MIND and a barrister's wife"; her brother in law, John Mills, "who prefers to fly himself to business trips"; and Martin McNeill "the son of a judge, a merchant banker and a keen member of the otter hunting set". The *Journal* then obligingly published photographs of the houses of four of the "well heeled" Labour councillors, together with current market values.

The rise in council rents was followed by bad news on housing repairs. The council had asked the government for £74m for its housing repairs programme, and the government had allocated only £44m.

---

12 One of the Conservative councillors had already reported the council to the district auditor following the rent freeze two years before, and now Derek Spencer, after accusing the Labour councillors of being "two faced and gutless" had again promised to contact the district auditor.

13 A vote had been called while Neil Fletcher was out of the committee room and, without warning, one of his Labour colleagues, Jonathan Sofer voted with the Conservatives.

14 Ellen Luby shouted down from the gallery: "You used to be able to hold your heads up high as Labour councillors –now you have to slink!" The abrasive Ivor Walker shouted back: "Shut up, you silly cow!"

This meant that the council would only be able to carry out those projects already under contract. "It is just absolutely astonishing", said Livingstone. "It is certainly the toughest cut that any council in the country has been dealt." The *Journal* blamed the new junior housing minister, Geoffrey Finsberg, and referred to the decision as "Finsberg's blitz". The point was emphasised by the front page story ("Baby dies after lift plunge") of twenty month old Ilia Stergines who fell through a five inch gap in the lift doors in Coram Street in Holborn.

The new Conservative government of 1979 had a duty, it declared, to curb the overspending of local authorities. Most of the offenders were inner city Labour authorities and all of them were dominated by left wing Labour Party councillors. The Thatcher government's method of attack was to reduce the rate support grant so that councils were left with the option of either putting up their rates or else cutting back on their expenditure. The result was usually a bit of both. In Camden, which then demanded the highest rate bill in London, the ruling group was faced with a particular problem as its own left wingers wanted a confrontation with the government even if it meant in the short term sacrificing the wellbeing of the very people who they were there to look after.

It was this unhappy situation that faced Roy Shaw in March 1980 when the rate was to be set. "We will not grovel to the government", he said, posing as a born again militant. "It would be morally wrong to neglect the very young, the elderly, the sick and the handicapped". He then proposed a 31% rate increase, the biggest rise for six years brought about by "the swingeing effect of government policy". He was backed by his deputy leader, John Mills who spoke both of the need for the rate increase and of Camden's "astonishing achievements". The Conservatives' reply was equally predictable in nature, if more colourful. Labour's budget, said Greengross, "was a fraudulent bucket shop prospectus which groans with padding and is riddled by loopholes." "Labour have saddled us with a £53m wages bill and the same amount in debt charges", said Julian Tobin. "That's £450 for every resident. By next year it will be £2,400 per person, nearly five times as much". The council was assured by its Conservative opposition: the Conservative government was not going to flinch from its election commitments.

Roy Shaw's strident line worked in that the left wing threat receded. There was no challenge to his leadership. Ken Livingstone was voted off as chairman of the housing committee and replaced by

Andrew Bethell. Other leading left wingers, Phil Turner and Sally Peltier, the outgoing mayor, also failed to get chairmanships. The only remaining committee chairman hostile to the leadership was Neil Fletcher, who kept his position unopposed. That, as Roy Shaw was soon to find out, was a mistake.

Within a month the new rates bills were in the post, accompanied by a council leaflet entitled *Camden Council –fighting to maintain your services*. It was, said Julian Tobin, the leader of the opposition, "a whitewash." "Why don't they say that most council wages have gone up by 66% in the past two years or that social services now employ more people than the whole council did in 1965?" "We have a very political government", said Roy Shaw, "and they are hitting local authorities, so obviously if we have to reply it has to be political". Things got worse towards the end of 1980. The secretary of state, Michael Heseltine, announced that he was cutting the rate support grant to thirteen overspending authorities. Camden was one of them and was due to lose £5m. Roy Shaw described this as an act of "pure vindictiveness against the borough". Frank Dobson said it was "immoral, illegal and would make poor people poorer".

In October Julian Tobin called an emergency meeting of the council to propose a motion of no confidence in the leadership. Labour's usual winning margin of seven was diminishing as Kevin Gould was unable to attend through sickness, Chris Gardiner had resigned from the council and Jonathan Sofer was now semi-detached from the Labour group.[15] Labour survived, but only after the Conservatives had extracted what publicity they could for pointing out that Labour had "fleeced" the ratepayers to fund "irrelevant and extravagant policies". Immediately after the meeting, Julian Tobin announced that "almost any service provided by the council could be run more cheaply by private enterprise" and revealed his own plans to cut a thousand jobs at the town hall by getting rid of the direct labour department and most of the employees in the architect's department.

The *Journal* sprang to the council's defence. Under a cartoon of the bearded Tobin holding an axe, it pointed out that his proposals "could mean mass dismissals at the town hall with all the agony and anger that would bring. The Tory plan -like Thatcher's style of government- is an attempt to put the clock back to the days of laissez faire capitalism.

119

---

15 Jonathan Sofer resigned from the council later in the month and Kevin Gould the following spring.

But who wants to live in Dickens's time again?" The *Ham & High* took a different view: "After two hours of debate that cost the ratepayers something like £70 a minute we were none the wiser as to what policies Labour Camden is to pursue to escape the dire consequences of the financial crisis it is in. The impotence of the majority party was pathetic, all the more so since the Tory attack was hardly brilliant. Yet not a single member of the Labour group was able to stand up last week and tell either their supporters or the ratepayers in general of any action that has or is about to be taken to alleviate that situation. All Labour Camden seems to have done is put on a blindfold, stuck a gag in its mouth and prostrated itself in the hope that the crisis will go away".[16]

Whatever Roy Shaw's public position, his private view was flexible. At the Labour Group meeting on the Monday after the council meeting in which he had so pooh-poohed the Tory suggestions, he announced his new plans. He was going to squeeze the direct labour and architect's departments. Any town hall job to fall vacant would be offered first to workers in those two departments. Unused council land was now to be sold off to private developers and the council would face the inevitable and put up council rents in April. "Where have we heard these ideas before?" screamed the *Journal*. "From the Tories! Roy Shaw has beaten Mrs Thatcher to it. He has made the first U-turn".

Roy Shaw, flanked by councillors Mills and Bethell, announced to a meeting of senior council officers that every department must find 10% of savings and that domestic rates would need to be raised by 40% next year simply to meet existing debts. Within a week he had revised his figures and felt obliged to write to all the council's employees[17] appealing for help and cooperation in difficult times and warning them that the rates may have to go up by 58%.

Things did not get any better. The district auditor began the first of his public hearings in the town hall to hear complaints against the council. Ken Avery and Derek Spencer made (with all the attendant publicity) three complaints on behalf of ratepayers: that the council had

---

16 The *Ham & High* or rather its editor, the formidable Gerry Isaaman, was generally supportive of Labour, especially of the party's leader, Hampstead resident Michael Foot. The following are taken from editorials in November 1980: "Mr Foot has time on his side not only to prepare the Labour Party for the next election but the chance to inspire it. That he alone has that ability is undeniable"; and under the headline LAME DAME it is noted that Margaret Thatcher is still often portrayed as "the determined Iron Lady." "She really ought to be depicted as Mrs Hopeless, Mrs Pathetic or Mrs Hole-in-your-Pocket."

17 Then 7,084 full time and 813 part time employees.

failed to collect rents as required by the law in that they had written off arrears; they had failed to put up council rents and so had unreasonably burdened ratepayers; and they had unlawfully introduced the "Camden supplement" to end the NUPE strike in the "winter of discontent". Roy Shaw thought it best to stay away, and instructed Labour councillors to do likewise as they had done nothing wrong.

And then William Barnes, Camden's 61 year old director of housing, resigned along with his assistant director. It was not a good time, but Roy Shaw made a point of playing down the problems. William Barnes would be missed, he said, not least because he "was a fantastic administrator with an unparalleled brain for getting to the root of the problem". But Barnes then went public with the reasons for his resignation. Within the week Roy Shaw had revised his opinion and told the press that Barnes "has a tendency to exaggerate and to over dramatise events..... It has become increasingly apparent over the last few months that he could not continue as director of housing".

Barnes's attack on the council –for it was nothing less- was very damaging. He described the Labour leadership as "a gaggle of ostriches who have buried their heads in the sand rather than face up to the realities of the Thatcher government." Although it had long been clear that cash for the borough's housing programme was going to be limited, Camden nevertheless "went on gaily committing itself to the hilt and beyond". There was "serious over-manning and inefficiency and a total unwillingness to tackle these in a businesslike way", and senior Labour members showed a profound unwillingness to take the necessary policy decisions.[18]

Barnes's attacks from inside the council were followed by Neil Fletcher's attack from inside the Labour group. Impressed by the *Ham & High* editorial after the last council meeting, he publicised his dissatisfaction with Roy Shaw's lacklustre defence of the council's policies and accused him of "dashing for cover" in the face of government threats to cut the rates support grant and of failing to take "positive action" . "We should come out of our corner and fight!" he said, in what was a clear launch of a leadership bid.

The following month, November, saw the council continue on its perennial campaign against the Right to Buy legislation. The council was obliged to send out application forms to interested council tenants,

121

---

18   Barnes was a son of Ernest Barnes, the controversialist bishop of Birmingham (the "bold, bad bishop" as he liked to call himself).

and had elected to send out with each form a leaflet pointing out the difficulties that might face a successful application: such as the high cost of a mortgage, repairs, insurance, and legal fees. Conservative councillors were scathing. It treated council tenants, said Ian Tomisson, "as if they are congenital idiots", and it constituted, said Mike Brahams, "a Socialist Party leaflet being sent out at the ratepayer's expense". "Not so", said Julian Fulbrook, "it is much *too* reasonable and *un*biased – you've had all your propaganda in the papers for weeks on end".

By the first week of November some two hundred completed applications had been returned to the council but were not being processed. The white collar union, NALGO, advised its members not to handle the applications as they amounted to extra work for which extra pay had not been negotiated. By the end of November, when the number of completed applications was approaching four hundred, NALGO held a ballot in which the council officers voted "to black the sales". Roy Shaw told the papers that he was "very disappointed", but did nothing[19]

Nevertheless, notwithstanding the increase in rates, by the end of the calendar year, the council was in difficulties. Following the reduction in the support grant, the wages bill was too high. The leadership looked around for a solution. Under the provisions of the new Local Government Planning & Land Act 1980 the council would have to start putting work out to tender after April 1981. One thing was clear: the building department was hopelessly oversized and internal discussions in the Labour group centred on whether or how to lay off 600 building workers.

The chairman of the building committee, Neil Fletcher, faced the leadership head on. Fletcher, a 36 year old Lancastrian sporting a beard, long hair and round spectacles, was a former member of the Workers Revolutionary Party. He worked as an education officer for NALGO. A personable man, he was, said the *Ham & High*, "reticent, almost shy", but he had a very different public persona. "If saving jobs means raising taxes", he shouted, "then the council must mount a massive publicity campaign to tell ratepayers why that is necessary". He called a meeting of all council tenants, and then announced that Roy Shaw had gagged him by preventing the notices of the meeting going out. "I am really shocked by his actions", said Fletcher. The accusation infuriated Shaw,

---

19 NALGO did not vote to stop blacking the applications until the following April after the government threatened sanctions.

not least because it was accurate. "He [Fletcher] has absolutely no authority whatsoever to call this meeting", he said. "He is deliberately trying to put pressure on the group".

The meeting went ahead, one of four such meetings in a week addressed by Fletcher, each of which voted overwhelmingly to back him. In each meeting he showed ever greater hostility to Roy Shaw and the Labour leadership who, he told the Hampstead Labour Party in Maoist terms, were "paper tigers" who "caved in when the going gets tough". Worse still for the leadership, at the December 1980 Labour group meeting, Fletcher won the day (by 18 votes to 13) with his "don't bow to the Tory government" proposal. Roy Shaw, John Mills and Andrew Bethell ("the staffing chief") threatened to resign and they, in the estimation of the *Camden Journal*, were "the three heavy men of substance in the group".

The opposition were of no help to Roy Shaw either. In the view of Ian Pasley-Tyler, Camden's crisis was self inflicted following its cosiness with the unions. The council's building workers had been guaranteed a 35 hour week and so could not compete with the more competitive rates being offered by the private sector. On top of that, 130 workers had been taken on in the last year at a time when there clearly was no planned expansion of work to be done.

The council needed more money and needed it quickly. The December 1980 council meeting agreed a supplementary rate of another 6%. It was a direct attempt to defeat the government's squeeze on rate support. The 6% would raise the £6m necessary to maintain services and would replace the £6m withdrawn by Heseltine from the rate support grant. Those electors of Camden who had to face the new rates bills would be left in no doubt by the council exactly who to blame for the increase.

It was a miserable Christmas for the Labour leadership. The internal threat from Neil Fletcher was growing and there seemed no way out. Roy Shaw could not change the direction in which the group's policy was hurtling, but he hoped at least to be able to prevent a nasty crash. By January Roy Shaw was singing a different tune to impress the Fletcher group. There would be "No cuts, no redundancies and a massive programme of housing repairs". There would also be a 60% rate increase to pay for them. The Conservatives were to blame: and to reinforce the point the Labour Party put out a leaflet showing Mrs Thatcher as a vampire, her fangs biting into a map of Camden. Neil Fletcher was delighted: "We want genuine savings, but we are not prepared to make

123

cuts in jobs or services". He had won: "The leadership did a U turn", he crowed to the *Journal*. The Camden Labour Party rallied round to put the blame for any future rate rises squarely on the Conservative government.

The party mood did not last, but Roy Shaw found his own position saved by the intervention of Ian Pickwell, the district auditor. In February 1981, Pickwell summoned to the Town Hall the leading councillors: Shaw, Mills, Bethell and, now that he was setting the pace, Fletcher. They were told what they were going to do: there would be no 60% rate rise, council rents were going to have to go up by £3.25 a week, half the building workers were to be laid off, and there would be a year's wage freeze for the council's fifteen hundred manual workers. As an afterthought, he cheerfully told them the bad news. He was issuing writs against all the Labour councillors who had voted for the Camden supplement, the "winter of discontent" supplementary pay award in 1979. He intended to get a court order surcharging them £60,000 each[20] and barring them from office.

The hurried Labour group meeting that followed was less bullish than it had been. Roy Shaw insisted that the district auditor's package be approved by the group and threatened to resign for the second time in two months. It was a risk the left wingers were willing to take. Fletcher and Livingstone accused the district auditor of "bullying and blackmail" and of being "an agent of the Tories". "Who is running local government, the elected representatives of the people or the district auditor?" "This is a night of shame", moaned Phil Turner, "I am as sick as a parrot. I feel like resigning from the council". Roy Shaw was pursued out of the six hour group meeting by Charlie Rossi, one of the GLC members, who shouted after him: "Gutless!" The *Journal* ran a headline: CAMDEN CRUSHED UNDER TORY HEEL.[21]

Camden's Labour councillors were deep in the mire. To many of them the spectre of being surcharged was a blast of icy air. For most it would mean bankruptcy. Neil Fletcher's leadership bid faltered. Having beaten Roy Shaw in "not bowing to the government", his support shied away under the glare of the district auditor. In February 1981, the Labour

20 Not that house prices are the perfect measure, but to put this in context: a £60,000 house in Camden in 1980 would sell for about £1.25m today.

21 The *Camden Journal* did not hold back from commenting on international affairs. The editorial for 7 March 1980 began: "Three cheers for Mr Mugabe, a great independence fighter, who, once reviled by the national media as a terrorist, is now rightly acclaimed as a responsible, moderate prime minister".

group re-elected Shaw by 17 votes to 11. Five councillors abstained.

That was not the end of things. On 4th March 1981 the council was due to set its rates for the coming financial year. It did not happen. The Labour proposal (put forward by John Mills) was for a 40.8% rise, a £3.50 increase in council rents and 600 job cuts in the council's building department. "This budget", shouted Cllr Fletcher to cheers from the gallery, "will betray the trust of the people of Camden. This is a kick in the teeth to major sections of the borough". Promising not to support "a single penny reduction" in expenditure, he proposed his own budget to increase the rates by £10 million. Fletcher's budget, said loyalist Nick Bosanquet, was "a leap into fantasy". Roy Shaw was careful not to antagonise the left. "All I can say is that the majority of the majority party have decided that the recommended budget represents a reasonable compromise in the circumstances. We are determined to maintain our services in the face of government attacks on them."

Knowing that the Fletcherites would not help, the leadership tried, rather desperately, to try to get the opposition to support them. They had "found" an extra £2.2m in savings which could be used to keep the rate increase down to 35.2% and tried again. But the Tories would not play ball. "Emboldened" said the *Ham & High*, "by the TV lights and the cameras of the BBC's *Panorama* programme in the chamber", Julian Tobin said he would only back a budget that produced a "substantial reduction in rates". "If Camden can produce £2.5m a week in savings out of a hat, it can wipe out the borough's debts within a few years" Tobin said. "The Socialists claim to be against indirect or regressive taxation, yet in Camden they have increased indirect taxation by virtually doubling the rates in two years and trebling their expenditure in five years from £37 million to over £100 million for next year. It is now time to stop this rake's progress!" Alan Greengross added: "Our housing and labour costs are not, as they claim, indications of how much the council cares, but are just indicative of how inefficient they are".

At the final vote, the ten left wingers abstained[22] and Roy Shaw could muster only nineteen votes for his two budget proposals. They were voted down by the twenty six Tories. It was the Labour group's first defeat in council since the 1971 election.

"This was not altogether unexpected", a grim faced Roy Shaw told the press after the event. A week of hurried diplomacy followed.

125

---

22 They were Bill Birtles, Anna Bowman, Tom Devine, Pat Driscoll, Neil Fletcher, Joan Hymans, Ken Livingstone, Phil Turner, John Tysoe and Jenny Willmott.

So polarised now were the two factions in the Labour group that they met in separate rooms in the town hall with messengers rushing between them. John Marlow, the director of finance, announced that "we could go out of business if no rate is set by 1 April 1981" "Camden cannot continue in this crazy fashion", thundered the *Ham & High* editorial. There could be no challenge to the district auditor's directions, but in order to buy off the left, the leadership would have to offer more, and that could only be done by putting the rates up even higher than they had first intended. The proposal now was for a 42.9% rise (as well as the £3.50 rent rise and the 600 job losses in the building department) but there would also be an extra £3½m towards urgently needed housing repairs. The *Ham & High* quoted a Labour rebel as saying: "It was just like they shook the magic tree and another nearly five million of goodies fell out of it".

When the rates setting meeting was reconvened a week later, all went smoothly and the heckling from the gallery was directed almost entirely at the Conservatives. ("Shut up, you shits!" shouted back Tony Kerpel, unable to hear himself above the barracking.) The only Labour rebel remaining was Tom Devine who rather limply abstained after making a fiery speech in which he described Tory Derek Spencer as "the unacceptable face of capitalism". Afterwards, Neil Fletcher was able to claim victory. The Tories were furious. 42.9% was far too high an increase. Roy Shaw had "paid off the Left at the ratepayer's expense" fumed Julian Tobin, knowing that this was about a third higher than the rate he had been offered a week before. "The left has called the tune and the ratepayers will have to pay for it". Roy Shaw was "gutless" said Alan Greengross. "We are more overstaffed than any other borough in the country".

It did not help the Labour Group that between the two rate setting council meetings, the Camden Commercial Ratepayers Group published *The Cost of Camden*, a report written by Alex Henney, a sharp tongued consultant who had been Haringey's director of housing until 1976. The report contained, noted the *Ham & High*, "charges of overstaffing, extravagance, waste, profligacy and sheer incompetence". Roy Shaw dismissed it out of hand, but it was a serious document. "Much that appears in the Henney Report has been published in our columns before, but obviously, brought together in one document it is a telling indictment of Labour's loss of control and inability to provide value for money". It also provided the Labour group with much food for thought, and the opposition with plenty of ammunition.

Nevertheless, the Labour group elections in April 1981 saw no challenge to Roy Shaw, and John Mills and Andrew Bethell saw off challenges for the chairmanship of the Policy & Resources and staffing committees from the left wingers Ken Livingstone and Phil Turner. More interesting were the opposition leadership elections. "Tory coup ousts the old guard" ran the headline in the *Ham & High* on 3 April 1981. Both Julian Tobin, a solicitor about to celebrate twenty five years as a councillor, and his deputy leader, Derek Spencer QC, stood for re-election. They were beaten by Tony Kerpel, ("an ebullient young man" said the *Ham & High*) a 36 year old, Belsize Park born, film examiner on the British Board of Film Censors, and Ian Pasley-Tyler, a planning officer at the Midland Bank, both from the non-lawyer end of the party. Although the *Ham & High* hoped it was an anti-Thatcherite coup, it was personal rather than political. Kerpel, a sociology graduate and a former national chairman of the Young Conservatives, had been a personal assistant to Edward Heath and a speech writer in the 1974 and 1979 general elections[23]. Kerpel's supporters were not after a policy shift, they just wanted someone to be more punchy in debate and to give the party a cutting edge in the run up to the 1982 borough elections. Reflecting on how Julian Tobin had never really been able to step out of Alan Greengross's shadow, the *Ham & High*, wrote of him: "He unfortunately lacks the necessary charisma that keeps leaders in power" and was "too much a gentleman". Derek Spencer on the other hand was "too arrogant, a man who upset his colleagues too easily without realising the damage he did. He invited being slapped down".

At the next council meeting the Conservatives proposed a motion of no confidence in Neil Fletcher who had just been re elected as the chairman of the Building Works and Services Committee. It was common ground by then that his department was overmanned and needed to be run down now that the law insisted on competitive tendering. The council had already agreed that the department be allowed to "adjust" its tenders downwards to submit artificially low bids. Or, as the Tories put it, to have the ratepayers subsidise the department which otherwise would not be able to compete on the open market. This decision had had a rough ride within the Labour group —John Thane in particular

---

23   As a founding member of the Coalition for Peace through Security (CPS), a body set up to counter CND, he was represented by the *New Statesman* as being one of the "Fruitcake Right". He had come within a whisker of being selected as the Conservative candidate for the safely Conservative S.E. London constituency in the 1979 Euro elections. He was beaten by Sir Brandon Rhys Williams Bt, the Kensington MP who falsely told the selectors that "Margaret" wanted him to be simultaneously an MP and an MEP.

was critical of Fletcher who had held up the process for four months by his politicking. But the Conservative motion was a great unifier, and the Labour group, except for John Thane who left the chamber rather than have to listen to anyone praise Fletcher, found themselves forced to express confidence in "Chairman" Fletcher, as the Tories now referred to him. The council defeated the motion by three votes.

Council activities were put on hold by the GLC elections which took place on 7 May 1981 and resulted in a Labour victory at City Hall. Alan Greengross bucked the trend by holding on in Hampstead for the Conservatives, albeit with a 9% swing against him (he beat Anna Bowman). Labour kept both the St Pancras seats with Charlie Rossi and Anne Sofer being elected (the latter despite her husband Jonathan having defected to the SDP). Also importantly for the council, Ken Livingstone won a GLC seat in Paddington. He had spent much time while a Camden councillor building up support among the other GLC candidates and on the day after the election was elected as leader of the GLC by the new left wing dominated Labour group. (The turnout had been low: one in five of London's electorate had voted Labour, and only half of those

had voted for left wing candidates.) The new Labour administration on the GLC took on a more aggressive stance. Ken Livingstone promised to use the GLC machinery as part of a political campaign against the Thatcher government and in defence of socialist policies.

Having failed to get elected to the GLC, Anna Bowman stayed on as Camden's social services chairman and threw herself into her campaign to make the borough a nuclear free zone. Following rumours that nuclear warheads were being transported through the borough on the St Pancras–Bedford line, she demanded a meeting with British Rail. At the same time, Michael Foot launched the Hampstead World Disarmament Campaign's petition which amounted, said Kerpel, "to 1930s style appeasement". Entering into the spirit of things the *Ham & High* printed a photo of six toddlers sitting on potties facing a sign which read BABIES AGINST THE BOMB.

In the wake of the Brixton riot, the summer of 1981 saw the launch of the Camden Council for Community Relations's campaign against police harassment of ethnic minorities. "The majority of black people in this country", explained George Shire, a Zimbabwean, "are now under attack from the police". Another committee member, Salman Rushdie, agreed: "Our business is to struggle against the police" he said, proposing that the CCCR sever all links with them. Attitudes had hardened on both sides. When the CCCR chairman, Michael Boye-Ananwomah, led a delegation to the council meeting in July, he was met with (said the *Ham & High*) "an almost unprecedented torrent of abuse from the Conservative benches" including widespread shouts of "rubbish!" and (from Julian Harrison) "bring on the water cannon!"

The leftward shift in the Labour Party had brought about its own strains. That same month, Nick Bosanquet, the housing chairman, resigned from the Labour Party (but not from the council) and joined the SDP, leaving the housing committee with six Labour and six opposition members.

Ken Livingstone's cheaper underground fares ("Fare's Fair") policy and the GLC's support of the ILEA budget resulted in a supplementary rate being levied through the London boroughs. The increase in rates had not formed part of the election manifesto. In September, Anne Sofer said that she had had enough of the confrontational direction the Labour Party on the GLC had taken. She had not been "elected to triple GLC precepts within a year or to promote a period of chaos and confrontation". She let it be known that she was going to resign at the next meeting of the St Pancras North Labour Party general management committee.

Rumours of her intention came in the week after Jock Stallard, the MP for St Pancras North, had collapsed and been taken to hospital with an inflamed pancreas. Frank Dobson wrote to Mrs Sofer: "Whatever the immediate impact on Jock's health, your resignation would put him under enormous pressure to get up from his sick bed long before he should".[24] It was no good. Anne Sofer attended the general management meeting and resigned. She announced that she had joined the SDP and would also resign as a member of the GLC, so forcing a by election. Her speech was received in silence and the committee then went on to mandate its conference delegate to vote to leave NATO, to leave the EEC without a referendum, to support the Palestine Liberation Organisation and to nationalise the banks and insurance companies. The GLC by election was called for 29 October, and would be of "national significance" promised another defector to the SDP, Ernest Wistrich.

The following week a special meeting of Camden council was called

129

---

24   Within a fortnight, Jock Stallard was up from his sick bed, not to deal with the Sofer issue, but to go to Brighton for the Labour Party conference where he and Frank Dobson voted for Tony Benn in the deputy leadership contest.

to raise a supplementary rate of 16.6p in the pound to meet the new GLC precept. On average each ratepayer would have to pay an extra £68 and each council tenant an extra £48. A Conservative motion to absorb the precept into the current rate was rejected, but two Labour members, Floss Parnell and Brian Duggan, both former mayors and both council tenants, were unhappy. Labour's GLC manifesto had said nothing about a supplementary rate demand, said Floss Parnell, and the people on her estate would not pay it. Backed by Conservative Ian Tomisson, Brian Duggan tabled an amendment to absorb £2.25m and set a supplementary rate of only 14½p in the pound. He failed, but only by 26 votes to 28.[25]

There was national interest in the October GLC by election in St Pancras North. It was, said The Times, "a test of Labour's decline". Ken Livingstone saw it as a vote of confidence in the GLC's confrontational position against the government. St Pancras North was on paper a safe Labour seat which Anne Sofer had won in May with 59% of the vote. She agreed to stand again as the SDP candidate, knowing that to win she would need a swing of 41% from the other parties. The Liberals chose not to stand, but instead endorsed Mrs Sofer. The Labour Party chose as their candidate a Hendon schoolteacher, Mildred Gordon, a one time member of the Revolutionary Communist Party. The Conservatives again chose Ian Pasley Tyler, their deputy leader on the council (this notwithstanding Martin Morton's suggestion that they should not put up a candidate, so as not to intrude on "a fight between two wings of the Labour Party").

It was a high profile affair: the leaders of the parliamentary and GLC Labour parties, Michael Foot and Ken Livingstone, entered the fray for Mrs Gordon; Shirley Williams, David Alton and William Rodgers did the same for Anne Sofer, and Tony Kerpel did his bit for Ian Pasley Tyler by calling Mrs Sofer "a shop soiled Labour drop out". The vote was emphatic. Anne Sofer won by 738 votes. She took about three thousand votes from each of the Labour and Conservative parties, helped perhaps, as Mildred Gordon morosely observed, by the election taking place only a few days after the supplementary rate demands had gone out.[26]

---

25 Duggan, Parnell and Bosanquet having voted with the Tories.

26 Mildred Gordon was luckier elsewhere. She served as the MP for Bow And Poplar from 1987 to 1997.

Within a fortnight, Brian Duggan had also defected to the SDP. The infighting in the Labour group, he said, was "terrible" and the moderate faction led by Roy Shaw was not strong enough to beat off the left in the coming borough elections. A Labour victory, he said, would see Camden run by "Bennites". The Labour majority on the council fell to three.

1982, a borough election year, began with the district auditor predicting that further high rate increases would give rise to "serious collection difficulties". At the same time he helpfully let the papers know that Camden had raised rates by 94% over the last four years, that "the average rate payment for a home was the highest in the whole country, and that Camden had the highest per capita spending of any council in London. Taking the hint, and notwithstanding Ken Livingstone's announcement that the GLC precept would increase by 93% that year, Roy Shaw announced that he hoped that Camden's own rate increase would be far below inflation (then running at 12%) in part because the Council was due an "unexpected" £6m windfall from the London Rate Equalisation Scheme. Kerpel was sardonic as ever: Shaw "was gambling on the electors suffering collective amnesia on polling day...The council budget will resemble an Ealing Comedy where the villain, having poured arsenic into auntie for years, now rouges her cheeks to deceive the visiting relatives that all is well. After the visit the arsenic treatment will begin again".

The February 1982 council meeting dragged on for seven hours, partly because Julian Tobin kept tabling amendments and partly because there was no overall Labour majority now that Ken Livingstone had been disqualified. He no longer appeared on the electoral register having moved from Kilburn to be eligible for his new GLC seat in Paddington. Maureen Robinson, the mayor, had to use her casting vote on three occasions to enable the Labour group to get its way. Not least was her contribution to defeating a SDP motion to reduce council spending and the rates by 7% which was supported by the Conservatives ("merely as a first step"). Council rents were put up by £2.54 a week. John Thane, who was not seeking re-election, during the debate on housing repairs lost his temper with Nick Bosanquet, the SDP defector, and threw two plastic cups at him (but missed).[27]

By comparison, the rate setting meeting which took place in early March, was a tame affair. The council voted to put up the rate by 7.9%,

131

---

27   Later that evening he apologised to the mayor "but not to Councillor Bosanquet".

rejecting the Conservative proposal for a 10% reduction. Kerpel held up a graph of his own making to demonstrate "the intriguing pattern in which rate increases sharply tailed off every four years just before an election". Not that their support was needed, the two SDP councillors voted for the Labour budget (although with Nick Bosanquet issuing a sharp attack on the council's inefficiency). The second March council meeting was the last of the term and was remarkable only for the fact that the Labour leadership suffered its second defeat in two years when the council voted to revoke planning consent on two buildings in Windmill Street in Bloomsbury. Following great pressure from local groups, Ivor Walker voted with the Tories and Floss Parnell abstained. It was a small victory.

The 1982 local government elections in England and Wales were the first real national test for the SDP and in Camden the election was closely fought, not least because the SDP appeared to represent a sizeable proportion of public opinion. The party had followed Anne Sofer's win in the St Pancras North by election, with two stunning parliamentary by election victories by Shirley Williams in Crosby (26 November 81) and Roy Jenkins in Hillhead (25 March 82). In Camden two of the SDP candidates were sitting councillors while another, Alan Evans, was a former Labour councillor. The new party had also been given sympathetic coverage in the local papers, although it met with bitter criticism in the letters pages from Conservative and Labour councillors. (Labour loyalist Roger Robinson, for instance, wrote in to remind people that, unlike Labour, the SDP was in favour of continuing membership of the EEC and was "pledged to maintain nuclear weapons to blow our society to the heavens".[28]) For the purposes of the borough elections, the SDP's modest position was that it was pledged to ensure open government and to keep rate rises no higher than inflation.

The Labour candidates concentrated their campaign on the council's stand against the Thatcher government, steering well clear of any controversy that would drive voters to the SDP. Their allies were not always so helpful. The CCCR's "Community Relations Officer",

---

28   One of Camden's founding councillors and then a Labour Party employee, Roger Robinson had come off the council for the second time in 1978 following instructions that he was to devote his energies to the coming general election by working in Transport House. He returned to the council in 1998.

Chris Adamson, a former NUPE official and self proclaimed socialist[29], launched an attack on the police for publishing ethnic figures for street crime (which showed that overwhelmingly most street robbers were black and most victims were white) as an "anti-Scarman plot". The CCCR's "Public education officer" Zareer Masani, who proved to be way ahead of his time, announced that "racism is now institutionalised in police officers". Both then opposed plans to set up a police liaison committee because, said Adamson, it would "not fulfil any of the aspirations of the ethnic minority groups" as the police were not doing enough to tackle racist crime. The Hampstead Labour Party joined in by condemning the appointment of Kenneth Newman as the next Metropolitan Police Commissioner. The CCCR also sent a questionnaire to all the council candidates to get them to sign a declaration to "reject utterly all forms of racial discrimination" (which Roy Shaw refused to sign as the "offensive" questions criticised the council which, he said, had done more than any other in the country to promote racial harmony).

The Conservatives were hopeful that, if the SDP managed to split the Labour vote in important wards, they could well be the main beneficiaries, but were just as fearful that the SDP would split the anti-Labour vote locally. In the run up to the election, an approach was made to the local SDP to see if some sort of deal could be made. A secret meeting was held between Tony Kerpel, Ian Pasley Tyler and Ron King on the one side and the Camden SDP leadership (including Ann Sofer) on the other. Various strategies were discussed, all involving the two parties agreeing not to field candidates in named wards. Agreement was eventually reached whereby in certain wards where two or three members were to be elected, one or other of the parties would put up no more than one candidate in the hope that the remaining second and third preference votes would be used to vote for other anti Labour candidates. The plan was such that Labour's grip on power in Camden would almost certainly have been broken. It was not to be. Kerpel then made the mistake of letting the agent for Greater London, Donald Stringer, know about his plans. Stringer, a former Military Policeman, was unbending. There were to be no local deals with the SDP under any circumstances, even if the consequence was continued Labour control.

29　And educated at Rugby. He is the son of Sir Campbell Adamson, one time director of the CBI.

For the opposition parties, it was back to the campaign. In the hope of emphasising that they were the only party capable of wresting power from Labour in Camden, Tory leaflets pointed out that had only 200 more people voted for them in 1978, no one would have suffered a Labour council for the last four years. The Conservative manifesto was headed "Putting Common Sense in charge in Camden" and Kerpel caricatured the Labour Party as "bigots viewing the world through an outdated, class ridden perspective". After eleven years of Labour rule, the council was "£500m in debt, rocketing rates had driven out jobs, the council is the biggest slum landlord and owner of empty properties in the borough and the standard of services has declined". The SDP councillors standing for re-election had been part of the Labour mafia and were clearly not to be trusted after voting for a 7% cut in rates, and then a fortnight later changing their minds to vote for a 10% increase.

As is traditionally always the case, the first shot came with a Camden council leaflet sent out with the new rate demands. The leaflet included the claim that "the 7% domestic rate rise is among the lowest in London", not mentioning, as Ian Pasley Tyler was quick to point out, the 43% rate rise in the previous year nor the fact the rates had doubled since the last council elections.[30]

A few days before the election, the High Court handed down its judgment in the district auditor's claim to surcharge thirty one Labour councillors. The court found no evidence that there had been collusion between the strikers and the councillors, and nothing to contradict the assertion that the sole reason for paying the "Camden supplement" was to end the strike. "It is not for this court to pass judgment on the wisdom or unwisdom of the wage settlement of March 1979" said Lord Justice Ormerod. "It was a case of the ratepayer's watchdog biting the wrong person." The district auditor was left with the bill for costs. The New Journal made its feelings clear by noting that Ken Avery and Derek Spencer, the two Conservative councillors who had set the ball rolling by making the initial complaint to the district auditor, were to face no penalty. "I am absolutely delighted", said Roy Shaw, "It's a vindication of our position and a great help to local government everywhere". No, said Kerpel, "it's a great blow to everyone paying rates in Camden".

---

30   Ian Pasley Tyler has since 1994 served as a councillor on Daventry District Council.

CAMDEN VOTES

"An endorsement of the policies we have pursued"
— Phil Turner

CAMDEN COUNCIL has more women councillors than ever before as a result of the May elections. The number of women members has almost doubled to represent 41 per cent of the council chamber — a total of 24 out of 59.

This change is represented across the parties with Labour boasting 18 women out of a total of 44 councillors, Conservatives five out of 11 and the SDP have one member of each sex.

Other steps to a more representative borough include the election of the first disabled Labour councillor Karen Newbury who won Brunswick from Conservative Kenneth Avery by just three votes.

Nirmal Roy, one of the new councillors from ethnic minority groups, won South End Ward with a majority of over 500. And for the first time Camden has two SDP members who took Fortune Green from Conservatives.

But the biggest change is the Labour majority in the Council — now 19 overall with 11 new seats.

Retiring Leader Phil Turner told *The Camden Magazine*: "This result is an endorsement of the policies we have pursued during the last four years as well as the plans we have put before the electorate for the next four.

"There is a considerable influx of new Labour councillors from very varied backgrounds who will bring a lot of new thinking and experience — and that's a big bonus."

Flick Rea SDP member for Fortune Green was delighted with the results. "Obviously we will not have a huge influence on the Council but we see ourselves as simply representing the people of Fortune Green. We will speak up for West Hampstead and hope to work closely with the other West Hampstead councillors.

Polling was high as usual in Camden, at 46 per cent. But the count was a more dramatic story with some marginal constituencies requiring several recounts. Swiss Cottage results were finally announced at 4.40am to a few stalwarts and wilting journalists.

Conservative Leader Stephen Moon who saw his party lose half their seats told reporters the results reflected the Government's unpopularity at the moment.

Rita Sanderson

OVER THE NEXT FEW PAGES READ WHO THE COUNCILLORS ARE — SOME NEW FACES, SOME OLD — AND TURN TO PAGE 18 TO FIND OUT WHAT WARD YOU LIVE IN AND WHO ARE THE NEW COMMITTEE CHAIRS.

ELECTION SPECIAL

CAMDEN

SHEILA FIELD is a parent of two children, and was herself once homeless and forced to live in bed and breakfast accommodation. She is concerned with problems faced by homeless families in Camden. She is currently secretary of her tenants association. (L)

SATNAM GILL has lived in Camden for the last six years and has worked as an equal opportunities officer and legal adviser. Satnam likes to spend time with his young family and is particularly interested in housing and social services. (L)

WEST END

KEVIN McDONNELL was born in London and now lives in Camden. He works for the Federation of Private Tenants in Brent. (L)

JULIA DEVOTE has lived in Camden for six years and is a local government worker. She has been active in campaigning against local Post Office closures, and on health issues. (L)

HAMPSTEAD TOWN

SELINA GEE has lived in Hampstead for three years and was previously a Barnet councillor. (C)

JACKIE JONES works in public relations. She was formerly a local journalist. (C)

HIGHGATE

MAGGIE COSIN was a local councillor in Waltham Forest where she was chair of social services. She has a son at Gospel Oak School and has lived in the area for 13 years. (L)

JOHN WAKEHAM is a representative on the Greater London Enterprise Board and was previously chair of the planning committee. A former teacher, he has lived in the area for 15 years. (L)

BARBARA BECK Second term as Highgate councillor, and chair of the race and community relations committee for the past year. She is a governor at Brookfield Primary School and has lived in Highgate for 27 years. (L)

KILBURN

ANGELA BIRTILL has been chair of the private sector housing sub-committee for the past year. She is a committed tenants activist and has lived in Kilburn since 1977. (L)

KATE ALLEN has lived in Kilburn for nine years and has represented Kilburn since 1982. She is particularly concerned about improving housing and community facilities in the borough. (L)

ALAN WOODS was previously chair of Camden's social services committee. He was born and bred in Stepney and worked as a teacher of children with special needs. He has two small children of his own. (L)

ELECTION SPECIAL

REGENTS PARK

DAVE HORAN lives locally in Regents Park, and comes from an active Labour party family. He is particularly interested in housing and educational issues. (L)

BOB LATHAM has been a Councillor for Regents Park since 1982. He is Chair of the Mornington Sports and Leisure Centre management committee and governor of Edith Nevill Primary School. (L)

GILL GREEN has been a Camden Councillor since 1982 and has been chair of housing management. She is a teacher at an Inner London secondary school. (L)

BLOOMSBURY

NICOLA KUTAPAN has lived in Bloomsbury for 21 years and also works locally. An active member of the Labour Party, she is also chair of her tenants association. (L)

BILL BUDD has a long record of public service. First elected in 1970 he served as Mayor of Camden in 1978. A member of the Labour Party since 1948, he is married with three children and four grandchildren. (L)

MIKE KIRK has been a Camden Councillor since 1982. Married with a young family, Mike has extensive experience on the Council particularly on housing and planning issues. (L)

CHALK FARM

JULIE FITZGERALD has been a Camden Councillor since 1982. A parent of two young children she is currently vice-chair of policy and resources committee and a council representative on the Hampstead Health Authority. (L)

JANET POPE works as an economist with the National Girobank and has lived in Camden for the last seven years. Chair of her tenants association, she has considerable experience in taking up housing and environmental issues. (L)

BRUNSWICK

PETER SKOLAR is a local doctor. He is interested in social services and education. (C)

KAREN NEWBURY has lived in Camden for 11 years and works for the ILEA as an equal opportunities officer. As a person with a disability, she is involved with the rights of disabled people particularly, with regard to transport and housing. (L)

FORTUNE GREEN

ROGER BILLINS is 31 years old, married with two children. A solicitor who likes to play cricket he is a founder member of the West Hampstead Community Cafe. (SDP)

FLICK REA has lived in West Hampstead for 25 years. She is married with two children and is an active member of West Hampstead Amenity and Transport Group and the London Regional Passengers Committee. An ex-actress she is interested in local history. (SDP)

ELECTION SPECIAL

ST. JOHNS

RICHARD SUMRAY has been a councillor for St. Johns for the last four years. He has served on many council committees and has previously been chair or leisure committee and vice chair of housing management. An administrator with a small public company Richard is also interested in issues affecting Third World countries. (L)

HILARY LOWE has lived in Camden for the last five years and originally comes from a small mining village in the North East. Hilary taught at Acland Burghly School for six years and now works for ILEA at County Hall. Hilary is particularly concerned to ensure that the interests of women are well represented on the Council. (L)

SWISS COTTAGE

ALAN RIPPINGTON has lived in West Hampstead for the past seven years. He is an active voluntary worker in mental health rehabilitation. (L)

GLORIA LAZENBY was born in West Hampstead and has lived in Camden for 30 years. She is currently working on an arts project with Haringey Council. (L)

ADRIAN STATES has been a member of the local Labour party for six years. He is a civil servant and an active trade unionist. (L)

CAVERSHAM

MARY CANE has been a Councillor since 1982 and has lived in Camden for the last ten years. Married with three daughters, she is governor of Parliament Hill School and has been chair of the development control sub-commitee dealing with all planning applications. (L)

GARETH SMYTH has lived in Kentish Town for six years and is a governor of Torriano Primary School. Gareth is also secretary of Peckwater Estate Tenants Association and has been a leading figure in the campaign to keep open Kentish Town Sainsburys. (L)

SOUTH END

NIRMAL ROY is a welfare benefits adviser and has lived in Camden for 30 years. He has been active on the Community Health Council and as a tenants representative. (L)

PAUL ORRETT was born in Liverpool and has lived locally for the past five years. He works as a management services team leader for the Post Office. (L)

ELECTION SPECIAL

BELSIZE

JUDITH BARNES is a solicitor and was previously a co-opted member of the social services committee. (C)

HUNTLEY SPENCE has been a councillor since 1971. He is married with two children and has been a member of the police sub-committee and leisure services committee. (C)

COLIN GLOVER is an accountant in the West End and is particularly interested in finance. (C)

ROSE HEAD has previously worked as a home help for Camden and is an active trade unionist. Widowed for over 33 years, she brought up her family on her own. (L)

HOLBORN

KEN HULME is Secretary of Holborn Labour Party and has lived in Holborn for six years. A GLC employee until its abolition, Ken organised many of the GLC's Festivals and concerts. A former carworker, Ken was a senior shop steward and secretary of Coventry Trades Council. (L)

BEN GRIFFITHS works as a research assistant to local MP Frank Dobson. Ben has been particularly active in publicising the adverse effects of private medicine on the National Health Service through his involvement with NHS Unlimited. He is interested in housing and planning issues. (L)

GOSPEL OAK

GRAHAM SHURETY has been a Camden councillor since 1982. Graham has lived in Gospel Oak all his life and teaches at a secondary school in Hackney. He is currently chair of the grants sub-committee in Camden. (L)

FITZJOHN'S

CATHLEEN MAINDS has been a Camden councillor since 1980 and is spokeswoman on housing management and housing development committee. (C)

RON KING is the opposition chief whip and spokesman on planning. (C)

ADELAIDE

STEPHEN MOON is Leader of the Conservative group and has been a councillor since 1982. He is 40 years old and is an industrial relations adviser. (C)

JULIAN TOBIN is a solicitor and has been a councillor for 30 years. He is deputy leader of the Conservative group and is active on housing and finance. (C)

IAN PASLEY TYLER a former leader of the Conservative group. He is financial controller of a major bank and is active on housing. (C)

ELECTION SPECIAL

SOMERS TOWN

TOM DEVINE has been a councillor for ten years and works in the National Health Service. Married with five daughters, Tom lived in Somers Town for over thirty years. He served as Mayor of Camden in 1982 and was chair of the employment committee between 1982-86. (L)

BILL SAUNDERS, a local shopkeeper, has lived in Camden all his life. Married with a grown up family, Bill was chair of the Godwin and Crowndale Tenants Association for over four years. Particularly interested in housing and planning issues he is currently chair of TRUST in Somers Town. (L)

KINGS CROSS

BARBARA HUGHES has been a Kings Cross councillor since 1982. A trade union official with British Telecom Barbara brought up her family on the Hillview Estate and lived there for over 25 years. She served as Mayor of Camden and as vice-chair of housing development. (L)

TONY DYKES has been a Camden councillor since 1982. Originally from Liverpool, Tony has lived in King's Cross for nine years. A worker with an educational charity, Tony was chair of the policy and resources committee. (L)

ST. PANCRAS

STEVE BEVINGTON has served as a Camden councillor since 1985 and is chair of housing management. Steve has lived in St Pancras for the last six years and has a family with a son of three years and a daughter of six months. (L)

SANDRA PLUMMER has been a Camden councillor since 1982 and is currently chair of the staff and management committee. Sandra has lived in Camden all her life and now lives in Somers Town with her fourteen year old son. (L)

PRIORY

JACKIE PEACOCK has been a co-opted member of the private sector housing sub-committee. She works for Brent Federation of Tenants. (L)

PHIL TURNER has been a member of Camden Council for 16 years and Leader for the past four. He works for the National Coal Board and is Prospective Parliamentary Candidate for Hampstead and Highgate. (L)

ELECTION SPECIAL

GRAFTON

ROY SHAW, born and bred in Camden, has represented Grafton since 1965 and previously served on the old St Pancras Council. Roy was Leader of the Council from 1975 to 1982 and has occupied many offices and chairs on the Council. (L)

PAT DENNY works as an administrator for a local financial advice centre. He is chair of his tenants association, a member of the housing management committee, and is also on the management group of the Harmood Community Centre. (L)

CASTLEHAVEN

GRAHAM GOOD lives in the ward and has been a councillor since 1982. Married with two young children, he has been a youth and community worker for 20 years. Currecently chair of leisure services committee at Camden, he also has an active interest in employment issues. (L)

JERRY WILLIAMS has lived in Camden for 25 years and worked for British Rail for over 30 years. A member of the London district council of the NUR he also helped found the Penhurst Tenants Association. Jerry is a school governor of a local primary school. (L)

FROGNAL

GWYNETH WILLIAMS is a school governor and has been a councillor since 1974. Her special interest is in social services. (C)

ALAN GREENGROSS former Camden Conservative leader and GLC opposition leader. (C)

IN FOR THE COUNT

HAVE WE? . . . OH, YES WE HAVE! Nirmal Roy, left, and Paul Orrett have a few anxious moments before the results are announced.

Meanwhile some calculating results in smiles — perhaps at how many women are in the new Council?

Photos: Chris Taylor and the Labour and Conservative parties

ELECTION SPECIAL
WHICH WARD DO YOU LIVE IN?

Council Department phone numbers

Department of Architecture and Surveying: 405 3411
Baths and Recreation Department: 267 9341
Building Department: 485 5636
Chief Engineer's Department: 435 7171
Chief Executives Department: 278 4444
Environmental Health and Consumer Services Department: 387 3456
Finance Department: 278 4444
Housing Department: 278 4444 ext 2283
Libraries and Arts Department: 278 4444 ext 2530
Planning and Communications Department: 278 4444 ext 2820
Social Services Department: 837 3363
Works Department: 435 7171 ext 318/319/320

Other useful numbers

Race Relations Unit: 278 4444 ext 2547
Civil Rights Unit: 278 4444 ext 2122
Women's Unit: 278 4444 ext 2738
Housing Benefits: 278 4444
Housing Aid Centres: (Euston Road) 388 0331
(West End Lane) 625 0251
Homeless Persons Unit: 837 4268

Council committee chairs

Policy & Resources: Julie Fitzgerald (C), Nirmal Roy (VC), Janet Pope (VC)
Grants Sub Committee: Graham Shurety (C)
Housing Management: Steve Bevington (C), Gareth Smyth (VC)
Housing Development: Alan Woods (C), Nirmal Roy (VC)
Private Sector: Angie Birtil (C), Jacky Peacock (VC)

Social Services: Richard Sumray (C), Julia Devote (VC)
Staff & Management Services: Sandra Plummer (C), Graham Shurety (VC)
Building, Works & Services: Phil Turner (C), Rose Hasd (VC)
Leisure: Graham Good (C), Dave Horan (VC)
Employment: Tom Devine (C), Paul Orrett (VC)

Race & Community Relations: Barbara Beck (C), Tony Dykes (VC)
Womens: Hilary Lowe (C), Jacky Peacock (VC)
Planning & Communications: John Wakeham (C), Bill Saunders (VC)
Development Control: Karen Newbury (C)
Police Sub Committee: Barbara Hughes (C), Adrian States (VC)

The Labour Party's defence to the election attacks by the other parties was the simple strategy of defending the high levels of rates. The government was forcing cuts on Camden, but the Labour Party recognised its responsibilities to "ordinary people". "We have resisted government cut backs", said John Mills, "but that costs money". Tory legislation, declared Tessa Jowell "was specifically designed to curtail the work of Camden council because in Camden the Tories see Socialism working in the interests of local people and they hate it!"

It was nevertheless an awkward campaign because the electorate were more than usually distracted by events far away from Camden. Election day was set for 6 May 1982 and April was devoted to campaigning by the candidates and their supporters. On 2 April 1982 Argentinian troops landed on the Falkland Islands. For the rest of the month the national news was dominated by the possibility of negotiations, the progress of the task force to the South Atlantic and eventually the RAF bombing raids. On 25 April, Royal Marine commandos recaptured South Georgia ("Rejoice! Rejoice!" was the prime minister's advice to the press waiting outside Downing Street) and on 2 May an Argentinian cruiser, the *Belgrano*, was sunk ("GOTCHA!" was the headline in the early editions of the *Sun*). Two days before the poll in Camden, on Tuesday 4 May, HMS Sheffield was disabled by an Exocet missile. Twenty crewmen were killed.

There was much talk even then of the "Falklands factor" in the elections. The 6 May poll fell on a bad time in the military campaign. Had the council elections taken place a few weeks later after a string of successes against the invaders, the Conservatives would undoubtedly have polled more —and especially at the time of national euphoria which followed the unconditional surrender of the Argentinian garrison on 14 June.

Camden's election results came as a massive relief to the many Labour candidates who genuinely felt that they were going to lose. Sharing that relief was the *New Journal*: "Back with the old firm....IT'S LABOUR" read the front page. The results were greeted with clenched fist salutes and (as always) with the singing of the *Red Flag*. The mood of the evening was best captured by the *Ham & High's* photograph of a cheering Bill Birtles, sporting a red rosette as big as his head, proclaiming: "The SDP are finished!"[31] None of the SDP candidates was elected. Their biggest name, Nick Bosanquet, lost by 400 votes in Caversham. In Labour strongholds the anti-Labour vote swung away from the Conservatives to the SDP. The Conservatives took two seats from Labour, and Labour took two back. The final result left Labour with 33 seats and the Conservatives with 26, the same as in 1978[32].

The share of the vote was Labour 40.37%, Conservatives 34.6% and, significantly, the SDP Liberal Alliance 24.8%. In 1978 the Liberal Party had managed only 3.24% of the votes cast. It was the beginning of the end for two horse races. As some ruefully noted, Labour had scraped home because there had been no Conservative/Alliance deal. If anyone deserved to be toasted by the Labour Party in Camden, it was Donald Stringer. Or perhaps, General Galtieri, for not invading the Falklands a month earlier.

The *Ham & High* ran a reflective editorial headed "Elephant Mandate".

> *Labour expected to lose at least a dozen seats to the SDP. Labour in Camden, after all, has suffered four years of the most poisoning publicity any local authority has experienced —and much of it deserved – but despite the scandals is still in charge.*
>
> *That, to some, is a miracle. And on that score perhaps Camden is something of a political Elephant Man – an unfortunate monster which manages to touch a sympathetic nerve at the crucial moment.*

136

31 Then a 37 year old barrister, Bill Birtles, a former member of the Communist Party, had been the treasurer of the St Pancras North Constituency Labour Party before being elected to Camden in the Grafton ward by election in October 1980. "The Tories are taking us back to the 1930s", he said. He had been selected as the candidate by one vote after it was agreed that an inquorate ward meeting could be made quorate by the participation of two outside members. One of those two members was Patricia Hewitt, who he married a few months later. The daughter of the chairman of Quantas, she earned herself a MI5 file purely on the strength of her marriage to Cllr Birtles. He now sits as a circuit judge. The Rt Hon Patricia Hewitt MP, PC, was Secretary of State for Health 2005-7.

32 In 1978 Labour had kept hold of power by winning the four most marginal seats by a total of 204 votes. In 1982, they managed to survive by taking the four most closely contested seats by 243 votes (22 votes in West End, 87 in Highgate and 150 in Regents Park ward).

6 |

Phil Turner:
the Left triumphant

Although he had won the election, Roy Shaw had lost the leadership. The writing had been on the wall for months. Some of his closest supporters had decided not to stand again, and some of the new candidates were known left wingers determined not to support him. "He knew that he wouldn't have stood a chance against the new wave of radicals", said the *New Journal*, with a certain amount of satisfaction.[1] On the day after the election a left wing caucus of 23 of the 33 Labour councillors met to elect his replacement. The three contenders were Phil Turner, Neil Fletcher and Anna Bowman. The 43 year old Turner, a personnel manager at the National Coal Board, was by far the favourite and, fearing a Fletcher victory, Roy Shaw described Turner as being "the best possible person in the group" to succeed him. Turner's election as leader was confirmed in the Labour group meeting on the following Monday. Neil Fletcher became deputy leader and Anna Bowman the chief whip. Phil Turner promised "more militant reaction to government cuts". In order to put into practice the new left wing agenda the group voted to set up new committees to cover women, race and community relations, health and police, each with three permanent staff costing in total £100,000 a year.

Phil Turner's first public act was to write to the *New Journal* "on behalf of all the newly elected Labour councillors" to let the public know

---

1   By 1982 Roy Shaw was hanging on by the skin of his teeth. After May 1982, the arithmetic was easy: he had lost Christopher Gardiner, Derek Jarman, Derek Godfrey, Antony Craig, Roderick Cordara, Floss Parnell, John Lipetz and John Thane. The new left wing intake unlikely to vote for him included Graham Good, Angie Birtill, Graham Shurety, Marion Chester, Tony Dykes, Jenny Willmot, Julie Fitzgerald, Barbara Beck, Kate Allen, Sandra Plummer and Alan Woods.

their views on the ongoing Falkland Islands conflict. "The Labour group deplores the loss of life which has already occurred on both sides and considers the way forward must be to seek a truce and a subsequent settlement through the United Nations. To facilitate this and to reduce the risk of further loss of life, the British task force should be withdrawn at least to South Georgia".[2] He then set off to join the peace vigil in Parliament Square and to present a 60,000 signature petition calling on the Thatcher government to disarm its nuclear weaponry.

The statutory council meeting or the "mayor making" in which the council elected Tom Devine "a fierce Irish nationalist" as mayor set the scene for the coming year. Because there were so many more committees than there had been, the Labour group felt that they could not guard their majority on the five service department committees (education, environment, housing, leisure and social services) if the proportions were kept the same as before. Two days before the meeting, Anna Bowman told the Tories that they were to cut opposition representation on all committees by one and demanded that a list be drawn up to nominate the councillors to be taken off. The mayor making, planned as a civic event with nothing other than formal council business, descended into a bitter squabble after the Labour whip determined who should sit on which committee. The results were not always happy. Julian Tobin, for instance, the opposition spokesman on planning, was taken off the planning committee.

The first of the new committees to be set up was the police committee, a body so close to Phil Turner's heart that he insisted on chairing it himself. His vice chairman was a lanky barrister, the newly elected Bob Latham, who told the press about his concerns about "corruption, relations with the black community, tactics at demonstrations and deaths in police custody". The committee was somewhat hampered in its aims as the Home Office did not allow police officers to sit on the committee or even to attend its meetings. It was a committee about the police, not a committee for them.[3]

---

2   The Falklands War ended a month later on 14 June with the Argentinian surrender of Port Stanley. It was celebrated in Camden that night by several thousand people crowding in and around the Falklands Arms on Bloomsbury Way, a run down pub decorated with photos of elephant seals. The pub has since been renamed "The Bull & Last" which a plaque on the exterior wall claims quite falsely to have been the original name.

3   Robert Latham and Roy Shaw met Douglas Hurd, the home secretary, later in the year to get the rule relaxed. It was not, but did lead to the 1986 Labour manifesto commitment to establish a police consultative group.

The new women's committee was chaired by Ken Livingstone's girlfriend, the fiercely opinionated Kate Allen. Sporting the same short haircut, her deputy was Julie Fitzgerald. The committee was immediately allocated £200,000 to divide between women's groups in the borough. Taking her lead from the way Phil Turner had a "police-free" police committee, Kate Allen announced a ban on men attending her committee and at the first meeting in early June ordered them out of the chamber. "Women feel inhibited when men are present", she explained firmly. Obediently most of the men left, including the Thames TV crew who had come along to watch the fun. Only Tony Kerpel and Ian Pasley-Tyler refused to leave, Kerpel making his point by shouting above the jeers "This meeting is sexist!" After attempts to remove them had failed, Kerpel and Pasley-Tyler sat through the first session alongside 200 women from across London, some representing themselves, and others representing groups such as Women Against Rape and the Women's Workshop. Irritated that there was no one to throw out the two Tories, Kate Allen was also irritated that the *Daily Mail* had written "a snide report" on the new committee under the headline "Men: Keep Away!". She announced the formation of a "women's unit" at the town hall, thereby creating three new jobs. "This unit will see the reports that go to all other council committees and will ensure that the policies that the council adopts are not discriminatory and that they recognise the special needs of women". If not exactly reflecting the spirit of the times, it certainly caught the mood of many. When in August the three new posts for the women's unit were advertised (at £12,000 a year), the council received 800 applications.

139

The creation of a race committee was something of a disappointment to the long established Camden Committee for Community Relations (CCCR) which was still receiving £320,000 a year from the council. In the two months before its annual meeting in July, the CCCR had been joined by 185 new Bengali members, half of whom lived outside the borough. The new members had been organised and recruited by CCCR staff and "clusters of application forms and ballot papers were completed by the same hand". There followed something of a coup when the old membership of 60 was easily outvoted by the new members who turned up to vote for what turned out to be an Asian slate of candidates for the committee.

The sitting chairman, Michael Boye-Ananwomah, was replaced by Gurmukh Singh, and the white (but no longer young) stalwarts who had kept the organisation going through thick and thin, Roger Jowell, Joan

Hymans and Tony Clarke, were unceremoniously and suddenly voted off. Several of the Afro-Caribbeans resigned. A proposal to prevent any one group dominating, by having committee members elected only by members of their own ethnic groups, was shouted down. The author Salman Rushdie, a long time committee member, feared that the CCCR would become "a ghetto organisation" if committee places were reserved for different ethnic groups. "I am deeply depressed", he said, "that we seem to spend more time fighting each other than fighting racism. I wish people would grow up". Writing from his Raveley Street address he dealt with the complaints in turn: "There's nothing sinister about a rise in membership just before an election"; "CCCR staff are specifically directed to encourage ethnic minorities to join and to help them fill in forms if necessary"; and, best of all, "if a large number of Asians wish to join us, why exactly is that a matter for concern?" His only concern was that, disgracefully, the ballot papers had been removed and inspected after the ballot. The resultant complaints from what the *New Journal* called "the Who's Who of the race relations field in Camden" made no difference. Gurmukh Singh was chairman and that was that. "The time is ripe", noted the *Ham & High*, "for the do-gooding liberals of old to be eased out".

When the council's own race and community relations committee was set up later in the year, it was chaired by the small, mop haired and bearded Richard Sumray. He at least had no fears of an Asian coup if only because, the Irish and Jews aside, Camden had no ethnic minority councillors and so the race committee was (unlike the CCCR) all white. Undaunted, Sumray announced his plans to co-opt a member from each of the Cypriot, Bengali, Chinese, Indian, Afro-Caribbean and Irish communities so that everyone could be represented.

The CCCR was not finished: its community relations officer, the permanently outraged Chris Adamson, complained that although the council had appointed race advisors to two departments, he was not happy. All was well, he said, in the case of George Shire[4] who had a post advising the housing department as Mr Shire was a black Zimbabwean refugee from the Smith regime who had shown little inclination to go back after independence in 1980. He was also a general council member of the CCCR. But in the social services department Mr Adamson was sorry to note that the race advisor was a white South African woman who, he felt, represented something of a lost opportunity. But then

---

4   Pronounced *Shee-ray*.

in October Shire was sacked for gross misconduct. This was of great concern to Mr Adamson: "It is very unusual for town hall staff to be dismissed", he said suspiciously. Mr Shire took the hint and claimed that the council had behaved towards him "in a racist manner".

The Labour group had greatly changed since the new intake, and there was a keenness to let the world know just that. Sandy Wynn, who now chaired the leisure committee, announced that an exhibition on the mining industry organised by the National Coal Board and the Arts Council at the Camden Arts Centre was to be cancelled because it was partly sponsored by that well known investor in Apartheid, Barclays Bank. "A political prank", sighed the *Ham & High*, pointing out that the new council had also banned Kit Kat bars and packets of Smarties and Polo mints from staff canteens because the confectioners Rowntree Mackintosh had a subsidiary in South Africa.[5]

The Conservative group also had its new intake of members holding robust views. Tony Kerpel had narrowly survived by two votes a leadership challenge from (Kerpel's words) "the more abrasive" Derek Spencer who had impressed some of the newcomers.[6] In the same month of the election, new councillors were given a "familiarisation tour" of the housing department buildings in Bidborough Street. There the newly elected Brian Rathbone spotted a notice board that had been set aside for the use of NALGO, the white collar trade union. Pinned to it were several political posters attacking the Conservative government. He tore them down. NALGO issued a statement to the effect that they were "blacking" all work for the opposition group until Councillor Rathbone apologised. He did not.

Rathbone, not in any way fazed by being a new boy, proposed a motion at the first proper council meeting offering "warm appreciation for the courage and fighting skill of our armed forces in the Falklands campaign" which had finished less than a month before. After the main council business was over, he stood up at 3am to propose his motion: "it is right that we in this council should play our small part in

---

5   The editorial also pointed out that the last time such a political prank had been played in Camden was in 1968 when Geoffrey Finsberg cancelled the East German Academy of Art's Heartfield exhibition in the aftermath of the Soviet invasion of Czechoslovakia.

6   Derek Spencer rather lost interest in Camden after this. He was elected (by seven votes) MP for Leicester South in 1983 and resigned from the council. He lost his seat in 1987, but was elected MP for Brighton Pavilion in 1992, a seat he lost in 1997. He was knighted in 1992 and served as Solicitor General to John Major's government from 1992 -97. His highly successful career at the Bar flourishes still.

giving thanks and congratulations to those who restored freedom to the islanders". In the public gallery was 20 year old Private Nick Rose, who had recently been in the thick of it on Mount Longdon. He and his family had been invited by the Conservative group, and Private Rose was wearing the uniform and red beret of the Paratroop Regiment. Some Labour members were furious. The Labour group as a whole instructed the deputy mayor Ron Hefferman not to welcome the young soldier. His presence was, said the easily excited Graham Shurety, a display of "reactionary and disgusting chauvinism". "Do you support the Argies?" shouted Cathleen Mainds. "Do you support fascism?" Private Rose's mother told the press that the Labour group had "insulted the country". "Every enemy of this country is a friend to the sneering detractors of the political left" said Bill Trite. "We wish to make it clear," said Phil Turner, "we meant no disrespect to the paratrooper and his family. We only regret he was used in a totally squalid way by the Tory Party".

In November 1982 the Holy Cross Church on Cromer Street, a short walk from the Town Hall, was occupied by a group of masked women claiming to be prostitutes in need of sanctuary as they were threatened by the police. The demonstration was organised by the English Collective of Prostitutes. The male police force, they said, harassed them but did little or nothing about either their pimps or their kerb crawling clients[7]. It was an argument which appealed to Kate Allen and the women's committee. The prostitutes were, after all, women victims and the police were men. After a couple of weeks the young bearded vicar of the Holy Cross, The Reverend Mr Trevor ("Trev the Rev") Richardson let the women know that although he had at first sympathised with their plight, they had outstayed their welcome. "We had no option" said their leader, "because otherwise no one would listen to us". Kate Allen told the women that the council would investigate their claims, and the women's committee voted to appoint a woman to monitor kerb crawling and police activity at King's Cross. With this assurance the occupation of the church ended. Mr Richardson wrote in his parish newsletter that he felt that the council had been "bullied" by an unrepresentative group. Mr Richardson, said, Kate Allen, was "a demagogue".

Spending was the council's most pressing problem. At the last council meeting of the year Julian Harrison pointed out that since the Turner administration had taken office in May, the council had recruited

---

7   "Kerb crawling" only became an offence under the 1985 Sexual Offences Act.

an extra 127 staff at a cost to the ratepayer of £1m. Phil Turner's reply illustrated the great gulf that there then was between the political parties. There were 10,500 unemployed people in Camden, he said, and it was the council's job to salvage people from the stress of unemployment. "When will the Tories get it out of their minds that the way to solve the country's ills is to throw more people on the scrap heap?"

Council debates were often marked by the need of each side to annoy the other rather than to carry out any proper council business. The *Ham & High* summed up the situation in an editorial in early November 1982 under the heading "The Pointless Marathon". "Not since 1971, when Camden councillors took it upon themselves to debate British government policy in Northern Ireland, has a full council meeting ended in the vicinity of 4am". At 2am Ian Pasley–Tyler launched an attack on the new race committee as "expensive window dressing" which did little more than add to the level of staff and bureaucracy in Camden. He was seconded by the barrister Brian Rathbone, forthright, insensitive and irascible, who added that "money was being spent on minorities to the disadvantage of the ethnic majority", a "disgraceful" view which "disgusted" Richard Sumray. The council decided to declare Camden a nuclear free zone which, sneered Tony Kerpel, had "as much effect as a borough calling itself a crime free zone –it all depends on what the burglars think". "Tory councillor David Neil Smith", reported the *Ham & High*, "showed just how far over the top a speech could still be at 2.20am. Unilateral disarmament, he shouted, 'could be an incitement to nuclear war'. He also suggested rather strongly that a large civil defence programme would give a much needed boost to the building industry". The evening, or rather, the morning, session was then topped off with a motion proposed by the Kilburn councillors, Alan Woods, Angie Birtill and Kate Allen, to condemn calls for disenfranchising Irish citizens resident in the United Kingdom. "The discussion", noted the *Ham & High*, "somewhat handicapped by Camden's lack of powers in Northern Ireland policy making and the home secretary's recent categorical denial that the government was contemplating removing Irish people's votes in this country, went on for thirty agonising minutes" before being passed.

In January 1983 the Ossulton Street Tenants Association made a delegation to the housing management committee. They complained that vacant flats on the estate were being allocated to Bengali rather than local families and that their councillors had been abusive to them. They had approached the mayor, Tom Devine, who had called them "the scum and dregs of Somers Town", and Barbara Hughes had called them "a racist rabble". Tom Devine knew of the intended delegation and determined to confront his enemies at the committee meeting. He rushed down from the Midlands to be there, but did not get to the town hall until after the delegates had made their point and left. Shortly afterwards, Tom Devine burst into the council chamber after his long train journey to find that he had missed his prey. He demanded that the committee pass a motion of his own composition calling on the tenants association to withdraw their allegation. The chairman, Julian Fulbrook, refused on the grounds that it would only inflame matters. Devine was furious. "You," he shouted at Fulbrook, before storming out, "are no longer a fit and proper person to chair this committee!" Before anyone could catch his breath, the door flew open and he burst back in having remembered what else he had to say. "Traitor!" he bellowed at Fulbrook. "Let the people of Basildon[8] know what you represent! A traitor is a traitor wherever he is!" Fulbrook was forgiving: Devine, he said, had been "tired and emotional".

Such dissatisfaction that there was in the Labour group with Devine's behaviour was soon mended by Tony Kerpel who proposed a motion of censure at the next council meeting. He was shouted down by Labour councillors when he attempted to play a recording of the mayor's intemperate outburst. The Labour group rallied round Devine agreeing that he was a "battler" and a "fighter for Somers Town", which was code for committed but noisy and dim. They also agreed with Phil Turner, that Kerpel's motion was "a particularly nasty example of the sort of smear tactics we have come to expect from the Tories". Four Conservative councillors refused to vote.

In March 1983, the Labour group chanced on a new way of annoying their enemies: by marking the centennial of the death of Karl Marx. There is, of course, a strong local connection. He lived for the last 27 years of his life within the boundaries of the borough. He is not only buried in the London Borough of Camden, but worked in the British Museum which is also in the borough, and he wrote most of the first volume of *Das Kapital* at his home in what was to become the Maitland Park estate off Haverstock Hill. Marx was a Camden man. Before the March council meeting the chairman of the Labour group, the bearded Hugh Bayley, invited the cameras in to record the historic moment of him presenting the mayor with a facsimile copy of

---

8   The charmless Essex new town where Julian Fulbrook was the Labour parliamentary candidate.

the first edition of the *Communist Manifesto*, the original of which had been printed in German in Holborn in 1848. Hugh Bayley had himself been presented with the copy on a recent visit to East Germany. In the council debate that followed there was no shortage of Labour councillors to sing Marx's praises. "The value of Marx's works", said Bob Latham, "lies not in political dogma but in illuminating the ills of society. He had not only inspired the working class movement in Britain but also the current liberation struggles in South Africa and Namibia". The Tories disagreed, especially Brian Rathbone who prepared a scathing speech. Unhappily for him, he had inadvertently left a copy of it in the members' room photocopier. It had been copied and handed out among the Labour councillors who, like a class learning by rote, read out in unison with him his description of Marx as an "appalling man" and an "evil man", "odious and intellectually weak".

At one o'clock in the afternoon of 14th March 1983, a hundred years after Marx had breathed his last, ambassadors from Cuba, Yugoslavia and the Soviet bloc countries queued up to lay wreaths in Highgate cemetery. On the roof of Camden Town Hall, Phil Turner stood with the mayor, Tom Devine, and Charlie Taylor, formerly a St Pancras alderman and a veteran of the raising of the red flag in 1958[9]. "We do this", said Turner, as they hoisted the flag, "to reaffirm our faith in socialism in this borough and as a sign of solidarity with socialist movements throughout the world". As the flag unfurled in a gentle breeze, he and the mayor treated the photographers to an impromptu rendition of *The Red Flag*. Several floors below them, in solitary protest, Tony Kerpel climbed out of his first floor office and perched precariously on the window ledge. His flared trousers flapping in the same breeze, he posed for the cameras while waving two union jacks at the deserted pavements of Bidborough Street.[10]

145

1983 was also a notable year in Camden's struggle for good race relations. The year began with the internal members appeal panel unanimously upholding George Shire's dismissal. "I intend to go on fighting until I have cleared my name", he said. "The issue has moved away from just me protesting my innocence to becoming a major political issue as far as the black community is concerned". Chris Adamson of

---

9   Charlie Taylor, a print union activist (in NATSOPA), was chairman of the St Pancras United Tenants Association during the 1960 rent strike. Alderman Taylor was one of those expelled from the Labour Party with John Lawrence. He never rejoined.

10 This was not entirely the end of the matter. In 1985, Julian Fulbrook, then the mayor, accepted from Viktor Popav, the Soviet ambassador, a bust of Marx as a somewhat belated centenary gift.

the CCCR expressed "extreme surprise and disappointment" and within a week CCCR members had announced an indefinite boycott of all town hall committees. Neil Fletcher took up the cause and presented the January Labour group meeting with a proposal to reinstate Shire. Phil Turner thought it "inappropriate" as the matter was going to an industrial tribunal, but Fletcher and six others pledged to continue the protest against the sacking. "This is", Fletcher told the press with some satisfaction, "the first major difference within the Labour Group".

In March 1983 Camden announced that it was hiring as head of the new race and community relations unit Rashid Mufti, a "45 year old British born Black", (said the *New Journal*) a sociology lecturer and spokesman for the Liverpool 8 Defence Committee. He was pictured in the *Ham & High* under a ZANU poster depicting two AK toting Mugabe supporters. His aim, he said, was to get as many people as possible to come to the Camden Race and Community Relations Committee.

Early in the year the Anti-Apartheid Movement moved its London headquarters to Selous Street, an unremarkable back street in Camden Town. In the previous decade, every town in Rhodesia had possessed a Selous Street named in honour of Frederick Courtney Selous, the great white hunter and explorer who had been killed fighting the Germans in 1916. Hugh Bayley, the ex-public schoolboy trade union official and anti-Apartheid campaigner, felt that a name change was in order and proposed calling the street Mandela Street. The idea was eagerly taken up by Richard Sumray who expressed the Labour group view at the planning committee meeting: "Nelson Mandela is a man of enormous courage who represents the changes we want to see in South Africa, and Selous is a symbol of the past which embarrasses many of us". The Tories were out of step. Julian Tobin's view was that the proposal was "racialist" and that "Selous had done more for the world than Mandela had ever done" and that "Mandela is a living politician who is neither better nor worse than other politicians of his background, whether white or black"[11]. The Labour group voted to change the name to Mandela Street.

The debate about Selous proved to be somewhat academic as it turned out that the street had been named not after the great African explorer Frederick Courtney Selous, but after his retiring uncle, Henry Courtney Selous, a frequent exhibitor at the Royal Academy who had

---

11   A view he later revised by stating that Mandela is a "terrorist".

lived until his death in 1890 in Bayham Street[12]. When this was pointed out, Hugh Bayley said, rather sniffily, that he had known all along (but perhaps had simply not bothered to tell anyone). Anyway, he said, the council must act to avoid confusion with the imperialist, and "I do not personally care for what I have seen of Henry Selous's paintings".

The Mandela Street decision was eclipsed by the announcement that the Round House, the large, crumbling Victorian engine turning shed in Chalk Farm which had been used in recent years to stage concerts and television debates, was to be bought jointly for £300,000 by the GLC and Camden council to house "Britain's first ever cultural complex for black artists". The Conservatives were against the idea. Martin Morton, their most sympathetic spokesman on matters of race, pointed out that the Round House had been losing £100,000 a year before it closed. Kerpel was against because other venues such as the Shaw theatre were underused and it would be bad for community relations to reserve the proposed new centre solely for Blacks. "Tory No to Black Arts", quipped the *Ham & High* headline. Richard Sumray (the Race Committee chairman) and Sandy Wynn (of the Leisure Committee) set out the majority view: "By supporting the Round House as a Black Arts Centre, Camden council and the GLC are demonstrating their commitment to a multi-racial society and their opposition to all forms of racist and Euro-centric thinking".

Within the council, the Camden left advanced. When Julian Fulbrook resigned as (a highly effective) chairman of the housing committee to concentrate on his parliamentary campaign in Basildon, he was replaced by the strident left winger and women's activist, Julie Fitzgerald, who had only been elected a year before. Neil Fletcher took over the chairmanship of yet another newly formed body, the Decentralisation Committee which was intended "to localise town hall services". In April the left wing of the Labour group heaped further humiliation on Roy Shaw and John Mills by replacing them with Phil Turner and Angie Birtill as Camden's representatives on the Association of Metropolitan Authorities. A hollow move, as the London Boroughs Association vetoed both appointments leaving Camden unrepresented. Disquiet at Roy Shaw's treatment materialised in the letter pages of the local papers. "It was good to see Roy Shaw's old friends coming to his

147

---

12 The street had formerly been known as Little Camden Street. The decision to honour Henry Selous was only taken in 1938 when some twenty streets in St Pancras were renamed to avoid confusion with similarly named streets both in the borough and across London.

defence", commented Neil Fletcher. "Sentiment plays a part in politics all too rarely".

1983 was also the year of the first general election called by Mrs Thatcher. In May she paid a visit to Euston Road and was met by a hostile demonstration. Among the protestors were several Camden councillors. One of them, Marion Chester, forced her way through the police cordon as the prime minister's car drew level, shouted "Down with Thatcher!" and threw an egg. The egg missed. Councillor Chester was arrested and later at Highbury Corner Magistrates' Court agreed to be bound over to be of good behaviour and to keep the peace for a year in the sum of £100.

Before the 1983 election, Camden's three parliamentary constituencies were amalgamated into two. St Pancras North was divided between the new Hampstead & Highgate and Holborn & St Pancras constituencies. Both were contested by the sitting MPs, Geoffrey Finsberg and Frank Dobson[13]. John McDonnell, the Labour candidate for Hampstead & Highgate, was a 31 year old Liverpudlian. He had been Ken Livingstone's right hand man on the GLC where he chaired the Finance Committee and, having an Irish father, was in charge of all things Irish. With Livingstone, he had managed to alienate right wing Labour Party supporters by inviting Sinn Fein spokesmen to address the GLC just after the Ballykelly disco bomb[14]. He was, he said, going for "the Peace Vote" and attended every CND rally he could find. He also wanted action on congestion in central London and an end to fox hunting. He described Finsberg as being "invisible". Finsberg described McDonnell as "an impertinent carpet bagger". The *Ham & High* expected a close election and gleefully reported that hundreds had packed Hampstead Town Hall for a Labour election rally addressed by John McDonnell and the Labour Party leader Michael Foot (a Hampstead resident). On the other hand Finsberg's election meeting in Beckford School in West Hampstead was attended by only one person (apart from party activists), and he claimed to be an "Indian Socialist".

---

13 Dobson had, "by a whisker" said the *New Journal,* been selected as candidate for the new Holborn & St Pancras constituency in preference to his rival, Jock Stallard, the MP for St Pancras North. Stallard never really left parliament as he was elevated to the House of Lords in the 1983 dissolution honours list. He died in 2008.

14 In December 1982 —sixteen dead.

In Holborn & St Pancras things were quieter. To liven things up, the Tories chose Tony Kerpel as their candidate, but Frank Dobson was quite safe, especially now that his old seat had been bolstered by a merger with most of the old St Pancras North seat. The SDP–Liberal Alliance, having failed at the council elections, was not expected to get far, especially in an election that was seen as a referendum on Mrs Thatcher. A deal had been struck between the SDP and the Liberal Party as to who should stand in what constituency, and the Liberal David Radford[15] was obliged to make way in Hampstead for the SDP's Anne Sofer, while the SDP stood aside in Holborn & St Pancras so that the the Liberals could chose Bill Jones as their candidate.

The candidates chased celebrities for their endorsements, Melvyn Bragg supported John McDonnell, Kingsley Amis backed Kerpel, and Finsberg got Judith Chalmers. Frank Dobson campaigned against Britain's membership of the European Community and against unemployment. "The dole", he announced, "is a Tory weapon to cow working people". The Camden Communist Party announced that they wanted to support Dobson and so would not be standing against him. Kerpel did not have unrealistic expectations, but hoped to make sufficient inroads to make the new seat a marginal. He went on the attack, pointing out that the Holborn & St Pancras Labour Party was run "by a rag bag of extremists" including Militant Tendency, supporters of Troops Out and the IRA, militant feminists and, his favourite, "rates funded rent-a-crowd CND activists".

As if to make Kerpel's point for him, to celebrate the "International Women's Day of Action Against Nuclear Weapons", Camden NALGO announced a half day strike in May. The *New Journal* was enthusiastic: "At 2pm women will link hands and encircle the town hall in support of the council's nuclear free zone policy. Then they will join a peace picnic in Argyle Square". And so they did. The day, according to the organisers, Women Against Cruise, was a great success. "A wonderful day", said Kate Allen. "The turnout is fantastic". Forty demonstrators broke away to perform "a three minute die-in" on Camden High Street to mimic the consequences of an atomic explosion.

The result was expected in that both Dobson and Finsberg won. In Hampstead & Highgate, McDonnell complained that the Alliance had split the "anti-Finsberg vote". In Holborn & St Pancras Kerpel blamed the Alliance for watering down the anti-Socialist vote. Finsberg's victory

149

---

15   And, having better things to do, it was the end of Radford's political career. He is now the Recorder of Redbridge, the presiding judge at Snaresbrook Crown Court.

was soured by his being sacked as junior health minister two days after the election, which cheered the *Ham & High*: "He has been invisible in the sense that he never gets out of the political rut and on many issues holds no known views". Being on the back benches will be "an excellent opportunity to get out and about more". Uncommented on at the time, it was also something of a triumph for the Alliance candidates. They came third in both constituencies, but in each case doubled the vote that the Liberals had managed in 1979, getting 25% of the vote in Hampstead & Highgate, and 21% in Holborn & St Pancras.[16]

George Shire's appeal against unfair dismissal was heard before the employment tribunal in early July. Peter Susman, Camden's counsel, opened gently. "Charming but inefficient" Mr Shire had behaved disgracefully. Shire was represented by William Panton, who had been instructed by the Commission for Racial Equality. Camden had "trumped up" charges against Shire he said, and without any written warning had sacked him for what was described as "hopeless incompetence". The chairman, Stella Hollis was unforgiving. She found that Shire "regards any criticism of him as racially motivated" and that when he was told off about his work, "he went berserk, threw a telephone on the floor and delivered a stream of abuse using the vilest of swear words". Such was her fear of being called racist, Shire's line manger had not immediately reported him because she did not want to jeopardise his chances of getting the post of race advisor to the social services department. Shire's behaviour, Miss Hollis ruled, amounted to gross misconduct following which Camden was entitled to sack him without warning. She also had harsh words for Neil Fletcher who had put "gross improper pressure" on the council to reinstate Shire.

The unrepentant Shire declared that the housing aid centre "is white, middle class and ethnocentric" and "run by middle class whites who held negative and stereotyped opinions of black people." His lawyer accused Miss Hollis of being "patronising, offensive and insulting". She had repeatedly interrupted him, she had corrected him when he called Indians "black", she had told him that there was no such thing as black politics, and she had called Mr Shire a bigot. His appeal to the High Court was heard and dismissed in the following January. Mr Justice Tudor-Evans accepted that Miss Hollis's remarks were "inappropriate and

150

---

16 And, wrote Tony Kerpel to the *Ham & High,* "Alliance members, having had their little fling can now retire to their preferred salon politics, nibbling quiche and sipping Chablis or whatever it is that these dilettantes do in between surfacing at election times".

unfortunate", but was "positively satisfied" that Shire had a fair hearing. Now describing himself as a "lecturer at London University", Shire was unbowed. "It simply shows the inbuilt racism in the tribunal system which Camden council has exploited to its advantage", he said.[17]

1983 was also the year in which the CCCR brought a complaint to the Press Council against Auberon Waugh, the wine correspondent of the *Tatler*. The case was much commented on in the national press. Waugh had criticised the lack of imagination used by wine writers when condemning poor wine. He proposed the use of increasingly preposterous images. "Their wine should be compared to a creaky old woman's bicycle in a Merseyside cul de sac; a bunch of dead chrysanthemums on the grave of a still born West Indian baby." Having received a complaint about the second part of the sentence, the CCCR took up the case because, as Chris Adamson explained, "A West Indian baby implies even greater condemnation than if it had been a stillborn white baby". The Press Council found Mr Waugh's piece "tasteless", but not racist. "The Press Council", sighed Adamson after the event, "clearly finds it difficult to understand the issues of racism we are talking about".

In a heated meeting in July, the Labour group discussed imposing the first rent rise for eighteen months. It was agreed to raise council rents in line with inflation, then running at 6%. The effect was an extra one or two pounds a week. Tom Devine stormed out threatening to leave the party "forthwith". Marion Chester threatened to resign her seat. Their mood had not mellowed when the council met two days later under a gallery packed with angry tenants' association representatives. Devine was in a furious mood. "The leadership has deserted our Socialist principles", he shouted to cheers from his supporters. "Our comrades have lost their way!" While the Labour group shouted at each other for one and a half hours, the Tories sat in silence and then backed the motion to raise rents. It was passed by 42 votes to seven[18]. The *Ham & High* was unimpressed: "If the voters of Camden had seen the ranting and raving that took place in the name of rational debate on Wednesday they would

---

17 Shire went onto higher things. Self appointed as ZANU(PF)'s UK spokesman he is frequently wheeled out on television news programmes to assert that Comrade Mugabe is a good thing and that Zimbabwe is doing well.

18 The seven were Tom Devine, Anna Bowman, Graham Shurety, John Wakeham, Sandra Plummer, Angela Birtill, and Marion Chester.

have realised, yet again, that the enemy is within Labour's own ranks and seems intent on suicide".

Under Neil Fletcher's guidance the council revealed its plans to fulfil Labour's election pledge to "go local". The idea was to set up area offices ("Mini town halls dotted around the borough", translated the *New Journal*) which, it soon became clear, could require another 120 new staff and up to £6m in extra expenditure. Fletcher was buoyant and, at least publicly, undismayed. "I am sure the electorate will be willing to pay the extra for the better speed and efficiency of services", he said while unveiling his plan to offer the borough one of three models of decentralisation. The most extravagant of these involved the setting up of twenty new area offices supported by five district offices.

The *Ham & High* reviewed the situation at the end of September and concluded that Camden risked losing its entire rate support grant.

> *"If Camden persists in following the policies in the manifesto on which it was elected, the rate rises will put Camden in a unique position once again and make it the inevitable target of harsh government punishment. The reasons are twofold. The first being that last year was a comparatively lucky one for Camden, it being able to soften its rate demand by calling on reserves and enjoying substantial windfalls. The second is that by increasing its workforce by almost 1,000 it will add £10m to its expenditure —and that money can only come from ratepayers. Apart from the money itself, the essence of the problem that confronts the council is credibility. How on earth can it convince anyone that the Draconian rate capping powers proposed by the government are unnecessary if the borough's inflated rate zooms into the stratosphere?"*

The last council meeting of the year was a caricature of its predecessors. Kate Allen, having made sure that her women supporters and Irish republican enthusiasts were present in numbers, proposed a motion condemning strip searches of women prisoners in Armagh Prison. The incidence of strip searching in that establishment, she claimed, was eight times that of women prisoners in English gaols. The Tories said that they did not believe it, it had nothing to do with Camden, and the council was not in the best position to comment on security considerations in that troubled province. They were shouted down and booed by Miss Allen's friends. The debate was wound up with an emotional speech by the "tired and emotional", "fierce Irish Nationalist", "battler" Tom Devine, who recounted the horrors of Black & Tans and ended by bellowing "Justice for my people!"

The first meeting in 1984 of the race and community relations committee discussed the long awaited report of its working party on the renaming of Cecil Rhodes House, a large brick 1930s council block on Crowndale Road between Camden Town and Kings Cross. "A change of name would be most welcome", enthused the head of Camden's race unit, Rashid Mufti, with Sumray's backing, "as Cecil Rhodes House is named after one of the arch imperialists and enemies of black people". The favoured alternatives were Zimbabwe Court or Azania Court "after the African name for South Africa". The committee summoned Pat Breen of the tenants association who, somewhat nervously, reported that although most of the tenants did not know who Rhodes was, they had rather got used to the name and did not really want to change it. Furthermore, as the *Ham & High* was careful to report, "Mr Breen stressed that tenants in the block had always supported council initiatives on anti-racism, and worked hard to counter racism and involve ethnic minority tenants in the association". The building was not renamed.[19]

Although the Conservative opposition was subject to its own differences of opinion, the most divisive matter for them was the contentious bill to abolish the GLC. Tony Kerpel led a delegation of Conservative councillors to Patrick Jenkin, secretary of state for the environment. "The government's generalised claim about savings was not enough", said Kerpel. "We're not entirely convinced that this is going to save the ratepayers money and we're going to ask the minister to carry out a cost exercise to show exactly what the proposals will mean in extra expenditure for each borough." Camden's Policy & Resources Committee was presented with a paper prepared by the chief executive's department in January 1984. It was blunt: the government plans for GLC abolition would not work because the time table was impossibly tight and the government had not considered the necessary costs of such a massive reorganisation. Both parties agreed to oppose the government's plans. Alan Greengross, who was a GLC as well as a Camden councillor, said "I am not pleading for the GLC as it now stands, but what the government are suggesting is not a workable solution. Giving power to quangos will not help anyone." Phil Turner described Greengross's address as "the most coherent and well argued demolition job" he had yet heard on the government's proposals. The government was not swayed, in part because other councils saw things differently.

153

---

19 Pat Breen was a journalist then in his mid twenties. According to his obituary in the *New Journal* in February 2008, he had been "a linchpin in the campaign to save the old *Camden Journal*" in 1980". He died aged only 50.

"Our own analysis proves the government is right", maintained Shirley Porter, the Westminster City council leader, in that abolition would cut Westminster's rates bill by £45m, and Camden's by £13m.

The fight against the Rates Bill dominated the council throughout the year, and the Labour Party used it to good effect to mobilise support. In February Phil Turner called a meeting of all the three hundred voluntary groups funded by Camden. Rate capping, he told them, would affect them all. Camden was planning to spend £125m on services in the coming year and £6½m of that was on grants to voluntary groups. The government had proposed to cap Camden's spending at £101m and so everyone was needed to campaign against the bill. It was, said Kerpel, "a discredited Socialist tradition" to cut funding to voluntary groups while refusing to cut unnecessary spending on the women's race and police committees and the nuclear free zone.

As it was, the 1984 rate rise was low; another 7.6% on domestic rates which rather took the sting out of the criticism offered by the Tories who had been led to believe (and rather hoped) it would be much higher. They still wanted some £15m taken out of the budget, and pointed out that Camden's expenditure was 25% more per capita than any other London authority.

154

The debate focussed on the work of the grants subcommittee. The St Pancras Boxing club, whose gym was in a parlous state of disrepair, feared losing its best members, but was refused a £20,000 grant. "I am personally very much against boxing", said the sub-committee chairman, Mary Cane. Tory activist Peter Slade wrote to the New Journal: "It really is quite appalling that this present council is prepared to equate the needs of such deserving organisations as the St Pancras Boxing Club with such groups of the loony left as Kentish Town Lesbian Women; Camden Women Against Cruise; Black Women for Wages for Housework; The English Collective of Prostitutes; Wages Due Lesbians; The Wages for Housework Campaign; the Prostitutes and Supporters Working Party; and the Lesbian Working Party of the council's women's committee." Tony Kerpel was particularly upset about the £13,650 grant to Camden Peace Groups Steering Committee, a gift to the CND so blatantly political which he predicted would be "the final nail in the coffin of section 137 of the Local Government Act", the legislation which allowed such grants to be made. [20]

The argument heated up with the passing of the Rates Act 1984

---

20 Much of which was repealed by the Local Government & Housing Act 1989 after lobbying from Conservative councillors in opposition in Labour controlled councils.

in June. It was another turn of the screw. Patrick Jenkin, the secretary of state, announced that Camden would have to cut its expenditure by £14m -10% of the total. "I wouldn't pretend that there aren't ways of improving efficiency", said Turner, throwing down the gauntlet, "but there's no way we can bridge the gap the government is talking about. The Labour group will not be prepared to co-operate with that kind of attack on services in Camden. I can't say yet exactly how we and the trade unions will resist, but I can say we will contest the government's plans all the way down the line". Kerpel was unsympathetic. The government were being "staggeringly generous". "Labour are behaving like a group of rich spoilt brats told that their Harrods credit card has been cancelled and they'll have to shop at Marks & Spencer instead". Finsberg advised people not to listen to the "squeals of anguish" from Camden until they cut back their expenditure and improved efficiency by putting out services such as refuse collection to tender. Ian Pasley-Tyler wrote to Patrick Jenkin to point out that only a third of Camden's population paid the full rate, and suggested that all councils where less than half the population paid the full rate should be stopped from fixing a rate altogether.

The move towards "Decentralisation", whereby real decision making power would be spread around the borough, began to stall. The main problems were the complexities of the proposed system and the staff costs that it would require. There was also the great difficulty of finding councillors willing to sit on all these extra bodies when they were already stretched with the new race, women's and police committees. The problem was in part dealt with by co-opting unelected people onto the new area committees. "Since 1982 Camden council has dramatically increased the number of co-options to committees", said Kerpel. "This means Labour activists being invited by Labour councillors to sit on council committees where they are then given voting rights. Labour has been ruthless in packing its side of the chamber with its socialist friends, all of whom are delighted to vote for spending public money on themselves and their pet schemes". He challenged Fletcher and Wakeham to name a single co-opted member of the race, police or women's committees who was not a Labour Party supporter. There was no answer.

The decentralisation debate was interrupted by the Labour Group elections. Phil Turner was unchallenged, but Neil Fletcher found himself isolated. His trusted lieutenant John Wakeham had decided to stand against him as deputy leader, but had then made the silly error of writing to all those who he hoped may support him. The letter was leaked to the press and published in the *Ham & High* before the group meeting. "We are not well served by our chief officers, although we have many good staff further down the line. In my view we need to sack some people at the top. It would save us money, it would give us self confidence and it would help our industrial relations". The chief executive, Frank Nickson, (on £35,000 a year) was "top of my list".

The other candidates were Tony Dykes, Kate Allen and Sandy Wynn, a 38 year old mother of two and former Labour Party agent in Hampstead. She won: VICTORIOUS WYNN, quipped the *New Journal*. "My main job will be to support Phil Turner", she said. As she had beaten both Fletcher and Kate Allen, the *Ham & High* saw it in political terms: "Labour delivers rebuff to Left" ran their headline, but it was not quite that. The criticism of Fletcher was simply that he was spending too much time with the Inner London Education Authority where he had been Camden's representative since 1979. He not only chaired their Further and Higher Education subcommittee, but was also a leading light in the battle to prevent the ILEA's abolition.

156

1984 was the GLC designated "Anti-Racist Year". Against the express wishes of Neil Kinnock, the Holborn & St Pancras Labour Party set up the first black section in London. Cllr Paul Boateng of the GLC addressed the Camden Black Workers Group and told them that it was "a scandal" that Camden had no black councillors. The Camden Ethnic Minorities Consortium and the Camden Anti-Racist and Anti-Fascist Alliance (CARAFA) were formed and the council looked about for suitable ways in which to celebrate anti-racism. The most imaginative suggestion came from an eager young officer in the works department, Peter Swingler, who suggested that the borough's dust carts should be named after black heroes such as Malcolm X, Martin Luther King and Nelson Mandela "using plaques like railway engines have". The July 1984 council meeting was preceded by a reception for Dave Kitson, a communist and a member of the military wing of the ANC, who had just been released after twenty years in a South African prison for "conspiring to instigate violent revolution". When the council meeting started, Kerpel and the Conservatives waited outside while the mayor presented Kitson with a portrait of Nelson Mandela. [21]

The GLC's Anti-Racist Year was celebrated by the CCCR by yet another bout of infighting. William Whyte, the black chairman of their employment committee, took out an injunction to scupper the annual elections as seven black members (as opposed to Asian members) had not received their ballot papers. The vice chairman, Zareer Masani tried to get Mr Whyte expelled as being "utterly undesirable". "We have been plagued by personalities", sighed ex-chairman John Lipetz. Chris Adamson declared the elections void because six people voted onto the committee were not even members.

As it was then the middle of the miners' strike, Tony Dykes proposed a motion to twin Camden with Bentley in Doncaster, where the pit was threatened with closure. The public gallery was filled with National Union of Miners supporters, plastered with badges supporting the strike. The purpose of twinning the borough with Bentley, said Dykes, was so the people of Camden could hear the miners' case first hand and the miners' children could use Camden's facilities. He then lectured the chamber on the need for coal rather than nuclear power. A delegation from South Yorkshire NUM addressed the council meeting while most of the Conservatives studiously read their newspapers. Tony Kerpel spoke against the motion: "It is sickening to hear councillors talking like Scargill's Cuban emissaries. This motion aligns the council with the intimidating mob tactics of people like the scum up there (indicating the delegation now jeering from the public gallery) who want to terrorise those miners who want to work." The motion was passed to the approval of the *New Journal* who devoted a page to the miners' struggle. Tom Devine told the council chamber: "If St Francis of Assisi is up there somewhere, and I believe he is, he would be saying 'long live the NUM'!"

Camden was in the news again in October when an appointments panel selected the Ceylon born Patrick Kodikara as the new director of social services in succession to the long serving Kenneth Urwin. The *New Journal* broke the news under the headline: "Black joins Town Hall

---

21   Later in the year the mayor, Barbara Hughes, wrote to the mayors of all twenty one towns in the United States also named Camden asking them to assist her in her struggle against nuclear weapons. The only publicised response to her request was that of the mayor of Camden, Maine. He told his local paper that politeness had prevented him from replying to "the mayor of Camden, England". He had read her letter and "thrown it in the trash".

top brass", describing Kodikara as "London's first black town hall chief". The appointments panel was made up of one Conservative and two Labour councillors. The chairman of the social services committee was delighted that Kodikara had accepted the job: "He's the best man for the job. He knows exactly what we're after". The Conservative panel member, Dr Peter Skolar was also enthusiastic: "He'll put a bomb under Social Services which is not before time".

The latter view was somewhat surprising because Kodikara was a Labour activist who had attracted national press coverage. "The question of race is political", he said. A former chairman of the Brick Lane Defence Committee, the Hackney and Tower Hamlets Defence Committee and the Hackney Community Relations Council, he was now as a Labour councillor chairing Hackney's social services committee. He also, only three years before, stood to deselect and replace the Hackney MP, Stanley Clinton Davis. Skolar had missed all this, and had not consulted Kerpel who had much to say on the subject. Kerpel had uncovered "an astonishing web of Labour councillors employed by Labour authorities."[22] Six Camden council officers were Labour councillors in other London boroughs, including George Meehan, the leader of the London borough of Haringey. Charlie Rossi of the GLC was a long term Camden employee (a rat catcher) who had just taken early retirement, but who had for the last three years been on sick leave on full pay. Mike Kirk, a Labour councillor who chaired Camden's housing committee, was employed by Hackney. Also Kodikara's record as the chairman of Hackney's social services committee was of concern to the Tories. He had adopted a policy of stopping trans-racial adoptions and fostering, he had been responsible for "dramatically increasing" the number of unqualified black social workers, and had made several highly political statements, amongst them the inflammatory assertion that the police had murdered Colin Roach (a disturbed young black man who had shot himself in Stoke Newington Police Station in the previous year).

Having jumped too early, Skolar changed tack and said that he would not have supported Kodikara's application had he known of his political background. In any event, he could not work with such a man. Joan Hymans of the CCCR demanded that the council ban Peter Skolar

---

22 The *Times* saw Kodikara's appointment as an example of "degenerating civic culture" in which "disinterested administration is made impossible [and] councillors play favourites with the general revenue".

from sitting on any future interview panels. After describing Skolar as "a very silly man", Alan Woods, in anticipation of Kodikara taking up his appointment, announced that the council might relax insistence on professional qualifications for social workers in order to recruit more non whites.

Kerpel's contribution to the local government debate at the Conservative conference in October in Brighton was well received. "Camden is spending £120 million on its own services, excluding education, for a population of only 160,000. When a council is in the grip of these hairy chested socialists –and I include their women councillors- (laughter, applause) then someone has to control their spending because they never will." He pointed out that only 30% of the electorate in Camden pay the full rate. "For those who do pay rates in Camden the Tory government is the only thing standing between them and the municipal pickpockets in the town hall".

It was a good speech, but was soon forgotten in the debris of an IRA attempt to assassinate the prime minister. In the early hours of 12 October 1984, a 100lb bomb exploded in the Grand Hotel. Five people were killed and many more terribly injured. The leader of Her Majesty's opposition, Neil Kinnock, was quick to express his "horror and outrage".

In Camden, reactions were less clear cut. The council met on the following Wednesday. There was no time to meet the administrative deadline to table a motion on the bombing, but Tony Kerpel tabled an amendment to an existing motion on the intimidatory violence of the striking coal miners. The mayor, Barbara Hughes, began the meeting by offering the council's condolences to all those who had suffered, but things did not run smoothly. Kerpel tabled his amendment condemning the outrage. It was not welcomed by the Labour group. Sandy Wynn tried to get him to withdraw it as it had nothing to do with the original motion. They then sat in silence through a contribution by the bearded John Wakeham: "I do not condone terrorist bombs. I do not condone the fact that innocent people were killed. I do not consider that the political intention behind the bombing is wicked, and I do not regard the target of that bomb, Mrs Thatcher, in any sense at all the innocent victim of that bombing." A furious Mike Farrer interrupted him: "Why don't you take a gun to her yourself?" Two Labour councillors, Kate Allen and Alan Woods, tried to invoke the standing orders to stop the debate altogether to prevent any condemnation of the IRA.

Kerpel's amendment was adopted because ten Labour members abstained and one, Andrew Bethell, voted with the Tories. Twenty one Labour councillors voted against it. Further amendments were tabled by Bob Latham "condemning unequivocally this attack on innocent people" and including the words "and equally condemns the loss of life in Northern Ireland". The final amended motion was passed by the Labour group, the Tories abstaining once their original had been watered down.

The press was unforgiving. The headline news was that twenty one Labour councillors in Camden had refused to condemn unequivocally the bombing. John Wakeham was widely quoted. The banner headline on *The Star* simply read: "SICK". The *Evening Standard* was even more critical, reporting Wakeham's speech as if he spoke for the majority, and in its initial coverage mentioned neither the mayor's opening remarks nor the final motion on which the Labour group did vote.[23] The Labour Party, noted the *Ham & High* a week after, had chosen not to discipline Wakeham. They "were putting their heads under the pillow in the hope that the embarrassment will disappear and be forgotten".

Council officers in the Housing Department's Homeless Persons Unit ("HPU") had been on strike since August. They were doing more work than ever before and they wanted more pay. In 1981 there had been sixty families in bed & breakfast accommodation. Now there were seven hundred. The council took a robust view and Sandy Wynn announced that there would be no negotiation while the strike continued, although the strikers' grievances would be listened to once they behaved themselves. Their union, NALGO, was furious and called for a strike ballot for the whole housing department. It was decisively rejected, but the HPU strike continued for the rest of the year, emergency cases being handled by senior officers. The strikers retaliated by encouraging homeless people to contact councillors on their home numbers. (Barbara Hughes, herself a council tenant, even awoke to a homeless Bengali family sleeping on her doorstep.)

Matters came to head when in November 1984 a Bengali woman, Shamin Karim, and her two children died in a fire at a bed and breakfast hotel in Marylebone where they had been temporarily housed by Camden. To protest at the poor state of their accommodation, some 89

---

23 Later the subject of a successful complaint by Camden's chief executive, Frank Nickson, to the Press Complaints Commission.

homeless Bengali families (or rather, about forty families –men, women and small children- and some others "representing" those absent) occupied the civic floor of the town hall and bedded themselves down in the council chamber and the committee rooms. Their negotiators called themselves the "Homeless Families Occupation Committee". The occupation had been the idea of some of the striking council officers from the homeless persons unit who now stayed on as "advisors". With them were two solicitors.[24] The demands were straightforward: all the families should be immediately re-housed, not in the temporary bed & breakfast hostels that they had come from and which were sometimes cramped, damp and dangerous, but in proper council flats with proper statutory tenancies. The occupiers were also unequivocally supported by the CCCR, one of whose members, Salman Rushdie, a frequent visitor to the occupation, wrote in the *Guardian* in florid terms: "If the deaths are to be treated as murders, then many of us would say that the murderers are to be found in Camden Town Hall".

On the first day of the occupation, Sandy Wynn addressed the occupiers but could not get them to shift. In the afternoon of the second day, a Friday, the housing chairman, Mike Kirk, together with Bob Latham and Richard Sumray went into the chamber to try to get things moving. It was not easy and the crowd was volatile. Mike Kirk read out a statement promising thirty vacant council houses and assurances to speed things along for those remaining. He was anxious to get away for the weekend, not least because his wife was about to give birth. While the occupation committee began to discuss the implications of his announcement, the three councillors made their way back to the door. A council worker, one of the striking homeless persons unit officers, shouted out that the council in fact had over fifty empty properties ready to be allocated. Sensing some trickery, the crowd immediately became angry and the councillors were stopped from leaving by a wall of protestors. The pleas of David Riddle, the deputy chief executive, shouted down from the visitors' gallery made no difference.

Although kept back from the door, the three councillors were able to talk to David Riddle. He left, having let them know that he was going to call the police. They did not deter him, imagining that a kindly local policeman would be able to calm things down. But Riddle's call, with its

24   The solicitors were Peter Norton, a legal aid lawyer from Tottenham, and Russell
      Campbell of the (council funded) Camden Law Centre. Campbell is now an
      immigration judge.

161

underlying message of an unruly mob and hostage taking, had a different effect on the police. They arrived in force some three hours after the three hostages were taken. Several vanloads of policemen with riot equipment parked outside the town hall and a superintendant made his way inside to assess the situation. From the visitors' gallery, he became involved in the negotiations which were led by David Riddle. Things began to settle down and an agreement was reached whereby the three hostages would be released. Without warning, an enthusiastic group of policemen burst into the council chamber. As the *Ham & High* reported, "the police stormed in and broke the human chain of protestors". The three councillors were freed. Although anyone who got in their way was roughly handled by the police, there were no injuries, and no arrests. But there was great anger at the way the matter had been handled. Much of that anger was directed at Bob Latham, who was chairman of both the race and the police committees, and who was now in some way seen as being responsible for the police action.

The occupation continued without the hostages. After the first weekend, Phil Turner paid the occupiers a visit and was given a tour of the committee rooms now transformed into makeshift dormitories. The plight of the homeless was distressing and he wept as they told him of their difficulties. The papers made much of this, and he wrote to the *Guardian* to say that he was not ashamed of weeping –it was through frustration at the council's impotence and with rage at the government who had brought about that impotence.

Something had to be done, especially as the occupiers showed no signs of leaving and were being fed by donations from local Bengali restaurants. A hastily convened meeting of the Labour group agreed to re-house the occupiers in council stock within a fortnight. Mike Kirk and Julie Fitzgerald, the chairman of the housing committee and his deputy, threatened to resign. There was no point in carefully managing a housing waiting list based upon assessed need and length of time in temporary accommodation if some people could get housed simply by making more fuss than those waiting quietly, or by sending a "representative" along to the occupation. Nevertheless, those with reservations were overruled and the eighty nine families were all housed (although some in temporary accommodation) by the weekend before Christmas. "We will go on from here to campaign for better treatment for homeless families", said Turner, and settled the HPU strike with a pay award backdated to February. He also had to placate NALGO who had issued letters to the council's chief officers (including Frank Nickson) threatening them with expulsion from the union for providing emergency cover during the strike.

There followed a great falling out of left wing Camden with the left wing Ken Livingstone at the GLC who saw an opportunity for self-publicity at the council's expense. He paid the occupiers several visits, and described the council's intransigence as "an outrage". He was particularly damning of Bob Latham: "I can think of nothing more disgusting", he said, "than the chair of the race committee and the police committee calling in the police. This decision places him outside the Labour movement." Livingstone had wanted to give the occupation committee a GLC grant, but the idea was dropped after representations from Camden council officers. It would have meant that the occupation of Camden council (run by the Labour Party) would have been funded by the GLC (also run by the Labour Party). Determined to get his photo opportunity, Livingstone managed to assemble the GLC Ethnic Minorities Committee to approve a one off cash disbursement so that he could dress up as Father Christmas, gather the press, and distribute Christmas presents to the Bengali children before Camden's housing officers could rehouse them. Several of Camden's Labour councillors made their feelings known to the papers. It was not as if, was the general message, Ken was any bloody good when he chaired the borough's housing committee.

Before the occupation was over, Rashid Mufti, the council's principal race advisor, resigned. He could no longer work, he said, with Councillor Latham. There were calls at the CCCR meeting in January for Latham to resign from the organisation. "Bob Latham showed total contempt for black people by calling the police", was the view of one member, Erroll Lawrence. Latham was expelled by the hard left City of London Anti-Apartheid Group and at the next meeting of Camden's race and community relations committee the chickens came home to roost. The "black" co-opted members proposed a motion of no confidence which was eagerly supported by the Tories whose only motive was to embarrass the Labour Party[25]. Latham said that he was sorry that the police had been called, but it was too late. The votes of the elected Labour members were not enough to save him, and he was forced to resign.

---

25 Everyone knew that had the Tories been in charge during the occupation, they would have had the protestors removed by the police within twenty four hours. This did not stop their spokesman on the committee, Bob Graham, piously arguing that Latham should have handled things better by "listening to what the occupiers had to say".

Ken Livingstone's girlfriend, Kate Allen, in a move that was to haunt her when she later stood for the group leader's job, wrote an article in *London Labour Briefing* attacking her fellow councillors for their behaviour during the occupation. Sandy Wynn had been "unsympathetic and defensive" when dealing with the occupiers and Bill Birtles had wanted to get the police to clear the chamber[26]. Other councillors, who had represented the occupiers as being a bunch of dupes led by black militants, or had argued that the Bengalis were queue jumping the housing list, had "prepared the way for a racist backlash". "The group", she said, "is more divided than ever it has been."

1985 began with something of a shock when John Mills, who had for years been Roy Shaw's chief lieutenant, resigned from the council. His company Fairtrade (UK) Ltd had gone into liquidation with losses of £250,000 in the run up to Christmas. He was, he said, facing ruin. In the consequent by election in Regents Park, Labour only narrowly survived a strong challenge from the SDP (and that was with the help of the housing department who, following the resignation, distributed a leaflet informing all tenants of the council's extravagant improvement plans for the Regents Park Estate).

The first half of 1985 was dominated by the government's insistence that the council set its rate within the confines of the 1984 Rates Act. The cap on Camden's spending was set at £117m, sixteen million short of Labour's planned expenditure in the coming financial year. The position of the Labour group was that they had decided what they were to spend, and so were simply unable to set a rate within the government's cap. In any event they did not know how it was that the government had arrived at the figure of £117m and so needed further information from the Department of the Environment before they could consider whether it was lawful.

In early February 1985, Phil Turner went to meet the Environment Secretary, Patrick Jenkin, with a delegation of leaders from other London boroughs threatened with being rate capped. They wanted an independent commission to look into local government finance. Jenkin was not helpful. Consequently, the rate capped authorities considered

---

26 Birtles was then the executive chairman of the National Campaign for Civil Liberties. His wife had been the general secretary of the NCCL, but had left to become Neil Kinnock's press secretary.

not setting a rate at all. If none of them did so, come 1 April they would all start to go broke and the government would have to step in and undertake the huge task of keeping council services running. And it would all be the Tories' fault. In any event, they declared somewhat hopefully, there was no piece of legislation that explicitly set out a duty to set a rate, in which case they would not be breaking the law.

At the end of the month the Labour Party organised a week of public meetings in protest against the Rates Act. The town hall staff went on a one day "Rate Cap Strike" to mark the TUC sponsored "Day of Action Against Rate Capping". The district auditor warned members against incurring extra expenditure through "wilful misconduct" on fear of being surcharged. His threats were on the back of Neil Kinnock's call to all Labour councillors to stick by their communities rather than break the law and risk disqualification. The Labour group met on 4 March to debate the chief executive's report advising that the rate had to be set by the end of May. Alan Woods and Julie Fitzgerald proposed that the council meet the government head on by bluntly refusing to set a rate "until the Rates Act is scrapped". Phil Turner faced "searing criticism of his leadership", especially from Woods who had already let the press know that he intended to stand for the leadership.[27] Turner, rather more cautiously, wanted to make sure there was a way out if things went wrong. He proposed that the council delay matters by claiming that as things stood a rate should not be set simply because Camden did not know exactly how the government had arrived at the figure of £117m. The ball could be thrown back into the government's court by demanding further and better particulars. A third group, the old moderates pushed aside by Turner three years before, were bluntly refusing to put their necks on the line. It was a bruising meeting and the group stood by their leader by 15 votes to 14 (he abstained in case he had to defend the policy he did not agree with).

In the meantime, the united front against the Rates Act collapsed when the GLC broke Labour ranks and, to the dismay of the left wingers, set a rate. Ken Livingstone who had campaigned against the Rates Act, had pledged that he would resist it to the end, safe in the knowledge that the Conservative opposition on the GLC would be joined by the right wingers in his Labour group and that a rate would

165

---

27 In January Woods had told the *Ham & High* that other councillors had asked him to stand. "I believe that we have got to have strong leadership in the coming months. There is an argument that we might have to have an election for leadership at a time of major crisis".

be set whichever way he voted. Alan Greengross, once the leader of the opposition on Camden and now the leader of the opposition on the GLC, called his bluff by announcing that the Conservatives were going to abstain instead. The result was that Livingstone and the other "defiers" would face surcharge and disqualification from public office if they continued along the path they had so noisily chosen. Livingstone could not afford that as he was already working on his parliamentary ambitions. At the last minute, he changed his mind. Charlie Rossi, the GLC member for Holborn & St Pancras, described Livingstone as "a spineless kipper". Livingstone's deputy, the hard line John McDonnell, resigned saying: "Ken and I may remain friends, but I'll never trust him again politically".[28]

The rate was due to be set at the March council meeting, but no one expected it to be. Public interest was such that Frank Nickson relocated the meeting from the council chamber to the much bigger Camden Centre at the back of the town hall. Thousands attended, spilling out into Bidborough Street where proceedings were relayed by loudspeakers. Confidence in the evening's outcome had produced something of a carnival atmosphere. In the council chamber two African dancing girls, clad only in bikinis, beads and grass skirts, gyrated to Lord Eric Agor Mmba's Sugumugu band. Phil Turner and Sandy Wynn, each holding a pole supporting a Labour Party banner, led their group in procession from the front entrance of the town hall on Judd Street and around the corner along Bidborough Street into the Camden Centre.

Tumultuous welcomes were given to deputations from the Caversham Nursery, the Tenants Against Rate Capping Organisation and the Camden Joint Trades Unions Steering Committee. The Mayor, Barbara Hughes, read out the long list of petitions received, with thousands of signatures. Phil Turner proposed the motion that the council should not set a rate. "This is a situation without precedent in English history", he said. The government was dictating what level of rates democratically elected local authorities could set. "There is a gap of £16m between what we consider should be spent and what Patrick Jenkin considers we can spend. In these circumstances therefore I am saying we cannot set a rate." At the end of his speech the crowd on the balcony broke into a chant of "The people / of Camden / united / will never be defeated!" After calling the Tories "a party of twits", Tom

166

28   Ken Livingstone gave a rather different account of this in his 1987 book *If voting changed anything they'd abolish it.* (Or, as Alan Greengross called it, *Mein Kenff.*)

Devine got the biggest cheer of the evening by shouting at the top of his voice: "No rate capping! Never ! Never! Never!"

The Conservative speakers were mercilessly heckled and shouted down, albeit mostly good humouredly as the outcome of the evening was not in doubt. Tory after Tory rose to point out that the council would have to give in and that it was madness to delay matters. When Alan Greengross rose to oppose the motion, a noose was lowered from the gallery. Martin Morton entered into the spirit of things: "There are more cracks in the Labour Party than the RAF inflicted on the Mohner Dam, and there are no bigger big damn moaners than Labour councillors faced with rate capping. Poor Old Phil Turner has marched his troops all the way up the hill only to have to march them down again." To cheers from the gallery, the council voted not to set a rate by 33 to 25.

As expected, the Conservatives, called an extraordinary meeting of the council at the very end of the month "to crack the nerve of the ruling Labour group". It became clear in the Labour group meeting on the Monday that the writing was on the wall. Roy Shaw announced that under no circumstances would he vote for the council to do anything illegal. Nine others took the same line. If they abstained, the Labour motion would be defeated. Alan Woods again proposed a hard line "no rate" option and again was beaten by 14 to 15 with Turner abstaining. Again it was agreed to toe the Turner line: no illegality yet, but to stall proceedings by claiming to declare the council "unable to set a rate pending negotiation and further information from the secretary of state".

On the night of the meeting "the public gallery –again full but not overflowing- perhaps sensing the inevitable defeat looming next month, abandoned the good humoured heckling of last month and poured a torrent of unpleasant abuse at every Conservative speaker". According to the *New Journal*, the crowd numbered 800: "The howling and foaming products of rent-a-mob" said Tory councillor Bill Trite.[29] Phil Turner again moved to defer setting a rate, this time because he was to meet Patrick Jenkin on 17 April, and so asked that a new council meeting be scheduled for a date not later than 25 April "to enable the matter to be considered in the light of circumstances then prevailing." To cheer those in the gallery he announced that "We have given the secretary of state a breathing space. We expect him to back down. If he does not back down, he is in confrontation with this council", and then added for good measure: "No cuts! Not next year or ever!"

167

---

29   Bill Trite, now a Purbeck District Councillor, was leader of Purbeck DC from 2000 – 2009.

"You are heading for a humiliating political defeat!" shouted Kerpel above the jeers from the Labour councillors and supporters. "You **will** set a legal rate, if not tonight then in a matter of days or weeks. The only question is whether you will crawl away from your defeat still holding the office of councillor or whether you crawl away from it disbarred from public office for five years".

The further adjournment allowed everyone to take stock of developments outside. Two more rebel councils, Lewisham and Haringey, voted to set rates in compliance with the act. Hackney was taken to the High Court and ordered to make a legal rate within six weeks. As far as Camden was concerned, the implication was that they were unlikely to be doing anything illegal if they kept pace with Hackney. The *New Journal* was supportive. Under the headline "Shattered Dreams" the front page was devoted to an account of how "Severely handicapped children in Camden are being denied a holiday because of the government's spending axe".

The next council meeting was set for the 24th April. The Labour group meeting that preceded it was presented with a paper prepared by Camden's director of finance, John Marlow. He showed that there were ways of reducing the £14m gap and of carrying the rest over as a deficit into the following year. This idea of carrying over, or "creative accounting", was seized upon by Roy Shaw and others as a way of avoiding both illegality and cuts. Andrew Bethell turned on Phil Turner and accused him of misleading them about the inevitability of cuts. The majority wanted to carry on not setting a rate. Feelings ran high. Ten Labour members led by Roy Shaw left the chamber with threats of expulsion and calls of "traitors" ringing in their ears. After a private consultation, they returned to say that they would not support the motion not to set a rate.

The council meeting was again held in the Camden Centre. Again, 800 attended. "It was packed but subdued", reported the *New Journal*. It had been agreed beforehand that only Phil Turner would speak for Labour. "The council cannot fight it out to the bitter end because a breakaway group among Labour members have withdrawn their support." There were shouts from the gallery of "Who are they?" and "They should resign!" The majority in the group, he explained, felt that they could not set a rate until the Rates Act was abolished and the rate support grant restored, and "the minority of the group consider we should do our best to maintain our programme during the coming year and fight to live another day".

The ten rebels sat apart and said nothing[30]. Kerpel was on form: "We are faced with a totally split Labour group. We have the nutters and the cowards. You plan to set a rate on May 15th. The only reason for delaying another three weeks is to knit a large enough white surrender flag and to cobble up the excuses for a humiliating defeat." Turner's reply was for the gallery: "The Tory verbiage was simply a smokescreen for the traditional Conservative solution to the deepening crisis of capitalism: renewed and savage attacks on the working class which Labour councillors are pledged to defend!" He was answered by the cheers of the 800. Again, the council failed to agree to set a rate.

Turner's immediate concern was not the Tories' savage attacks on the working class so much as his inability to control his own group. The Labour group meeting planned for the following Monday was preceded by a left wing caucus meeting to which Roy Shaw's rebels were not invited. The traitors were to be punished. On the Monday it was decided to strip those who chaired committees of their positions. And for good measure they did the same to Richard Sumray for "flirting" with the rebels. Turner wrote a long letter to the *Ham & High* setting out the position and was rewarded with a damning editorial: "He gives no explanation why he thought fit this week to attend a secret meeting of the hard left at which he stitched up a deal to save his own shame and position, a move which earned him the ephitet of 'puppet' from a colleague".

By the time the council next met on 15th May, another left wing Labour council, Sheffield, had made a rate. The mood of the 800 Labour supporters in the gallery of the Camden Centre had not changed. They dearly wanted no rate to be set, but the Labour group was in deadlock. Roy Shaw rose to propose a motion to set a rate to shouts of "scab" from the gallery. He was barracked throughout and was barely audible to those around him. Other councils had given in, he said. It was pointless to continue to defy the law. It was a difficult decision but one that had to be made. His motion was seconded by Bill Birtles whose short speech (apart from the phrase "it's political suicide") was entirely drowned out by shouting. Only one other councillor, David Neil-Smith, the "maverick Tory", voted with them.

The Conservatives then proposed to set a rate, and were defeated. Turner rose again to propose that the rate setting be deferred yet again.

169

---

30 They were Roy Shaw , Andrew Bethell, Bill Birtles, Mike Kirk, Mary Cane, Richard Stein, Julian Fulbrook, Hugh Bayley, Gill Green and Tessa Jowell.

He was seconded by Julie Fitzgerald who did so by introducing to the council to great cheers, ex-alderman Charlie Taylor for his part in defying the Tory council in the St Pancras rent strike of 1960. Eggs were thrown at the Tory benches, mostly wide of the mark, and Phil Turner's motion was also defeated. Roy Shaw rose again to seek to amend, but both the Tories and the Labour benches refused him an extension of time and the meeting ended in complete deadlock.

The *Ham & High* turned its ire on Tony Kerpel. Shaw's amendment, which was about to be moved when the time bell went could have put an end to the arguments and set a rate. Their editorial was headed: "Misguided Tories."

> "Mr Kerpel and his colleagues accepted political gain and so-called advantage before the good of the borough and it residents with a juvenile gesture that is not the tactical victory they claim but a disgrace. We have had enough of these silly posturings.
>
> "It means now that Roy Shaw, undoubtedly Camden's most respected politician, will have to walk the gangplank again to a chorus of jeers of 'scab' and 'traitor' in another attempt to set a rate and bring to a halt the council's loss of more than £150,000 a week in interest revenue alone.
>
> "He has the courage to do it. He has, after all, devoted his life to sensible local government, playing a vital role in Camden in some of its proudest years and, unlike many who pay lip service to democracy, fought for freedom as a tank officer.
>
> We sincerely hope he will be successful in bringing back home commonsense to Camden."[31]

It was a bit unfair as Kerpel had no idea what motion Roy Shaw had up his sleeve, and Roy Shaw had voted down all Conservative attempts to set a rate not only earlier that evening, but at the preceding three meetings as well. But the comment certainly reflected the sense of exasperation felt by many observers as the debate was drawn out into weeks and months with no progress.

The next rate setting meeting came on 5th June. It was also held in the Camden Centre although the crowd had dwindled down to a hard core of 400. Just before 11 o'clock a delegation of twenty supporters from Lambeth came in waving flags with the glad tidyings that Lambeth had again refused to set a rate. Some of the "no rate" demonstrators

---

31 Kerpel later asked Gerry Isaaman, the editor of the *Ham & High*, why he no longer attended council meetings himself. "Because it breaks my heart", was the reply.

managed to occupy the area set aside for Tory councillors and Julian Fulbrook, the new mayor, had great difficulty in keeping control. The meeting was adjourned to the council chamber where the security was better. As the councillors filed in, the crowd attempted to surge in behind them and there were a few minutes of pushing and shoving, and even fists flying, with the security staff.

The debate consisted of a long series of new amendments from the Tories and the Labour rebels. The rebels would not vote for any cuts, and the Tories insisted on setting not just a rate, but a budget as well. There were fourteen formal divisions. After the violence and the move to the council chamber, said the *Ham & High*: "the Tory resolve had by now clearly broken. Having begun by proposing major spending cuts and rejecting creative accounting, they now went for compromise in a series of defeated amendments, their leader Tony Kerpel admitting: 'these motions do not meet our objectives' ".

The group leaders could not negotiate. Turner loathed Kerpel and Kerpel loathed Turner. The Labour left wanted to challenge the government, and the Tory right wanted the left to be crushed by the government. There seemed no way out. "There were lunatics on both sides wanting to fight the good fight", said Alan Greengross. "Without compromising our principles, Roy Shaw knew and I knew that there was a council that needed running". Finally in a brief adjournment not long before 3am, the old guard took control. Greengross pulled Roy Shaw aside and said: "Look: you've got to bloody well set a rate and here's how you're going to do it." They scribbled a new amendment: "This council resolves to make the maximum rate permitted by law and to instruct the relevant committee and officers to take all necessary steps to put this into effect". It worked. Shaw's rebels voted with the Conservatives and at 3am after eight hours of the fifth council meeting, the fighting was over, by 34 votes to 23[32]. The councillors filed out to shouts of "traitors!" and "Judas!" from the public gallery. "It might mean defeat," said Hugh Bayley, "but it is better than letting the Tories take over the council".[33]

The Conservatives felt a sense of victory. Even if they had not got everything they wanted, the new legislation had left their enemies

---

[32]   The Labour rebels were Roy Shaw, Gill Green, Hugh Bayley, Bill Birtles, Andrew Bethell, Tessa Jowell, Richard Stein, Mike Kirk and Mary Cane.

[33]   Having married a lady from St Kitts in 1984, Hugh Bayley stood down from the council in 1986 to lecture in social policy at York University. Since 1992 he has been the MP for York.

humiliated and divided, and they had rubbed their noses in it. "I feel angry and annoyed and of course I feel a sense of betrayal", Phil Turner told the *New Journal* as he left the town hall. "We'll begin building the campaign against rate capping once again for next year", and then added, darkly: "But we have to ensure we create a Labour group that will see that campaign through to victory next time." Others were more forthright. "The rebels must be driven out of the Labour movement forever!" snarled Graham Shurety, adding that he was "ashamed to be in the Labour Party tonight". Tom Devine agreed and, it having been a long night, shouted across at Roy Shaw: "Don't think you can get away with your treachery!"

Within a fortnight, Kerpel resigned as leader of the opposition. His letter, ostensibly written to his group members was framed in the most insulting of terms and he gave a copy to all the local papers. He wrote:

> "The deep involvement in council work brought by group leadership has multiplied my exposure to the socialists and their co-opted mercenaries, and I have to say I feel soiled by contact with these people, many of whom have no business in public life.
>
> "I am not prepared to accept the loss of self respect entailed in sitting with these people, being forced to listen to their endless verbal garbage, and accepting defeat in committee and council on policies which sicken most ordinary people."

The *New Journal* was delighted: "Camden's Tory leader huffed out of his job with an extraordinary outburst this week –and slammed the door behind him". But it was the best way a leader of the opposition could go: he had just won the big match and had, as it turned out, walked off to play in a different league. Phil Turner shed no tears: "It has confirmed what many of us thought for months. The man has completely lost his marbles. His departure will not be lamented by us either personally or politically".[34]

Kerpel was replaced by deputy leader, the quieter Stephen Moon, a 39 year old industrial relations officer at the Building Employers' Association who lived on Gloucester Crescent. The *New Journal* liked the idea: "Wet to lead Camden Tories" read its headline: "In contrast to

---

34 No other leader of the opposition has since matched Tony Kerpel's stinging attacks on the leadership. Neil Fletcher describes him as "the most effective Tory figure I came across in Camden", summing him up as "waspish". He certainly managed to hurt. Roy Shaw, so often Kerpel's victim in council debate, and disapproving of Kerpel's national rather than municipal political interests, described him as "a bloody lightweight".

172

his predecessor Tony Kerpel's brawling, Moon fits into the gentlemanly style that has characterised Tory leadership in Camden."

John McDonnell, Livingstone's deputy at the GLC, and distinguished from Livingstone by being even more determined to follow a hard left agenda whatever the consequences, was out of the blue appointed by the council to fill the new post of principal policy advisor to the council on a salary of £20,500. This was, said the Conservatives, a clear case of jobs for the boys –a left wing council providing a job for a left winger who found himself unemployed and unlikely to get himself a proper job in the outside world. "His politics are so extreme that his appointment is an insult to Camden", said Moon. To Alan Greengross there was something laughable in appointing as a policy advisor "the one person at the GLC who, at budget time, proved he had no idea at all how to evolve or carry through any sort of policy". He was an "outstanding candidate", said Phil Turner.

Tony Kerpel was back in the news in January when he announced that he was to join the Department of the Environment as the "Special Adviser" to the Secretary of State, Kenneth Baker. One of his tasks would be to advise on the implementation of policies designed to curb the excesses of high spending Labour councils. "After twelve frustrating years of being in opposition in Camden putting up with all their nonsense, it'll be nice to know I'm going to be in a position to curb the antics of loony boroughs like Camden". His message to Labour was: "watch out, I've got my eye on you", said the New Journal. "It's jobs for the boys", said Tony Dykes.

As the 1986 borough elections approached, it was clear that the Tories were in trouble. The national polls were against them. In January 1986 Stephen Moon announced that he would be standing not as the candidate for the dangerously marginal South End ward which he represented, but for the safe Tory ward of Adelaide. Brian Rathbone, whose Monday Club views had left him somewhat isolated in the Conservative group, was deselected as a candidate in Bloomsbury and replaced by Martine Kushner, Stephen Moon's wife.

Rathbone no longer cared who disagreed with him. When the women's committee voted to provide premises for the Camden Lesbian Centre Project, he objected because it would obviously encourage lesbianism. "It is not a criminal offence and they can do it in their own homes or on premises for which they pay themselves, but I would not wish council premises to be used for that kind of thing". The howls of protest encouraged him further: "I am of course sorry for lesbians individually, as they are presumably unable to lead a normal life. However I do not believe that lesbianism should be encouraged".

The issue returned a few months later when the development control sub-committee allowed the change of use of a shop premises in Phoenix Road off Euston to house the lesbian club. Betty Wilson of the Ossulton Street Tenants Association and her supporters were ejected from the chamber for engaging in a noisy slanging match with their local councillor, Barbara Hughes. The lesbians, they pointed out, would be a menace to local schoolgirls. But when the Policy & Resources Committee voted to put up a new £129,000 advice unit to provide advice for gays and lesbians, it was too much even for Martin Morton. Council officers had prepared a report estimating that there were as many as 17,000 gays and lesbians in the borough (over 10% of the adult population) but that "most of them live their lives in secret". Martin Morton, the most unlikely of gay bashers, said rather mildly that he really was not convinced that there was a problem that required that sort of expenditure. "Whenever the word 'gay' is mentioned", said Kate Allen sharply, "the Tories have apoplexy".

In February 1986 the council agreed a new policy of banning all News International ("the Murdoch press") newspapers from the members' room and the borough's libraries. The leading proponent of this policy was Graham Good[35], the chairman of the leisure committee, who wanted to support those Camden residents caught up in "the historic struggle" at Wapping where pickets were, often violently, protesting against Rupert Murdoch's use of non unionised labour to produce the *Times* and the *Sun*, rather than the unionised print workers of Fleet Street. "As a committed trade unionist", said Good, "I can't metaphorically cross the picket lines and buy News International papers". News International launched a legal challenge in the High Court.

The Labour Party made an election issue of the Conservative government's plans for council housing. The "Right to Buy" legislation was not only "immoral" but was, they said, only a first step in the government's planned wholesale sell off of council estates to private companies interested only in profit. There were no such government plans, but the accusations were repeated again and again. Much was

---

35 Graham Good was a youth worker at the council funded Winchester Project ("the Winch") based in a converted pub on Winchester Road, Swiss Cottage.

done through letters to the press written by supposedly unattached members of the public pointing out that the Tory Housing and Planning Bill would result in whole council blocks being sold to developers to house greedy yuppies.

The Camden Tory manifesto for the 1986 election predictably concentrated on Labour's wasteful spending. They would abolish all those newly created committees for women, race and police, impose a freeze on town hall recruiting and raise money by selling commercial property. But to many none of that mattered while the suspicion remained that the Tories were considering selling off the estates. Defensively, but wholly unnecessarily, the manifesto included the words: "where tenants agree we'll transfer council estates or parts of them to housing associations or co-operatives –not to private landlords." But denials of the hidden plan were not enough. "They clearly believe, like Dr Goebbels, that if they repeat it often enough some tenants might believe them", said Moon.

The Camden Labour manifesto confidently repeated the successful theme of past years: "No cuts in jobs or services". £5.6m was pledged to voluntary organisations in the coming year as extra help was needed for those organisations in the borough that had previously relied on GLC grants. Frank Dobson endorsed the local party's efforts: "Having Labour in power here will make it easier for the next Labour government to bring in policies to fight poverty and unemployment", he said. There was a homelessness crisis and one person in six was unemployed. "The question is", said Turner, "which party is most likely to defend services? There can only be one answer".

At the last council meeting, in March 1986, the rate was set at a cautious 1% rise (to £227.92 in the pound) which was all the government's cap allowed, leaving the council with a budget of £133m. The problem was that the council's own budget exceeded that by £30m and, notwithstanding the creative accounting, still left it £9m short of its expenditure plans for the coming year. Phil Turner reaffirmed his pledge that there would be no cuts in jobs or services. "When capitalism is in crisis as it is now", he told the council, "the Tories attack the standards of living and spending on services to working people". He then proposed what the *Ham & High* described as "a blatant self congratulatory piece of propaganda" noting "with pride" the expansion and improvement in council services over the last four years. Over a thousand new jobs had been created within the council, services had been expanded by 20% and eight thousand households had been rehoused. Alan Greengross, standing in for Stephen Moon who was at this critical juncture in a hospital bed suffering from angina, saw things differently: "Camden has got through £500 million since this Labour administration took over and has achieved absolutely nothing". He then challenged Phil Turner to find a single council tenant prepared to say that he was satisfied with his council housing. "We need another Labour council in Camden like we need a hole in the head."

The meeting was brought to a standstill by two hundred council tenants who began a noisy protest when their spokesman, Alf Barrett of the Tybalds Close Tenants Association, was refused permission to speak. The mayor, the very reasonable Julian Fulbrook, suspended the meeting for five minutes, during which time the chamber was treated to a football chant of "Labour out – Tories in!" and a hearty rendition of "Land of Hope and Glory" by a boisterous gallery. Alf Barrett was then allowed to speak, so long as a spokeswoman for the CCCR could reply. The council's race relations policy, he said, placed ethnic minorities on a pedestal. "All we hear about is the amount of racism in the borough" while local people suffered prejudice in getting a council home. The protestors were racists, answered Jay Ugoala of the CCCR, and were "helping the spread of racialism". Phil Turner agreed: "I hope you're proud of what you just said", he shouted at Barrett, and added that the council "had no intention of changing its policy towards priority groups".[36]

Although the New Journal had reported the council election campaign in early April as being "the toughest poll battle", all doubt about the outcome had evaporated by polling day. The polls nationally and in London, where the abolition of the GLC was especially resented, showed the Conservatives far behind Labour. By the end of the month, under the headline "Labour set for bigger majority", the New Journal accurately reported that the Tories were concentrating on damage limitation. "The last four years of Camden have been the worst, a period of bitter internecine wrangling coupled with the inability to spend money wisely, control staff, fill empty houses, repair pot holes and broken pavements and much else", declared the Ham & High, but "The Tories are onto a hiding to nothing. And they know it."

So confident were the more experienced Labour councillors that their minds turned from thoughts of winning the council election to

---

36 Alf Barrett died in 1990 aged only 60. He was held in such affection that his name was chosen by the tenants association for the Alf Barrett Playground which was opened in 1995 on Old Gloucester Street.

thoughts of winning the leadership election. Now that Phil Turner had been chosen as the Labour parliamentary candidate for the Hampstead constituency (albeit narrowly, by 42 votes to 32 over the determined Kate Allen), he needed to concentrate on the campaign ahead. In particular, he needed to show the confidence exhibited by Geoffrey Finsberg in 1970 when he stood down as leader. Turner announced his resignation. He had good reason to be confident. The MORI poll commissioned by the *Guardian* in January 1986 predicted that in the event of a general election, Phil Turner would win Hampstead with 42% of the vote with the Alliance taking 32%. Finsberg, suggested the poll, would come in third with the remaining 26%.

The hard left caucus, which met in Angela Birtill's house, agreed that Kate Allen should be leader of the council and that her two deputies would be John Wakeham and Sandra Plummer. The broad left caucus met to agree that their two candidates for leadership would be Tony Dykes and Alan Woods, the understanding being that should they both stand, the loser's votes would be transferred to the winner so that whatever happened they would have the satisfaction of stopping Kate Allen. The difference between the two groups, the *New Journal* helpfully told its readers, was that the hard left wanted to take on the government, whereas the broad left wanted to take on the town hall unions.

7 |

Tony Dykes: left and far left

"WE'RE BACK" ran the headline on the *New Journal*, reporting a massive Labour victory. The new Camden council had 44 Labour councillors, 13 Conservative and, for the first time, two Liberal SDP Alliance councillors. It was the worst result for the Conservatives since their defeat in 1971. The *Ham & High* relegated the story about the council election to page seven and ran the news under a headline "The foregone conclusion". The Tories were "sunk" said the *New Journal* (who liked the *Belgrano* metaphor) by "the Maggie Factor". The turnout was high, 47%. Of those who had voted, 52% had voted for Labour, 28% Conservative and 20% Alliance. There had been an 11% swing.

Phil Turner was delighted: "It was an excellent result", he told the *Chronicle*, "and a resounding endorsement of our policies over the last four years. It was also a positive vote for our plans for the next four years". The Conservative agent, Peter Golds, offered a different analysis: there was an anti-government backlash, a higher than usual turnout of Labour supporters and determined canvassing concentrating on national issues. On top of that, he said, Conservative voters, not all of whom liked Mrs Thatcher, stayed at home. If only people had voted on local issues, said Stephen Moon, the outcome would have been very different.

The Tories had lost half their seats. Martin Morton, by far the best known name among the Conservatives, crashed out of Highgate[1]. Bob Graham lost by fifteen votes in Swiss Cottage and Ken Avery lost by three

---

1   Morton's distinguished career on the council came to a humiliating end. He polled more than 500 votes fewer than the last Labour candidate, and on their results page the *Ham & High* misspelt his name as Merton.

1986 - 1990

votes in Brunswick. The latter result was particularly galling as Avery had stopped knocking up likely voters so that he could help out in nearby Bloomsbury where he felt the Conservatives needed more assistance than he did. He was right in that they lost their seats in Bloomsbury as well, leaving Peter Skolar the only Conservative councillor outside the old Hampstead borough boundary. The only ward in which the Labour vote did not increase was Holborn where Alf Barrett, the disgruntled tenants' representative, beat the Conservatives into second place.[2]

In neighbouring Islington, no Conservatives were elected, and the Liberal–SDP Alliance formed the opposition with sixteen councillors. In Camden their candidates had performed respectably, but not well. Their target ward in Regents Park was easily held by Labour once the best SDP campaigner in the south of the borough, Ken Workman, had pulled out because he was moving house. But they did meet with better success in the north where their only success came not against Labour, but against the Conservatives in Fortune Green where Flick Rea, the local housewife with local issues, won on her third attempt against a declining Tory vote[3]. With her was a young solicitor, Roger Billins, an experienced campaigner who had stood in Hampstead for the GLC, Kilburn for Camden council and Brent South in the General election.

On the front page of the *New Journal* was a picture of Nirmal Roy, a small bespectacled Indian, with the caption "Nirmal Roy –one of Labour's three black councillors".[4] The description drew an angry letter from a Mr Sunil Kumar Pal of Abbey Road. "I also come from India", he wrote. "If anyone identifies me as black I know that that person is a racist". Blacks were blacks and Indians were Indians. Nirmal Roy was even angrier than Mr Pal had been in the first place. "I am black", he insisted, and Mr Pal was guilty of "outrageous ethnocentricity and divisive presumptions".

The Inner London Education Authority (ILEA) survived the wreck of the GLC and held its only direct elections at the same time as the borough elections. In Camden, the two parliamentary constituencies each returned two members. The SDP and the Liberal Party agreed to put up one candidate in each seat so as to share the vote. Labour won

---

2   The Conservatives missed a chance here. The combined Barrett/Conservative vote easily outnumbered those cast for Labour. They may well have taken at least one seat in Holborn had they got Alf Barratt to stand for them in place of one of their two inept and inexperienced candidates, Peter Smaill and Piers Wauchope.

3   She had managed 514 votes in the 1980 by election in Fortune Green, and 649 votes in 1982. Her winning score in 1986 was 677 (which gave her a majority of 99).

4   The other two were Satnam Gill and Jerry Williams.

with comparative ease, Neil Fletcher topped the poll in Holborn & St Pancras over 10,000 votes ahead of the leading Tory, the *Sunday Express* columnist, Lady Olga Maitland. In each case the Tories came second, narrowly ahead of the Liberal-SDP candidate.

At Camden, the planned election of a broad left candidate for the leadership of the Labour group did not run smoothly. The hard left of the group called a Saturday meeting of not only the new councillors but also the party's Local Government Committee of activists where a vote was taken to choose a new leader. With the assistance of the activists' votes, Kate Allen was elected by a majority of one (38 votes to 37). "The joint group/party meeting was a democratic process", she told the press, "-the most democratic yet employed within the party." Wholly unsurprisingly, her triumph was short lived once the Regional Labour Party became involved. It had been an unconstitutional coup. A second ballot was ordered for the following Monday in which only Labour councillors could vote. Tony Dykes won by 24 to 19 votes. "I deplore", said Miss Allen, "the decision of a narrow majority of the Labour group to ignore the views of the Labour Party".

Tony Dykes, the son of a slaughterman, was then a thirty five year old Liverpudlian who advertised the fact by wearing an Everton Football Club shirt to council meetings. He had passed through grammar school, Lanchester Poly in Coventry for a BA in social studies and a further education course, and now worked in Islington for the World University Service, "an educational charity working for refugees". The *New Journal* described him as being "one of the polytechnic tendency". Dykes was at pains to say that he was not the right wing candidate and emphasised the strong influence the Nicaraguan Sandinista government had over his politics.

The first meeting of the new council was somewhat enlivened by the presence of half a dozen National Front supporters who, angered by an eviction in Holborn, threw insults and eggs from the gallery, roughed up a hapless bystander who had tried to stop them and made a noisy exit. After they had gone, Tony Dykes proposed and had unanimous cross party support for an emergency motion condemning such people and their behaviour.[5] The council then heard from Penny Abraham of ALARM (Alert London Against Radioactive Material) who led a delegation of

---

5   The egg stains were visible on the carpet for the next six years.

concerned groups (Friends of the Earth, CND and Teachers for Peace) in support of the council's adoption of the new anti nuclear power policy proposed by Graham Good. The Liberal and Labour members voted to express their disapproval of both the use of nuclear power (which then generated 17% of the nation's electricity), and of any trains that may carry nuclear waste through the borough.

Tony Dykes's biggest decision in the first few weeks of the new council also turned out to be the one that would cause Camden the most trouble. Since the Conservative government that had prevented socialists from behaving like socialists by rate capping them, the Labour Party had searched for ways around the problem. Two other Labour councils, Ealing and Hammersmith & Fulham, had set up an ingenious method of borrowing large sums of money. They had entered into arrangements with banks whereby the banks would pay for capital projects so freeing up money for the councils to spend as they chose. Hammersmith had been advised in their financial adventure by Camden's director of finance, John Marlow, and Camden's principal policy advisor, John McDonnell.

In July the Policy & Resources Executive sub-Committee approved Camden's own loan with the Banque Paribas. The loan was for £100m. There were to be no repayments for the first four years and after that the council would pay off the debt over a further ten years. Tony Dykes accepted there were risks. If interest rates were running at 10% (as they then were) the total repayments would be in the region of £200m, and so, he said, the council required some sort of a guarantee from a future Labour government that the council would be protected. "We will have a contractual obligation to pay back the loan, and also to continue funding services and jobs. There could be a crunch". An unattributed (and, frankly, implausible) Labour Party source at Transport House was quoted in the *Ham & High* as saying that the leadership of the Labour Party nationally had given the required guarantee that a future Labour government would make good the debt. The words used were: "Every local authority in the country will find their coffers replenished". The loan, Dykes added cheerfully, will enable the borough to freeze council rents for the third year running. The council has to borrow in this way, said Julie Fitzgerald, to get round the government's "stupid legislation". John Marlow, with the authority of *Old Moore's Almanack*, told the press that the cost of the loan would be £167m.

Others were less sure. The deputy chief executive, David Riddle, described the move as "inherently risky". It was "an unwise decision", said Stephen Moon. Tony Dykes was putting Camden into pawn and throwing away the ticket, said Sir Alan Greengross[6] in the council debate. "The Labour Party sticks its head in the sand and hopes reality will go away. But you will need two miracles. First you will need a Labour government –a remote possibility at the best of times- and secondly that Labour government will not merely have to absolve Camden council from anything it has done, it must pay your debts for you." He had hit a raw nerve. Tony Dykes disagreed, rather strongly: "Crap, crap, crap", he replied. "It's a load of shit! The Tories do not give a damn about defending jobs and services for people in Camden".

On the shoulders of their election success, the Labour group decided to invite Sinn Fein to send a spokesman to address the council at its October meeting. The proposal, which was backed by Tony Dykes and Phil Turner, caused division within the Labour group and from the beginning nine councillors announced that they would boycott the meeting.[7] Amongst them was Roy Shaw, who said that he was not going to listen unless they condemned the continuing senseless violence in Northern Ireland. The newly elected Ken Hulme wanted to invite representatives from the SDLP and the Northern Irish trade unions rather than have "the right wing nationalists of Sinn Fein" give "a promo for the Provos".

The build up in the press was predictable. The Tories were against inviting Sinn Fein, but Stephen Moon challenged them to a public debate. It did not happen. On the night the Liberals invited the SDLP MP Seamus Mallon to a meeting in the Town Hall which was attended by two Labour councillors, Gareth Smyth and Ken Hulme. Nine Labour councillors boycotted the council meeting. Tony Dykes, who had started the ball rolling, was on holiday in Amalfi. Outside, five placard holding Sinn Fein supporters stood somewhat exposed with their backs to the town hall under the watchful eye of the police. On the other side of the road a larger group stood bellowing insults through a megaphone

183

---

6   He had just been knighted in the Queen's birthday honours list for services to local
     government as leader of the opposition on the GLC. There was to be no Sir Ken.
     "Basically, the honours system is a bit of a joke", said Livingstone, "I'd abolish it".

7   Bill Budd, Maggie Cosin, Pat Denny, Ben Griffith, Ken Hulme, Nicola Kutapan, Roy Shaw,
     Gareth Smyth and Jerry Williams.

under a banner which read DEATH TO I.R.A. MURDERING SCUM. The Sinn Fein spokesman, Pat Treanor, a Monaghan councillor with a criminal conviction for IRA membership, was invited by the mayor to address the chamber. Stephen Moon proposed a motion to stop him being heard, but was voted down by the twenty five Labour members present. At this the Tories walked out, followed, after a hurried consultation, by the two Liberals. One of the Labour dissidents, Maggie Cosin, held her own meeting on the steps of the Town Hall where she told the press that Sinn Fein was "anti working class" for putting people on the dole and "opposing many of Camden's policies on abortion, divorce and gay and lesbian rights". Inside the chamber, Pat Treanor read out a five minute speech calling for British troops to be withdrawn from Northern Ireland. There were no questions, and no debate. In the absence of any opposition (other than Flick Rea and Roger Billins who had returned to occupy the Tory benches) the rest of the council business was over in three minutes and the council rose at 7.25pm. Meanwhile, as Dykes was away, Pat Treanor was whisked off to the leader's office where the council's principal policy advisor and well known Sinn Fein enthusiast, John McDonnell, hosted a press conference.

What had been billed as a major political event proved a damp squib. There had been no debate, just Mr Treanor's statement, the contents of which were reported nowhere. Not only had Dykes not been there, he had made himself look foolish by forcing the decision on the Labour group without thinking through the consequences. He had recently won the leadership election by only four votes, and now he had seriously harmed his reputation with at least nine of the councillors who had voted for him. "What happened last week in Camden", groaned the *Ham & High*, "was another malignant example of the Labour Party tearing itself to pieces without significant cause, making a puerile political gesture, instead of, as it believed, a big bang. For sheer political incompetence, let alone anything else, it takes your breath away".

The pledge to expand services was also going to prove difficult. The leadership planned to spend £200m in the coming year, which was £60m over the rate cap, and the workforce was to reach 8,588 in 1987, an increase of over two thousand since 1982. The council's difficult financial position was no secret, especially after details of a special meeting of Labour councillors addressed by Dykes and Julie Fitzgerald were leaked in November. The leadership had put all their eggs in one basket. They needed a Labour win in the coming general election and they needed a pledge from the national party that a future

Labour government would bail them out. "If a Labour government is elected and abolishes rate capping without assisting Camden financially, we would need to levy an average rate increase of £5 per week [£260 p.a.] in the year prior to our next local elections".

Despite the coming financial squeeze, there were still plenty of demands for extra spending. In October 1986, the Race & Community Relations Committee allocated £225,000 to appoint two racial harassment officers to tackle town hall racism, and to distribute cash to community groups to tackle racial harassment outside. Later in the month the committee approved the setting up of a £100,000 pool to fund anti-apartheid initiatives organised by groups based in the borough, and the Policy & Resources Committee agreed to boycott twenty five firms with significant South African links.

The expectations of minority group activists ran high. Not satisfied with the seven co-opted places (with full voting rights) on the council's race and women's committees, the CCCR demanded black representation on all council committees because, said Yvonne Joseph, the acting community relations officer, "black interests are being marginalised". Dykes said that he agreed in principle, but did nothing. Julian Tobin described it as "the most racist notion I have heard". Seven workers in the housing department's own race relations unit accused the council in a letter of using "racist delaying tactics" because of a two year delay in implementing a plan to expand their unit. They were supported by the CCCR and AFRICA (African Families Resident in Camden). "Had we been white officers", they wrote, "we would have been treated differently". When it was suggested that the "Housing Department Race Relations Unit Seven" might be disciplined for accusing their employers of being racist, the whole department went on strike.

The Roundhouse "Black Arts" project had rather fallen apart a couple of weeks before the 1986 election. In its dying moments, the GLC had bequeathed £8m to Camden for the scheme. Other boroughs challenged the payment and the House of Lords ruled it unlawful. The cash should instead be transferred to the London Residuary Body to be more widely distributed throughout the 32 London boroughs. "it is a great pity that a project of this importance to the black community should be part of a political football game", said Camden's lead member on the board of the Roundhouse Trust, Richard Sumray, giving it one last kick. Now, post election, the council put all its hopes on a "scaled down" £1m option which relied on a grant of £250k from the Arts Council. Having paid out £330k three years before, Camden was still left with

185

an annual bill of £60k for security a remaining deficit of £270k, and the Roundhouse stood derelict. Sumray warned that the whole project was in danger. His fears were answered by Remi Kapo, the project's coordinator: "If this had been a white project they wouldn't have had to wait three years to launch it". Kapo then sacked three employees for whom, he said, there was not enough work, and they noisily complained that he had sacked them because they had reported him for sexually harassing them.

After being regaled with a rendition of the catchy *Free-ee Nelson Mandela* by a deputation from the City of London Anti-Apartheid Group, the November 1986 council meeting agreed to create an eleven member Gay & Lesbian Committee. The Gay & Lesbian Unit was to employ eight council officers at a total cost of some £250,000 a year. Pointing out that there was now a £10m overspend not covered by "creative accounting" measures, Stephen Moon described this as "a criminal waste of resources". Not so, said Tony Dykes. "Gay men and lesbians have said if we are to combat the discrimination they face because of their sexual orientation, we need a unit and we need a committee". The Labour whip had a difficult time. Ten Labour members refused to come into the chamber for the division and the proposal was passed by only nine votes.[8]

The council's ban on "all Murdoch's newspapers" lasted until November 1986. The council action was justified said Dykes, who had approved a grant of £4,600 to the Camden Printworkers Support Group to assist their "historic struggle", because "News International has thrown hundreds of Camden residents out of work" by moving to Wapping with non-unionised labour. The High Court disagreed, set aside the ban as being "*ultra vires* and void" and awarded costs against the council.

The financial situation worsened. Also in November, the council was warned by the district auditor, Brian Skinner, over the failure to collect over £7m arrears of rent and a further £2.4m from the DHSS in bed and breakfast payments for the homeless. The national Labour Party had still not issued a statement to bail out those local authorities who had incurred debts to keep their socialist programmes alive. A confidential report from Dykes and Julie Fitzgerald to a special meeting

---

8   1986 was also the year in which Camden held an anti-racist and anti-sexist version of the pantomime *Aladdin* in the council funded Shaw Theatre. A black actor, Norman Beaton (who even then was old enough to play Aladdin's grandfather), played an Aladdin who donates his massive fortune to the city of Peking.

of Labour councillors in November 1986 made the position clear. "If a Labour government is elected and abolishes rate capping without assisting Camden financially, we would need to levy an average rate increase of £5 per week in the year prior to the next local elections". The current plans were to spend £200m in the coming year, which was £64m above the rate cap, and to increase the workforce to 8,588 council employees. (There were 6,577 in 1982.) "I do not accept the word blackmail", said Dykes, but then instructed John McDonnell to write to Jack Cunningham (then of the National Executive's Local Government Advisory Committee) to demand that he set out his plans for bailing out London councils or else face "a major backlash" from the membership.

Over the Christmas break in 1986, Stephen Moon resigned as leader of the opposition, citing work commitments and poor health. The Tories looked around for a replacement. The old guard, Tobin and Greengross, declined. The bluff Dr Peter Skolar, the no nonsense local GP who shared a precarious seat in Bloomsbury with Labour, stepped into the breach. Born in Brunswick ward, Cambridge educated, he had run a surgery in Brunswick for the last seventeen years. "The doctor who wants to cure Camden's ills", as the *Chronicle* described him: "His bluntness is his great strength". [9]

187

By January 1987, the council's plans for the coming financial year were in disarray. The planned expenditure had been for £64m more than could legally be raised on the rates, but new housing subsidy arrangements had since pushed the gap up to £72m. Each department was instructed to find savings that could be approved by the leadership. The result was amended spending plans which had been, somewhat modestly, reduced from £198m to £190m, still £54m over the cap of £136m. It was, said Alan Greengross, "the economics of the bucket shop. Labour in Camden is building a debt mountain for future generations which makes the EEC mountains look like sandcastles. I hate government interference but the lunatic left in Camden is not only asking for it, but apparently craving it." "We remain committed to defending and improving jobs and services", said Dykes. "The alternative is unthinkable".

---

9   Fed up with the Thatcher government, the *Ham & High* was less interested. Its first editorial of 1987 read: "All that augurs well on the horizon of 1987 is its decisive defeat. There's a provocative thought. Happy New Year."

Never mind the common front against the dreadful Thatcher government, the Camden Labour group continued to tear itself apart. The inaugural meeting of the new Police Consultative Group was held in the first week of January. It was to include local politicians, representatives of local organisations and, of course, the police. The idea was that people could express their views on policing policy directly to those responsible for carrying it out. The Labour Party had pledged in its manifesto to take part in the scheme for a trial twelve month period. It was not an idea that found universal favour within the group. Adrian States, who was the vice chairman of the council's police committee (to whose meetings the police were not invited), called for a boycott and mass picket of the meeting. "Many black groups and women's, gay and lesbian groups are against it," he said, and that, as the Labour group had agreed to go along with the project in December 2005, the twelve months was now up. Kate Allen agreed. Support for the consultative group was, she said, "a real mistake".

When the meeting took place, it was heavily picketed by council workers belonging to NALGO, the Camden Black Workers Group, Black Women for Wages for Housework, Wages Due Lesbians, the English Collective of Prostitutes, the King's Cross Women's Centre, and the CCCR. Three Labour councillors pushed their way through the crush to chants of "no collaboration" and "rubber necklace". Barbara Hughes (who was elected chairman of the Police Consultative Group that night) and Ken Hulme complained of being assaulted. Less convincingly, the demonstrators claimed that Hulme had assaulted them. Bob Latham and Ken Hulme reported three senior council officers for blocking their way.[10] "It was a deliberate attempt to stop elected members carrying out a manifesto commitment", said Ken Hulme, demanding disciplinary action be taken against the offenders. Geoffrey Finsberg was not there, he had been invited to the meeting. He was delighted. It was, he said, "a perfect example of what happens when the Labour Party lets the evil spirit out of the bottle" and promised to turn up at future meetings, commitments permitting.

The unions were not happy and called a meeting in February to be addressed by the campaigning journalist Paul Foot. Representatives of many of the community groups funded by Camden attended. Protestors stood outside holding placards listing police crimes and

---

10   The three named were Johanna Fawkes of the public relations department, Judy Watson, who headed the Women's Unit, and Azim Hajee of the Camden Law Centre.

the names of people said to have been murdered by the police. "The decision by the council to take part in the police consultative group", said Nina Lopez of the King's Cross Women's Centre, "is tantamount to condoning the rape, assault and murder of black people and women by the police".

The following month, February 1987, the Labour group considered Angie Birtill's motion to withdraw any disciplinary proceedings against the council officers who took part in the picket. The complaint, she said, brought by the two "clowns", Latham and Hulme, amounted to "victimisation of union members". There was something of a compromise: the group passed her motion by 21-17, but also agreed by the same majority to continue for the time being in the police consultative group. They then voted not even to discuss Bob Latham's motion to remove Adrian States from the council's police committee. The success of Angie Birtill's motion was, said Roy Shaw "a serious blow to the management of the council's services". Feeling bound by the political decision, Frank Nickson took no action against the pickets[11].

Finance was still the main worry. The papers printed a series of leaked reports from Labour councillors back to their constituency or ward committees. John Wakeham, now firmly in the anti-Dykes faction, described the council's finances as a "leaking pool" and that the urgent task was not to put more funds into the pool but to stop the leaks: "We have too many chief officers and too many separate departments and committees", was his analysis. Ben Griffith concluded that "everyone recognises that whatever happens at the next election, Camden will not be bailed out –so someone will have to pay, maybe our ratepayers many of whom are real working class people". Bob Latham attacked the council's mismanagement pointing out that there had been a 63% increase in the housing budget over the last four years but rents had only been increased by £1 which "blunts any accountability to tenants". Roy Shaw's view was that "we have far too many inexperienced members who find themselves in positions of authority with no training and no experience in managing, or rather, managing the managers".

The council's woes piled up. In February, the Audit Commission issued a critical report on how certain Labour run London boroughs (Brent, Camden, Hackney, Haringey and Islington) were spending more

189

---

11   The second meeting of the police consultative group was held in May. To ensure security, it was held in the marriage room in the town hall. Only ten members of the public made it past the demonstrators.

than other councils, but were less efficient and often provided worse services. They employed twice as many staff per local resident as the most deprived boroughs, and a third more than other London authorities. They suffered difficulty in recruiting and retaining senior staff. In Camden, the report noted, 69% of senior officers had left in the three years up to the end of 1986. Council rents were lower but arrears were three times higher than in other boroughs. Refuse collection, children in residential care and vehicle maintenance all cost more, but with results no better than in other boroughs. An angry Tony Dykes wrote to the controller of the Audit Commission pointing out that he considered the report to be "unbalanced, inaccurate and misleading –the truth is that a great deal is being achieved against enormous odds".

Almost by way of reply, the district auditor, Brian Skinner, issued yet another damning report on the council's financial difficulties, interpreted by the *Ham & High* as "Camden is on the road to ruin." "The purpose of this report is to underline the extremely serious situation the council faces", he wrote. "The council is putting seriously at risk its ability to meet the future financial demands which will inevitably be placed upon it". He also disapproved of the council's plans to raise money by selling property and equipment and then leasing them back. This, he wrote, "is not a conventional transaction in local government". But the council had committed itself. By the end of the financial year, Camden had raised a total of £23m in somewhat desperate circumstances. Funds were raised through the deferred purchase scheme, and by selling and leasing back the freeholds of four office blocks, a million library books, and thousands of parking meters and street lamps.

In March 1987 the council set its rate. It went up by a mere 1.7% (which added £13 to an average annual rates bill), as much as the government's rate cap allowed. Julie Fitzgerald announced to jeers from the opposition that "the council's finances are safe in our hands". Skolar replied that the ratepayers should thank their lucky stars that there was a rate cap as the £56m overspend would otherwise have generated a 43% rate increase.

The Conservatives had hoped to discuss the state of Camden further in a motion of no confidence in the Labour leadership. Such were the divisions in the Labour group, and so vulnerable was the leadership to criticism from within, that Tony Dykes took the unprecedented step of deciding beforehand that the mayor should not allow a debate on the motion. Mary Cane, the mayor, was told instead move straight to a vote, thereby preventing both the Conservatives and any disaffected

Labour members from making their points. On the night, the mayor forgot her instructions and called a proposer for the motion. Alan Woods, the chief whip, leapt to his feet: "You have made a mistake! I challenge your ruling!" he shouted at her. "You, like me, are subject to the ruling of the Labour group!" The historic procedures of the Labour movement, he said, overrode the council's own standing orders. Mary Cane obediently called for an immediate vote, which of course the Conservatives lost, although not before Stephen Moon had shouted out across the table to Woods: "Your squalid behaviour on behalf of your group is the reason why democracy has failed in the chambers of local authorities around London".

The future did not look rosy. When Neil Kinnock's campaign manager, Bryan Gould, came to address an audience in the borough he was ambushed by the *Ham & High*. He was forced to confirm that a future Labour government would not bail out Camden whose actions, he intimated, were something of an embarrassment. The national party, he said, were informally warning Camden "to be aware of the effect of their actions on the national stage".

In April, in a move without precedent, the homeless persons unit closed its doors for a month in order to clear its unmanageable backlog. "Homelessness is worse than anything we've seen in forty years", explained Steve Bevington, the new housing chairman. Last year the unit had been approached by ten thousand people. The council had put over 1,200 applicants into bed and breakfast and 500 others into temporary accommodation elsewhere. There was no sympathy from Skolar: "It serves them damn well right", he said. "Camden is now renowned for taking on anybody. The borough is a soft touch and people are coming from all over the world to be rehoused".

191

In the run up to the 1987 general election, Phil Turner found photo opportunities everywhere: Launching a recycling campaign, campaigning (as Finsberg once had, before being accused of "Imperialism" by Whitaker) for the transfer of Hampstead Heath to Camden, and sombrely putting a ballot paper in a dummy ballot box for the Anti Apartheid Movement's "Vote Mandela Campaign". The election campaign started with the Conservative candidate for Holborn & St Pancras, the young Peter Luff, announcing that he had found an "obscene" leaflet starkly entitled "Sex" in one of Camden's libraries. It was written "in uncompromisingly idiomatic language with explicit cartoons of homosexual acts". The leaflet had been published by the Terrance Higgins Trust who had placed copies in Camden's libraries where it would be found by those gay people who do not go to the pubs and clubs where the leaflet is otherwise available. "It was an affront to normal decency and to normal people", Peter Skolar said. Mr Luff told the press that he was "terrified" that it would fall into the hands of innocent children, and so had referred the matter to the Director of Public Prosecutions. Frank Dobson was disapproving. Candidates should not make political capital out of AIDS: "If Mr Luff was interested in the issues rather than a cheapjack stunt he should've approached the council", he said. (The *Ham & High* was against him on that: "Come on Frank. You can do better than that", read the editorial.)

Just as the general election was announced for 11th June, the Somers Town by election took place to replace Tom Devine, who had died in March, aged only sixty. Labour's Caroline Holding, a community project worker, won it but with a 17% swing to the Alliance which, said the Tories hopefully, made Dobson's seat a marginal. (The Alliance candidate, Betty Wilson, had out-Toried the Tories by making strong statements on housing the homeless from outside the borough. She was the same Betty Wilson who eighteen months before had made a name for herself by objecting to a lesbian centre in Euston on the ground that the lesbians might interfere with local school girls.)

In the Labour group annual meeting in May, John Wakeham stood against Dykes for the leadership (and lost 38-4) and for the vacant chair of the Policy & Resources Committee where he was beaten by the surprising choice of a new councillor, Satnam Gill. Alan Woods remained chief whip, and Kate Allen was elected to chair the staff committee. Sandra Plummer, a mother of one but now openly lesbian, was elected to chair the new Gay and Lesbian Committee. Adrian States was kicked off the police committee.

Also in May 1987 was the leadership election for the Inner London Education Authority. Neil Fletcher won by a single vote, defeating the "autocratic and remote" Frances Morrell under whose leadership "we were firing on one cylinder", he said. "My first priority is to rebuild our present industrial relations shambles. I like working with unions."

The council announced a raft of "creative accounting" measures to cover the £56m budget gap between anticipated income and expenditure. Labour members reluctantly, for the first time in four years, raised council rents in line with inflation to raise £2½m.[12] There was, said the deputy chief executive, David Riddle, an acute threat of government intervention: the council's property sell-offs had ground to a halt, the market was cold and there was "an acute threat" of government intervention. Having received a better offer from Welwyn Hatfield District Council, he then handed in his notice, telling the press that "the future in Camden is bleak".

Everyone was in full general election mode during the May council meeting, and the Tories made the most of the council's financial discomfort. "Let me make it absolutely clear," bellowed Skolar, "There is not, I repeat not, going to be a Labour government coming to your rescue like the Seventh Cavalry. It's going to be more like Custer's last stand!" Greengross was no kinder: "You've already taken Camden to the pawnbroker's and now all you can offer is to take the borough to the liquidator's. Looking at your faces! I can see that you know it! You're down the drain and you're taking Camden with you and you ought to be ashamed of yourselves!"

In the marginal seat of Hampstead & Highgate, Phil Turner's campaign got something of a boost from the National Tactical Voting Campaign, an anti-Conservative group, who offered to help squeeze the Alliance vote to get rid of Finsberg. "Our canvassing", said Turner, "shows we are heading for victory with a three or four thousand majority". The Alliance candidate, the former GLC member Ann Sofer in turn responded by hitting out as hard as she could at both her opponents, both of whom had held positions of responsibility in the past. The Royal Free Hospital was left in a poor state when Finsberg was the junior minister for health, she said, and Camden's old people's homes had been in a scandalous state when the council was run by Turner who was high on the Alliance Party's list of the "100 Damnations", the hard left Labour candidates standing in the general election.

There was the usual scramble for photo opportunities with the famous. Finsberg was photographed variously with Margaret Thatcher and Norman Tebbit, and Phil Turner with not only John Prescott and Robin Cook, but also Maureen Lipman and Ben Elton. Turner attacked the Tories on their record: "After eight years of industrial decline", he asked, "do the voters want a welfare state or a poor law state?" Finsberg

193

---

12   Rents were raised on average by 65p, bringing the average weekly rent to 16.88p a week.

wanted to stick to local government. Councils should have to apply for special legislation if they want to waste money on race, police, gay and lesbian committees and nuclear free zones and as for Turner: " His council record", said Finsberg "is all that he has to offer, and I certainly would not be proud of it under his leadership". Turner was happy with his record (*pace* the *Ham & High*). Finsberg was "unsatisfactory, lazy and arrogant", he said, and attacked him on the Tory plans for the poll tax. The average domestic rate was now £745, but the new tax would cost every adult in the borough £769 so that a household of two adults would pay over twice what they now pay. Not so, said Finsberg, "safety netting" would reduce the charge to £421, some 4% less than the average per-adult rate bill. "The poll tax will benefit Mr Average", he said, but turned down Phil Turner's demands for a public debate. Although the *Ham & High* did not admire Phil Turner, it disliked Finsberg more. "Is Sir Geoffrey a tired knight", wondered the editorial a fortnight before polling day, "who, at sixty, no longer has the stomach for the game and really does not care much for meeting the people? The voters will decide".

By contrast, the Holborn & St Pancras election campaign could not be presented as close, not even by Peter Luff getting his picture taken with Ted Heath and Peter Walker. Dobson's majority was safe even with an Alliance candidate standing. Nor was he threatened from the left by Mick Gavan, "co-ordinator" of the council funded Camden Unemployed Action Group, who stood for Red Banner, a new party launched by the Revolutionary Communist Party.

Frank Dobson won comfortably, but in Hampstead it was close. Finsberg won with a reduced majority. The Labour vote went up by 2019, Finsberg's went up by 870, and Anne Sofer's vote was squeezed and went down by 2294. Finsberg attributed his success in Hampstead to the antics of Camden council. The Conservatives won their third general election in a row. Nationally, they lost only twenty two seats and were left with a parliamentary majority of a hundred. "I weep tonight", said Turner, "for the people who are homeless in this country. I weep for the people who are poor".

In Camden, Conservative celebrations were marred by Stephen Moon's sudden announcement that he was leaving the party altogether. He had not canvassed for Finsberg during the election because he had joined the SDP. "I am well past the point at which I should have left the Tory Party", he said, citing government policies rather than his otherwise good relationship with his council colleagues. He had delayed making the announcement because he did not want Turner to make any political capital out of it during the election. "The most I can be accused of", he said, "is that I am a rat joining a sinking ship".[13]

The Conservative victory in the general election left Camden somewhat exposed. The leadership had staked everything on there being a Labour government that would in some way allow them credits or funding to get them out of the financial mess they were in. The council faced a budget deficit of some £13m which it needed to bridge by 15th July. There were three options. Either the Labour members would have to defy the law and risk personal bankruptcy and disqualification from public office, or they could resign en masse leaving the Tories to make the cuts. Or else they could bite the bullet and make cuts themselves. "The manifesto is now right out of the window", said Alan Woods, the chief whip. "We took a gamble and lost". Dykes also faced a new difficulty in that the Labour group was split three ways. The right wingers despised his soft left group who had got the council where it was in financial terms, and were fed up with the hard left group who wanted to fight the government notwithstanding the general election defeat. Ken Hulme, one of the most vocal on the right wing of the group, was quite open in his disappointment: "We are in crisis, deep crisis. We may scrape it by minor cuts this year, although there is still a gap of over ten million pounds to close by July 15th". On the other hand, the left wingers were furious at any talk of toeing the government's line. "The choice ahead", said Angie Birtill, "is that either we capitulate and carry out the Tory cuts or we attempt to resist the government cuts by mobilising the community against them".

The director of finance prepared a paper for the Labour group in June pointing out that failure to act now would invite intervention by the district auditor. His suggested package of action included a freeze on recruitment, a moratorium on temporary staff and 10% less overtime in order to save £6m. The group agreed to accept the advice, but not without angry opposition from the left, including Steve Bevington and Kate Allen, who chaired the housing and staff committees. Angie Birtill circulated her own paper calling for "unqualified resistance" and for the group "to begin the process of mobilisation with mass meetings of tenants and ratepayers". Sandra Plummer called on the group "to arm the workers" (presumably, the Ham & High hazarded a guess, she was

195

---

13 His place on the council was taken by Bob Graham (one of the losers in Swiss Cottage in 1986) in a by election on 23 July 1987.

referring to "the firepower of words and information").

"We are trying not to panic", said Dykes after the meeting. "We are supporting a series of measures to hold the line in the short term". Dr Skolar offered no sympathy. "They are going to have to get rid of staff. They employed 'em and they're going to have to sack 'em", he said, before adding helpfully: "If they don't want to do it, I'm prepared to take control of the council tomorrow and do it for them".

Skolar was back in the papers the following week when he attended the inaugural meeting of the Gay & Lesbian Committee. Pink carnations were handed out to those present by way of celebration. "After listening to a series of speeches heralding the new committee as a breakthrough for gay and lesbian rights", reported the *Ham & High*, "Dr Skolar could hold his tongue no longer". Hardly audible above the hisses and boos, he assured everyone that he was not a homophobe. He pointed out that the cost of the committee and department was £100,000 a year and asked whether at a time when the council faced a £13m deficit anyone could be surprised if there were a backlash. "Is it reasonable to form a gay and lesbian committee at this time?" "Yes!" they all shouted, and he left. "This is more than a joke", he told the reporters outside, "it is a sick joke". [14] Sandra Plummer was unmoved: "Lesbians and gays have suffered in silence much too long", she said. "We pay our rates too and we intend to defend our rights".

The Conservatives wanted to keep the pressure on Labour on the main issue of the day: the council's finances. They called an emergency meeting of the council in early July to discuss the package of savings already agreed by the Labour group. Much of Labour's dirty linen was washed in public. The Labour right misbehaved: Bob Latham accused Dykes "of fudging and running away from difficult decisions" (and then rather theatrically passed around sweets which he described

14   Peter Skolar's account is this: "When the first meeting was called, I could not get any of our group to attend so I volunteered myself. I sat through the first stages where each member stood up and introduced themselves as my name is so and so and I am the chair of the GLC gay and lesbian committee and I am gay. Then, I am the vice chair and I am a lesbian etc. This went on for ten minutes to great applause with each announcement until I was the only one left sitting in splendid isolation on our benches so I introduced myself as 'Cllr. Peter Skolar, I am white male and heterosexual and happily married for 20 years and leader of the Tory group'. The boos and hisses could be heard from one end of Camden to the other. After 2-3 minutes of this, I got up and walked out. None of our group ever attended another meeting of the Gay and Lesbian Committee."

as "Camden fudge"), and the hard left led by Kate Allen argued that the savings package "would turn the anger of the workforce and the people of Camden against us instead of against the government". Eight hard left Labour councillors, describing themselves as the Camden Briefing Group[15], voted against the whip, but the leadership got its way: a package of cuts now and a further debate on cuts in October.

The bitterness in the Labour group came to a head at the next meeting of the grants sub-committee, chaired by Graham Shurety who allowed the allocation of full grants to twenty five groups on the agenda. Dykes was furious: "No committee chair who lives in the real world", he said, "would say to the voluntary sector: here's your full year grant but we're ten million pounds short and we don't know if we can finance the gap. That's no more than a provisional grant. It would be playing silly games with the electorate".

Within the week the Policy & Resources Committee, under the obedient Satnam Gill, removed all members of the Camden Briefing Group from the committees they chaired. Suddenly Kate Allen and Angie Birtill were no longer on the staff committee and Bevington was no longer on Housing Management. Sandra Plummer and Adrian States were taken off the Gay & Lesbian Committee and, importantly, States was taken off the grants sub committee.

197

The seriousness of the decisions to come was somewhat underlined in August 1987 when all 59 of the people who had been councillors in 1985 received a letter from the district auditor demanding that they explain their voting behaviour between April and June of that year when the rate was set three months late incurring interest charges. Only 26 of the 59 were still councillors. "About bloody time too!" was Skolar's view. "The Labour group who voted again and again to delay the rate deserve surcharge!"

By the time the October council meeting was called, the split in the Labour group was past mending. Dykes had announced that there was no alternative to making cuts. Angie Birtill announced that she was "appalled at Dykes's arrogance", adding that "we either fight or go under and this applies to everyone who works or lives in the borough".

---

15   Named after the *London Labour Briefing*, the left wing monthly of the hard left. They were Kate Allen, Steve Bevington, Angie Birtill, Caroline Holding, Gloria Lazenby, Karen Newbury, Sandra Plummer and Adrian States.

The majority of the group accepted Dykes's proposal for a 20% reduction in the coming year's budget to avoid a "vast and illegal" £40m deficit.

But there were further humiliations before the meeting. Camden had the second worst record in London for "Right to Buy" sales of council homes under the 1981 legislation. Camden had sold off only 595 of its properties compared, for instance, to neighbouring Barnet where 5,000 council homes had been sold. This was the result, explained Alan Woods, of careful valuations by Camden. The Department of the Environment, he said, wanted the borough to act in a "reckless" way. Finsberg had complained to the DoE "quite satisfied that there is a go slow policy" (which there was). The DoE threatened to take over the council's home ownership department unless the outstanding right to buy applications were processed by the end of the year. There was nothing else for it: the council announced that it was taking on nineteen new employees to deal with the backlog. The unions were less happy. "The only area they are keeping full staffing", moaned Dave Eggmore, the secretary of Camden NALGO, "is the one where they follow government actions down the line".

And in mid October, following an internal investigation, all fifty council employees in the homeless persons unit were suspended, sent home and barred from returning to work. A block booking policy had resulted in £48,000 a week being spent by the council on 635 bed and breakfast places that were not being taken up. There were, said Frank Nickson, "severe accounting discrepancies". Loyally, but quite incorrectly, the New Journal blamed not the hopelessly incompetent Camden staff who kept making and paying for the block bookings, but "racketeering hoteliers who are pocketing millions of pounds by booking tourists into rooms meant for homeless families and paid for by Camden". Dykes knew nothing about it. He was "shocked". NALGO helpfully called for the suspension of Ann Clarke, the director of housing. The Ham & High was despondent: "There may be some arguments over who carries the can, but in our book, Camden's humiliation is complete".

The council meeting at the end of October 1987 was the most heavily guarded yet. Councillors (other than those known to be left wingers) were jostled, punched and spat at by angry protestors. Such was the noise and the crush that some members of the delegations could not get in. It was "institutionalised racism" said John Oke of the CCCR. "It takes a white man to ask another white man whether we can be allowed in". The council voted for the cuts already agreed by the Labour group. Any other vote, said Dykes, was for "suicide and oblivion". Expenditure on the architects, engineers, finance and chief executive's departments was to be cut by between 30 and 40%, environmental health, libraries, recreation and planning by 25%, and housing, social services, building, grants and equalities by 20%. The proposals were voted against by eleven Labour rebels, calling themselves the "Manifesto Group" because, despite the economic squeeze, they still wanted Labour's election manifesto honoured in full.[16] "We are not prepared to stand by and watch the people of Camden be smashed", cried Graham Shurety with emphasis. "We now have a fortress Camden policed by security guards, only two years after we met with the full support of more than two thousand workers". Shurety and his friends were, said Alan Woods dismissively, "a small gang of mavericks trying to hold the group to ransom".

The bitterness of the splits within the Labour group were further demonstrated in November 1987 when members of the Manifesto Group briefed the *Guardian* on Camden's "repatriation" policy for homeless Irish families. Having replaced Steve Bevington on housing management, Gareth Smyth had introduced a policy (which had been mooted when Bevington was in charge, and which had been agreed by the group as a whole) to ease the burden on the housing list by not housing Irish applicants who had no links with Camden and who could be housed in Ireland. The law allowed councils to treat homeless Irish in the same way as homeless Britons. If a person is housed or can be housed in his home town, then he cannot have a right to be housed in another town.[17] Under a front page headline "Labour council is repatriating Irish homeless: Camden may offer Bangladeshis airline tickets" the *Guardian* mischievously speculated whether the policy would apply to Bangladeshi families. It gave examples of two applications then being considered by the council. Both concerned men living in London who had been joined in each case by a wife and five children from Bangladesh. Had they come from Ireland, said Donald MacArthur, of the housing department "decisions would be made which would avoid a call on Camden's housing resources".

The *Guardian* articles had their effect on the Labour group. Satnam

199

---

16 They were the Camden Briefing Group, now joined by Graham Shurety, Dave Horan and Graham Good.

17 *R v Bristol City Council ex parte Browne* [1979] 1 WLR 1347.

Gill said of the nine Irish applicants who had already left with their travel warrants, "The families should not have been sent back", and hotly added, when asked by the paper, "Over my dead body will a Bangladeshi family be sent back to Bangladesh". Having generated the articles, the Manifesto Group then tabled a motion before the Labour group meeting on 16 November: Smyth had been operating "a unilateral immigration policy" which was "racist and undoubtedly discriminatory", and Smyth should resign. A counter motion was also tabled calling for the expulsion of the Manifesto people from the Labour group. No one resigned or was expelled, and the spat soon paled into insignificance in the light of the King's Cross fire.

On 18 November 1987 thirty one people died horribly in the King's Cross underground station. A discarded cigarette had combined with the slovenly practices of station staff who had allowed a build up of inflammable rubbish under a wooden escalator. Across the road, the tragedy spread new gloom in Camden town hall where things seemed to be about as bad as they could get. Council officers were drawing up lists of council property to be sold by auction at the Connaught Rooms. The schedule included houses, factory premises, offices, shops and three derelict blocks of council flats in the hope of raising £17m before the end of the financial year and another £20m in the next. Even then, as Dykes pointed out, it was still unclear whether the budget with its £43m cuts would be a legal budget as it still exceeded the government's cap by £20m. Council officers were sent away to see which libraries should be closed and sold off.

In the last council meeting of 1987, after words of condolence for the victims of the King's Cross fire and their families, the Labour group again exposed its wounds in public. Hulme castigated the Manifesto Group rebels for their "hypocrisy and duplicity", Gareth Smyth accused them of being "Trotskyists". Tony Dykes was made to outline the proposed cuts in council services. "We had all these services in 1982" said Skolar, "why can't we keep them in 1987?" "Your compassion is a veneer and a sham!" shouted Dykes. "We reject your crocodile tears!" Listening to Dykes extolling the need for cuts and prudent spending, said Greengross "was like listening to Herod making an appeal on behalf of the NSPCC". The leadership got its way but, with the Manifesto Group voting with the Conservatives, the majority was down to only four.

Shurety had been replaced as chairman of the grants committee by Ken Hulme who spent two hours in open session in the week before

Christmas striking out grant funding for the coming year.[18] In all, 250 voluntary groups had their grants cut making a saving of £2.7m. Winston Pinder, the general secretary of the Afro-Caribbean Organisation, on behalf of the Camden Black & Ethnic People's Consortium, declared that the cuts in grants were "racist and sexist". Hulme was, said the *New Journal*, "Camden's Mr Scrooge". He was also the first councillor to fire a shot across the bows of the CCCR. He cut their £555,000 funding by 12½% (£70,000) and told them that if they failed to balance their budget, they would get nothing next year. "The effect of this", said their spokesman, Charles Wright, "will be the virtual end of community relations in Camden".

The new year of 1988 began with Mary Cane, the previous mayor, making a public attack on Dykes's leadership. "We should never have borrowed on the scale we did. I feel ashamed I did not make a bolder, noisier objection at the time". She described Alan Woods, the chief whip, as acting "like a spoilt child". Dykes, she said, was "so obsessed with his left wing credentials he has around him a bunch of people who are, with the conspicuous exception of Barbara Hughes, wheeler dealers and trimmers". Her conclusion was blunt: "The time has come for a new leadership. The only person with the stature and experience is Roy Shaw". Woods described her as being "very confused and very distressed".

But Mary Cane was not the real threat if only because she and those who thought like her would be sure to vote for Dykes against the threat from the left. It was clear that he would have to make an example of the eleven strong Manifesto Group. "We've won key votes at council meetings more by fluke than planning", he admitted. The whip was withheld from all of them for an initial term of six weeks. It changed little. "The Labour leadership can't fight for the welfare state", Graham Shurety told a Camden Fights Back rally at Swiss Cottage, "because it is wedded to capitalism".

There was more trouble at the council meeting to set the rate in March. Somewhat nervously, the chairman of the Policy & Resources Committee, Satnam Gill, opened his budget speech with the words: "It has been a difficult year..." and was silenced by the barrage of laughter and jeers from the Tory benches. The Conservatives and the Manifesto

201

---

18   Groups to lose all their funding included: Camden Women's Bus (£61,109), Housewives in Dialogue (£27,873), the Maternity Alliance (£4,623), Sex, Race & Class (£7,203), the Camden/Doncaster Twinning Association (£3,000), Central London Law Centre (£55,496) and the Irish in Britain Representation Group (£55,471).

Group[19] voted against the budget (and the two Liberal SDP Alliance councillors sportingly voted in different ways), but the Labour majority was too big to be concerned. "We end up with the Labour majority group implementing a Tory rate and now a Tory budget" said Graham Shurety. "You are slaughtering our troops out there!"

A few days before, the council had announced the sudden retirement of Patrick Kodikara who had handed his notice in on a Friday and then disappeared on a five week holiday to his native Sri Lanka. He was being paid off with, Skolar had heard, £27,000 a year for three years to run a consultancy. Richard Sumray, the chairman of the social services committee, did his best, but without referring to the figures: "Mr Kodikara is planning to set up a research, advisory and training consultancy in the area of transcultural service delivery." The silence that followed was broken by Dr Skolar: "I've never heard such rubbish", he said. "That's the biggest whitewash I've ever heard in this chamber".

Bit by bit, as the months went by, more and more detail about Kodikara's departure was leaked. There seemed no end of favours that had been done by the Labour council in Camden to this Labour councillor in Hackney. He had been given a retirement package, a years' salary and a £27,000 grant to his new consultancy, and his car loan had been waived by the council, several thousand pounds worth of audiovisual equipment, and £1500 worth of furniture from his office (including the coffee table). Dykes told the press that he knew "nothing at all" about it. "It's all part of his grant", said Sumray, but did not say more other than letting people know that only he and Frank Nickson knew the details. Judith Barnes referred the matter to the district auditor, and Ken Hulme asked the Local Government Ombudsman to investigate.

Kodikara hit back in a way that had not occurred to Sumray. "Nearly two thousand people left Camden in the last few months including numerous senior officers", he said. "Why is it only the black director who is receiving this treatment?" Sumray then wrote a confidential letter to councillors (which was immediately printed in the press) setting out the deal in full which had been hammered out between him and Kodikara. He had, in effect sacked Kodikara. This got a sharp reply through the press from Kodikara to say that Sumray

19 Now somewhat weakened by the resignation of Steve Bevington, who had moved to
    live with his sister in Leeds having tired of the experience of bringing up a young family
    in a short life property. In 1989 he emigrated to Melbourne where he met with great
    success. He is now the managing director of Community Housing Ltd and chairman of the
    Community Housing Association of Australia. He is also greatly respected in East Timor.

was not telling the truth. Kodikara resigned, said Kodikara, because he "could not tolerate the severe cuts" being imposed on his department. He then threatened action for defamation. And so, observed the *Ham & High*, "one by one all the chaotic chickens come home to roost".

Withholding the whip from the eleven left wingers helped Dykes's supporters in the group elections. The remaining left wing candidates each lost eleven votes. To some it was a return to sensible, middle of the road Labour policies. The *Ham & High* rather hopefully thought it could see the possibility of a comeback by Roy Shaw who gave the appearance of being more valued off the council at the Audit Commission than he was on it. He hoped, in the absence of the Manifesto Group, to replace Satnam Gill from the chairmanship of the Policy & Resources Committee. It was close, but was not to be. "Instead of just coming back with reductions", said Gill, having survived by one vote, "I can develop the policy side along with improving service delivery to make the council an effective and efficient socialist authority". Ken Hulme's bid to take one of the deputy leadership posts also failed. Nirmal Roy was elected to chair the Race Committee, and Mary Helsdon, who had been elected only four days before in the St Pancras ward by election (to replace Steve Bevington), was elected to chair the women's committee.

A financial report prepared for the Labour group in October 1988 sparked further infighting. The spending gap for the coming year was still over £25m. The council would be paying £9½m on interest charges. All "creative accounting" ploys had been spent and the council's "fat" had been removed. There would need to be a 7% cut in overall expenditure, 17% reduction in voluntary grants, rent increases would have to be higher than demanded by the government's housing subsidy scheme, £15m would have to be raised by selling property, and staff costs would have to be cut by maintaining a 10% vacancy rate. All seemed well at first, but the agreement to pursue the belt tightening measures was scuppered in December when the Labour group changed its collective mind. The right wingers argued that the cuts were in the wrong places and the left wing did not want any cuts at all. "People accepted it in October", said Dykes. "It doesn't show the Labour group in a good light".

In the middle of all this, Angie Birtill and Kate Allen tried to get the council to debate the use of plastic bullets in Northern Ireland. They were unsuccessful, but did manage to invite a delegation from

203

the United Campaign Against Plastic Bullets so that Jim McCabe, whose wife had been killed by a plastic bullet, could address the council. It caused a minor stir, but only because the Tories and half the Labour group, suspecting a Sinn Fein stunt, did not come into the chamber until it was over. "They didn't even have the courage to boycott the meeting", said Kate Allen, angry that no one was making a fuss. "They just sent apologies for lateness, or just stood outside the council chamber having a drink".

In February 1989 the district auditor, Brian Skinner, at last released his report into the conduct of the Labour councillors who had refused to set a rate in 1985. He found that the delay caused by the councillors had incurred costs of £2m to the tax payers in lost interest charges. He found that as they had all received unequivocal advice from council officers, all twenty two councillors[20] had acted "with wilful misconduct by failing to support the making of a rate on June 5-6, knowing that it was wrong to do so or at least being recklessly indifferent as to whether it was wrong". However, as a rate was set on 6th June, their actions did not warrant a surcharge or disqualification.

Observers outside the Labour group were astonished. Skinner had, said a "shocked and appalled" Skolar, made a mockery of the district audit system. He had reduced his office to that of a "useless, toothless quango". It was a decision, said the Ham & High that flies in the face of the facts. The 22 had consistently voted against setting a rate and had deliberately and unlawfully wasted £2m of the taxpayer's money and would face no sanction. David Cooksey, the chairman of the Audit Commission, was so embarrassed by Skinner's decision that he issued a statement emphasising there had been a finding of unlawful conduct. Cooksey agreed to meet Finsberg to discuss Skinner's "inexplicable decision" and described the action of the 22 councillors as having been "totally unacceptable", but regretted that he had no powers to seek a judicial review of a decision of a district auditor. "We consider", said the Ham & High, "that Mr Skinner has done a disservice to both the embattled remains of local government and to the need to protect ratepayers from maverick councillors who have now been let off the hook and can celebrate their good fortune. Lucky they are indeed!"

---

20   It had been twenty three, but Tom Devine had since died.

Spurred on by this, seven members of the Labour group[21] voted against the whip in the setting of a modest £2.17 rent rise. The housing service was going to get worse because of the cuts, ran the argument, and to increase the rent would add insult to injury. The in fighting flared up immediately. There was not enough time on the agenda to deal with them at the following group meeting, but Ken Hulme went straight to the press, saying that the whip should have been immediately removed from the "not-so-magnificent seven" for being "the Tories' best friends". "That some members of the group should be demanding that action be taken against us rather than against the government is not only depressing," said Angie Birtill, "it is absolutely terrifying."

The rumblings continued at the meeting to set the rate. Satnam Gill introduced the budget again, and fluffed his first line: "Any rational analysis shows that rates in Camden have gone up less than the rate of inflation in the last three years. In fact Camden's rates have been steady for the past five years. There have been no increases whatsoever." This was a red rag to the Tory bull. Skolar leapt to his feet. "I've never heard such a load of absolute nonsense", he shouted. "It's not surprising rates have risen less than the rate of inflation. You're rate capped, you blithering idiot!" Poor Gill could not cope with the burly doctor, nor with the laughter that followed the intervention. Dykes sprang to his feet to say that Gill should have said eight years which would include the period before rate capping, and eventually after much jeering and laughter, Gill was able to read out the rest of his speech and proposed a rate of £210.69p in the pound. Greengross made the point that in the last seven years the borough had spent a billion pounds while presiding over a steady decline in services. The new rate was passed, but six Labour councillors abstained. The Tory motion to condemn Skinner's decision not to surcharge those who had deliberately cost the ratepayers £2m was defeated, and Angie Birtill kept old wounds open within the group by proposing a motion recognising the contribution made by the Irish to the "political, social, economic and cultural fabric of Camden". This proved to be little more than a vehicle for her angry diatribe on the Prevention of Terrorism Bill, which caused Roy Shaw to criticise her for her intemperate language and her failure to condemn the IRA.

At the next group meeting, the rebels by a series of narrow votes were allowed back into the fold, except for Adrian States who

205

---

21 Cllrs Angie Birtill, Kate Allen, Adrian States, Dave Horan, Caroline Holding, Sandra Plummer and Graham Shurety.

was expelled from the group for three months. He appealed to the London Regional Labour Party who ordered his reinstatement with the observation that singling him out for suspension while only issuing the others with a warning amounted to "a clear miscarriage of justice". It was, said States, "a vindictive witch hunt by the right".

The crunch came at the Labour group elections in May 89. Dykes, the political survivor, made a new deal with the left. He was unchallenged as leader. The right wingers were kicked off everything. Gareth Smyth, who was replaced as housing chairman by Jackie Peacock, complained of "a squalid deal between the Leadership Group and the hard left Briefing Group"[22]. As if to make his point for him, Dave Horan took over as chair of the staff committee, and Graham Shurety was put back in charge of grants. Maggie Cosin, who lost to Horan, told the press that the Labour group was "on a kamikaze course". Roy Shaw pointed to the "disastrous effect" on officers' morale. It was "a setback to those who believe in responsible mainstream Labour policies". Dykes was above all this. "If the Labour group just gets bedevilled by wrangling," he said, "that ain't going to get us anywhere". It was, said Peter Skolar, rubbing his hands together, "a disaster for the ratepayers".

Having suspended the left wingers in the past, Alan Woods of the Leadership Group, stood down as whip and was given the chairmanship of the new education committee. The new chief whip was Mary Helsdon (who had only been on the council for a year) of the Briefing Group. Over the following weekend she worked out the committee allocations in such a way that the left wingers would form a majority on as many committees as she and her friends felt they could bear to sit. Some of the left wingers were allocated to sit on as many as four committees, whereas some of the (often more experienced) moderates were allocated only two places. Mary Helsdon was unfazed by the resultant fuss: "We just have to try and ignore these things —there are much more important things for us to concentrate our time and effort on". Before doing nothing, Tony Dykes said the right things: "I will suggest to the whip that she look at this again".

The immediate effect of the group elections and the allocations was that the right wing was pushed into formally organising itself. On 15th May, the Camden 1990 Group was formed by fifteen councillors

---

22 As the 1986 manifesto faded into memory, the Manifesto Group had reverted to calling themselves the Briefing Group.

with Roy Shaw as its leader.[23]

The divisions flared up spectacularly at the next council meeting during a debate on a report of the Housing Investigation Panel which had been set up to look into the losses of over a million pounds between 1985 and 1987 on bookings for bed and breakfast accommodation. Gareth Smyth described the report as "a sham and a device to distract responsibility. It is a disgrace to this borough". His main complaint was that the investigation panel had been chaired by Julie Fitzgerald who had also chaired the Policy & Resources Committee during the period under investigation. She had had financial control over the homeless persons unit which in turn had handed over large sums of money for bed & breakfast. Alan Woods (who outside council hours shared a bed with Julie Fitzgerald) shouted him down: "We should be looking into why Councillor Smyth threatened to bomb the Camden Labour Centre!" he yelled. Smyth turned round and yelled back "Shut up!", and to the mayor: "Can't you stop this thug? Are you chairing this meeting or not?" Woods then had much to say of a loyal nature of the integrity of Julie Fitzgerald, and indeed of the housing Investigation Panel as a whole. But when the press eagerly sought clarification of the bomb threat accusation afterwards, he was less than forthcoming: "Bomb. I certainly can't remember saying that." Others were less forgiving. "When he starts accusing councillors of terrorist activity", said Ken Hulme, "that's a sure sign he needs a rest".

The *Ham & High* reporter, Matthew Lewin was not impressed: "As usual, the fury was being directed not across the chamber at political opponents, but across the Labour benches in the time honoured tradition of Labour councillors reserving their vitriol for their own number". He walked out in disgust. "There are only a handful of councillors with the calibre and gravity to command real attention when they speak, many fewer than in the heady days of the 1970s when Camden was a respected borough with pioneering policies".[24]

*   *   *

---

23 Bill Budd, Mary Cane, Maggie Cosin, Pat Denny, Ken Hulme, Mike Kirk, Nicola Kutapan, Bob Latham, Paul Orrett, Janet Pope, Bill Saunders, Roy Shaw, Gareth Smyth, Jerry Williams and John Wakeham.

24 He went on: "It was interesting to note, for example, that there was a dry council meeting earlier this year –caused by a delay in the liquor licence for the foyer- and that meeting was the only one in living memory to end well before the 11.15pm deadline. Whether that was because councillors were more sober, or whether they were merely anxious to finish the meeting early enough to get to the pub across the road, is debateable."

Domestic rates were to be abolished in April 1990 and replaced by the Community Charge, the Conservative government's poll tax. The idea was simply that as everyone uses local services, so everyone who can pay should pay for those services, regardless of the value, rateable or otherwise, of where they live. The intention was to make more accountable to the public those left wing Labour councils such as Camden, who had upset so many by funding political adventures which were so clearly surplus to the needs of good local government.

Anti-poll tax protests built up throughout 1989. Mass campaigns were orchestrated by the Labour Party and groups to the left. In Camden, where the tax was expected to average £438 per adult, rising eventually to £639, the Stop the Poll Tax Campaign was chaired by Adrian States. He urged "collective action" to defeat the government and arranged displays of public burnings of poll tax demands. He hoped this would be reminiscent of the burning by Africans of their passes in protest against the South African pass laws, although in Camden's case the effect was somewhat limited as the council had been so slow in getting the demands out. A motion was placed before the council in July expressing hostility to the poll tax but nevertheless accepting that the council would have to gather it. Adrian States was furious. "Tonight's paper", he shouted, wearing his AXE THE POLL TAX T-shirt, "is not even Camden's Munich. It is our surrender!" Only Angie Birtill voted with him.

In August, nine months before the borough elections, Roy Shaw launched his Camden 1990 Group campaign manifesto. It was entitled "Time for a change", a title used before and since by the Conservative group. It read like a Conservative manifesto:

> Most people see the ill swept streets, the cracked and uneven paving stones, the general air of neglect in the borough. Council tenants will have experienced the difficulties of getting repairs done, the unkept promises of improvement, the general disrepair of many estates. But all this is only the tip of the iceberg. There has been a general deterioration in the management of our services. Part of the responsibility lies with the Tory government, part with the officers of the council, but the main responsibility lies with the elected members.

An opportunity presented itself in Hampstead Town ward to test the local appetite for the poll tax following the resignation of Selina Gee, one of the Conservative councillors. The Labour candidate was Myra "Bubbles" Polya, one of Hampstead's ILEA members. She urged voters to "give Mrs Thatcher and her servile Sir Geoffrey Finsberg a salutary lesson in Town ward". The Social Liberal Democrats (the SLD) were hopeful in that their candidate had lost by less than a hundred votes in 1986 when he had stood for the Liberal-SDP Alliance. Irritatingly for them, following some internal bickering, the Liberal-SDP Alliance agent for the 1986 election was also standing, but as a rival candidate. Not that it made any difference (outside SDP/SLD/Liberal circles). After a careful door to door campaign, Rita Pomfret doubled the Tory majority in a 31% turnout and Labour came third. In Hampstead at least, the poll tax had affected nothing.

By the beginning of 1989, the government was so concerned over Camden's failure to implement the legislation granting council tenants the "Right to Buy" their homes that the minister, David Trippier, summoned Tony Dykes to explain himself. After the meeting Camden put out a press release to the effect that the minister had been satisfied that Camden "had made good progress on processing tenants' right to buy applications". Trippier was furious when he heard this, and issued his own press release to say that "Camden's backlog is by far the worst in the country", which was the cue for Finsberg to pose his stock question on Camden council: "Are they deliberately lying or is it incompetence?"

209

The Right to Buy legislation, not liked by the council, was nothing to the fuss caused by Camden's response to compulsory competitive tendering (CCT). CCT was introduced in 1989 by the Thatcher government, hoping to wean councils off inefficient and costly housing maintenance and waste disposal departments. Councils were to put certain services out to tender to encourage efficiency and economy. Camden was obliged to put the rubbish collection and street cleaning contract up for tender. The council's response was to allow its own direct services department (DSD) to tender for the contract and despite a competing tender from an Anglo-French consortium, the result surprised no one. On 1st August the council announced that the DSD had won the £4m contract having agreed to carry out the work with 279 council employees.

It was a disastrous move. Within a month the service had all but collapsed. The chairman of the Direct Services Committee, Bill Budd, was at first forced to admit that the DSD had too many employees. He told the council there were 303, but tried to excuse this surplus by adding that sickness and absenteeism meant that the actual workforce available was no more than 230. There were immediate allegations that Camden had "competed" unfairly by awarding itself the contract, and was acting illegally by subsidising the DSD over and above the £4m contract price that the other bidders had tendered for. Within a week it was estimated that the surplus staff in the DSD would cost the borough £500,000 by the end of the year. They were given an ultimatum to accept jobs elsewhere on the council's payroll. Predictably, Camden NUPE called a strike ballot. "Everything will come to standstill", warned their secretary, Bob Hall.

In October the council admitted that the DSD had 82 surplus employees and the department was heading for a £2.5m deficit just two months after being awarded the contract. Both Tony Dykes and Frank Nickson were somewhat reticent on the subject, but a report to the Labour group, signed by Dykes, Budd and Graham Good, the chairman of the Public Health subcommittee, was leaked to the press at the end of the month. "The quality of the service leaves much to be desired", it read. "This has been due to a combination of problems —weak and incompetent management going back for some time, obviously budget cuts, and, let's be honest, some work practices e.g.: regular non attendance for no good reason". And importantly, the mechanics of CCT had neither been taken seriously nor properly considered.

Keen that the subject should not be debated in council, Dykes issued a statement at the October council meeting (in the part of the agenda reserved for committee reports) that an extra £500,000 was going to be diverted from other council departments and ploughed back into rubbish collection and street cleaning in order, suggested the *Ham & High*, "to find the missing streets which have not been seen since they disappeared under piles of rubbish on August 1st". The Tories tabled a motion on the DSD, but the Labour group voted not to allow any debate on the subject until the end of the agenda, after the debates on South Africa, the Guildford Four, dog registration, and ambulances.

Bill Budd was howled down by the Tories when he said that things were getting better and Tobin said that the filth would remain so long "as this filthy lot are in charge". Complaining that Camden was "disgusting, dirty, filthy and knee deep in rubbish, black sacks and rats", Skolar led the Conservative group out of the chamber rather than remain for the other debates. "I think it ought to be noted" shrieked Julie Fitzgerald, in case any Tories were listening outside the chamber while she sought the council's approval of the release of the Guildford Four, "that the opposition have left during this motion". The meeting ended at 10.30, so if they had stayed, said Dykes, they could have had their debate on the direct services department after all.

The Department of the Environment became involved at the behest of Judith Barnes who wrote to the minister, David Hunt, with a list of accusations against the DSD and the old building department which had overcharged the housing department (i.e.: been subsidised by the taxpayer) by £100,000 for housing maintenance. If there has been a breach of the Local Government Act, there will be sanctions, warned the minister, giving the council a month in which to answer the accusations.

In the meantime the in-house boiler workers went on strike in October in the knowledge that their own department was facing CCT in December. Not only were they intent on striking throughout the winter months, they had each clocked up some five weeks of sick leave. The 42 staff had been off sick on average for 24 days each in the six months leading up to October. The council decided nevertheless to award the contract to the in house team provided they came back to work, which they refused to do, and all 109 tenders were awarded to the next bidder.

The Labour Party, as usual, exposed all its selection agonies to public view. In November the party's Local Government Committee rejected Steve Taylor and Terry Flanagan as being unsuitable candidates for the borough elections as they were too left wing, which was something of a turn around as in 1986 the committee had rejected three right wingers. John Mills, who had left the council in 1985, reapplied to be a candidate. He was rejected by the committee in January because he was a "controversial candidate" with a disreputable past, although his real crime was that as an ally of Roy Shaw he was disliked by the Hampstead branch for being right wing.[25] (At his selection meeting Ramen Bhattacharyya, a future councillor and mayor of Camden, laid out on the delegates' chairs copies of a document entitled "The sordid

211

---

25 Within ten months of leaving the council in 1985, Mills was appointed the deputy chairman of the London Docklands Development Board (LDDA) where his Labour Party connections were valued in the negotiations with the Labour run councils concerned. In December 1987 a *World in Action* television exposé made much of his past: "In 1976 one of his companies went into liquidation owing a quarter of a million pounds to creditors. In 1985 another of his companies went into liquidation, this time with debts of nearly half a million...Then in 1986 he pleaded guilty to a series of offences involving selling gold plated jewellery which was in fact made of brass." The minister, Nicholas Ridley, sacked him from the LDDA on the day the TV programme was broadcast.

saga behind the John Mills affair".) Mills and Flanagan were reinstated by the London Regional Labour Party.

By the new year over half the sitting Labour councillors had announced that they were not planning to stand again. Of the right wingers, Hulme, Griffith, Smyth and Latham had had enough.[26] Richard Sumray also stood down, exhausted by the infighting.[27] On the left, Angie Birtill and Adrian States were not standing because Camden had betrayed the working class by implementing the poll tax. King's Cross ward, with a membership still smarting over the cuts in the 1987 budget, deselected both their councillors, Tony Dykes and Barbara Hughes, and selected left wingers Gloria Lazenby and John White. Gospel Oak dumped Alan Woods and Rose Head and replaced them with John Mills and Wyn Parsons. The Tories had difficulties of another nature, as their inadequate new agent, David Fisher, let the press know that they could not find candidates and in February were still twelve short.

The poll tax had dominated the thoughts of politicians on both sides of the divide in the six months before its implementation in April 1990. The director of finance, Peter Derrick, had first announced that the borough's poll tax would be £586 per adult. This was well above the government's own calculation, the "standard spending assessment" (SSA), of £344 which led to fears that the council would be capped for the sixth year running. The council, advised Derrick, would certainly be capped if the tax was £500 or more, and may well be capped even if the tax is as low as £400 per head, a level which would require about £21m in budget cuts. He outlined his package of "radical options": more property sales, increased parking charges, speedier sales of council housing, "critical examination" of housing services and "tougher value for money scrutiny" of grants to the voluntary sector. Skolar thought otherwise: "Rubbish! No one will really know until the grants are announced and until then how the hell can anyone make any predictions? This is a scare tactic that will backfire on them". To great applause from the Conservative conference at Blackpool, he predicted

---

26 Gareth Smyth left the Labour Party in 1990 and took up journalism becoming the *Financial Times's* man in the Middle East, the Iraq war, and then (until 2007) Iran. Robert Latham has lived and worked in the borough ever since. In 2008 at the Legal Aid Lawyer of the Year awards he was named as the "Barrister of the Year" for "having led the way in applying the Disability Discrimination Act to residential housing".

27 Richard Sumray became the chief executive of London International Sport which initiated the bid for the London Olympics, and now chairs the London 2012 Forum. He was a member of the Metropolitan Police Authority for eight years until 2008, and since 2001 he has chaired Haringey's NHS Primary Care Trust.

that by exposing the cost of Camden "the poll tax will ensure that we take control of the borough in May 1990".

The final gasp of the ILEA came in March 1990. Its schools and budget was transferred to the twelve inner London boroughs. The bishop of London, Graham Leonard, held a special farewell service at St Paul's in which he gave thanks for "our educators and their administrators", but ordained that politics should not raise its unruly head in front of the congregation. He allowed Neil Fletcher to read the lesson, choosing for him the passage from St Luke where the child Jesus is found debating with the elders in the Temple. Fletcher, without warning anyone, chose instead two passages from Isaiah which he felt more appropriate for Mrs Thatcher and her cabinet: "Woe to you O destroyer...when you stop destroying you shall be destroyed", and "Come here, you sons of a sorceress, you offspring of adulterers and prostitutes".[28]

In March the Labour group (overcoming by 30-8 a motion proposed by Adrian States and Angie Birtill not to impose the tax at all) agreed to reduce the budget to £184m and set the poll tax at £555, which was 22% above the government's SSA. The council meeting that followed was subject to unprecedented security with policemen patrolling outside and security staff guarding the doors letting in ticket holders only. The Town Hall was besieged by placard waving demonstrators from the Camden Stop the Poll Tax Campaign who, frustrated at not being able to get into the Town Hall, periodically broke out onto the Euston Road to chant and dance in the box junction at the end of Judd Street.

The meeting, held beneath packed galleries, began with the mayor, Barbara Hughes warning that she would clear the galleries if the occupants did not behave. Dykes then rose to his feet to announce that the meeting was going to be suspended for forty five minutes. It transpired that he had fresh information to the effect that the government was planning to cap only those councils whose budgets were 20% above the SSA. If the council set its budget a penny below the 20% mark, the council would avoid being capped. There was a period of desperate figure crunching in the leader's office with Frank Nickson and Peter Derrick, in what the *Ham & High* described as "an eleventh hour financial soft shoe shuffle" that resulted in "a complicated set of manoeuvres

213

---

28   "That was disgraceful", said the bishop afterwards, declining to shake hands. Neil Fletcher has since been NALGO's education officer, the executive head of education at the Local Government Association, a governor of the London School of Economics and chairman of the City Literary Institute.

including some rescheduling of debts and changing the 'sinking fund rate' which governs the rate of debt repayments". The result was more "creative accounting". Another £2.84m was knocked off the budget for the coming year to be, of course, paid in years to come.

When Dykes returned new papers were circulated with an amended motion setting the poll tax at £534 a head, which happened to be 19.9% above the SSA. The debate that followed was short and all the speakers were drowned out by shouts and chanting from the gallery. The barracking stopped only for Adrian States who rose, made a clenched fist salute to his supporters, and gave a short speech beginning "Of all the measures introduced by the Tories since 1979, the poll tax is clearly the most unjust, the most indefensible, the most pernicious..." No other speaker could get heard and the council moved to a vote, which was won by 35 votes to 16. "It is absolutely clear to me", said Skolar to the press afterwards, letting them have the full blast of what he would have said inside if only he could have made himself heard, "that this was a cynical and desperate exercise designed purely to get expenditure just under the level at which people expect the government to start capping". And of course the tax was too high: "We could reduce the community charge to £417 by merely removing growth and without making any cuts at all".

That was not the end of it. In April the government announced that Camden was going to be capped in any event. The cap would not be at the original SSA of £151m, but at a new concessionary level of £177m which was a mere £4.4m below Camden's budget. Just as it looked as if this modest lowering of the bar would cause problems the government then gave Camden permission to increase its borrowing by £12m. The poll tax was reset at £500, and all went quiet(ish). The Camden Trades Council called off their anti-poll tax day of action march with Tony Benn when only thirty people turned up.

In December 1989, Geoffrey Finsberg unexpectedly announced that he would not stand again for parliament. Now that his wife had died, he said, he could not face politics without her support. The *Ham & High* then gleefully published details that he had got married "in secret" by special licence at Camden Town Hall to a glamorous Irish divorcee[29]. The papers took much interest in the selection procedures

---

29   After the 1992 general election he was made a life peer (Baron Finsberg of Hampstead). He died in 1996.

15. 1984: "Evening all –anyone want a smack?"
The police rescue the town hall hostages. *(Camden)*

16. 1984: The town hall occupation. Ken Livingstone spreads
goodwill *(although not to Labour councillors)*. *(Nigel Sutton)*

17. 1985: The great "shall we set a rate?" debate. Tony Dykes, Phil Turner, Sandy Wynn and Neil Fletcher. *(Chris Taylor)*

18. Hands up to say: "No we shan't!" *(Nigel Sutton)*

19. 1987: Tony Dykes watches as Julie Christie and Julian Fulbrook raise the Nicaraguan flag. *(Nigel Sutton)*

20. 1987: Bob Latham (in spectacles) and Ken Hulme (in black jacket) go to the Police Consultative Committee meeting. David Riddle waits in the doorway with an agenda. *(Nigel Sutton)*

21. Stephen Moon the Tory leader who defected to the SDP. *(Nigel Sutton)*

22. Peter Skolar, "the doctor who would cure Camden's ills". *(Nigel Sutton)*

23. 1990. Through gritted teeth: the three party leaders, Flick Rea, Julie Fitzgerald and Judith Barnes. *(Camden)*

24. 1996. Night of the Long Jackets: Richard Arthur (right) with his "Dream Team", Steve Bundred and Amanda Kelly. *(Camden)*

25. John Mills: the safe pair of hands. *(Nigel Sutton)*

26. Glenda Jackson: triumphant in 1992.
    (Nigel Sutton)

27. Pam Chesters, the saviour of the
    libraries in 1999.

28. Going nowhere in 2002. Andrew Marshall and Piers Wauchope
    launch the Conservative manifesto. *(Camden New Journal)*

29. Dame Jane Roberts and Richard Sumray.
(Camden New Journal)

30. Before the fall. Raj Chada (right) and Tony Blair wait to be questioned by
Richard Osley of the Camden New Journal. *(Camden New Journal)*

LIB DEMS TRIUMPH

● **LABOUR LOSE TOWN HALL FOR FIRST TIME IN 35 YEARS** ● No outright control ● Lib Dems and Tories discuss power-sharing pact ● Lib Dem vote rockets ● First Green councillors ● Labour leader loses seat ● Veteran Labour councillors lose seats – Cabinet members kicked out ● Worst Labour results for a generation ● Tory leader loses seat ● 'We're gutted' say Labour ● Massive turnout ● www.camdennewjournal.co.uk for full results

Winning smiles: Lib Dem leader Keith Moffitt

31. ...and the winner is: Keith Moffitt on the front of the Camden New Journal May 2006. *(Camden New Journal)*

that followed. The Conservatives attracted two hundred applications, but eventually plumped for Oliver Letwin, the thirty three year old head of privatisation at Rothschilds Bank, who had been brought up and educated in Hampstead before being sent off to Eton. As a policy Advisor to Conservative Central Office he was said to be one of the chief architects of the community charge: the "The Poll Tax Tory" (*Ham & High*), or the "Poll Tax Maestro" (*New Journal*).

On the other side of the fence, Glenda Jackson had been first mentioned as a possible Labour candidate in the summer when a group of local activists had been encouraged to invite her to apply. The attraction was obvious: she was an internationally known, highly successful and glamorous film star and, living as she did in Blackheath, she was not tarnished by any association with Labour in Camden. "I don't know Hampstead very well", was her opening gambit, but she was, she said, flattered by the suggestion that she should stand. Local candidates had been mooted. Neil Fletcher had shown an early interest but soon ruled himself out, as had Tessa Jowell who instead got herself selected for Dulwich, Glenda Jackson's own constituency (almost). But the main contender was Kate Allen who had so nearly been the party's choice last time, and who had so nearly been the leader of the council. It was another near miss: she took Glenda Jackson to a third ballot when the party assembled in March 1990, but glamour won.[30] The line up pleased the *Ham & High*: "Mr Letwin and Miss Jackson make excellent opponents. They come from different worlds and extol two different ideologies. There's a real choice for you when the time comes".

Given the circumstances, the last council meeting before the borough elections passed off predictably enough. Dykes made the point that if the government stopped clipping Camden for the £75 a head safety net "to help more wealthy boroughs like Tory held Wandsworth", or if Camden was allowed the extra £20m given to Tory Westminster, or was given the same grant as Wandsworth, the poll tax would be £203. "Rubbish", said Skolar, it was Labour's fault that we all had to dig so deep in our pockets because Labour cannot stop spending. Council expenditure was up 14% when, taking into account inflation, it should only be 7.7% which would take the budget down to the rate initially set

215

---

30   Kate Allen turned her back on Camden after this: she went to the Refugee Council, became an advisor to the Home Office and is now the director of Amnesty International (UK). She threw Ken Livingstone out for his philandering in 2001. She lives in Brighton.

by the government at the beginning of the year. The LibDems proposed a local income tax.

Skolar then went further and launched the election campaign with a leaflet promising a poll tax of £335. No one really feared the Conservatives. "A Labour victory is all but assured", the *Ham & High* confidently predicted. Nationally, the opinion polls made dire reading for Mrs Thatcher's government, but the sheer cheek of Skolar's leaflet rankled. "It's not a teaser", he told the press, "it's a guarantee", and, whenever asked, went straight into his list: "If you remove five council officers like the nuclear free zone officer, at £25,000 a head, that would immediately knock one pound off the poll tax; then you collect the rate arrears of £20 million, remove all squatters and illegal tenants from council housing to reduce the bed & breakfast bill, cut bureaucracy and unnecessary costs...."

It was all bravado. The Conservatives suffered from "Thatcher Factor blues", said the *New Journal*. "Tory morale is so low they have thrown in the towel in virtually the whole of the southern part of the borough". They were not going to win, and the only matter of interest to party activists was whether they were going to be utterly crushed by popular dislike of the poll tax and of Mrs Thatcher, now in her eleventh year as prime minister.

As in the 1986 election, the Labour Party was confident enough to take time off the campaign to start plotting for the succession. Dykes no longer had the support he needed. He had fallen out with the left wing, who, to be fair, would have fallen out with anyone, and to keep the left wing on board he had fallen out perhaps even more badly with the right wing, Roy Shaw's Campaign 1990 group. The new champion of the Leadership-Briefing alliance was Julie Fitzgerald, a former deputy leader, who had, said the *Ham & High* (consistently loyal to Roy Shaw) "made little impact". "Hers is a kind of fire brigade campaign, trying to mount a 'We-Must-Stop-Shaw' momentum".

Of the Tories, Sir Alan Greengross had had enough and announced that he was not standing again, having been on Holborn and then Camden councils since 1957. Gwynneth Williams, now eighty one, also stood down after sixteen years on the council, as did Colin Glover, a Belsize ward councillor elected in 1986, who in the council chamber had never once found anything he wanted to say.

8 |

Julie Fitzgerald:
into the buffers

L abour won, but not by as much as they had anticipated. The Conservatives had held on and had even managed, slightly, to improve their position. The great anti-poll tax vote had not happened. "Landslide Dashed", was the disappointed headline in the *New Journal*. The turnout even fell by half a percentage point to 46.1%. The "Thatcher effect", if it existed, had lost the Tories only a thousand votes, but Labour's vote had gone down by 6,000.

Peter Skolar paid the price of leading from the front. His seat in Brunswick, the only Tory seat in the south of the borough, was in a ward shared precariously with Labour. He refused to do as Stephen Moon had done four years before –flee to a safe seat– and, quite predictably, he lost, albeit defiantly. "I shall be back!" he told the *Chronicle*, disappointed that the poll tax bills were not due to go out until after the election. The Labour attack on the marginal Belsize ward was unsuccessful, and the only change on the political map, outside Brunswick, came somewhat unexpectedly in Swiss Cottage where the Conservatives took all three seats from Labour, unseating Sandra Plummer and Barbara Beck.

The closest result turned out to be in Hampstead Town where third time unlucky LibDem candidate David Brierley lost by one vote to Rita Pomfret. The LibDems consolidated their position in Fortune Green, where the Tories had given up and fallen into third place. And the Greens, who won no seats, gleefully pointed out that they had got more votes than the Lib Dems in 17 of the 22 seats which they had both contested. All this was something of an irrelevance in the short term as the council was still crushingly Labour with forty two councillors to fifteen Tories and two LibDems.

After the usual weekend of canvassing the newly elected Labour councillors, the Labour group meeting on the following Tuesday produced a new leader. Tony Dykes was elbowed out of the way before the voting began and stood down, knowing that he could not win, but consummate survivalist that he was, he was able to strike a deal whereby he became chairman of the policy & resources committee. He was replaced by 35 year old Julie Fitzgerald, a small, blonde, bespectacled mother of two, formerly on Ken Livingstone's policy team at the GLC and then an administrator at the ILEA. She had been Dykes's deputy and was his choice of successor. With the help of the eleven Manifesto Group members on the new council, she beat Roy Shaw 23-19. The left had won, but it was not a clean sweep: the right wingers Roy Shaw and Bill Saunders were elected her two deputy leaders. "The borough election results", Julie Fitzgerald told the papers, "proved people's willingness to pay a high poll tax in order to maintain a wide variety of services".

The new leader of the opposition, Judith Barnes, was elected unopposed. A solicitor, she had a capacity for hard work and an appetite for detail. The *Ham & High* described her as "a true behind the scenes performer, burrowing away at agendas and reports, nagging council officers for information, much of which takes months to surface". Skolar had been hard hitting and strident, but was of a jolly, slap-dash disposition and was generally liked on both sides of the chamber. Judith Barnes was hard hitting and strident. There was to be no honeymoon period. She told the *Chronicle* that "Julie Fitzgerald will be a disaster as she is one of the architects of the mess in which Camden finds itself in at present". Flick Rea remained as leader of what was now the two woman Lib Dem group. For the only time in Camden's history, all three party leaders were women.

The new administration also saw a new chief executive, Jeremy Smith, a barrister who had joined Camden nine months before as the chief law officer. He was described by the *Ham & High* as "a smooth 42 year old, seen as the candidate of the old GLC left" having been a Labour Party man, Ken Livingstone's legal advisor and "deeply involved in the development of radical Labour policies, most of which of course ended in disaster". The *Ham & High* gave his predecessor less than full marks. "Polite Mr Nickson's reign was disastrously flawed. He may, politically, have shielded the left wing councillors from the law, but whatever happened to decentralisation? What happened to the so called officers steering group and the loss of many talented senior staff? What happened over the huge deficit on the bed & breakfast account? And that's just to identify a few matters of serious importance, not forgetting the sick Kodikara saga".

The problems did not go away. Within a month the Department of the Environment had served a "Section 13 Order" on Camden forcing the council to put the refuse contract out for retender on the open market. There was nothing to stop the Direct Services Department from reapplying, but if they failed the council would have to make 274 redundancy payments. "It is my whole hearted desire", said Julie Fitzgerald, "that we make the refuse contract work with the DSD". It was to be an uphill battle, the consequence, said Judith Barnes, "of ten years of the council pandering to the unions at every step, creating a workforce incapable of doing the job. They buried their heads in the sand".

Putting aside the Labour Party's election pledge of no redundancies, the staff committee gave senior officers powers to issue redundancy notices to fifteen council workers should alternative employment not be available for them. This provoked an occupation by NALGO and NUPE workers of the council chamber during the July Labour group meeting. It also provoked an attack on Labour by one of the two Tory trade unionists at the next council meeting. Bob Graham made the claim that Labour was the party of compulsory redundancies and that people would be selected for redundancy "because of their union activities", an "absolutely disgraceful" allegation said Phil Turner, now reduced to chairing the staff committee. He then had to face Judith Barnes's motion concerning the auditor's report that Camden's 25% absenteeism rate "was a shocking statistic". "People in Camden work in difficult, stressful conditions, having to deal with major social problems created by the present government and their policies", he said, recommending that Judith Barnes's motion "should be thrown out with the contempt it deserves".

By August it was clear that the DSD was facing an annual loss of £750,000, and was dead in the water in that it had only managed to win two of the three housing maintenance contracts, and then only because the council was entitled under the rules to factor in the cost of redundancy should they lose. In any event, a further 200 redundancies were now on the cards. New figures showed just how badly the DSD was doing: in January not a single street in the north of the borough had been swept all month ("and yet" said the *Ham & High*, "Camden still has the gall to retender").

The contract could not be reassigned until next April which brought the obvious complaint from Judith Barnes: "If they'd been sacked eight months ago we'd already have an efficient replacement". "It was regrettable", was the leader's reply, "that the opposition had directed all its concern on getting the private sector to take over council services. They have expressed no interest or support for the vast majority of people who have made substantial improvements and the increased effort made by workers".

David Summersgill, the director of DSD then resigned with a modest resignation package. Judith Barnes demanded details: "I want to be sure we're not having a repetition of the Kodikara fiasco", she said. Maggie Cosin told her to "stop whining". NALGO, NUPE and UCATT announced they were planning a rolling programme of two and seven day strikes.

Just before Christmas 1990 the Department of the Environment did what it had been itching to do for some time: it issued a notice preventing the DSD from tendering for the refuse contract. The decision was "perverse and irrational" and "a travesty" said Jeremy Smith because the DSD had so much improved over the last few months. A new director had been appointed, three senior managers had been drafted in and the workers were pulling their weight. "No one can deny", said Bill Budd, "that they've done a fantastic job". Nevertheless, with the DoE taking the stance it was, plans were made to disband the department. Camden NUPE promised to fund a judicial review of the DoE's decision. Their secretary, Bob Hall, declared somewhat mysteriously that the "Tory councillors have betrayed the people of Camden" and predicted that the cost of the contract would "dramatically increase" under a private contractor.

The council did challenge the DoE decision and within a fortnight the DoE backed down. In the March 1991 council meeting, Bill Budd and Phil Turner proposed a motion condemning the Conservatives' "bigoted antagonism" towards the DSD. Judith Barnes noted that "they did nothing about the filth in the streets and they only reacted when there was a danger of the direct services department losing the contract".

The victory over the DoE was short term. When the tenders were submitted, the DSD's bid of £7m did not stand a chance, especially as (thanks to NUPE) their workers were being paid for 35 rather than 40 hour weeks. Onyx UK Waste (a subsidiary of Companie Generale d'Enterprise Automobile, the biggest refuse company in Europe) undercut them by £2m. The workforce were in for a shock. Onyx was happy to interview them, but offered them longer hours and a cut in pay of £100 a week.

* * *

The merger of the Gay & Lesbian, Race and Women's committees and their departments into a single equalities department was proposed in October 1990 in a paper requested by Julie Fitzgerald. "In no way", she said, somewhat defensively, "is Camden's support for minority groups softening". It was a move "long overdue", said Judith Barnes: "These committees are totally counterproductive and get people's backs up". Getting the backs up of people like Miss Barnes was not the purpose of the committees, but it was the icing on the cake. Within two months Sandra Plummer was arguing that "since Julie's paper has seen the light of day, there has already been an increase in harassment cases and in many cases management are already disregarding the council's equal opportunities policies".

The race committee survived the merger of the Gay & Lesbian and Women's committee in March. After nine years, the women's committee was no more. Its last chairman, Gloria Lazenby, (who had wanted the council to introduce special refuse collections by all women teams) was furious: "Coming at a time when women are again under attack it is a retrograde step that attempts to place us back to where we were in the 1960s. The white middle class male officers who run this council are crowing at our demise".

The cuts in funding hit hardest at those voluntary groups dependent on council grants. Amongst those threatened by the cuts were several Cypriot groups, in particular the Cypriot Arts Forum. At the beginning of the year, funds from the council's race unit were used to host a reception for the Cypriot High Commissioner in the town hall. Graham Shurety, who was married to a Greek Cypriot, was now again the chairman of the grants committee. Over Easter Julie Fitzgerald and her family, together with Graham Shurety and his family, and Chris Jeffrey, the head of member services, went on a ten day holiday to Cyprus. They flew on "discounted flights" subsided by the Cypriot High Commission in London and their hotel was paid for by an aspiring Cypriot film director, Panicos Chrysanthou, who was then invited by the Camden funded Cypriot Arts Forum to their summer festival in London. Chrysanthou claimed that he paid for the hotel accommodation with £700 he had received "in donations from Cypriot friends". Members of the Cypriot Arts Forum were in Cyprus while Julie Fitzgerald was there, as was the trip organiser, Dr Niazi Kizilyurek, one of Chrysanthou's friends. Kizilyurek was in the meantime being paid a £15,000 consultancy fee by Camden for "a report on Cypriot needs in the borough". Shurety had authorised Dr Kizilyurek's consultancy

221

fee following a meeting of officers and councillors four months before the Cyprus trip.

There is, said Judith Barnes through pursed lips, no such thing as a free lunch, especially when the annual grants budget was £10m. She reported the matter to the district auditor, the Metropolitan Police and to Neil Kinnock. "Absolutely extraordinary behaviour", said Julie Fitzgerald. "If I was her, I'd be highly embarrassed." The trip was "a great political success" which had informed her on "the politically correct" treatment of Greek and Turkish Cypriots in Camden. There had been no need to declare the trip on the list of members' interests because the gifts were not from those who stood to gain from council expenditure. And the trip had to be kept secret, said Graham Shurety, because otherwise their travels north of the Green Line risked being "politically endangered". Judith Barnes was "a public nuisance", he said, "for misusing council procedures". But the criticism hurt. Julie Fitzgerald told the Holborn & St Pancras Labour Party general committee meeting in May not only that she would answer no questions on the subject, but that she had taken legal advice and any party member raising the issue could face legal action.

222

Adrian States in the meantime kept up the pressure on his erstwhile colleagues on the Labour benches by direct action by his Stop the Poll Tax Campaign. Predicting that there would be 11,000 poll tax defaulters in January alone, the council block booked Highbury Corner magistrates' court so that a thousand community charge cases could be heard a day. Those found to be in default were to be left to the bailiffs. In protest, council meetings were disrupted by placard wavers, and in November 1990 by bags of soot which were thrown from the gallery onto the Tory benches below (all of which missed save one bag which exploded on Maureen Braun's head) and forced the council to reconvene for a while in the Camden Centre until the mess was mopped up.

At seven on a cold Monday morning in November, thirty chanting protestors laid siege to Julie Fitzgerald's house in Primrose Hill, "screaming, whistling and beating on the door and windows". With her was her former chief whip, Alan Woods, who told them to go away. The police were called. The leader of the council was appalled. Her two children, both under the age of ten, were present. It was an outrage. Not so, said Comrade States: "Bailiffs visited a man in Castlehaven ward on Friday who has a wife and two young children as well. People like him are now being betrayed by Labour councillors". Ken Livingstone rather agreed. Speaking of Julie Fitzgerald and Camden council, he said: "I think the people running things now are just like the Vichy regime in France under the Nazis. They convince themselves that they can make a difference, but in reality the occupying power relies on them".

The council was also heavily criticised by the new district auditor, Kash Pandya who produced a new report into the Kodikara pay off. Some of the payments, said the district auditor, "bordered on illegality". The writing off of the £6,000 car loan was "a gift from the ratepayer", and a £14,000 redundancy payment (which had never before been admitted by the council) was clearly wrong as Mr Kodikara was patently not made redundant. Frank Nickson had misdirected himself. Pandya urged the council to take legal advice to recoup £20,000 of what was now estimated to be a package worth £127,000. The simple fact that it took three years to discover what had been paid to Kodikara was, said Judith Barnes, "shocking".

On top of that the district auditor noted that there was only £100,000 contingency fund in the £181m budget for the current year, a predicted overspend of £12m which was inadequately covered by a package of cuts and was based on an assumption that £7½m overpaid to Thames Water would be recovered. The DSD was generally financially incompetent and uncompetitive, and on top of that, Camden had the worst managed local authority pension scheme in the country.

The fuss provoked a detailed, defensive letter to the *Ham & High* from Julie Fitzgerald in January 1991. The paper responded a week later, commenting unfavourably on the points she had made under the headline: "The gall of Julie". Tellingly, Jeremy Smith wrote to the paper in the week following that. If the readers had no confidence in the leader of the council, he appeared to say, at least the chief executive knew what he was doing. "I welcome", he said, somewhat magisterially, "the role that a strong local press can play in keeping local government on its toes" and then went on to say that the district auditor's findings were old hat. Things are now on the up, thanks to "my management team". The *Ham & High* did not reply, but printed on the same page two letters calling for Julie Fitzgerald's resignation.

The squeeze was on grants. The Labour group agreed to cut back by £500,000. It meant hitting their friends: Graham Shurety, the chairman of the grants committee, was called "a Judas", "traitor" and "racist" when the £41,000 funding to the Afro-Caribbean Organisation was cut. In February the committee cut funding for the Swiss Cottage and Hampstead Citizen Advice Bureaux which handled 34,000 enquiries a year. Priority, said Shurety, was to be given to deprived areas. Finsberg put on his angry face and wrote to Julie Fitzgerald asking her to revoke the decision: "Do not, please, come back and say that it is because the government charge capped your council. If you had collected even a fraction of your uncollected rents you would have had the money available for the CABs".

The allusion to the housing department was topical: rent collection was poor, as was the department's knowledge of who was in their properties. The corpse of a sixty three year old Irish tenant had been found in his flat on the Regents Park estate. He had lain there for a year before being discovered not by council officers, but by would-be squatters who broke in. In the same week a seventy six year old woman died in Gospel Oak during the cold snap. The boilers in her council block had not worked for weeks.

Another failing service was the council's old people's homes. A scathing report commissioned by the council four years earlier had made 115 recommendations for change. Following the report, Judith Barnes had made regular visits to all the council's homes in rotation. The clear lack of improvement provided not only embarrassment for the council but also an excuse for Oliver Letwin and Judith Barnes to call on Virginia Bottomley, the health minister, who promised an enquiry into the borough's old people's homes. The *Ham & High* compared the Labour party's attitude to the DSD ("blinkered extremist posturing") with the council's treatment of the old ("so called socialist caring aims").

As finances got tighter, Belsize Library faced closure (again) in September 1991 in order to save £38,000 a year. Although closing the library was "a matter of regret", said Barbara Hughes, who chaired the Leisure Committee, close it must. As Belsize was a Tory held ward, Judith Barnes, in her capacity as a local councillor, saw the announcement as "blatant and completely outrageous political bias", and added, rather helpfully as it turned out: "How they expect Glenda Jackson to win Hampstead & Highgate with this cut I do not know".

The Belsize Public Libraries Users Group ("Belsize PLUG") organised an all night sit in and led by Chris Burley, a solicitor who lived next door, applied for an injunction against the council. Three hundred people attended a meeting in the Hampstead old town hall to be addressed on the subject by the filmmaker (and wife of Michael Foot) Jill Craigie and David Wrede, the LibDem parliamentary candidate, a gynaecologist. Glenda Jackson sent a letter of support.

224

The Hampstead & Highgate Labour party under the chairmanship of Roger Robinson agreed to affiliate to Belsize PLUG, and pointed out that the council's own *Camden Citizen* magazine cost the council £75,000 a year, twice as much as the library. Mr Justice Popplewell gave the leave for a judicial review which had been taken out in the name of Dorothy Ralphs, a sixty five year old library user who would not be in a position to pay the council's costs should the council win the case. The council did not back down, but the Labour group did. They voted in October to keep the library open, albeit with reduced opening hours. It would be bad politically in a target ward in a target constituency. A review of opening hours across the borough could save £550,000 without a single closure.

Local annoyances aside, the great difficulty was going to be in the coming budget. The council was looking at a £12m overspend in 1991/2 and was having to find some £20m in savings to keep within the government's cap. On top of that there came the sudden realisation that the Banque Paribas loan was due to be paid. "£24m loan that Camden forgot" was the *Ham & High*'s headline. The budget deficit had grown overnight by £24m and no one had seen it coming. The background was simple enough. In 1986, early in his administration, Tony Dykes had authorised a £75m loan from Banque Paribas, gambling then that a Labour victory in the general election would bail the council out, or at least provide the council with a way to repay the loan. The original terms were that the council would have a four year period before any payments were due. Julie Fitzgerald, who then chaired the Policy & Resources Committee, described it as "like taking a mortgage". In 1988, after Labour had lost the general election, the council renegotiated the loan to extend the first payment date to 1991.

All had gone quiet after the 1988 negotiations until the Banque Paribas wrote to the council in April 1991 to ask why the council had not made any further approaches about refinancing. It was too late. In August 1991 the council paid, as it was contractually bound to do, £25m. That money was taken out of the current year's budget, leaving a deficit. Under the rules, the council could borrow no more and so was forced to apply to the Department of the Environment for supplementary credit approvals. Without refinancing, the capital budget for the current year would be completely undermined.

The Department of the Environment refused to allow Camden

to borrow more. The environment minister, Michael Portillo, was unsympathetic. "I am amazed that Camden forgot about this loan, and that strikes me as an extraordinary piece of mismanagement". The government should not get involved, he said: "I just feel sorry that it's the poor people of Camden who have to pick up the tab".

As the council could not raise the money by putting up the poll tax because the government was waiting to cap them, it was indeed the poor who would have to pick up the tab. In October the Labour group agonised and then agreed to put up council rents by £11 a week from £30 to £41 –a 35% increase[1]. Eight of the eleven pounds was to repay Paribas. Sue Berger of the Camden Federation of Tenants made their position clear: "It is completely unjust for this burden to be borne by council tenants". At the next council meeting the poll tax demonstrators were rather sidelined by Camden Federation members waving placards reading "Camden Tenants say No Rent Increase".

The social workers had been on strike since June because the council had not implemented a national pay agreement. As the crisis developed, Ken Dixon, the director of social services who had been on sick leave for three months suffering from nervous exhaustion, resigned in protest at the proposed cuts. Just after he left, the department issued seven hundred voluntary redundancy notices. The council announced that it hoped to save £25m by reducing the workforce by 750. Jeremy Smith read the riot act to councillors and managers alike. The days of the council spending beyond its means were over. Five months into their industrial action, the social workers were threatened with the sack and NALGO threatened an all out strike.

Jeremy Smith and John Mabey, the acting director of finance, ordered a freeze on all spending except that to which there was a contractual obligation. Judith Barnes described Mabey as having an "inescapable duty" to apply for a Section 114 Notice –that is to inform the Department of the Environment that the borough was unlikely to balance the books at the end of the year, and to invite the minister to order a statutory spending freeze. "We are", she said, "just wading further and further into the mire. We are at the end of the road". Mabey rather dismissively let her know that things were not that bad, but within a month he had relented, issued the Section 114 notice and got a statutory order freezing expenditure for the rest of the year. Rather

---

[1]   Rents had already been put up £3.70 in April, the total annual increase was 54%, the second highest rise in the country.

embarrassingly he found that in the month in which he had issued an informal freeze, the deficit had increased by another million making the anticipated shortfall £6m. Judith Barnes wrote to Portillo demanding that the borough be subjected to an "extraordinary audit".

The pressure mounted. In early November the Hampstead & Highgate Labour party had a vote of no confidence in Julie Fitzgerald. It was narrowly defeated, and a fortnight later Holborn & St Pancras went through the same exercise. She survived by two votes but, as the papers were quick to point out, there were three abstentions, one of whom was Julian Fulbrook who was clearly waiting to succeed her. The no confidence motion had been instigated by Neil Kinnock's office in Walworth Road. "It was", said an inside source, "a right wing orchestrated coup and it failed. They got their numbers wrong". But only just. Ten members of the Labour group had refused to back their leader[2].

The town hall staff offered no sympathy. In early December Camden NALGO paid for full page advertisements in the local papers urging people to join a march on the town hall to petition the December council meeting. The union "condemned" the government for the destruction of local services, but also "we condemn the chief executive and the senior management of Camden whose mismanagement has fanned the present crisis". On 11th December "thousands of town hall staff" (said the New Journal) marched from Kentish Town chanting "Get up off your knees Camden! Fight back now!"

Sympathetic though many Labour councillors were, they had in their minds the "surcharge warning" that had been issued by the district auditor. They risked both surcharge and disqualification unless they took immediate steps to balance the crippling budget deficit. To do otherwise would be to invite government commissioners to step in and run the borough. The council voted to cut the budget by £30m[3].

Mary Helsdon resigned from the Labour Party (but not from the council) "in disgust" at Neil Kinnock's support for Trident. John "IRA" Wakeham moved to Bristol and offered to resign from the council, but his ward wanted him to stay on to avoid a by election. "I am ashamed of

227

---

2   They were Roy Shaw, John Mills, Julian Fulbrook, Richard Arthur, Terry Comerford, Jane Roberts, Jerry Williams, Maggie Cosin, Simon McDonald and Bubbles Polya.

3   The education budget was to be cut by £3.36m, environment by £4.8m, leisure by £2.6m, social services by £5.6m, grants by £865,000 and central services by £6.3m.

the lack of drive shown by the past three Camden regimes", he told them (and the press), before launching into a critique on the failings of Phil Turner, Tony Dykes and Julie Fitzgerald. The *Ham & High* printed a letter from Ken Hulme in their Christmas edition: "Nothing can excuse the very poor performance of Camden council's leadership in the past year", he wrote. "Poor financial management, 'forgotten' loan repayments and the failure to act on the sound advice of the district auditor, combined with a lack of purpose, vision or direction have turned a bad situation into a disaster. Julie Fitzgerald should resign".

AT the beginning of 1992, the 39 year old Steve Bundred took up his post as the director of finance. He had an unusual background in that he had been an unsuccessful Labour candidate in the European elections in 1979[4], and in 1981 he was elected in Islington to the GLC where he was prominent as one of Livingstone's allies. Since then his career had taken a rather more conventional direction which included accountancy qualifications and a post as the assistant director at Hackney. His selection had not been easy in that he was up against John Mabey, the acting director, and Tony Dykes had used his casting vote to get him the job, but Bundred had the approval of Julian Tobin who, disapproving of his past politics, thought him a good accountant. The *Ham & High* introduced him to their readership with a profile: "He speaks softly....the distinct remnants of his Liverpudlian accent giving his speech a gentle form of authority, even a mild touch of menace..."

"There is a clear recognition on the part of elected members", said Bundred, "that the difficulties they find themselves in now are a consequence of decisions in the 1980s, and that there now needs to be a very different approach. It will be a painful process. In constructing the 1992/93 budget, necessary decisions will mean service reduction of £25m, and further staff reductions, and you can't make that level of cuts without a real impact on services."

It was not to be an auspicious start in that the Labour group, against his advice, dropped plans they had agreed earlier to cut a further £6m from the coming budget, and hoped to make up some of the shortfall by lowering the contingency reserve from £5m to £2.1m. But when the Policy & Resources committee met to agree

228

4   He stood in S.E.London where he lost to Sir Brandon Rhys Williams, who had so narrowly been selected in favour of Tony Kerpel.

the new budget, a letter from Kash Pandya, the district auditor, was hand delivered to the town hall. The contents took everyone by surprise. Pandya asserted that the council was about to fail in its duty to set a lawful budget and demanded that the council set a higher poll tax to avoid not balancing the 1992/92 budget. He added the reminder that the councillors would face being surcharged if they failed in their statutory duty. The Policy & Resources committee meeting was cancelled. "To deliver a letter an hour before the budget meeting questions his professionalism," said Fitzgerald of Pandya.

There had to be a general election before 10th June 1992. All the polls showed that it was going to be close, and many predicted a Labour victory. The March council meeting was infected by election fever. Labour had something of an advantage, as the *Ham & High* noted of the introduction of question time: "Peeved at having to fend off awkward probing from their Tory and Liberal Democrat opponents, Labour's leaders can now field placed questions from their colleagues and ramble on to their hearts' content". Judith Barnes, who was herself standing as the Conservative candidate in Sunderland, attacked the council's housing building campaign in the mid-1970s costing double the rate of the private sector, the longest construction timescales in the country in 1980 and "funny money" deals in the mid-80s, before ending rather limply with "heating problems on the Alexandra Road estate in West Hampstead where tenants were either freezing or frying eggs on their kitchen floors." Andrew Marshall asked why no members of the Labour front bench would allow themselves to be photographed with either Fitzgerald or Dykes.

When, in March, the election was announced for 9 April, the parties were ready. Glenda Jackson and Frank Dobson had a joint campaign launch in Haverstock School on the boundary of the two constituencies. To the stirring music of *Jerusalem*, they fought their way through crowds of supporters and foreign press reporters (all there for Glenda, not Frank) for the formal adoption meeting where they were greeted by Harry "Loadsamoney" Enfield who urged the faithful to dig deep. The *New Journal* marvelled at the "razmataz presidential style campaign tactics." "This election", said Miss Jackson, "is the most important since the second world war. Our nation is trapped in the midst of the longest, the deepest recession this century. Industry decimated, businesses bankrupt, our infrastructure crumbling at the seams. And the people of this country, the people who are its lifeblood, find themselves under unrelenting attack from poverty, from crime, from unemployment, from all the things that in the year 1992 should be anathema to any civilised society".

Letwin's adoption meeting at the Clive Hotel a week later was just as glitzy (but without Harry Enfield). He was accompanied into the packed and applauding conference room ("US razzmatazz style" said the *Ham & High*) to stirring Andrew Lloyd Webber music by a troop of drippy looking Young Conservatives in pale blue "Let's Win with Letwin" sweat shirts. Each held aloft a placard with a flattering photograph of the candidate.

Dr Wrede, the LibDem gynaecologist, drove round Hampstead in an old orange VW Camper van. He did what he could, but he knew that he could afford to relax. A fortnight before the election Corals the bookies had Glenda the favourite at odds of 1/6 on, and Letwin trailing at 11/4.

Frank Dobson's campaign was so much in the shadow of the Glenda Jackson campaign that it became something of an effort for the press to even mention it. This even applied to the local papers. As part of the Labour front bench team touring the country, Dobson was rarely in the constituency. The only real press coverage achieved by Andrew McHallam, the Conservative candidate, was his complaint that he had been jostled by the Workers Against Racism supporters in Camden High Street. (Not so, said the WAR candidate, Nigel Lewis, who complained of one of his people being punched by a Tory.[5])

Having failed to bring down Finsberg, despite a twenty two year campaign, the *Ham & High* put the boot in on Letwin. It did so in the week of the election. "Disgust as Tory plays the race card", was the front page headline. The four candidates had been invited to Hampstead Synagogue for a public debate in which a member of the audience asked the candidates for their views on something that had not been mentioned in the campaign before, the Immigration Bill. Letwin backed it. "I don't want this society to be turned into a quite different society" he said. "If we don't want this society torn apart, we do have to have controls". The Green Party candidate, Stephen Games, heckled him with the question: "Is this the 'Rivers of Blood'

230

---

5   Nigel Lewis (or Castledine on his birth certificate) was a member of the Revolutionary Communist Party. He had proved an extraordinary organiser of angry Bengali youths complaining about the police, racist attacks and society generally. He suffered a brain haemorrhage two months after the election and died, aged 29.

speech, Oliver?" Letwin said it was not.

It was not a major part of the debate, although it got a half column in the *New Journal*, but the *Ham & High* reporter pursued the other candidates after the event and gave them a second chance to respond to what Letwin had said. His remarks, said Glenda, were "shocking and distasteful" and had made the audience feel uncomfortable. "Very disturbing" agreed Dr Wrede, thankful at the opportunity of saying that which he had not said in the meeting. "What remarks like that do is encourage racial intolerance. To stir it up as an issue, particularly in a Jewish meeting, was very disturbing." Letwin had, reported the *Ham & High*, "incensed all three of his opponents".

This headline, on the Friday before polling day had Letwin chasing his tail for the rest of the week, urgently composing and then distributing tens of thousands of copies of a single sheet letter from him pointing out that he is "the son of immigrants, the grandson of refugees and someone whose relations were persecuted by Nazis", and that he wanted to guarantee sanctuary to genuine refugees but not bogus asylum seekers. He wrote to the editor to set the record straight: "I am shocked at the disgraceful personal slur contained in the headline of the *Ham & High*". His complaint was obligingly printed on their front page but, of course, that happened a day after he had lost the seat to Glenda Jackson.

Finsberg won in 1987 with just over 2,000 more votes than Phil Turner. Glenda Jackson also got 2,000 more votes than Turner, but Letwin managed 1,500 fewer votes than Finsberg. The swing to Labour was 4.15%. When the count finished at three, Miss Jackson said what needed to be said: "The people of Hampstead have returned this seat to Labour because they feel that never before has this seat been needed by the Labour Party as it is now to help the homeless, the frail and the sick". She then left by a side door to avoid the photographers and disappeared into the night.

Letwin blamed his defeat on the collapse of the LibDems, whose vote had almost collapsed by half to fewer than five thousand: "I was quite optimistic before the count, but when I saw how small the piles of votes for the LibDems were, I knew things were bad", and then, echoing the prediction made by Martin Morton after the 1971 borough elections, he added: "This seat is only on loan to the Labour Party". Dr Wrede's singular analysis was that "the fear and uncertainty over proportional representation drove voters into the arms of the Labour Party". The *Ham & High*, who rather approved of Dr Wrede, blamed his lack of success on tactical voting. In Holborn & St Pancras Frank Dobson's majority increased while his vote stood still and both the Conservative Andrew McHallam and the LibDem Jenny Horne-Roberts saw their support shrink by two and a half thousand votes each.[6]

The general election over, the Labour group settled down to its own elections. Julie Fitzgerald was challenged head on by Julian Fulbrook, the new candidate of the centre-right. She won, but narrowly by 22 votes to 18. Roy Shaw remained as one of the two deputy leaders, but was joined by Phil Turner (who replaced Bill Saunders who had recently died). John Mills was replaced in housing by the newcomer Charlie Hedges, a gargantuan breeder of Great Danes who had until recently chaired the Camden Fed.

In the fall out of the Paribas affair, Jeremy Smith had commissioned Andrew Arden QC to carry out an enquiry into why the council had not anticipated the loan repayment that fell due in 1991. Although it had been expected in the spring, Arden produced his report in July 1992. Its contents were highly embarrassing for the council. The report described an inadequately staffed legal department pressurised by the political leadership into making catastrophic decisions. Arden identified "the profound error" as taking place in January 1988 when a paper issued by the finance department misleadingly stated that the first half of the loan would be repaid in five years time, rather than five years from 1986. Tony Watts, the acting head of the legal department, admitted to Arden that he had not fully understood the documents he had signed on behalf of the council. At the time, he said, he was under extreme pressure from the financial directorate, his department was on the verge of collapse and he was nearing physical and mental exhaustion. Furthermore, the opposition were unable to get information to which they were entitled because the then chief executive, Frank Nickson, had failed to give adequate answers to their enquiries.

The Conservatives were angry because, as Judith Barnes said, the report hit the wrong target. Arden's narrow terms of reference had been defined by Jeremy Smith with Fitzgerald and Dykes breathing down his neck. They had specifically forbidden Arden from looking at the role of councillors. The Labour leadership had been let off the hook before the enquiry had begun. It proves, said Barnes, that there

---

6   Or rather, the LibDem Mrs Horne-Roberts got 2,500 fewer votes than had the Liberal candidate Simon McGrath in the 1987 general election. Jenny Horne-Roberts was in a former life the glamorous Labour Camden councillor Jenny Horne and Labour parliamentary candidate for Fareham.

is no political accountability in this borough. Ken Hulme[7], writing from beyond the political grave but still persistently a thorn in the side of the Fitzgerald/Dykes faction, wrote to Arden: "How can an enquiry overlook the confusion of roles and responsibilities which took place between senior managers, policy advisors and elected members? The buck cannot stop with some unfortunate officer who may or may not have made a mistake". It did.

As the report had not been allowed to look into the role of the leadership, it could not blame the leadership and so, the leadership was able to proclaim that it had not been criticised. In any event, said Fitzgerald, speaking of the council officers concerned: "There was no scandal in the sense that they took no personal gain".

Allegations of personal gain came from elsewhere in that the Cyprus scandal would not go away. Judith Barnes had pressed for answers and was told that Dr Niazi Kizilyurek, who had arranged the trip and who had already received £9,000 (of the agreed £15,000) for writing a report that had not materialised twenty months after its commission. "I'm pissed off" said Shurety, "That we haven't seen a report", and the council threatened to sue. Twenty months after he was commissioned to do the work, Kizilyurek duly presented the council with a 156 page report mostly (said Bubbles Polya) "a rambling, biased history of Cyprus". Local Cypriot groups complained that he had not consulted them and that the report was "worthless". Nevertheless, the Equalities committee agreed to pay him £11,500. Although she had not read all of the report, the account of Cyprus's history, said Gloria Lazenby, was "very helpful".

The following council meeting brought the most direct accusation of corruption against the leader yet. The Cyprus report, spat Judith Barnes, was "a useless wad of paper and a disgusting waste of money. Apart from Dr Kizilyurek, who received £11,500 of public money, only one other person had benefitted from all this: "The leader of the council to the tune of ten days in a high class hotel in Cyprus". There was no reply.[8]

233

---

7   Ken Hulme, now the leader and sole member of the Labour group on Saddleworth Parish Council and an outspoken critic of the Greater Manchester Passenger Transport Executive's plans for congestion charging.

8   The story rather fizzled after this as the district auditor did not publish his report until November 1993, when both Julie Fitzgerald and Graham Shurety were politically passé. According to the report, the appointment of Dr Kizilyurek as a consultant was "very unsatisfactory" but not illegal, and it was noted that the council had since tightened up the rules on consultation.

* * *

In Hampstead, 1992 was the year of McDonalds. Hampstead has long had tea rooms and cafés, bistros and pizzerias (although, in part due to its proximity to the West End, decent restaurants have always been scarce), but it had never had anything quite so disturbingly vulgar as a fast food outlet. Although low property prices had forced the village into an egalitarian phase that had lasted into the seventies, Hampstead no longer had a need for Woolworths. In 1980 McDonalds had purchased the old Woolworths building (now Waterstones) on the High Street. McDonalds applied for planning permission. The Hampstead & Old Heath Society and pretty well every other group in the parish subscribed to Hampstead's "Burger Off" campaign. They had unexpected allies on the left who saw McDonalds as being an unwelcome arm of American imperialism. Tory and Labour councillors united and refused planning permission to change the use of the building from retail to restaurant. McDonalds appealed, but Michael Heseltine, then at the Department of the Environment ruled against McDonalds, who then sold the building.

In 1991, McDonalds planned to open on the other side of the High Street where a former Pizza shop was up for sale. Towards the end of the pizza shop's lease the premises had been for a short while a second hand bookshop. McDonalds held that they did not need planning permission, and the council officers agreed with them. The chairman and his deputy of the planning committee, Ernest James and Paul Stinchcombe[9], both barristers, thought otherwise. If McDonalds did not apply to the council for change of use, the committee would enforce a breach of planning rules. The restaurant use, said James, had lapsed when the second hand bookshop began trading.

McDonalds complied and applied to the planning committee to change the use of the property back to a restaurant. The council officers advised the committee to allow the change, but Ernest James now had the bit between his teeth. He persuaded the committee, who took little persuading, to trust him as a lawyer and to refuse the application. "Our aim", he told the press afterwards, "is to preserve our policy of

---

9   They were described by the *New Journal* as "The Rumpole Brothers". Then still in his twenties, Stinchcombe became the MP for Wellingborough in the Labour landslide of 1997, beating the Conservative incumbent by 187 votes. He won again in 2002, but lost by 687 votes in 2005.

maintaining retail shops in core retail areas, of which this is one".[10]

McDonalds appealed to the High Court and won. Camden's case had been made difficult in that the council officers who had advised that the change of use be allowed, had then been obliged to argue that their own advice was wrong and that, in effect, Councillor James's was right. James refused to back down, and announced that the council would appeal the High Court decision. "I have nothing against McDonalds" he said, "although I think I trod in one once". The Court of Appeal upheld the High Court and awarded £25,000 costs against the council.[11]

In the July 1992 council meeting, following a barrage of eggs, flour, icing sugar and smoke bombs onto the Tory benches (and onto Julian Tobin in particular), Andrew Marshall, the Conservative spokesman on social services, pointed out that the council's bad debts had risen from £86m last year to £101m this year. His analysis was to be echoed through the council for years to come: "The Labour group has ignored financial health issues and now they have lost control of the council not to the Conservative Party, but to the unelected director of finance". A few days later, as if to make his point for him, Bundred told the Policy & Resources committee that "Camden faces at least another year of severe financial constraints on all fronts".

235

The most difficult of the cuts fell on the voluntary sector –not difficult in that they would necessarily cause more hurt, but difficult in that the many voluntary organisations were themselves urging their workers, supporters and beneficiaries to campaign against the cuts. They were for the most part those very people who had marched time and time again to the town hall for Phil Turner for the rate setting debates in 1985. The special grants meeting at which the first cuts were to be made was besieged by hundreds of pensioners and schoolchildren waving banners outside the town hall. The committee was presented with a list of 41 organisations whose funding was to be reviewed –community

---

10 In the middle of all this, Ernest James got himself into the papers again for being seized by the gaoler at Southwark Crown Court for cheeking Judge Butler.

11 Planning permission was granted subject to the facade being painted black rather than the usual garish red and yellow, and subject to the provision of litter patrols. Peggy Jay, one of the leaders of the Burger Off campaign, was spotted eating a burger there when McDonalds finally opened the doors in June 1993. "It was very tasty", she said. Peter Gorb, chairman of the Hampstead & Old Heath Society, was forgiving: "I'm delighted", he said, "that she enjoyed her meal in the company of children and other undiscerning eaters".

associations, youth clubs, law centres, and even the Camden Fed.

Bundred in a television interview in September 1992 made it clear that he was prepared to take drastic action, notably a spending freeze, if the councillors did not vote through the cuts he felt necessary. When the Labour group came again to consider the cuts (with 700 demonstrators outside the town hall), the proposal met with opposition. The leaders of the dissidents were the disgruntled right wing, led by John Mills, and the disgruntled left wing, led by Graham Good, a youth worker whose own job was at risk. The group voted to reduce the cuts from £3.2m to £1.5m, giving some hope to the demonstrators outside, but sending out a strong signal that the Labour group did not have the stomach to carry through Bundred's £32m programme of cutbacks. It was "a bloody open rebellion", remarked the *New Journal* enthusiastically. "The leadership budget is in tatters".

At the October council meeting, councillors were again met outside by 700 placard waving demonstrators, this time being addressed by Graham Good from the back of a Camden Community Transport van: "Make sure you harass the councillors as they go in. Make their lives hell! If you're not on the list of cuts this year, you'll be on the list next year! Keep on campaigning! Camden will be the laughing stock of London if they go through with these cuts. All we'll have left is the town hall and the chief executive!"

It was clear that spending was still not under control. In November, Steve Bundred announced that the council was heading for a £9.9m deficit by the end of the year and issued the second Section 114 notice in a year. "Bundred takes over" was the headline in the *New Journal*. He had taken control of the council and "removed all spending decisions from the councillors". Camden's expenditure was frozen until the end of the financial year. The council, he said, had been bankrupt for months.

"What a shambles," said Judith Barnes. "This was going to be the year in which we got the finances right." For Julie Fitzgerald, the penny had dropped. "Local government has become", she wrote, "merely an agent of central government, with little or no power to vary provision to suit local needs". Times had changed. In 1990, Camden had 9,600 employees. There were now only 6,800, almost 30% fewer.

At the end of the month, Bundred called a special council meeting because he had word that the district auditor had expressed himself to be "increasingly concerned about the council's financial health" and was about to issue a public interest report. The council meeting, despite grumbling, voted through Bundred's medicine of £10m cuts by the end of the year and for him to lift the Section 114 notice. The cuts were felt in every department. In March 1993, much was made of the council's 320 school kitchen staff, half of whom were made redundant to help meet the £7m cut in the education budget. Schools were to get ready cooked meals and new staff were to be taken on at lower pay scales. "The council", said Bob Hall, now the NUPE Camden branch chairman, "are playing Russian roulette with the dinner ladies".

Also In March 1993, Camden celebrated the end of the poll tax and set its first council tax. Its Band D tax was set at £717 a household, nearly £200 more than most other authorities and the highest in Inner London. As it was replacing a poll tax of £375 per adult, it hit hardest those living alone. It is, said Glenda Jackson, "a disaster." Judith Barnes claimed that the tax could be set at £500 "if only the council had the conviction to tackle bureaucracy and staff benefits", which, countered Phil Turner, would mean the unacceptable cutting of staff, and cutting the earnings and benefits of the survivors, which would provoke prolonged strikes. "We are paying for the follies of the past", persisted Miss Barnes. "Of £38m this coming year alone, £16m was to pay for cover for bad debts, £10m on the infamous French bank loan, £7m on a leaseback deal that Camden messed up, and £5m to repay other councils that have bailed Camden out of its constant budget deficits".

It was all over for Julie Fitzgerald. The Bundred intervention had been the final straw and amid whispered promises that she was going, she finally announced her intention to resign in April and to stand down from the council in the elections. "I'm proud," she said, "to have been leader during the period where we've run the best schools in inner London, and the best housing benefits system in the country, and put an end to the use of bed and breakfast accommodation for homeless families". Others were less kind. She had, noted the *Ham & High*, led Camden through three years of turmoil.

The Labour group was presented with the old choice of left and right. Eight years after he stepped down as leader, Phil Turner threw his hat back into the ring. An act, suggested the *Ham & High*, of "mere *chutzpah*" by "the man responsible for so many of Camden's woes because of his blinkered belief that the council could ignore the threat of a Tory government in the hope that a Labour victory would eventually take the self impaled Camden off the hook."

Julian Fulbrook, who had been tipped by the *New Journal* to be the next Labour leader, declined the challenge saying that he had a family and in any event was working on a book on health and safety law. The

237

right wing of the party was instead represented by Richard Arthur, a forty nine year old father of three and a venture capitalist. He had been on the council in the early 1970s (before resigning and causing the by election that let Morton back) and had then spent ten years in Singapore, and more recently had been working in Poland. He had only returned to the council in 1990, and had since then been the chairman of the social services committee which had been in the thick of the cuts. Ernest James, the anti-establishment, anti-McDonalds barrister, stood for the awkward squad.

It was close. When James lost in the first round, all his votes went to Turner, leaving the party divided with twenty votes each for Arthur and Turner. Arthur won the third ballot 22-19. "The right wing of the Labour group", spat the *New Journal*, "has taken control of Camden council in an orchestrated move. Senior councillors on the left were unceremoniously dumped." The *Ham & High* saw it as the end of an era: "The ghosts of Livingstone and Dobson have been exorcised". Arthur had inherited a divided Labour group. Although one of the two deputy leaders was the "respected veteran" Roy Shaw, the other was Tony Dykes "a former leader guilty of political blindness". But Dykes was the only left winger left standing and, importantly, John Mills took over the Policy & Resources Committee. The Arthur/Mills partnership was to prove both enduring and effective. Times had changed: the Labour group was in the hands of a banker and a man with a mail order business[12]. The face of real socialism, Julie Fitzgerald, who a few minutes before had been the leader of the council, could not now even get elected to chair the public health committee.

12 John Mills, the mail order man, was also the husband of the Director of Public Prosecutions. His wife, Barbara Mills, had been appointed to the post in 1992 following the sudden resignation of the previous director, Sir Alan Green, who had accepted a police caution for cruising around Kings Cross in his Jaguar in search of a bit of rough. Dame Barbara is currently the Adjudicator for HM Revenue and Customs.

JULIE FITZGERALD: INTO THE BUFFERS

9 |

The end of politics:
Richard Arthur

"What I hope is fresh about my leadership," said Richard Arthur, "is that we won't face the same financial crisis and cuts we have seen in the last three years. We now have a stable budget and we can build on that". "Stability", observed the *Ham & High* approvingly, "appears to be Mr Arthur's watchword."

The one obvious piece of unfinished business from the Fitzgerald era was the direct service departments. In the week that Arthur was elected leader, Judith Barnes pointed out that the DSDs had lost £10m since 1989 and the Labour group had voted to keep the in house building maintenance department going despite its losses of £5m against Bundred's advice to the contrary. The Labour group followed Bill Budd's plaintive plea that the department should be kept going "for six months to give it a chance to make a profit". Poor old Bill Budd represented, said Skolar, "the worst piece of Labour rose tinted spectacles and fable and mythology I have seen in my life"[1]. He was right, and Arthur and Bundred were not going to help. The borough's building maintenance, highways & sewerage, vehicle maintenance and new construction departments hit the buffers. The crunch came in August when John Gummer, the Environment Secretary, announced that they were to be wound up for failing to meet their statutory 5% profit targets. "Extremely disappointing", said Arthur, cheerfully.

Norman Lamont's March budget had given the council an unexpected windfall. He lifted the restraints there had been on

239

---

1   Skolar had been back on the council since May 1992 following a by election in Swiss Cottage.

the proceeds of property sales so that they could all be spent on capital projects. The "holiday" from the regulations would end on 31st December and so Camden concentrated on getting in as much as it could. By the deadline the council had raised some £30m on commercial and residential property sales, including the Hillview estate of short-life properties in King's Cross, Holly Court School in Highgate and, after years of trying, the Roundhouse (which went for £900,000 in May).

By the end of 1993 the council was confident enough to announce that council tax bills would fall massively in the coming year just before the local elections. The government was not going to cut its grant funding. Just before Christmas, Arthur set out his main priorities to the press: to balance the budget, to maintain or lower council tax and to increase spending on capital assets by way of spending more on repairs.

Also by the end of the year, it became clear that the new regime was no longer likely to be under threat. Julie Fitzgerald, Tony Dykes, Graham Shurety and Graham Good all announced they were standing down.[2] The left wing had abdicated. Phil Turner was the only left winger of note to get reselected. "The left is to be relegated to the fringes of power for the first time since 1981", enthused the Ham & High.

To make the point, the council tax was cut in March, not by as much as John Mills had enthusiastically predicted, but (at Band D) it came down by £66 (9.2%) from £717 to £651. The payroll had been reduced by a fifth. "The best reduction in the country", said Mills. And the council rents went up, without a squeak, by £2.50 a week. The budget process was overseen by Steve Bundred ("or Mr Grumpy as he is affectionately known by the councillors", reported the Ham & High, following one of Ernest James's informal briefings). The direction that he and Arthur were going was just the way that Judith Barnes wanted to go. The Tories could not oppose the cuts but instead argued, somewhat awkwardly, for cuts of a further £10½m to reduce Band D tax to £492. Bundred's budget was voted through. "Mr Grumpy", reported the Ham & High, "looked decidedly grumpy at the result".

At about the same time, UNISON, the newly named town hall union, revealed that of the thirty staff laid off in the housing department, twenty were black. Dave Eggmore, the Camden branch secretary, tried to get things going. "It stank of racism", he said. "Nothing has changed".

---

2   In 1993 Tony Dykes became Christian Aid's regional manager for Southern Africa. He left in 2007 to become the director of Action South Africa (ACTSA), the successor body to the Anti-Apartheid Movement.

But there were no takers. The left wing was silent or resigned to resign. Not a single councillor took up the cause, which was settled by a stern letter from the director of housing passed through the council's public relations department. The department was in a "complex process" of "restructuring" in which jobs were "ring fenced" and "housing officers" were "selected" or "deselected".

The Conservative manifesto ("Common Sense in Camden") was launched later in the month. Twice a week refuse collections would be reintroduced, parking fines would be imposed rather than clamping, and traffic calming measures would be used instead of road closures. Council tax would be reduced by a further £167 by instituting a strict billing regime, implementing staff incentives and eliminating staff perks. The last item was a live issue, especially as, only a year before, Jeremy Smith had described the council's terms and conditions of employment as "generous to the point of illegality". Richard Arthur took another view: "Only a party with no expectation of winning could come up with such a profoundly barmy programme", he said. "So Councillor Arthur thinks it barmy to make efficiency programmes to reduce the council tax and improve services", answered Barnes. "He gives a new twist to the expression 'loony left'". Labour's own manifesto ("Our Values Our Vision") promised greater efficiency. "We have a good deal to be proud of", said Arthur.

241

The reality was that few were interested in the council anymore, and bickering between rival councillors interested no one. The voters did not take the election as an opportunity to comment on the great changes in Camden or on the failures of the Fitzgerald years. They took it as an opportunity to comment on the state of John Major's government.

"Tory Blues", cheered the headline in the *New Journal*. "Labour romp to a record majority" explained the *Ham & High*. On the same 46% turnout as in 1990, Labour won the election by 47 seats, leaving only seven Conservatives and five LibDems. The sheer scale of the win came as something of a happy surprise to the Labour Party campaigners. It had been thought that support for the Tories could not dive lower than it had been on the introduction of the poll tax at the end of the Thatcher era. But the Major factor turned out to be more significant than the Thatcher factor. "It shows," said Richard Arthur, "the disarray of the Tory Party and is an endorsement of our policies in Camden". Fifteen years of Conservative government, and now the economic fallout of Black

Monday, had encouraged Labour activism. While the Conservatives were left to stew, Labour, from a position of strength, went on the attack. They targeted three Conservative wards taking back all three seats in Swiss Cottage, two of the three seats in Adelaide, and one of the three seats in Belsize[3].

The LibDems were also on the attack. In 1990 they lost in Hampstead Town by a single vote. Now, after a long campaign and with both Conservative councillors standing down, they took both seats by a wide margin of over double the Tory vote. They also took, against a Labour fight back, one of the two seats in West Hampstead. Significantly, their five seats did not properly reflect the scale of their advance: they gained 18½% of the vote against the Conservatives' 22½% and Labour's 53%. Had seats been allocated under a system of proportional representation, they would have doubled their number. "There is a yellow tide washing itself up against the Labour Party in Camden", gushed the New Journal in a hopeful editorial to be repeated by the paper at every election time for the next twelve years[4]. "It was a fantastic night for us", said Flick Rea. "We fought hard on local issues and these results prove that our potential in Camden is huge."

And the Green Party contested eighteen wards, coming bottom of the poll in fourteen, but managing to beat the Tories in two hopelessly Labour seats, and the LibDems in Highgate.

It had been a bad night for the Conservatives nationally. In neighbouring Barnet, the Tories lost control of the council after twenty nine years to an alliance of Labour and LibDems. In Camden, the Tories, although impregnable now only in their two strongholds of Fitzjohns and Frognal, had seen their vote slip in every other ward. They lost eight seats and were left with only seven. It had been by far their worst result since the birth of Camden. "This is", said Judith Barnes, "a sad day for local democracy because national issues dominated the vote. It is certainly not a resounding vote of confidence in Labour's running of this council." The Ham & High was not sympathetic. The paper had taken against Judith Barnes in much the same way it had once taken against

---

3   One of the losers in Swiss Cottage was Peter Skolar. It was his last Camden election, although his interest in municipal politics continued first on Barnet and then on Oxford County Council. He now chairs Oxfordshire's Health Scrutiny panel. Huntly Spence was the Tory loser in Belsize where three women were elected. He attributed his defeat to there being "too many feminists" in the ward.

4   The New Journal's line was consistent: the people would punish New Labour for ditching socialism, and the means of that punishment would be the LibDems.

Finsberg: "The Tories cannot shrug off their defeat and blame it on the John Major government. That would be far too easy an answer and very much like the complacency which led the electorate to reject them in the first place". In Hampstead, "no one has worked harder than Flick Rea, Jane Schopflin and their colleagues".

The editorial bought in a sharp letter from Judith Barnes setting out how the only significant opposition on the council had come from the Tories, and how the swing against them had been far less than had been the case nationally. It was an incitement for activists from the other parties to write in. The newly elected Labour councillor Gerry Harrison put it this way:

> *"Councillor Barnes reminds one of the Black Knight in Monty Python and the Holy Grail who in a duel with King Arthur (geddit?) loses, one by one, each limb and finally his head, yet still believes that somehow he is the winner. Someone should tell her the truth."*

The first Labour group meeting of the new council was flooded with new councillors, and although the left wingers were in a minority, it was not an easy arrangement. There was no challenge to Arthur for the leadership: the only tussle of note being the replacement of Roy Shaw by Jane Roberts as joint deputy leader with Phil Turner.

243

Following his reinstatement, Richard Arthur's first act was to go on the offensive at the town hall unions. Before the election he had referred to Judith Barnes's attacks on staff perks as being "barmy", but with the election over he adopted her plans to end the entitlement to "extra holiday, forty weeks annual adoption leave and fifty days sickness dependency leave" which was then costing the council £15m a year. His modest proposal was to sack all the council's 6,032 employees and reemploy them on new contracts. An "absurd, outrageous and ridiculous" solution, said Dave Eggmore of UNISON.

Having expensively failed in the Court of Appeal to stop McDonalds getting planning permission in Hampstead, the council now took on the Americans in Kings Cross. McDonalds applied for change of use for part of the old Post Office building opposite the station. A local resident, Harvey Bass, collected a petition signed by 1,400 (including Glenda Jackson and Frank Dobson) and handed it to the planning committee. A late opening McDonalds "would give pimps and drug dealers a legitimate excuse to hang around late at night". The council's own planning officers advised the committee to grant planning approval as there were no arguable grounds for refusal. In September 1994 the committee refused the application. "A great victory for the local community", said Mr Bass, but, like the early victory in Hampstead, not one that would last.

In September 1994, Charlie Rossi, the former Camden rat catcher and then GLC councillor, died aged 66. A big, heavy man with an impressive laugh, the papers gave him a big, if coded, send off. Although he had a Neapolitan grandfather, he was described as a larger than life Glaswegian, which was a polite way of saying that he was aggressive and had a loud laugh. But those who had liked him, had liked him very much. As the *New Journal* put it, he had been "the people's champ".

On the same day that Rossi's death was reported in the papers, the closure was announced of the Mornington Sports Centre (on Arlington Road) which Rossi had founded[5]. "Who are the guilty men?" roared the *New Journal*, as if the shrine of a saint had been desecrated. They answered the question with photographs of the council's deputy leader, Phil Turner, and "finance chief" John Mills, who had taken the decision to close the centre because it was £28,000 in debt and had no way of paying its bills as it had already received its grant for the year.

This last piece of news came as something of a surprise as grants to voluntary organisations were paid by the council in quarterly instalments. It soon became clear that the chairman of the grants subcommittee, Dave Horan, who was also a director of the centre, had ordered a council officer to change the minutes of the December meeting when the grant had been approved. He told the officer to add a clause to the minutes to say that the committee had agreed to make the £32,000 grant payable in one lump sum. That was, he said, exactly what the committee had decided and the minutes had left out that important point. He had done no more than ensure their accuracy, and would be happy to stand up in court to say just that.

Embarrassingly, no one else remembered it that way, not even his vice chairman, Terry Comerford, who was also the Labour whip. Neither the committee clerk, who had made a full note of the meeting, nor any other officer or member of the committee then present could

---

5   Long since reopened and run "in partnership" with Greenwich Leisure Limited as the Mornington Sports and Fitness Centre.

agree Horan's version. The borough solicitor, Amanda Kelly, prepared a report on the affair. A week before it was to be published, Horan resigned. Never mind that he had stepped down from the chair in the December meeting, the report concluded, his action had materially helped an organisation of which he was a director. If he had not done what he had done, without reference to other councillors, the centre would have got a payment of £8,000 rather than £32,000. The larger sum had now disappeared into the black hole of the centre's finances. "This," said Judith Barnes, "is definitely sleaze".

Another embarrassment for the council came by way of the High Court. In January 1995 Sir Charles McCullough scuppered Camden's plans for a controlled parking zone (CPZ) in the Primrose Hill area, which had a knock on effect on the planned CPZs in Belsize, Kentish Town and Highgate. The basis of the ruling was that Camden was bound to consult, and Camden's consultation had been poor. There had been an "informal consultation" by letter in December 1990 which prompted the formation of the Primrose Hill Action Group (PHAG). The council wanted daily parking restrictions from 9.30am to 6.30pm. PHAG wanted restrictions from 8am to 10am only. The council did not answer PHAG's letters. "Two councillors –Brian Woodrow and Julie Fitzgerald- behaved outrageously badly, like old fashioned bullies", said PHAG's leader, Mark Cran QC. "PHAG were treated with scorn and derision and Camden behaved as though a policy had been adopted which nobody had any right to challenge". PHAG called a public meeting which was attended by 300 people including the two local councillors, Harriet Garland and Julie Fitzgerald. Notwithstanding Julie Fitzgerald's attempts to stop them doing so, the organisers called for a vote in which 95% of those present expressed hostility to the council's proposals. "I conclude," said Sir Charles, "that her resistance to a vote indicated that she was already committed to the introduction of controlled parking in Primrose Hill". Richard Arthur set up a working party on consultation.

245

Judith Barnes told the papers that the judgment "exposed the council as a completely tyrannical organisation whose commitment to consultation was nothing but lip service". But it was no good. The *Ham & High* was by now firmly on Arthur's side. He was a sensible, pragmatic leader, a worthy successor to Roy Shaw. He represented the type of Labour politician of whom the paper approved, whereas Julie Fitzgerald had been something else. Richard Arthur's call for people unhappy with the council's consultation to come forward and give him their suggestions was "commendable".

The papers also made much of the pay rises awarded to the senior council officers. Camden could not afford to lag behind. The Labour group voted to raise the chief executive's pay by 8% to £77,000, and the pay of directors and assistant directors by 5%. The Town Hall was besieged by demonstrators against cuts, including a dozen Bengali youths complaining about the limited opening hours of their youth club. They were helpfully supplied with Socialist Workers placards which read STOP CAMDEN BOSSES PAY BONANZA. The feared rebellion within the group fizzled out, but eleven Labour councillors voted against the rises.[6]

Not that anything had gone disastrously wrong, but by the annual Labour Group meeting Arthur was in trouble. Many of the councillors did not like his pragmatic politics, many did not like his style of leadership and many did not like him. Phil Turner was expected to stand again, but changed his mind at the last moment. The malcontents pushed Charlie Hedges to the front –the 25 stone, chain smoking housing chairman who bred Great Danes from his Kilburn council flat. He wanted to scrap the Policy Group, Arthur's "inner cabinet". Camden, he said, "was a reactive council bumbling along from crisis to crisis" and the policy of asset stripping has "left us waiting for dodgy developers to ransack Camden".

Arthur's chief lieutenant, John Mills, the chairman of the policy and resources committee, was challenged by Ernest James, who the *Ham & High* described "as something of a Dennis Skinner figure in the Labour group". Maggie Cosin, who chaired the corporate services committee, had lost popularity because of her support for the large pay awards and was challenged by the newly elected trade unionist Bob Hall.

It was close. Arthur and Mills survived by nine and three votes respectively, but Bob Hall beat Maggie Cosin. Her support for the pay awards had cost her the post. Charlie Hedges was made deputy leader with Jane Roberts. Left wingers Angus Walker and John White ousted Terry Comerford and Julian Fulbrook as whip and as education chairman and, in "the most bizarre result" (said the *Ham & High*), Dave Horan was voted in as assistant whip. Gloria Lazenby was made deputy mayor. "The Labour Left", enthused the *New Journal,* "has delivered a sharp kick to Arthur's administration".

* * *

---

6   They were Ernest James, Ray Adamson, Bob Hall, Mahmud Hasan, Angus Walker, Jim Turner, Bernard Kissen, Gloria Lazenby, Sybil Shine, Anne Swain and Pat Weir.

At the end of the year, the Tories chose their candidate to wrest back Hampstead & Highgate from Glenda Jackson. She was Elizabeth Gibson, a part time teacher, "devout catholic" and "a John Major loyalist to the marrow". She was also the wife of Keith Best, the one time Tory MP (for Ynys Môn until 1987), who had since seen the inside of Brixton Prison for making dishonest and multiple share applications during the British Telecom privatisation, and who was now, somewhat unfashionably, an agitator for more immigration. Oliver Letwin had been a nice chap but a bit wet, was the wisdom of the day, and politeness had somewhat handicapped him from going for Glenda in the way that only a woman could. Labour had won the seat with a humourless old boot, we'll win it back with one. "I'm fifteen years younger and fitter than Glenda Jackson", said Miss Gibson, graciously. "I didn't need an all women short list to be selected. Like cream I rise to the top".

John Dickie, the bright young LibDem who had succeeded in kicking the Tories out of Hampstead Town ward, had been making waves in his own party since his election. He edited *The Reformer*, a LibDem policy journal in which he celebrated the election of Tony Blair as the new Labour leader. LibDems should rejoice now that the Labour leadership had moved towards the LibDem position. He criticised those (such as Paddy Ashdown) for seeking "artificial philosophical differences" between the parties. To talk of the LibDems replacing Labour was, wrote Dickie, "clearly nonsense". Mr Ashdown was not amused.

247

Not only was the 30 year old management consultant (as an ex-SDP man) an admirer of Tony Blair, he had developed "a passionate belief that we need a Labour government". At the same time he had developed, through close association, a sense of the intellectual limitations of his fellow LibDem councillors. "Being in a political party is like being in a relationship. You have to ask yourself if you are really happy. If you are not, you should leave", he told the press when in December 1995 he took the Labour whip. By this time his relationship with the LibDem group had so broken down that he did not tell them of his intentions. "He should stand down: it is verging on the fraudulent not to", fumed his party leader, Flick Rea. "It is not as if he is joining a party with passionate convictions".

The most important change to the council in December 1995 was the appointment of a new chief executive. In September, Jeremy Smith had announced that he was leaving Camden to take up the directorship of the Local Government International Bureau in January. Interviews were to take place in November, giving the strongest internal candidate, Steve Bundred, plenty of time to prepare.

In October Bundred told the policy and resources committee that external debt was now less than £500m as opposed to the £800m when he had first taken up his post as director of finance. The council was going to be in surplus by £3½m by the end of the year, a happy position, he explained, "entirely due to the financial management of the authority". (An achievement only possible, as Julian Tobin put it, because the capital programme was so far behind. "Aren't we congratulating ourselves for not maintaining the capital budget?" he asked.) Richard Arthur let all the candidates know that he was making himself available to have a "chat" with them, which brought complaints that he was holding private interviews. "If anyone's worried about the process", he added, "they can have a chat with me too".

The final selection took place just before Christmas: Bundred, still only 43, was the clear winner. "This decision is an indication of the confidence of our members in the progress Camden has made over the past three years", said Bundred. "Camden in the 1990s is led by politicians who are realistic about the constraints under which they operate, the financial limits permitted by the government, and who are passionately committed to delivering services to the communities they serve". The *Ham & High* was delighted and ran articles and editorials throughout the year praising the new chief. "The parachute has finally closed on lesbian skydiving on the rates. Today instead of acting as a banker to loony left schemes, the talk at Camden is of presenting a 'building society' image". Two members of the selection panel voted against him, the two opposition leaders, Judith Barnes and Flick Rea, who both found his solid Labour Party credentials unattractive.

In the February 1996 council meeting, Judith Barnes demanded details of what benefits Dave Horan had received from council's loans made to the Migrant Training Company (MTC), a charity of which Horan was a director and the chairman. Over a three year period, up to 1992, the MTC had received loans from the council. MTC had been set up to provide training for unemployed Irish immigrants, but according to a whistleblower from within the council, Warren Garrett, "it was apparent that the money was not being used for training". Horan was furious: it was a slur that should be retracted: local Tories were "desperate to use vulnerable, often traumatised refugees as scapegoats for, and justifications of, their heartless racist inspired Asylum Act"

Steve Bundred was obliged to reply to Judith Barnes's subsequent enquiries which were summarised by the *New Journal* in a lengthy headline: "Almost £1m worth of loans —made without 'appropriate authority' were approved by the council to enable one of its own councillors to avoid a criminal offence". In 1993 a loan arrangement had been made whereby MTC, which had no assets, owed the council £½m. The agreement allowed the company's directors to avoid trading whilst insolvent. Without the loan Horan would have been made liable for the company's debts and bankrupted. As Judith Barnes was quick to point out, the MTC was wholly inefficient when compared with similar operations. It assisted only ten Camden residents a year, and only 124 people across London. Dave Horan, should, she said, resign. Richard Arthur ordered an enquiry.

The dispute over the new contracts for council employees rolled on into 1996. In March Camden UNISON (formerly NALGO) balloted its 3,000 members on strike action. Fewer than half returned their ballots, but those who did voted by a majority of fifty to strike. Nevertheless, the national union refused to back a strike based on such limited support. The strike threat crumpled and in May a thousand employees were sacked and reemployed on the new contracts.

Richard Arthur survived another leadership ballot in May 1996, this time narrowly beating off the delayed challenge by Phil Turner by 25 votes to 20. Gloria Lazenby, who described herself as "a fully paid up member of the awkward squad" became mayor.

The Migrant Training scandal would not go away, despite a report by Brian Heiser, the senior investigations officer for the deputy chief executive, Amanda Kelly. Tom Connor, a former Camden officer, had signed off one loan and had prepared another for MTC while both he and his wife were directors of the company. No declaration of interest was made for three years. The deputy chief executive nevertheless found that there was "no evidence of deliberate attempts to deceive or defraud". The report and Miss Kelly's response, said Judith Barnes, was "a feeble attempt at a whitewash". The council turned down her call for a public enquiry for the MTC loans and a further £500,000 that had been illegally used to bail out Interchange, another training organisation. "Who", asked Julian Tobin, "is protecting whom?"

In June 1996 Steve Bundred arbitrarily ordered that all the *New Journal's* distribution racks be removed from the town hall and the

249

borough's libraries. The *New Journal* complained to its friends in the Labour group. The chief executive justified his order on the ground that the council was at risk from defamation actions if it distributed the paper with any libel that may be printed in it. He was asked to reverse his order, but refused on the ground that he only took orders from the council, not from individual councillors and he would only follow a properly minuted decision from a council committee. The *Ham & High* was delighted: Bundred was "absolutely correct". It repeated John Thane's description of the *New Journal* as "an undistinguished rag" and devoted an editorial to the subject of how in the bad old days Labour councillors had been able to boss senior council officers around without getting proper democratic authority.

All was not well in Camden's education department. In July 1996 a special education committee decided to close down Saint Richard of Chichester Roman Catholic Comprehensive school in Kentish Town as it was verging on being "the worst in London". The school had failed an Ofsted inspection in 1994 and faced being taken over by government administrators and closed (as had happened at Hackney Downs Boys School in 1995) unless it came up to scratch within two years. The two years were up and a new inspector's report showed that less than half the lessons were taught satisfactorily and that there was "considerable underachievement" in two thirds of the classes. By closing the school and transferring the pupils to Acland Burghley School, the council would spare itself the supreme embarrassment of government intervention. The staff responded, somewhat hopefully, by petitioning the Vatican.

John Major's government put off the evil day of a general election until the very end. From 1995 they had hoped to find a favourable moment to go to the country, but no such moment came. Their popularity sank, and by the time they were forced to call the election, they were 20% behind Labour in the opinion polls. It meant that Frank Dobson was safer than he had ever been, and even Glenda Jackson could relax. Not that she did: the only thing that made the Hampstead campaign in any way interesting was that the Tories needed only a 2.7% swing to take the seat back. But they were swinging nowhere, and the boundary changes had already dashed their hopes. Central Office was of no help —all their efforts in the 1997 campaign were concerned with holding what they had, not with taking seats from Labour.

Camden council played its part by ensuring that it did nothing to upset the political mood. A minor but telling example of this followed the meeting of the Education (Youth and Community Education) Subcommittee in January 1997. Grants of £1050 were approved to the Kings Cross Brunswick Neighbourhood Association and the Somers Town Youth Club to take some of their members for a bracing trip up Mount Snowdon. There was no difficulty there, but the subcommittee also approved several small donations to gay and lesbian groups, and the press picked up on a particular donation of £500 to the Male Out Group. This was to fund a trip by young gay and bisexual men aged between 17 and 24 to Amsterdam "where they could experience holding hands in the street without feeling fear, and experience an environment where gay and lesbian sexuality is accepted". Labour councillors not on the subcommittee wanted the decision revoked. Arguably the grant was illegal under Clause 28 of the Local Government Act which forbad councils promoting homosexuality. Judith Barnes said she was "speechless", but managed to add: "I hope that all the boys will be doing is holding hands".

It was not the sort of publicity the Labour Party needed immediately before an election. The Tory leaflets would be full of it. The council leadership withdrew the grant. In February, the council tax went up a mere 2% (£11 on Band D to £799).

The two Tory challengers worked hard. In Hampstead, Elizabeth Gibson pushed her two young children Phoebe and Ophelia in front of the cameras whenever she could, and in Holborn, Julian Smith spent his time pushing leaflets through letterboxes. The only outside help came from *The Field*, a magazine aimed at the huntin' and shootin' set, which launched its own poster campaign against Glenda Jackson entitled "Get shot of her". It all counted for nothing. Nationally the Conservatives were up against the wall and there were no big name visitors, except Ann Widdecombe. Both the Referendum Party and UKIP put up candidates to lure voters away from the Conservatives, but to little effect. It was not going to be close, and the result when it came was of little surprise. Labour won.

Nationally, the general election of 1 May 1997 was a disaster for the Conservatives. John Major's majority of 21 seats in 1992 became a Tony Blair majority of 178 in 1997. The LibDems gained 28 seats to take their total to 46. In Holborn & St Pancras Frank Dobson stormed home with 65% of the vote on a 65% turnout. In Hampstead and Highgate Glenda Jackson got 57% of the vote on a 68% turn out, giving her a majority of 13,284, more even than Henry Brooke had managed in 1959. She more than doubled the total Conservative vote with a swing of 12.4%, which was even greater than had been Jack Cooper's swing against Brooke in 1964. The LibDem vote, about 12.5% in both constituencies, showed little change from 1992.

"We are at last free", Glenda Jackson told her exultant supporters on the night, "from this miasma of Conservatism that has hung over this country like a dehabilitating fog for far too long". Both the Conservative candidates were booed and jeered after the counts when they made political speeches predicting that Labour would not last more than a term. "Night of a Thousand Smiles", declared the headline in the *New Journal*, itself sighing with relief at no longer having to appear disinterested in the outcome. It printed happy pictures of Glenda and Dobson, and photographs of the two "worthy" LibDem candidates, but nothing of defeated Tories, the memory of whom was now too distasteful to revisit.

For the first time in eighteen years there was a Labour government, albeit it one pledged to follow the Tory spending plans for the first two years, and pledged not to favour Labour councils. Frank Dobson was appointed the new Secretary of State for Health and, surprisingly, Glenda Jackson was made the new Minister for Transport. The appointment gave her many opportunities to pose next to buses for the local papers, and gave Flick Rea many opportunities to accuse her of breaking a promise to save the double decker Routemaster bus from extinction.

For the council it was back to business. The public mood was so pro-Labour that any shortcomings were easily blamed on the constraints of the adopted Tory spending plans. Even reports of fraud caused few ripples. In July 1997 UCLAF[7], the EU's anti –fraud branch, issued a report showing the full extent of the MTC scandal. Camden was among the eight London boroughs to have rubberstamped false claims amounting to £550,000 which now had to be paid back to the EU. Another million pounds could not be accounted for and Camden (as well as other boroughs) had since lost its paperwork. There was, said the report, "no evidence of personal gain" but nevertheless MTC had defrauded the EU by representing loans from boroughs as grants that could be matched by EU funding. The EU now demanded £54,285 back from Camden. There was something of a sigh of relief that the figure was so small.

---

7   Unité de Coordination de La Lutte Anti-Fraude.

Immediately after the 1997 general election, Brian Weekes, the chairman of the housing committee made it clear that an extra £300m was needed to bring Camden's housing "up to the high standards tenants deserve". The external repairs programme had already been suspended for a year leaving a £45m backlog. The much trumpeted capital receipts initiative announced by the new government was a mere £14m over two years. Whichever way one juggled the figures, Camden was still £50m short. As the 1998 election approached, arguably the biggest embarrassment facing the council was the funding of its repairs programme on its estates. Tough solutions were needed. Desperate to raise cash, Brian Weekes started a consultation on local housing corporations, private finance initiatives and the sale of commercial properties. Camden set about selling residential properties occupied only by short life tenants. The press was not supportive. When the Policy & Resources Committee agreed to sell three houses for £3m to avoid having to pay £800,000 for repairs, the New Journal headline read: "Outrage over sale of houses". Tenants were to be "thrown on the street by Camden council so their valuable houses can be sold to wealthy bidders".

In order to claw back £21m in government funding Camden challenged the government for sticking to its "no favour" policy towards London boroughs. It cost the council dear. In March 1998 the House of Lords found for the government who, as a sop, left Camden with a promise "to look at payments afresh". In 1998 the council tax went up by 9.98% putting Band D house up by £79 to £878. "We have had", said John Mills, "a very difficult revenue support grant from the government". The excuses did not impress Judith Barnes, not that anyone was listening. "Camden is top heavy with middle and senior managers", was her analysis. "They push up council tax each year, while services do not improve".

253

By far the hottest issue in the run up to the local elections was Camden's libraries. KPMG issued a preliminary report in September 1997 concluding that there were too many libraries in the borough and that savings could be made if eight were closed, leaving the borough with five. The council could instead invest in "kiosks" at popular sites such as supermarkets and tube stations. There was an immediate howl of protest. The final report came out in October favouring seven "community libraries", seven "mobile libraries" and sixteen "community library access points". The closure of seven libraries would save £¾m a year. "We need to improve library services rather than library buildings", said Tim Walker, the chairman of the leisure committee, and promised that nothing would happen without "the biggest and most comprehensive public consultation process that we have ever carried out. We want to consult everyone and we particularly want to consult people who are not using the service to find out why not".

A public meeting at the Keats Library in Hampstead was called. The building was packed with local worthies. Melvyn Bragg told the gathered bibliophiles: "It seems to me the most magnificent idea in a democratic country that books of all sorts and denominations should be available to whoever wants to read them". Underinvestment, he said, was the problem. Michael Foot nodded in the audience. "What we are trying to do", said the now rather defensive Tim Walker, "is start a debate".

The Conservatives seized on the libraries as all that was wrong with Camden. Judith Barnes pointed out that Camden already spent more on libraries than did any comparable London borough, but opened its libraries for fewer hours. Camden spent more on library staff than did other boroughs, but had fewer than average professional staff. "Libraries are a classical example of what has gone wrong in Camden". Her remarks came in the middle of the council's effort to restructure the staffing in the libraries. True to form, on 26 February 1998, UNISON called a libraries strike which lasted until the borough elections in May.

In the meantime, the North London literary world had much to say on the proposed closures: not just Melvyn Bragg, but now Fay Weldon, Margaret Foster, Doris Lessing, Margaret Drabble, Imelda Staunton, Maureen Lipman and Roger Lloyd Pack. So scandalised was Joan Bakewell that she said that she was not going to vote Labour. Determined not to back down, Richard Arthur was nevertheless conciliatory. He emphasised that all the council's options were open. "We will listen very carefully to the consultation", was the official line, "and if the outcome is that it's best to continue as we are then we shall do just that". But in fact, the tough decision had already been made, as had the decision not to announce it until after the election.

The election campaign had started as early as November 1997 with the launch of the *Camden Plan* ("A vision for Camden") by the lacklustre minister for local government, Hilary Armstrong. It was the first of its kind to be launched in the country, underscoring Camden's

New Labour credentials. The *Plan* set a hundred and eleven specific targets for a miscellany of services to be improved and new projects to be set up. Security was to be improved in 75% of council homes by April 1999, the council would distribute ten thousand smoke alarms by the end of the month, and would ensure smoke free seating in fifty restaurants by September 1998, and provide training for 500 local people by March 1998 and so on. New Labour was going to make a difference.

The Labour manifesto ("Our Vision, Our Values") made much of the recent success of the council in attracting more than £150m of government regeneration funds and lottery money, the best exam results in Inner London and cutting external debt by £219m. The Tory manifesto promised a £50 refund in council tax to every council tax payer, a pledge not only to keep all the libraries but to open them all for five days each week, a pledge to intensify refuse collection and to deal with fly posting. Cheekily, in the wild hope that it would attract the discerning Bengali voter, there was also a pledge "to consult parents about setting up a Muslim school in the south of the borough". The LibDems ("Choice, Caring & Commonsense") promised "more money into libraries and schools and large cuts in central bureaucracy at the town hall".

Rather than stand for re-election in Belsize, Judith Barnes chose to stand in Highgate, Richard Arthur's ward. The reality was that she had had enough. If there was a big enough swing to the Tories to enable them to win in Highgate, the new council would be Conservative too and it would be worth staying on as leader. But another term as leader of the opposition against a big Labour majority was a dreary prospect for someone who had just endured eight long thankless years of it. The *Chronicle* saw the Highgate contest as an epitome of the whole election. "The Richard and Judy Show!" read their headline above a contrived photograph of the two smiling candidates each wearing a boxing glove. Not good on sporting metaphors, Miss Barnes was quoted as saying: "I'm aiming to knock Richard for six".

As the election neared, the parties brought out the big guns. David Blunkett and Geoffrey Robinson, the paymaster General, turned out for Labour, as did Gordon Brown (with, the *Ham & High* felt compelled to report, an unseemly split in his trousers revealed when he bent down to do up his shoe laces). The Tories managed Norman Fowler and, amid Tory flyers demanding NO LIBRARY CLOSURES IN CAMDEN, Jeffrey Archer, who told the press that closing libraries was a "loony leftwing policy". Tim Yeo, the well known Suffolk MP and adulterer,

255

gave the candidates their pre-election pep talk. The elections would be "a measure of how well the Conservative leadership is doing".

Smaller parties made little impact. The only non-aligned candidate to spark the press's interest was Jane Owen, author of the racy novel *Camden Girls,* who stood for her own Right to Party and posed for photos swigging from a bottle of pils.[8]

But, however hard the parties tried to make things appear important, in the wake of the Blair landslide, politics had rather gone off the boil. In 1997 at the general elections hustings in South Hampstead School, six hundred people had turned out to hear Glenda Jackson debate the issues with her challengers. A year on only three hundred made it to boo Richard Arthur's library plans. The reality was that although there were things to quibble over, the council had greatly changed. Libraries excepted, the Arthur/Bundred administration had purged the council of its ability to generate anger. "Dramatic strides have been made in improving services, cutting waste and stamping down on inefficiency," said the *Ham & High*. "Letters to the *Ham & High* complaining about refuse collection, street cleaning and other council services have all but dried up. There is no longer an ongoing financial crisis at the town hall, no endless overspending, and indeed Camden's financial resources are the envy of other boroughs".

So pleased with Richard Arthur was the *Ham & High*, that when Judith Barnes wrote to the paper to point out the council's many deficiencies, the paper launched an attack on her. "She is an outstanding local councillor with a prodigious ability to muster facts and understand complex issues. She is certainly admired by her ward constituents, and she has dug up numerous scandals for which Camden rightly deserves castigation. But her negative style has reduced her effectiveness in the council and the public arena". She had not given credit where it was due. "The voters' verdict is that Conservative approach to local government is hostile, misconceived and outdated. The sooner Ms Barnes and her colleagues realise this, the sooner we may have a chance of seeing a strong and vibrant opposition at Camden Town Hall again".[9]

---

8   The novel, according to its review in the *Independent,* "features a crew of horny, Lycra-clad boozing babes on the prowl in North London's coolest quarter".

9   Not that it mattered in the great scheme of things, and not that Matthew Lewin's editorial influenced a single voter, it was nevertheless a grossly unfair attack and, if this book demonstrates anything, it was also wholly incorrect. In any event, the paper had, as Judith Barnes quite rightly pointed out, "showed a radical misunderstanding of the nature of effective opposition".

But things were to change dramatically in the weeks before the election. There was a breakdown within Camden's "dream team": the chief executive and his deputy fell out, and the council used the courts to gag the press. Overnight, the *Ham & High* abandoned its stance of admiring all that Bundred and Arthur did (libraries apart), and attacked them in every way it could.

The cracks had first appeared in July 1997 when Amanda Kelly had appeared on the shortlist to take over as secretary of the Association of London Government, a Labour leaning organisation. The vacancy had arisen because the previous incumbent, John McDonnell, formerly Camden's "principal policy advisor", had at last got elected to parliament as the member for Hayes & Harlington. Tellingly, the £60,000 salary was over twenty thousand less than she was being paid by Camden, but once the shortlist was spotted by the local press, she withdrew her name and announced that she was not leaving after all.

Things were clearly not going well. In September she stayed away from work, sick "with a stress related illness", and in late October announced that she had taken Camden to the Industrial Tribunal because she had been victimised and sexually discriminated against by Steve Bundred. She then promptly went holiday to Cyprus. Bundred told the papers that the allegations were "totally untrue and totally without foundation", and Richard Arthur, somewhat bemused by what had been going on, was left to mumble something about "unfortunate management difficulties" which he hoped would soon be resolved.

It was not going to be easy. Back from holiday, Amanda Kelly returned to her desk letting everyone know that she was pressing ahead with her complaint to the Industrial Tribunal unless a satisfactory agreement was reached. Matters grumbled on for a few months until February 2007 when, quite bizarrely and wholly wrongly, the North London Industrial Tribunals regional chairman made a restricted reporting order. Any newspaper carrying a report as to what was happening with the case would be in contempt of court. The local papers were furious, but impotent. Not even able to identify Camden as the culprit, the *Ham & High* complained that the order "is being used to save a local authority employer from embarrassment during the run up to local authority elections –and that cannot be right".

Although the local papers did not have the funding to make a legal challenge, rescue came in the unlikely form of the *Mail on Sunday* newspaper who applied to the High Court to quash the order. Just over a week before the local elections Mr Justice Keane did just that, describing

257

the reasoning behind the restricted reporting order as "perverse and irrational". The council then announced that it was going to appeal the decision and so although Camden had lost in the High Court, the restricted reporting order remained in force pending appeal and the papers were still unable to report what the allegations against Bundred and the council were. Then suddenly, some might say predictably, once the last edition of the *Ham & High* before the borough elections had been printed, on the Friday before polling day, Camden changed its mind and announced its acceptance of the High Court ruling. "There was", said Richard Arthur, vainly hoping that someone might believe him, "zero political input in this".

So incensed was the *Ham & High*, that in an act of impotent rage it went to the expense of issuing a free four page "Special Extra Edition" on the Saturday before the polls. In attacking the council, the editorial concluded; "Legal costs are so far approaching £200,000, and fighting the tribunal could cost another £1 million or more. How many libraries could be kept open for that kind of money?"

The turnout at the election was 30.96%, the lowest in the borough's history. Labour had just won a general election on the back of a great popular urge to get rid of the Tories. The electorate now sat back exhausted, not liking the Tories, but no longer really concerned. The Labour vote had dropped by what could have been a disastrous fifteen thousand, but the Conservative vote had also shrunk by three thousand. The changes were negligible. The Conservatives took three seats back from Labour (two in Adelaide and one in Swiss Cottage[10]) and the LibDems took one from Labour in West Hampstead. In Highgate Richard Arthur, as expected, was re-elected and Judith Barnes was not. She had wiped six hundred votes off the Labour majority, but was still two hundred behind. "Judith has always worked hard for her cause", said Arthur generously, "but this time she set her target too high".

---

10   The Swiss Cottage result had much to do with luck. Bob Hall, the deputy mayor, had been deselected by his own ward, Gospel Oak. He was then selected for Swiss Cottage in place of the former chief whip, John Macdonald, who then stood (as was then allowed under the rules) as "Labour Councillor Seeking Re-Election", which rather queered the pitch in that he got 600 votes, more than any other independent in the borough's history. Many or most of these votes were cast by confused Labour voters who thought that they were voting for the three Labour candidates. The consequence was that the first of the Conservatives on the ballot, the city lawyer Stephen Hocking, managed to sneak in at the expense of the old time leftie Bernie Moss, the last official Labour candidate on the ballot.

The *Chronicle* reprinted its photograph of the two in boxing gloves under a headline they had worked on for weeks: "Knock out blow".

The Conservatives had been assisted in making their modest gains by the planned library closures. Once the election was out of the way, the library staff ended their strike action. Or, as the *Chronicle* put it, having saved up another headline, "Strike is a closed book".

The poor turnout was despite the extra point of interest that had been offered to the electorate. There was a London wide referendum on whether there was to be a mayor of London. Of those who voted in Camden, 81.2% voted in favour of the idea. (Or, to put it another way, of the 135,131 people entitled to vote in Camden, only 41,846 chose to do so. Of those, 36,007 voted in favour of a London mayor, an endorsement of 27% of the electorate.)

With the state of the parties now being 43 Labour, 10 Conservative and 6 LibDems, there was no material shift in power on the council. Richard Arthur was elected as leader unopposed, with Charlie Hedges and Maggie Cosin as his deputies (Maggie Cosin only beating Ernest James on the third ballot). Dermot Greene was elected chief whip.[11] Rather exhausted by the libraries dispute, Tim Walker stood down as chairman of the leisure committee and was replaced by Phil Turner. Pam Chesters took over as leader of the opposition.

The details of the Bundred /Kelly case became clearer after the election as the Industrial Tribunal case continued. There could have been little to damage the council in the election as the case essentially involved two people who found it difficult to work together. The worst that could be said was that the male dominated council had backed the male chief executive rather than his female deputy. The £200,000 lost legal costs in fighting the *Mail on Sunday* were unnecessarily and quite disgracefully wasted. Amanda Kelly claimed that she could not work with Bundred because he had lost his temper, shouted abuse at her, threatened her with dismissal, and had refused to do anything about her complaint that in 1994 she had been sexually assaulted by a council officer. When she had made the complaint to the industrial tribunal, Richard Arthur had written to her suggesting that she may care to be seconded elsewhere, which she said, "was like bundling an unmarried daughter off to an asylum when the family discovered she was pregnant".

---

11 He managed to keep the job for the next eight years up until the 2006 elections –no small achievement given that whoever was chief whip had been voted out of office every year since Richard Arthur became leader.

The council was "misogynistic", she said. Bundred was "sexist". Richard Arthur had commented on her appearance "in a patronising way", and a council officer had pulled the hair of a senior female colleague "and said that she looked like a schoolgirl".

As Amanda Kelly had run the legal department, the decision was taken to use outside lawyers to conduct the case. No expense was to be spared. The city law firm Simmons & Simmons was instructed to defend the case, who in turn instructed Elizabeth Slade QC. Miss Kelly, they argued, was "unable to take criticism", was "obsessed by status" and "consumed by professional jealousy" because she had her eye on Bundred's job and was continually undermining him. The local papers loved it —the *New Journal* devoting as many as five pages to the story in one edition. Amanda Kelly's own solicitor Gillian Howard, saw the potential for publicity in the case and released to the press a soft focus photograph of herself in pendant earrings to give the impression that she had a part in *Dallas*. [12]

As counteraccusation followed every accusation, each successive hearing was the cause of further embarrassment. At the end of May the council let the press know that an £80,000 package for Amanda Kelly had been agreed and accepted. It was wishful thinking. The information had been released "in error". Michael Rabin, the tribunal chairman, described the council's behaviour as "extraordinarily inept". By July he had had enough and adjourned the hearing to encourage negotiation. The dispute, he said, "had brought the council and possibly the whole of local government into disrepute". The *Ham & High* took its cue: "Settle the Kelly case", it advised sternly, "or the district auditor may show an interest".

The cost of lawyers to Camden was prohibitive. The bill to the taxpayer at that point had already exceeded £600,000. It would have been far cheaper to have settled with Amanda Kelly at double her demands than enter into the dispute, and the case had now degenerated into mudslinging. There followed a curious informal meeting, without lawyers, between Amanda Kelly and the leaders of all three parties. A package was hurriedly drawn up. Amanda Kelly accepted £85,000 severance pay, £5,000 plus VAT legal fees for drawing up the agreement, £3,500 plus VAT for counselling, two weeks special leave and a reference.

---

12 At the hearing, Miss Howard wore "huge pinwheel earrings" and a Moschino top bearing the legend "This T-Shirt has no sense of humour". She describes herself on her website as "the Rottweiler with a handbag".

It was not the end as far as the opposition was concerned. Pam Chesters immediately called for an independent enquiry into how the council came to foot such a massive bill for costs. The *Ham & High* called for an inquest along the lines of the Arden report on the Parisbas loan that the council had subjected itself to in 1991 (although, as the *Ham & High* should have well remembered, a fat lot of good that did). After the summer break, Pam Chesters gathered sufficient signatures together to call an extraordinary meeting of the council to demand, in a joint motion with the LibDems, an inquiry into the Kelly affair. The Labour Party voted it down. Richard Arthur explained that as the Kelly dispute "had cost the taxpayer well over £600,000 and brought the council into national disrepute", he wanted "to avoid digging into old sores". He added an amendment to the effect that Huw Jones-Owen, the secretary of the Greater London Employers Association, would carry out an enquiry into the wider issue of the council's policy towards industrial tribunals. It was to be an enquiry into the general principles of how the council should conduct industrial tribunal claims that may be lodged in the future.[13] The Jones-Owen report, at further cost to the taxpayer, was eventually presented to the council in May 1999. It was met with uncomplicated derision from the Conservative benches. "All it seems to include", observed Pam Chesters, "is a list of administrative procedures. I could have written the report on the back of an envelope in a pub". It was the end of the Kelly affair.

261

Migrant Training raised its head but briefly. UCLAF issued a second report, this time naming certain Camden officers, including the one time director of finance, Steve Bundred, as being guilty of misconduct. The Financial and Resources Committee refused to make the report public but reviewed an officer's account of it which declared it to be flawed because the investigators had not interviewed Bundred to give his side of the story. It was "a complete whitewash" said Pam Chesters, who demanded and was refused the report's immediate publication[14].

13 "Labour U-Turn kicks off enquiry...Kelly probe to go ahead...Labour councillors vote for wide ranging enquiry" reported Lee Gordon in the *New Journal*, getting his wires well and truly crossed in what the paper had taken to describing as the "Kellygate Town Hall Sex Case".

14 "Eurogate: the report they tried to bury", shouted Lee Gordon in the *New Journal*. Lee Gordon, by far the most colourful local reporter left the *New Journal* to cover the Iraq war in 2002. The profession suffered a great loss when he gave up journalism in 2004.

Bundred asked for and was given a month to answer the allegations and the council agreed to hold an independent enquiry. In the meantime, Chesters went on the attack: "It was inexplicable that Bundred had not asked to see the UCLAF investigating team before now", and "instead of blaming UCLAF for a much delayed report, Labour should be explaining why the council never investigated this matter properly in the first place". When Bundred did respond, it was to say that the UCLAF report was "riddled with errors" and its findings were "grossly unfair and inaccurate".

At the end of the year, a special committee chaired by Richard Arthur sat to clear Bundred of wrongdoing in the MTC case. The five selected councillors sat for six hours to consider the chief executive's 25,000 word response to the report. As a public relations exercise it achieved little as Pam Chesters voted against, saying "I remain convinced that there has been a cover up". The council agreed to set up an independent enquiry, and all mention of MTC was forgotten while the council turned its attention to the libraries.

The build up to the implementation of the Libraries Plan was slow. It culminated in a MORI report which showed that young people favoured the council's plans to close libraries and to invest the savings in those remaining. In February 1999 the Leisure Committee voted to close down Chalk Farm, Belsize and Kilburn libraries. It was time, said Gerry Harrison, "to bite the bullet". The Camden Public Libraries Users Group threatened legal action. And all was not well within the Labour group. To some (such as Ernest James) the libraries presented themselves as an opportunity to get at Arthur, and the old left did not like the idea of closing any council services. Andrew Mennear, the Conservative spokesman, demanded more spending. The mayor, Bob Hall, once Camden's NUPE (and later UNISON) chief, said that he would vote against closures[15]. At the council's budget meeting in March, the libraries review was pushed through by only 29 votes to 20. The figures were ominous. Ten Labour members had stayed away and four had voted with the opposition. The four library rebels (Ernest James, Aileen Hammond, Gloria Lazenby and Pat Nightingale) were then barred from attending any Labour group meetings until the annual meeting in May.

---

15   In part at least because, to commemorate the brief association of the Filipino hero with the area, he had just opened the Rizal Memorial Garden at Chalk Farm Library, one of those threatened with closure.

In April 1999 Labour lost the Swiss Cottage by election which had been needlessly brought about by the sitting councillor, Mary Ryan, having inadvisedly got herself selected and elected while she was, as a teacher, a Camden employee and so ineligible. The big campaigning issue for the Tories was the library closures which did not affect Swiss Cottage, and on a dismal 24% turnout the Conservative Honora Morrissey won by a 150 vote margin. It was the first time a seat had changed hands in a by election since Frank Dobson resigned in 1977.[16] At the time its significance seemed to be no more than that, but the resultant substitution of that single Labour loyalist by a Conservative was to prove decisive in the library votes yet to come.

Ernest James, who led the library rebels (living as he does almost next door to Belsize library) made his move at the May Labour group meeting and challenged Richard Arthur for the leadership, as did John Mills. Arthur held on by 22 votes to Mills's 11. James got eight, but then narrowly missed being made deputy leader, getting 19 votes to the 22 votes for Charlie Hedges. The Arthur loyalists then turned on James and elected Bernard Kissen as chairman of licensing in his place.

The *New Journal*, who approved of James but not of Arthur, responded by printing a series of hagiographical letters (all from women) extolling the virtues of the wronged Ernest James. They also stirred things up by printing a letter from Bernard Kissen saying that James was "a bad loser". That was perhaps something of a mistake on Kissen's part, because at the very next licensing committee meeting he was ambushed by Ernest James who got Pat Nightingale (another member of the awkward squad and one of James's many female admirers) and the opposition members on the subcommittee to vote him back into the chair in Kissen's place. James then compounded his sins by managing to get Ewan Cameron elected as his vice chairman, only the second Conservative councillor to hold any post on the council since 1971[17].

The Labour leadership was unamused, as were, overwhelmingly, the Labour group. But retribution could not be swift because the library

263

---

16 The Tories were greatly encouraged. Their very able agent, David Douglas, told everyone who would listen that "two years ago Labour had two seats in Adelaide, and now they can't even get a quarter of the vote".

17 Real anoraks will thank me for this: the other occasion was in 1987 when Ron King was elected vice chairman of the North West Area Development Control Sub Committee. Only two of the five Labour members turned up and were outvoted by the opposition councillors there. His proposer was Flick Rea.

closures were still vulnerable to a vote. It was not a time to make enemies. If the four rebels and ten abstainers voted together, the Libraries Plan was dead.

A bigger distraction by far began as a minor spat at the beginning of the year 1999, but ended by sending the *New Journal* into paroxysms of moralising. The Hampstead Theatre, housed since 1962 in a Swiss Cottage shack, had obtained significant funding to build a new theatre nearby, and applied to the council for planning permission. Three councillors (Flick Rea, Dave Horan and John Thane) sat on the board of the Hampstead Theatre. They were advised by the borough solicitor not to take part in the planning decision when it came before the development control subcommittee on which they also sat. They all attended the meeting, declared their non pecuniary interests, and then all voted for the application. In fact, their actions altered nothing as the planning application was passed with a majority of more than three, but they were nevertheless criticised.

The Conservatives, who did not like the theatre plans for reasons of detail rather than principle, made what fuss they could. Julie Tomalin, a quiet, inoffensive young reporter on the *New Journal*, phoned John Thane to ask if he had taken independent legal advice before going against the borough solicitor's advice. He told her he had. In writing up her report, she wrote that "John Thane claimed to have taken legal advice". The phrase, "claimed to", irritated Thane greatly. He read out a speech for the March council meeting attacking the *New Journal*'s reporting of the affair. It ended with the words: "I will not accept the implication of lying from someone like Julie Tomalin who has the integrity of a used sanitary towel". And sat down to what the *Ham & High* described as "an exquisitely embarrassed silence".

The *New Journal* was furious. Their deputy editor, the shaven headed Andrew Johnson, felt it sexist in the extreme. There were immediate calls for Thane's resignation. Forced to apologise, Thane emailed all the members of the Labour group, the leaders of the opposition parties, the chief executive and "the serious local newspapers" for using the phrase he did. But he would not apologise to Miss Tomalin. The *New Journal* responded with an article headed "Why won't this man resign?" in which were quoted a series of (often anonymous) opinions concerning Thane's shortcomings, his rudeness and his need for psychiatric help. Alongside, it printed a cartoon of a dinosaur with Thane's mug shot superimposed on its head: "And you thought men like this were extinct", read the caption.

Thane was reported to the Independent Standards Panel[18] who produced a report finding Thane's behaviour fell a long way below the ethical standards expected of councillors. The words complained of were "insulting, disgusting and inexcusable". The panel suggested that he should at least face a motion of censure. He was duly censured by the council, and stayed on as chairman of the environment committee.

In May 1999 Roy Shaw became mayor. His outstanding career as a Camden councillor made him the obvious choice to be Camden's first citizen during the millennium celebrations. He insisted on having Julian Tobin, who had been the leader of the opposition when he was leader of the council, as one of his two deputy mayors for the year. Both Shaw and Tobin had first been elected as metropolitan borough councillors in May 1956, and both had been councillors ever since.[19]

In June 1999, the leader of the opposition, Pam Chesters, hatched her own plan for the libraries. Encouraged by the dissident voices of Ernest James and Bob Hall on the Labour benches, she called an extraordinary meeting of the council on 22 June to overturn the policy that had been approved in March. There was by then a particular urgency as the council had announced that Chalk Farm Library was to close by the end of the week and Belsize library within a month.

The pressure grew. The Camden Public Libraries Users Group (CPLUG), ably led by Tom Selwyn, busily lobbied Labour members. Those Labour councillors in the two affected wards, Chalk Farm and Belsize, were given dispensations to abstain from the vote[20]. Nevertheless, in the days before the vote, Dermot Greene, the chief whip, was certain of one thing only: the vote was going to be too close to call. He advised Arthur and the Labour Group officers not to go ahead with the closures, but Arthur was determined. He found, he said, the slowness of it all so frustrating. There was to be no turning back.

265

---

18 The panel of three was then made up of the barrister Mark Hapgood, a former chairman of the Holborn & St Pancras Conservative Association; Rabbi Julia Neuberger (now a LibDem peer, Baroness Neuberger of Primrose Hill) and Labour's choice, the black barrister Lincoln Crawford.

19 This was the only year in which there were two deputy mayors. The reasoning was that as convention dictated that the mayor is succeeded by his deputy, Shaw would be succeeded by the other deputy mayor, Heather Johnson. Julian Tobin, one of the best of councillors, died in November 1999, half way through his term of office.

20 Aileen Hammond, John White and Bill Budd. There was no pressure on the Kilburn councillors as their library in Cottleigh Road was to be replaced with a smart new building on the High Road.

On 22 June 1999, CPLUG and others ensured that the public benches were packed for the occasion. They had enlisted the support of local celebrities, some of whom appeared at the council meeting. Notably present was the highly versatile actor Roger Lloyd Pack[21] who had made himself the face of the objectors during the campaign. The mayor allowed several delegations to speak, including one who had set up large video screens on which pleas were heard from Camden celebs including Joan Bakewell, Alan Bennett and Jonathan Miller (who had said that "he thought his arm would melt before he voted anything other than Labour".) In the packed and often unruly public gallery, a five man choir sang a song written for the occasion. Someone had brought along a trumpet. Those Labour councillors still determined to toe the party line and support the closures were heckled and howled down.

Encouraged by the enthusiasm of the protestors, a few more Labour councillors had joined the rebels. They were now loosely led by John White, who as one of the two Chalk Farm councillors had been given a dispensation to abstain from the vote. They proposed their own motion to stop the closures which was supported by the opposition councillors and only defeated on the casting vote of the mayor, Roy Shaw. There was a recorded vote in which each member had to call out "For" or "Against" as the chief executive read out his or her name from the list. Each successive declaration of "Against" by a Labour councillor was met with shouts of "Shame!" from the gallery. The abstainers were jeered and the Labour rebels were cheered.

Pam Chesters rose to her feet. It was her finest hour on the council. To great cheers from the gallery, she proposed an amendment to the original motion to close the libraries by adding the following words: "except that all library closures be deferred until 1 January 2000 to enable a public consultation to be carried out in strict accordance with the council's consultation standards as defined by the 'We're Listening' report". Her intention was not to give the libraries a six month reprieve, but to scupper the policy altogether in the confident hope that any public consultation was bound to show a massive majority in favour of retaining the libraries.

In the few minutes between the first vote and the second, the pressure from the public gallery proved crucial. One of the abstainers

---

21 Lloyd-Pack is best known (no doubt to his continuing irritation) as Trigger in *Only Fools and Horses*.

decided to vote with the Labour leadership, but two of the others decided to defy the Labour whip. Bill Budd and Pat Callaghan, both with great shows of reluctance, voted for the Tory amendment. Others wavered. Edward Cousins, put his hand up to vote for the amendment, but had it pulled down by Nick Smith, acting as a deputy whip.[22]

The amendment was passed by 29 votes to 28. It was the first defeat for the Labour leadership in the council chamber since Phil Turner was overruled on setting a rate in 1985. A single vote had made the difference. Had the Conservatives not won the Swiss Cottage by election, or had any one of the opposition members or the Labour rebels stayed away that night, the libraries would have been closed on the mayor's casting vote.[23]

The consultation that followed could only have one result. Those who did not use the libraries had no motivation to fill in the questionnaire, whereas library users did. There was no attempt by the leadership to win or reopen the argument. Council officers carelessly drafted a questionnaire that contained the usual page of race monitoring questions, but failed to ask for the consultee's name and address. Piles of questionnaires were left in Camden's libraries for users to complete. Anyone wanting to keep the libraries open was free to remove armfuls of them, fill them all out in identical terms, and then return them to the Town Hall (post paid). That is what happened. The consultation resulted in an overwhelming defeat for the libraries' plan.

267

In September 1999 the MTC scandal ended in something of a damp squib. The council commissioned SOLACE, the Society of Local Authority Chief Executives, to prepare a report for £60,000. The authors, John Harris, a former chief executive, and Alex Ritchie, an accountant, delivered what the *New Journal* described as "a slap in the face for UCLAF". The European fraud investigators had been uncooperative and had no more helped in the SOLACE enquiry than Camden had assisted UCLAF in theirs. The authors took Steve Bundred's position:

---

22   Eddie Cousins distinguished himself by never once uttering a word in any council meeting in his four years on the council. Since 2003 he has been the Adjudicator to HM Land Registry.

23   Every opposition member was present and voted against closure. The twelve Labour rebels were: Bill Budd, Pat Callaghan, Bob Hall, Aileen Hammond, Gerry Harrison, Dave Horan, Ernest James, Gloria Lazenby, Pat Nightingale Sybil Shine, Anne Swain and John White.

as UCLAF had not interviewed the Camden employees and councillors (which it had not the power to do), it had no right to accuse them. In the absence of a police style investigation, UCLAF's conclusions were worthless. No one named as culpable in the UCLAF report was in fact culpable of anything, the report concluded. The procedure was the only culprit. Camden made serious errors in its dealings with MTC, but there was no evidence that its actions were improperly motivated. Procedures should be tightened up, the report recommended, and it criticised the practice of councillors sitting on outside bodies. "The report was so skewed towards scoring points off UCLAF", said Pam Chesters, that the question still remained unanswered: "Was the MTC affair a cock up or a conspiracy?" The *Ham & High* reminded its readers that the council tax payers had been left to pay £189,000 (£54,000 attributable to the MTC) to the EU, and that the report revealed "ample evidence of hopeless monitoring procedures, conflicts of interest, and a lamentable failure promptly to investigate problems". "We have been", gushed Richard Arthur, "completely cleared".

The libraries defeat saw Richard Arthur's leadership on a downward slide. The final blow came later in the year in the form of the Blair government's plans to modernise local government. The 1999 Local Government Bill[24] proposed the "democratic renewal" of councils. No longer would there be numerous committees wastefully overseeing all aspects of council work. Councillors would be released to "spend more time with their constituents" while the running of the council would be left to an executive committee or a cabinet. Backbench councillors would then be able to serve on scrutiny committees which would either be standing committees to cover the work of the old committees, or else would be set up on an ad hoc basis to look into certain matters as they arose.

It was clear from the outset that the perceived need for legislation on this matter had grown from the Labour dominated Northern councils, unused to opposition from outside the Labour group. Councillors would no longer gain experience on the job by learning how council departments worked. They would no longer get experience of working with council officers. Scrutiny would (in Camden's case) be limited to those topics chosen by the Labour group, and politics within the

---

24 Now the Local Government Act 2000 which, after much debate, only squeezed through the House of Lords on 24 July 2000 following a mysterious deal struck between the government and the LibDems.

council would be confined to council meetings in which the leaders of the opposition parties would each be allowed three minutes to speak.

The proposals met with universal hostility from the opposition benches, and almost universal hostility from the Labour benches. Only three New Labour loyalists spoke up for the new system: Maggie Cosin, Nick Smith and, unhappily for him, Richard Arthur. It was a poor choice of principle on which to take a stand as support or opposition would achieve little. Once parliament had determined the law, the council would be obliged to implement it, as it had over the years with (for instance) Fair Rents, or the poll tax, or the abolition of the business rate and aldermen.

Richard Arthur's public downfall came in November 1999 when the council held a debate on the Local Government Bill. Phil Turner led the debate with great eloquence denouncing the new proposals. Speaker after speaker from every party backed his motion to let the government know of the council's opposition. When it came to the vote, Arthur and his faithful lieutenant, Nick Smith, were in a minority of two. By way of compromise, Arthur abstained rather than vote against.

It was the end. He had fought hard to ensure that his new managerial style of local government would chase out the left, and he had won. As in so many matters New Labour, an independent observer would have had difficulty in finding any ideological difference between him and his Conservative (or LibDem) opponents. Aged tribal considerations were all that were left. The internal enemy had been vanquished but not destroyed. The costs thrown away on the Amanda Kelly case were seen as having been spent to protect not the council so much as Steve Bundred. Indeed, the very decision to support Bundred had damaged him in some quarters. Once that choice was taken, Richard Arthur took, and the council took, the mud that was thrown at the chief executive, including all the untested allegations of sexism, misogyny and bullying. Arthur could be removed, Bundred could not.

269

Camden's Library Plan, which he had championed to save money, had failed leaving a jeering opposition and a badly fractured Labour group. First the *Ham & High* and then the *New Journal* had turned against him. His treatment of the impossible Ernest James had even been described as "Stalinesque". Finally, his loyalty to the Labour government had found him horribly isolated when it came to objecting to the provisions of what would become the Local Government Act 2000. He was no longer loved. The council had stopped being political and had become merely managerial. Arthur had somehow taken the romance out of local government in Camden.

In the run up to the Labour group elections in May 2000, Arthur intended to stand as party leader for an unprecedented ninth year. Dermot Greene, the chief whip, took soundings. It was clear that Arthur would not win and with some difficulty he was persuaded of that fact. "With some regret", he stood down, citing "personal reasons" for his decision.

There were two front runners for the position, Julian Fulbrook and Jane Roberts. The very experienced Fulbrook, a law lecturer at the LSE with a PhD from Cambridge was a former mayor and had variously chaired the housing, education and social services committees. He had also stood unsuccessfully for parliament in Basildon in both 1983 and 1987.[25] Fulbrook, who had been firmly in the anti-Bundred party during the Amanda Kelly affair, issued a statement to his fellow Labour councillors outlining his intention to sack the chief executive[26]. To many, this was an attractive idea, but to the mainstream he raised the spectre of another great Camden unfair dismissal case in the wake of the Amanda Kelly settlement. It amounted to an invitation to "vote for me and watch the fireworks", and helped the waverers make up their minds.

The second candidate was Jane Roberts, a 45 year old child psychiatrist, who had first been elected in 1990 and who had the advantage of having held the education portfolio, the borough's flagship service inherited from the ILEA. An unmarried mother of one, she, somewhat unusually for someone of her age, wore very long black hair which she complemented with a wooden watch and mid calf length skirts. She held a strong sense of injustice, of glass ceilings and of the enemy being "men in suits", and she offered the excitement of a

270

---

25 It had been a close thing: in 1983 he had lost by just over a thousand votes when his pitch was somewhat queered by the challenge of Sue Slipman, the earnest one-time president of the NUS, who stood for the SDP. Each time he was beaten by David Amess, a Redbridge councillor and a graduate of the Bournemouth School of Technology (and later the MP for Southend West and the vice chairman of the All Party Girlguiding Group). A Cambridge University Labour Society contemporary of Fulbrook's, Martin Smith, remembers "of all our contemporaries at Cambridge, Julian is the one you would have tipped for being in a future Labour cabinet".

26 The Kelly affair had "incapacitated" Bundred, said Fulbrook who would offer him "an honourable exit". Pam Chesters reported him to the Standards Panel who, a year later, issued a report to say that Fulbrook's campaign had been "inappropriate and wrong".

daring return to sensible left wing politics. Arthur, on the other hand, had simply given up politics and become a manager. He had become "one of the men in suits". [27]

Jane Roberts won comfortably by 24 votes to 14. (The third candidate, John White, stood for the awkward left as a successor to Ernest James, and got three votes.) For the second time since Millie Miller became leader in 1971, and set the party on an unbroken run of eight outright election victories, the party chose a woman.

The leader of the opposition, Pam Chesters, the libraries' champion, also resigned. She had been selected by the Conservatives to fight the marginal parliamentary seat of Bristol West, which William Waldegrave had lost to Labour by fifteen hundred votes in 1997. All political interests outside Bristol had to be sacrificed. Her parting gift to the Camden Conservative group was to prevent a scramble for succession. She named Piers Wauchope as her successor.[28]

On Thursday 4 May 2000, the London mayoral elections took place. Ken Livingstone became the first Mayor of London despite having been forced to stand as an independent after the Labour Party rejected him as a candidate for his past sins. Frank Dobson had been the unsuccessful Labour candidate[29]. The Conservatives had been forced to choose the affable Steve Norris after their first choice, Jeffrey Archer, was proved to have told a lie too many. The LibDems chose Sue Kramer, in the mistaken hope that a candidate that knew nothing of anything (but who would nevertheless talk about it at length) would somehow get the women's vote.

The electorate generally stayed at home and the turnout was a dismal 33%. The first members of the new Greater London Assembly

271

---

27 Jane Roberts was also the co-editor of a 1996 book of academic texts, *Politics of Attachment: Towards a Secure Society*. Patricia Hewitt wrote the forward and among the contributors were Tessa Jowell, Helena Kennedy, Mo Mowlam and Beatrix Campbell, who, the back cover announces, "draw on recent research and debate in developmental psychology and political science to provide a unique dialogue between the psychological and the social - a political grasp of ordinary human needs."

28 Pam Chesters went on to chair the Royal Free Hampstead NHS Trust and, after several disappointing Conservative parliamentary selections, was in 2009 appointed as Mayor Boris Johnson's "Advisor on Health and Youth Opportunities".

29 The London Labour Party had also rejected Glenda Jackson who, after an unhappy year as a junior minister, had been encouraged to resign so that she might stand, only to see the party choose Frank Dobson instead.

(the GLA), with a role of scrutinising the mayor, but with little real power except an ability to reject the mayoral budget, were also elected. The new GLA had attracted much interest from local politicians, but little from the press and less still from the electorate. For GLA purposes, Camden found itself in a new Barnet/Camden constituency where Labour dominated in the south and the Conservatives in the north. Both parties chose Barnet councillors as their candidates, Brian Coleman for the Tories and Labour chose Helen Gordon over the Camden candidates, Richard Arthur, Maggie Cosin, Nick Smith and Jane Roberts.

The count for both elections was conducted by the as yet untried electronic readers and soon descended into confusion. Livingstone won throughout Camden with ease, but Brian Coleman won in the constituency by 500 votes, a miniscule amount against the 126,000 votes cast (let alone the total electorate of 360,704). It was by far the closest result in the new GLA. There was a strong suspicion after the count, shared by the returning officer, Steve Bundred, that 300 votes had been counted twice. The difficulties with the new electronically scanned ballot papers and the second count for the mayoral vote meant that the count did not take place until almost noon and as the hall had been booked out to someone else in the afternoon there simply was no way of arranging a recount. On top of that there were 8,000 spoiled ballot papers, almost all of them being blank assembly slips. People had come along to vote for the mayor, and had in puzzlement simply discarded into the ballot box their unmarked assembly ballot papers.[30]

---

30   Steve Bundred was left in the position of the referee who, having allowed a goal, is after the match shown TV coverage of the hand of God. "I am", he has since said, "one of those, together I think with Brian Coleman, who do not think he got more votes than the Labour candidate". He was also critical of the electronic readers which could not distinguish the nature of the mark on the ballot paper: "So if someone wrote 'Wanker' alongside Dobson's name, it still counted as a vote for Dobson".

|0|

Jane Roberts:
searching for a cause

Richard Arthur had given the impression that the single purpose of his leadership was to ensure that Camden was run as an efficient authority. In order to achieve this, John Mills and Steve Bundred kept a firm grip on the finances. The two mammoth departments of housing and environment were in the safe hands of Brian Weekes and John Thane. Politically, it was a no frills affair. In many fields for most of the time the managers provided the leadership while the politicians looked on. But it is in the nature of councillors to want to make their mark. They do not join political parties and fight sometimes bitter elections to sit on the sidelines to watch the management getting on with things. They hankered after the pre-Arthur days when the managers acted under the direction of the politicians. In the old days too much time had been spent "fire fighting" the harsh economic realities, but the new financial stability could allow a return to politics, especially as Mills and Bundred were still in office. Jane Roberts's aim was for the Labour Party to breathe life back into Camden, so that an invigorated Camden would in turn put life back into the Labour Party.

It was a bold idea, but the sad reality was that the battles with Whitehall and the district auditor had been lost long ago. Straight after her appointment in May 2000 Jane Roberts addressed the Central Management Team of senior council officers and let them know what she was after. She followed up her address with a letter to the chief executive in which she set out her priorities for Camden's future. The correspondence was leaked almost immediately. Of its eleven or so paragraphs, only one (of five and a half lines) dealt with "excellence in service provision". It was for many on the council an introduction to her two interests: "inclusion" and "engagement", words which so often translated as "ethnic minorities" and "presentation".

> "A local authority is a political institution and the majority group must reassert its political values... A local authority is after all a political institution for the delivery of local government, not just a deliverer or enabler of services....our insistent focus should be on reducing inequality.... and improving communication within the Labour Group.... crucially, we must work with the party to ensure that we attract and retain candidates for the next local election who are more representative of [the] local community: younger candidates, women and black and Asian candidates...as a Labour council the real "wicked"[1] issue is social inclusion...inequalities.... engaging with the electorate....I would like Camden to have a clear political identity"

This was a novel way to write to a chief executive. It confused or even merged the Labour Party and the London Borough of Camden. Bundred had once been a Labour councillor, but the demand that "we must work with the party" was too much. She had misjudged his position. He replied:

> "Your letter states that you want the council and your party to be itself more representative of all the local communities. These are not matters for officers; but I believe it is entirely legitimate for the council to put effort, including resources, into developing more active citizens and community representatives, thus widening the pool of potential candidates for all parties."

His letter underlined his view of what the relationship was between the professional council officers and the members, between those who are directed from the chief executive's office and those part time dilettantes who sit in the council chamber. None of her points, so urgently pressed, were answered with any encouragement. He instead somewhat blandly gave her the Camden council response. Where she had used a term such as "service provision" or "social inclusion", it seemed that he simply pressed a button which in each case pasted a two or three paragraph automatic response. Even her insistence on reducing inequalities was doused with cold water. "The vision set out in the draft community strategy makes explicit that we want to create a society where inequalities in the borough are reduced." It was a letter

---

1   Her son was then almost ten.

to an outsider, a way of saying: 'It is good of you to show an interest, but the council is doing great things, thank you very much.'

The use of the word "we" in each case was also instructive. She used it to refer to the council in which she hoped to give direction. When she wrote "we", she meant to include him. He used it to refer to a council that already had his direction. When he wrote "we" he did not mean to include her. She said: we should do this. He said: we are already doing it. "A lot of thought went into the draft community strategy and we feel it in large measure provides the bold and imaginative thinking you want to see." And then, in case she had missed the point, he finished by saying:

> *"The Camden Plan and the Corporate Plan that preceded it played an important role in the council's recent success, and officers at all levels are now geared up to recognise the Community Strategy as the successor to the Camden Plan —which will set the agenda for staff over the next few years and form the reference point for performance management systems that are now deeply embedded within the council. Yours sincerely, Steven Bundred, Chief Executive".*

Or, to put it another way: the managers have taken over.

275

National politics had changed greatly since Tony Blair became the leader of the Labour Party, Voters found it increasingly difficult to differentiate between the policies offered by the three main parties. The same became true of municipal politics. In practice, in the delivery of services, there was no longer anything left wing about Camden. For the entire Jane Roberts period, it is difficult to identify a single policy concerning service delivery that could not just as comfortably have been carried out by a council run by either the LibDems or Tories. Politics had given way to management. Council officers were forever producing papers concerned with the better management of the council, or with meeting government targets set to ensure better management. The councillors were left to present the managers' decisions to each other. New policies were not generated by politicians, but by council managers concerned with government initiatives and targets.

Although Jane Roberts had set out with other ideas, she was soon defeated by the sheer tedium of the Camden Plan, the Corporate Plan and the Community Strategy, all deeply embedded in the minds of senior and middle ranking council officers. The knowledge that council officers had written them and would use them as an excuse not to do anything that in their interpretation was not in them, wore her down.

The reality was that the change in leadership brought about no real change in the running of the council. There was instead a distinct change in the council's aspirations. In order to make her mark, Jane Roberts was reduced to looking at areas alongside the Camden Plan. The council could be a bold political body by making bold statements that at times would have little to do with council business. The managers would manage, but the councillors would engage in bold peripheral activity. The council could assert its influence beyond its immediate boundaries, and Jane Roberts could at the same time ensure the future of the Labour Party by more closely connecting with the young and the ethnic minorities.

Behind her interest lay the belief that when there is a low turnout, Labour fares badly. Those most determined to vote are the middle classes and the elderly. As groups they are less likely to vote Labour than those groups who show less determination to vote, such as the under 25s and the ethnic minorities. If only all kids voted, Labour would have the advantage. Kids know that Tories are boring men in suits and that Labour represents ordinary people and is interested in fairness and the Third World and green stuff. If the voting age were lowered to 16, then there would be more kids on the register and so more Labour votes than there would otherwise be. Black and Asian people will vote Labour because only Labour genuinely has their needs at heart and will always ensure that funding is provided to projects concerned with ethnic minorities. So, the thinking goes, if only we can get more young people and ethnic minorities to vote, the proportion of people who will vote Labour will also increase.

The opposition did not like it. To them, Jane Roberts, the Labour politician, was determined to spend public money to encourage Labour friendly groups to vote. Experience shows that whether there is a low or a big turnout, the proportion of those not interested in politics (and so disinclined to vote) remains low. It is the fluctuating interest of the majority population which determines whether there is a high turnout or not. High turnouts happen not because civil servants and council officers have targeted groups thought more likely to vote Labour, they happen because political parties have given the impression that there is something to vote for or against. It was not an argument that appealed to Jane Roberts.

Within the first six months of her leadership, she oversaw the early appointment of a "Faith Communities Coordinator", a junior council officer whose time would be spent in getting together leaders of religious groups and inviting them to council functions where Labour Party members would lie in wait. It was clear from the beginning that the council's urge to connect with these pious people was less than altruistic. There was a need to engage and to get them involved in local democracy. They had to be urged to get their marks on ballot papers. "We're not looking so much to meet Anglicans from Hampstead", said John Thane when the proposal was first debated in public, "but those from faiths who need to be more involved in democracy". The council was to employ an officer to go where the Labour Party canvassers were unwilling or too idle to go. This was presented as a matter of great importance. Jane Roberts ended her address to the council by shouting out the word "Justice!" The *Ham & High*, now edited by a young Scotsman, Ross Lydall, was most impressed by her passionate plea and resented any opposition to the proposal. "Does the leader of the Camden's Conservative Party have a problem with race?" the paper asked. "Councillor Wauchope surely cannot know how it feels to be black". But black had nothing to do with it. A marriage (or at least a civil partnership) was needed between the modern, vibrant, gays-and-women's rights friendly Camden Labour Party and those adherents of the most conservative of all religious groups, the old-world, exclusive, rigid, patriarchal, gays-and-women's rights unfriendly Muslims.

The consequence was a series of bean feasts with religious leaders. There were no invitations for councillors outside the Labour Party. Church of England clergymen, Roman Catholic priests, non conformist ministers and rabbis, indeed pretty well everyone who was asked to attend, were flattered that they should be involved in what was seen as a sort of council organised, ecumenical experiment. Although unable to guide their flocks at election time, the presence of the clergymen and rabbis was necessary to snare the target groups. The leaders of the Muslim community in Camden were correctly identified as being quite a different thing. They were overwhelmingly from the Bengali community, that great milch cow of untapped Labour votes. They were already in receipt of council and government grants (allocated by the council) on which their various organisations and community centres depended. They had real clout inside the Bengali community and could be, and shortly would be, very impressed by what the Labour council would be able to do to support them.

* * *

Another bold gesture came in October 2001 when she made a submission to the Home Affairs Select Committee on Drugs. The council was invited to take a stance on decriminalisation. It is a dangerous argument to get involved in, especially so in those areas where drug use and crime go hand in hand. Camden's submission approved the fact that the police were concentrating on arresting people for possession and supply of some Class A drugs such as crack and heroin. It recommended that, so as to allow the police to continue their current pursuit of heroin and crack dealers, recreational drug use should be decriminalised. Recreational drug use was not defined –but clearly ecstasy[2] (Class A) and cannabis were intended and, although it was not mentioned, one supposes cocaine (also Class A). Furthermore, the drugs market should be managed by providing a legal supply of drugs "with the provision of an indoor space where drugs, both legal and illegal, can be injected safely". There was no input by anyone outside the Labour Party and, within the Labour group, no discussion of it before publication. It was a singular view simply delivered complete to the executive who voted it through as if it were a collective will of all ten of them on behalf of the borough as a whole.

It was a mistaken and a wholly unnecessary action taken with the confidence of a party that saw its majority as unassailable. There were no votes in it and it gave the opposition a stick to beat Labour with at the next two elections: the opposition wanted a crackdown on crime in Camden. It wanted drug dealers off our streets, and here the Labour council was suggesting that drugs should be decriminalised. That the criminal gangs of Somalis and Gambians selling drugs along the High Street should not be interfered with.

Under the provisions of the Local Government Act 2000, each local authority is obliged to formulate a strategy to promote well being and to consult with such persons as they think appropriate. To this end the council set up the Strategic Local Partnership, on which Camden council would be represented by the leader who would be surrounded by a wholly arbitrary selection of local worthies. In Camden this disparate group included the (no doubt utterly bewildered) top fireman, the top policeman, someone from University College London (which is in the borough), the local business association, the joint chair of school

278

---

2   Or, specifically, methylenedioxymethylamphetamine.

governors (naturally, a member of the Labour Party), someone from the primary care trust and a number of representatives to speak for the voluntary sector. The only councillor with a place on the Strategic Local Partnership was Jane Roberts, who chaired the meetings. Sitting amongst them "engaging" were council officers and the occasional otherwise unoccupied Labour Party executive member able to make two hour meetings during working hours.

Faced with this new idea of being somehow in a state of partnership with local government, the police were easily seduced into playing the game as if they were themselves up for election. They had plenty to bring to meetings of the Strategic Local Partnership to let everyone know of new initiatives and plans and of how well the police are working "in partnership" with the local authority. The police provided material for Camden press releases would even provide articles where the borough commander could be photographed by a local newspaper while letting them know in his own words how well he is doing. As the political parties increasingly used crime as a political issue, so the borough commander found himself increasingly invited to pat himself on the back at election time.

The result of this was simply that no one believed the police. So intent were they on describing their success, in describing the emperor's clothes, they lost all perspective as to why they had to explain themselves in the first place. Police work to them became like council work. You need not actually do anything, and certainly not do anything effectively, you just had to keep telling people that you were doing plenty and doing it well.

Jane Roberts's election as council leader was followed almost immediately by news that Jake Turnbull, a 27 year old Labour councillor for Bloomsbury ward, was no longer living in the borough and had only turned up to one council meeting in the year. He had his excuses ready and was, the papers found, refreshingly Old Labour for one so young. "Tory Toffs forced me out, says Jake", was the headline in the New Journal. "It's all very well, these well-heeled Tory toffs, sitting back in their mansions in the posh end of town", read his press release, "but whilst the Tories are sitting in Camden committee rooms, behaving like they are taking part in a private school-boy debating society, I am out with the real people trying to do my bit". The solution, he felt, was to have full time councillors paid enough to enable them to live in the areas they represent. He would like to resign, he said, but the Labour chief whip, Dermot Greene, would not let him do so until a by election date after the summer holidays could be guaranteed. These were still the days when students were expected to vote Labour. In May, Turnbull's majority had been 151 votes, a margin too narrow to risk on a reduced turnout before the start of the academic year. "We just want a good turnout", said Greene, with his fingers crossed behind his back. "We would come in for criticism if we held an election when the students were away".

Dermot Greene was right, and delay brought further help to the Labour Party by way of Archie Norman MP, then the shadow environment minister, who made an extraordinarily unnecessary speech at the housing conference at Harrogate in June. Registered social landlords were good, he felt, and council housing was bad. Within the first five year term of the next Conservative government, he promised, all housing stock would be taken out of the hands of local authorities[3]. Brian Weekes, Camden's housing chairman was listening in the hall and was, metaphorically at least, rubbing his hands with glee. When the by election was set for 28 September 2000, with the students comfortably back at University College, the Labour Party made sure that everyone in Bloomsbury knew of Archie Norman's plans for council housing (or, at least, Brian Weekes's version of Archie Norman's plans). Every council flat was to be sold to greedy, heartless Thatcherite developers.[4] Labour held the seat by 19 votes.[5]

The "Democratic Renewal" provisions of the Local Government Act 2000[6] were unpopular with all parties in Camden. In the interests

---

3   A policy broadly adopted by the Labour government with varying success in 2003 when it insisted on arms length management organisations (ALMOs), private finance initiatives (PFI) or stock transfer.

4   Nor did it help the Tories when, two days before the by election, Jeffrey Archer was charged with perjury. After a long illness, Brian Weekes died, much regretted by all, shortly after the 2002 elections.

5   It was a sign of changing times: the last Bloomsbury by election had taken place only five years before in 1995 under the Major government. Labour's Pat Callaghan got 1271 votes, beating the Conservative David Whittaker by over 900. Now that Tony Blair was prime minister, Peter Brayshaw beat Patsy Prince in September 2000 managing only 495 votes to her 476: the Labour vote had shrunk by 60%, the Tory vote increased by 40%.

6   Reliant on LibDem support, the government forced the legislation through the (as yet unreformed) House of Lords on 24 July 2000.

of efficiency, the government was determined to get rid of the committee system "so that councillors could spend more time with their constituents". The legislation allowed one of three options: an executive mayor, an elected leader with a chief executive, or a cabinet style executive. Of these, the councillors overwhelmingly felt the last to be the least bad. The local press preferred the idea of an elected mayor[7]. The council carried out "the most extensive consultation on the subject in the country", a postal survey of residents and local groups to confirm support for the status quo. Although there were over a thousand responses, they still represented less than one percent of the electorate and underlined public apathy on the point. When the council petitioned the government with the outcome of the consultation, the environment minister, Beverly Hughes, was unimpressed: "White, fairly well heeled people from social classes one and two were grossly over represented and people from the poorer parts of Camden were grossly underrepresented". Jane Roberts led a cross party delegation to plead with Hilary Armstrong, the minister for local government, for an exemption, but to no effect.

Interested members were invited to join a Scrutiny Working Panel chaired by John Dickie to beat out a new constitution as required by the new law. The government provided no template for this and so local authorities were frantically cribbing off one another to come up with what was best. The draft constitution was drafted by the borough solicitor's department, circulated and then pored over in committee where amendments were made. It felt like a long process[8], but the reality was a rushed draft. Alison Lowton, the borough solicitor, explained away the document's many defects in that it was "only meant for the current make up of the council". The final version, where the only real care had been to ensure the fewest number of opposition members sat on the scrutiny commission and panels, was adopted against vociferous opposition[9]. Even if the Local Government

281

---

7   The *New Journal* changed tack once it discovered that Steve Bundred favoured the elected mayor option.

8   In a meeting of the Scrutiny Working Panel in May 2001, Roy Shaw slipped me a note which read: "I estimate that 46,707,873 angels can dance on the head of a needle. Or is it a pin?"

9   Membership of both the scrutiny commission and the panels was allocated to the parties on the basis of proportionality. The proportionality was calculated not with reference to the available councillors (that is, the non-executive members on the council), but on the total number of councillors, so it was overwhelmingly a Labour body (with only two opposition members until 2002 and three thereafter).

Act permanently damaged local democracy, John Dickie pointed out in the final debate, there simply was no public interest in local government reform. The public gallery was empty. Even Mrs Luby had gone to bed.

The 2001 general election was, for the two Camden constituencies as well as for the rest of the country, the dreariest election of modern times. The country was content and the economy was still growing. The John Major government was still a lingering distasteful memory, and although the intensity of the wind that had blown Tony Blair into power had somewhat diminished, it was still blowing in the same direction. Conservative Central Office was under no illusions as to the likely outcome. Few seats were targeted and they concentrated on defending those they already held. The two Camden seats were far beyond their modest ambitions. All activists in the borough were instructed to devote their time to the nearest "marginal" constituency, Finchley & Golders Green. Andrew Mennear, councillor for Fitzjohns ward, was chosen as the Tory candidate for Hampstead & Highgate on the basis that he would work hard and make much noise and, although he was not expected to win, any inroad into Glenda Jackson's majority would be welcome. In Holborn & St Pancras, the Tories chose Roseanne Serelli, a lawyer from Essex with even less of a chance, but who photographed well. It was hopeless in both cases.

The turnout on 7 June 2001 was poor nationally, down from 72% to under 60%, the lowest percentage turnout since the introduction of universal suffrage in 1928. There was little change. The Conservatives overall gained only one seat, and the LibDems six. Tony Blair was left with a working majority of 166. The turnout in Hampstead & Highgate was only 54%. Glenda Jackson lost nearly nine thousand votes but still won with a margin of almost eight thousand, and the Conservative vote slumped by three thousand leaving Mennear with 8,725. No Conservative candidate in Hampstead had ever polled less[10]. In Holborn & St Pancras the turnout was under 50% and Frank Dobson lost an easily affordable eight thousand votes but still got over half the votes cast. The only point of interest in the results concerned the LibDem

282

---

10 Although, as the Labour vote had in percentage terms fallen more than the Tory vote he was able to claim (when he later applied to stand in the marginal Finchley & Golders Green in the 2005 general election) that he had brought about "a 4% swing from Labour to the Conservatives".

candidates. In Hampstead & Highgate, Jonathan Simpson, had crept up on the Conservatives and got 20% of the vote, not quite up to Anne Sofer's 25% in 1983, but getting there. In Holborn & St Pancras Nat Green overtook the Conservatives and came second with almost six thousand votes, although still eleven thousand votes behind Dobson.[11]

On the council, the "democratically renewed" system of an executive and a scrutiny commission came into operation in September 2001. The hostility to the system that had been professed by everyone before its implementation, was soon replaced by a general enthusiasm by those in the executive, and by Janet Guthrie who had been elected to chair the scrutiny commission. To the executive members the stipends were better than ever before, they did not have to share information with anyone outside their immediate circle and they no longer faced any systematic scrutiny. Unlike the old committee chairmen who had to be ahead at every committee meeting, the executive members could work or not work, but they got paid.

The scrutiny commission was made up of councillors not on the executive. Topics for scrutiny were chosen by the commission and were then scrutinised by a panel of non-executive members. The system in its operation was a scandal, designed to prevent councillors from doing anything useful. It was paid for by the tax payer to ensure that councillors were never in a position to challenge the executive, and soon became a waste of time because it was made a waste of time.

283

The conduct of three of the early scrutiny panels was instructive, and set the style for future panels.

In 2000, West Hampstead Housing Association had teetered on the brink of insolvency before being bailed out by the Housing Corporation with a £4½m guarantee. Had the Housing Association not acted, thousands of tenants may have lost their homes. Camden had sold several properties to WHHA at a discount on the agreement that Camden would retain the nomination rights (that is, the right to decide who on its housing list should be housed in the properties once WHHA had done them up). If any of the properties were sold, the council retained the right to claw-back the money. In 2001, as part of the rescue package with the Housing Association, the council was

---

11 Pam Chesters was pushed into third place by the LibDems in Bristol West, as was Stephen Hocking in Streatham.

obliged to waive its claw-back so that WHHA could sell the properties —now renovated- on the open market to clear its debts. These were houses that Camden had transferred to the WHHA to provide housing for families on Camden's housing list. Camden had favoured the WHHA whose housing portfolio had been built up over the years with help from Camden council. The situation was particularly embarrassing for Camden because the association had been set up and run by Anna Bowman, a former Labour councillor. People wanted to know what business Camden had in transferring properties to an inept housing association run by one of its former councillors. Such was the anger, that Jane Roberts promised a scrutiny panel to investigate.

But when the panel was set up, the terms of reference were so tight that the panel was confined to considering whether the council "could reasonably have been expected to know the extent of the problems facing WHHA". Camden was safe on this. There was no mechanism whereby Camden could have known. Not even the regulatory body, the Housing Corporation, had seen the danger. In a sense it was a rerun of the Arden enquiry into the Paribas loan in 1992. The panel was not charged to investigate what was of interest, it was only charged to investigate that which was of marginal interest and which could not damage the council's reputation. The chairman of the panel, John Rolfe, was given the task of blaming the Housing Corporation for not effectively monitoring the WHHA. Camden was not criticised for giving birth to the WHHA as an autonomous body and leaving it in the hands of Anna Bowman who was, within the political memory of many Labour councillors, not only a former member of the Labour group but also a leadership contender. [12]

The first LibDem to chair anything on the council was Flick Rea, who chaired the scrutiny panel on the council's administration of its commercial properties. It was written by a council officer, overseen by a panel dominated by Labour councillors, and contained mild criticism of the council in a field free of electoral danger. In February 2002 she presented the report to the executive and outlined its conclusions with the words "We're not actually very good landlords". She was met with great rudeness. The executive sat back to watch the fun as John

---

12 Two panel members, Julian Fulbrook and Heather Johnson, were so concerned that the single Tory panelist would attempt to blame the WHHA mess on the former Labour councillors Anna Bowman and David Lines (who until 1998 had been an observer on the board of the WHHA) that they submitted written statements to the panel so that they could consider their own submissions as evidence when the time came to agree the report.

Thane (executive member for the environment) told her that the panel's conclusions were "confused" and that overall it was "a pig's breakfast". The report, like so many, was then noted and, in real terms, forgotten.

The only panel that actually provided the opposition with a good opportunity to gain publicity was the School Run Scrutiny panel which had been suggested and then chaired by Mike Greene, the new councillor for Frognal[13]. Hampstead is school rich, and most of the children who attend the schools are brought in from outside the borough, and many of those who live in the borough still rely on being driven. There are traffic jams entirely attributable to school run traffic and the local amenity groups, often run by the retired, detest the school run traffic.

When offered the chairmanship of one of the scrutiny panels, the Conservatives seized upon this one. It was of great help to them. Mike Greene lived in Hampstead Town ward but represented Frognal. Frognal was to be amalgamated with Fitzjohns in the boundary changes that were to take effect for the 2002 borough elections, and there was to be no place for Greene in the new ward. If he was to stay on the council, he would have to win in Town. The new, larger Town ward was to include a small part of Frognal (and a larger part of Fitzjohns) so that Mike Greene would have his entree into the campaign as a sitting councillor.

285

Mike Greene met with great success. He chaired the panel with skill and charm. There was great public interest in the subject. The locals wanted less traffic, the parents wanted their children safely deposited at the school gates. There could also be little or no criticism of the council, in fact the very existence of the panel showed that the council was doing something rather than nothing. By the end of the process half of Hampstead had come forward to give evidence and Greene was in frequent contact with every tenants group. The panel made recommendations concerning parking dispensation schemes, green travel plans, school buses, remote drop off places and car sharing. Its recommendations pleased the local groups (whose members voted in Town), and displeased the school-runners (who had no votes in Town). He presented his report in March 2002, and was ready for the borough elections in six weeks time.

*   *   *

13   He had won the by election in 2000 called following the resignation of Pam Chesters.

In March 2002, two months before the local elections, Camden was named "Council of the Year" by the *Local Government Chronicle*.[14] It was an award that Steve Bundred had been angling for for years. He had been until the year before a columnist on the *LGC* when Camden had first entered the council of the year award and had been "highly commended". The 2001 award instead went to Suffolk, a Labour council facing elections in that year. Bundred took stock of what needed to be done, gave up his column, and Camden positioned itself to win. The award was then in its infancy with no more than half a dozen councils showing serious interest each year. The *LGC* busily promoted its "local government Oscar ceremony" in the hope that it could produce something a bit more exciting than whatever came out of the Audit Commission or IDeA. It required cooperation from the councils it was to consider, and so the councils had to enter the competition and put aside officer time to be able to compete. It could not merely be an award given to an unsuspecting council for good performance. The award was restricted to the small number of councils who entered the competition. There was not a shortlist, so much as a line up of the councils who had made the considerable effort to enter. An assessment was carried out in categories that were never published in full by the *LGC* and were not revealed by Camden. Many councils did not enter because they knew they would not win. But also many councils, in particular those high performing Inner London boroughs such as Westminster and Kensington & Chelsea, did not enter on the simple grounds that the expense was not warranted by any benefit to the council taxpayers. They also thought it rather beneath their dignity to enter[15].

The Conservative response was simply to answer in kind. The government had insisted on councils assessing themselves against performance indicators and from year to year would change the

14 Not quite *The Council of the Year*, as the award was shared with Labour run Blackburn with Darwen Borough. The two councils treated the awards rather differently. Blackburn looked upon the award as a celebration of all things Blackburn and brought opposition members to the awards junket in London. Camden saw the award as being a celebration of all things Labour and invited only Labour members and council officers.

15 The leader of Westminster City Council, Simon Milton, allowed his officers to enter the competition the following year and won the award in 2004. Neither he nor the ruling Tory group had anything to gain by it. There were no banners over City Hall and nothing on the notepaper. He succumbed, he said, purely to pressure from his officers (with an eye on their CVs) who were so affected by the fuss Camden made.

"basket" of those indicators so that councils could be assessed on a shifting basis. At the same time that the *Local Government Chronicle* had named Camden as the joint Council of the Year, Camden's own officers had prepared a "beacon basket" of 68 performance indicators from the lists prepared by DTLR (the Department of Transport, Local Government and the Regions) and IDeA, considered to be the most important. Camden was ranked fourth in Inner London behind the three Conservative run boroughs of Westminster, Wandsworth and Kensington & Chelsea[16]. Wandsworth, the Tory run council so loathed by everyone in the Labour establishment, had gone further and arranged for its officers to assess every London borough on as many performance indicators as possible. The resultant "Rank of Ranks", based on 168 performance indicators, ranked Wandsworth as first in Inner London. The Rank of Ranks was then distributed to the press, initially to embarrass Labour run Ealing who were ranked bottom. Of the thirty two London boroughs, Camden came fourth from bottom. To emphasise the point, the Conservatives launched their manifesto against a backdrop of posters which repeated round the room the simple legend "29*th*".

The reality was that the press was not really interested in a bout of self congratulation. They reported the award and reported the criticisms of the award. An exasperated Jane Roberts wrote to the *Ham & High* to complain of "the scant coverage" of "this prestigious award –the Oscar of local government". "Of course, I know that we have much more to do and that we must bring all our services up to the standard of the very best", she pleaded, "but just as your readers should know when we have made a mistake, surely they have a right to know when we succeed?" Her letter was lost on a page of lengthy complaints from Conservative councillors complaining of high council tax and the poor ranking on the government's performance indicators. "What is wanted" wrote the leader of the opposition, matching her letter for both predictability and crassness, "is a council dedicated to good services, rather than one dedicated to telling the rest of us how good it is".

But the letters page of the *Ham & High* was one thing: Jane Roberts got her message across in a thousand ways a day that could not be answered. Within a week, every piece of mail emanating from the town hall was franked with COUNCIL OF THE YEAR 2002. Council

287

---

16 Whose council tax at Band D was set, respectively, at £445, £398, and £762. Camden charged £1006.

stationery was not far behind. Camden's fleet of vehicles were soon emblazoned with the message, and the news went out with every council tax demand. Two storey high banners were draped over the front of the town hall building on Judd Street proclaiming the award. On the marble staircase inside the town hall, where couples fresh from the registrar's office pose for their first wedding photographs, there appeared a twelve foot green banner with the same legend, so that in years to come those newlywed couples may look back on Camden's happy event as well as their own.

As the 2002 borough elections approached, the Labour Party candidate selections brought about many changes. The old wards had been merged, reducing the council from 57 members (representing 25 wards of two or three members each) to 54 members (representing 18 wards of three members each). Many of the councillors were of an age when retirement was a happy release, and the rebels had been made to feel not welcome. Twelve councillors, including Richard Arthur, did not stand again; two others (Pat Nightingale and Aileen Hammond) were selected to fight Belsize where the boundary changes did not favour them; and one (Gloria Lazenby) stood as an independent. With the sole Asian councillor, Nirmal Roy, standing down, there was a sense of urgency in selecting more non white faces. Five Asians were chosen for safe Labour seats.

The Conservative selection process was centralised in Camden, where Pam Chesters chaired a committee of both the constituency associations. The leader of the opposition was an observer only (although not necessarily slow to offer advice) so that if any awkward decision needed to be taken, the blame would rest with the panel rather than the group leader. The selection process included the application of the dietician, "Dr" Gillian McKeith, then wholly unknown but who had recently been the "healthy living expert" on the *Joan Rivers Show* in California[17]. She wanted to become a councillor so that she could become the MP for Hampstead. It was a short lived application which she withdrew a few weeks later, and the closest the committee came to a celebrity selection was that of Sheila Gunn, who had been John Major's press secretary in at the kill in 1997.

---

17 Her husband, Howard Magaziner, was confident that Gilliam McKeith would soon be "better known than Glenda Jackson". He may well be right.

The panel also declined to nominate for Swiss Cottage Honora Morrissey, the victor of the Swiss Cottage by election, and instead selected her to fight the safe Labour seat of Kilburn. Within two months she resigned from the party and joined the LibDems, which caused slight embarrassment at the time. There was fear that she could be looked upon as having been hard done by, but helpfully a script was drafted for her and she announced that she did not like the Conservatives who, under Iain Duncan Smith, were now too right wing.[18]

Although the Conservatives hoped to achieve great things against Labour in Highgate and Bloomsbury, and against the Liberals with Mike Greene in Hampstead Town, they had much to fear from the effect of the boundary changes. Two of their wards had been amalgamated (Frognal and Fitzjohns) and another (Adelaide) had been split between four adjoining wards. The LibDems, on the other hand, were rather favoured by the new boundaries in that the three wards in which they appeared secure (Hampstead Town, West End and Fortune Green) were expanded to return three councillors in each rather than two. The LibDems hoped to have nine councillors in their three (expanded) wards and perhaps something in the new, awkwardly named, Camden Town with Primrose Hill ward.

289

Nevertheless, it was clear to everyone that even if there were gains by the opposition parties, Labour was going to win. The electorate, so soon after the re-election of the Blair government, was not going to vote for change. Camden was after all, as Jane Roberts and John Dickie were keen to point out at the Labour manifesto launch, the "Council of the Year".

The Conservatives put on a confident show at the launch of their manifesto at "Finsberg House" on Heath Hurst Road, making much of Camden's position as being 29th out of 32 London boroughs on the government's performance indicators. They pledged to reduce council tax by £21 by making savings in thirty key areas (in "a budget carefully costed by Andrew Marshall"). Photos in the press followed of the leader of the opposition posing with the glamorous, bare midriffed Fiona Béry-Cook next to a street sign on Boundary Road (where she lived) and which runs between Camden and Westminster. Each held a placard to illustrate the difference in council tax between the

---

18 John Dickie, who had defected from the LibDems in 1995, described her defection as having "increased the average IQ of both the Conservative and LibDem groups".

two boroughs. Westminster charged £445 for a property at Band D, whereas Camden charged £1006.[19]

In the run up to the election, the *New Journal* all but lost interest in the main parties: Labour for not being socialist and the Tories for being Tories, while the LibDems were again only of interest if they were to punish Labour for its lack of socialism. The paper's editorial a fortnight before the elections blamed the Local Government Act whereby "a century old system of committee run local government was hollowed out and replaced almost overnight by a Labour autocracy". However, it continued, "there are signs however faint –that interest in politics is coming back into vogue. It can be seen in the growing attraction of the Greens, and the stir such independent candidates David Reed[20] in the Kilburn ward and Gloria Lazenby in the Primrose Hill with Camden Town ward are making". The paper then gave more coverage to Gloria Lazenby than to the established opposition parties together. "Former Labour mayor Gloria Lazenby, an old Labour stalwart dismissed from the party could produce a shock result" wrote their senior reporter under the headline SHOCK RESULT LOOMS AT PRIMROSE HILL. For the first time the Green Party fielded a full slate of candidates across the borough.

The council ensured that the voters were also guided by a glossy purple card distributed by the council (complete with Camden logo) on which was a photograph of the gangsta rappers More Fire Crew: four surly, baggy trousered black youths making V signs for the camera. The caption read: "More Fire Crew say Oi vote!" [21]

Not necessarily because of More Fire Crew, Labour won. The state of the parties immediately after the election was 35 Labour, 11 Conservative and 8 LibDems. "Labour defies London swing", read the

---

19 She later revealed that she had been a *Penthouse* Playmate of the Month in 1993. To Stephen Hocking the photographs were reminiscent of "that period when Sam Fox [late of Page 3] got religion and appeared in pictures alongside bemused looking elderly clergymen".

20 David Reed lives near to what was then referred to as the Swiss Cottage site. He disapproved of the nature of the development and by way of protest stood in Kilburn against Phil Turner, the executive member responsible. Reed got a respectable 174 votes despite the Kilburn electorate having no interest in anything at Swiss Cottage.

21 Unhappily, the voting records of Ozzie, Shaunie, Neeko and Lethal Bizzle were not disclosed. This card was followed by Camden's own MAD ("Make A Difference") magazine for distribution in secondary schools. Aiming to explain to the young what the council did, it featured a photograph of two baggy trousered rappers on the front and an assurance by Jane Roberts that "We're not a bunch of boring people in suits".

Ham & High headline, but told only part of the story. At 28%, the turnout for the 2002 borough election was the lowest in Camden's history, 5% down on 1998. The Labour share of the vote in the 1998 election had been 44%, but in the 2002 election Labour's share had shrunk to 34%, with the Tories on 26% and the Lib Dems on 23%. The improvement in the share of the vote for the opposition parties did not translate into seats won. Both the Conservatives and the LibDems increased their majorities in the seats they held, but made insufficient headway in Labour wards. As predicted by the *New Journal*, there was a shock result in the new Camden Town with Primrose Hill ward, but not in the way the paper had anticipated. The LibDems took one of the three seats from Labour, which came as something of a surprise to their winning candidate, Justin Barnard, who, claiming that he disliked confrontation and could not cope with stress, promptly resigned.[22] That slender (and short lived) victory sweetened for the LibDems an otherwise disappointing night following the result in Hampstead Town, a ward which in the 1998 election they had won with a thousand votes and 60% of the ballot. In 2002 they managed only one of the three seats. Mike Greene and Brian Cattell took two for the Conservatives, but could not dislodge the sitting councillor Margaret Little. "I think it was an extraordinarily difficult campaign and some of the abuse was quite shameful", said Flick Rea after the result. "It does not please me as a democrat to see elections full of personal vilification and slurs".

There were disappointments for the Conservatives elsewhere. Their expectations in Bloomsbury had been high, especially after the Conservatives had successfully appealed against the ward boundary initially proposed by the Boundaries Commission[23]. They failed by less

---

22 Having fallen out with the Labour Party, Gloria Lazenby stood as an independent in Camden Town with Primrose Hill. Backed by the *New Journal*, she took 603 votes (beating John Macdonald's record for an independent in 1998 by three votes). She split the Labour vote and (alphabetically) the last Labour candidate, Jake Sumner, lost out. He won the ensuing by election in June by 50 votes, the first Labour gain in a by election since 1970. Since the 1998 Political Parties Registration Act, independents have been prevented from describing themselves on the ballot. If Mrs Lazenby had been allowed to stand as a "Labour councillor seeking re-election" (as had John Macdonald) she may well have won. Barnard's resignation was to Flick Rea "far more hurtful than Dickie's defection had been, or Simpson's defection was in 2005".

23 This was down to the hard work of Ken Avery, formerly a Brunswick councillor (and in 1968 at 24 was the youngest member of the council). The Conservatives succeeded in getting a Bloomsbury ward that lay from east to west to include part of the old Brunswick ward, which seemed at the time more promising than the proposed ward that lay from north to south and included Covent Garden. Ken Avery died in 2008.

than a hundred votes, behind Labour who had sensibly begun their campaign by signing up Bengalis (whose turn out is traditionally poor) as postal voters. Over a hundred Bengali postal votes were cast in the election and the Conservatives lost by a margin of just under a hundred. Labour also hung on in Highgate, less than 50 votes ahead of both the Conservatives and the Greens.

The Labour newcomers to the council were impressive, especially as six of them were young, articulate and university educated and who were to dominate the front bench as the term wore on (Lucy Anderson, Theo Blackwell, Anna Stewart, Geethika Jayatilaka, Raj Chada, and – after the Camden Town with Primrose Hill by election- Jake Sumner).[24] The LibDems were joined by Jonathan Simpson, their parliamentary candidate in Hampstead & Highgate. Also elected were the first Muslim Bengalis (Nasim Ali, Fazlul Chowdhury and Abdul Quadir)[25]. Ali was promptly elected deputy mayor by the Labour group so that he would be mayor after only a year on the council, the same honour that had been granted to Jerry Williams in 1986 for being the first West Indian councillor.[26] In Swiss Cottage the Conservative Don Williams became Camden's first Jamaican councillor.

292

In August 2002 Camden launched its attack on the 1981 "Right to Buy" (RTB) legislation by which council tenants may apply to buy at a discount the properties they live in. Of the properties sold by Camden under RTB about half of them were then still occupied by the original purchasers, while the other half had been either sold on or sublet. Those who sell on (in a time of rising prices) may make a profit, and that (although not the central issue) was nevertheless a matter deeply distasteful to those hostile to the scheme. Much was made of this aspect in the press.

The council produced four glossy booklets enclosed in a folder colourfully designed with a picture of a big toe sticking out of a sock and

24 To jump forward: in 2006 the last two lost their seats, Lucy Anderson resigned soon afterwards, and the remaining four announced in 2009 that they were not standing again.

25 The former Labour councillors Nirmal Roy and Ramen Bhattacharyya were Bengali, but not Muslim.

26 Making a councillor deputy mayor immediately on his first election to the council was not without precedent. The same had happened to Brian Duggan in 1971 and Jim Turner in 1990. In Ali's case the principal change was that in order in to get him to take the job, he became the first mayor to receive a special responsibility allowance, giving him the same remuneration as an executive member.

the legend *HOUSING the hole in Social Policy*. Jane Roberts launched the campaign by posing, po-faced, behind a theatrical set of scales on which a toy house inscribed "182 New" was outweighed by a heavier house marked "761 Sold" to illustrate the fact that more council houses were being sold than social housing units were being built. The *New Journal* loved it. The Right to Buy (RTB) policy was one of "the morally flawed policies hammered through parliament by Margaret Thatcher". But how could the Labour leadership "shake their heads over the damage done by RTB when some of their own elected members have benefitted over the years from the wheeling and dealing that goes with it?" Although he was not the only councillor to have sinned, they singled out the deputy mayor, Nasim Ali, who was then living on the Regents Park Estate in a flat which had been bought by his family under the RTB scheme earlier in the year. He was now in the process of buying a former council flat in Gospel Oak. He was at pains to point out that he disapproved of RTB but that the flat had already been sold by the council and was being sold on. "It's not a right-to-buy sale", he said carefully, "otherwise I wouldn't be buying it". He was, in a sense, handling stolen goods, but not actually stealing. The *New Journal* was mollified. "He is a victim of the housing shortage!" proclaimed its next editorial. "This was caused by Mrs Thatcher!"[27]

The anti-Right to Buy campaign was followed by another arbitrary decision without debate in council. Jane Roberts ordered the removal from the town hall of all the portraits of former mayors of the metropolitan boroughs of Hampstead, Holborn and St Pancras. These stately oil paintings of dead white men were stuffy and no longer relevant to a borough as vibrant and diverse as modern, forward-looking Camden. To reinvent itself, the council must cut free the past. There was no consultation, no warning, simply a sudden disappearance.[28]

The Tories made much of it, as did the newspapers. The phrase "loony left" was levelled at Camden for the first time in a decade. No plan had been made as to what was to replace the pictures. For months the walls of the committee rooms were bare, and when they

293

---

27 Nasim Ali and his family (he was then a teenager) took part in and were housed by Camden following the homeless families occupation of the Town Hall in 1984 (see pages 160-164).

28 "It's positive discrimination against white male councillors", said Jonny Bucknell, the new Belsize councillor whose grandfather had been a mayor of Hampstead and whose father chaired the housing committee in St Pancras. "Perhaps I should take it to the Commission for Racial Equality".

were eventually filled, it was with enthusiastic daubs of poster paint on paper, collectively provided by the children of the agreeably diverse primary school on nearby Argyle Square, or with colour photographs of the mayor and her deputy in full regalia engaging with local people. Later the gaps were filled by drearily unattractive examples of naïve art in the form of large oils of buildings in the borough painted by a depressed Irishman.[29]

Another gesture, made without consultation, and meaningless because so few councillors attended, was the fixing of the annual civic Remembrance Day service at the St Pancras new church on the Euston Road. As Camden was an amalgamation of three old metropolitan boroughs, the conciliatory tradition had been to hold the civic service at a different church each year, alternating between parishes in Hampstead, Holborn and St Pancras (and occasionally including the Catholic churches). This did not please Jane Roberts, in no small part because the clergymen were likely to dwell on matters concerning those who fell in the two world wars. What she wanted was a clergyman who could represent, in a sort of muted Christian way, her own view of what should be said in the pulpit. The incumbent of St Pancras, the Reverend Mr Paul Hawkins ("Father Paul") spoke her language. Avoiding any reference to the British dead (unless forced to because he wanted to refer to Iraqi civilian losses), each year he delivered sermons concerning water privatisation in the Third World, fair trade, world poverty, the politics of Nigeria and Uzbekistan, praise for the council on its strategy for inclusiveness, and the reading of Sufi verse. For the six years that Jane Roberts was leader, the civic service was held at St Pancras.[30]

In November 2002 Steve Bundred resigned as chief executive to take up the post of executive director of the Improvement and Development Agency for Local Government (IDeA)[31]. He had once, he said, intended to measure his success as a chief executive by the number of decent

---

29 Who shortly afterwards joined the dead white men his pictures had replaced by committing suicide.

30 So adept was the Rev Mr Hawkins in engendering decidedly unChristian thoughts in those who mistakenly imagined he was holding a service of remembrance that Dawn Somper was deputised to attend for the Conservatives while the leader of the opposition and others went elsewhere.

31 He was not there for long. Since 1 September 2003 he has been the chief executive of the Audit Commission.

restaurants that opened on the Euston Road. "There is", he said in parody of the leader, "still much to do".

However, restaurants aside, he had done much. In the following month, the Audit Commission described Camden as an "Excellent" authority. The *New Journal* was in a congratulatory mood: "Relieved Labour councillors now feel they can relax after seeing Camden Council among the top teams in the Premier League of local authorities. Their sense of self-satisfaction is matched with hidden dismay by their opponents on the floor of the council chamber". They were right: it was a great achievement for a council that only ten years before had been subject to a statutory spending freeze for not being able to balance its books. "We have come from being a basket case to a beacon council!" Jane Roberts told the council. "We know we provide many excellent services, but we are not complacent and know that we have much more to do".

Nevertheless, as the Tories were quick to point out, the Audit Commission had lowered the bar to allow it to happen. Council services were given marks out of four. Four points was "excellent", three points was "good", two was "adequate" and one was "failing". It had originally been intended to designate as "excellent" only those councils scoring the maximum four marks in each category, but this excluded all Inner London boroughs under Labour control. The rules were consequently relaxed and Camden, together with Hammersmith & Fulham, made the grade even though they scored four points in fewer than half the categories. Only two of Camden's departments (education and benefits) were given top marks.[32]

A great loss to Camden though Bundred was, the political fallout from the resignation of the deputy leader, John Dickie, was by far the greater. Before Bundred had left his desk, Dickie announced that he had accepted the position of head of Parliamentary and Political Affairs at the BBC and was obliged to resign from the council.[33] Dickie was clearly among the most able of councillors, and Jane Roberts placed great reliance on

295

---

32   *In Camden,* the housing, social services, environment, and leisure departments had each been awarded only three points. Nevertheless, two "excellent" and four "good" departments, made Camden an "excellent" authority overall rather than merely a "good" one, thereby bracketing Camden together with other "excellent" London boroughs who had scored top marks in all categories.

33   Dickie did very well there, going on to become the BBC's director of corporate affairs. He left in 2008 to take up a new position as director of strategy and policy at London First.

him as her deputy leader. The timing of his resignation was of the very worst, and the consequences were serious. Haverstock ward, which Dickie represented with Jane Roberts and Roy Shaw, was the third safest Labour ward in the borough. The majority over the LibDems had been 430 (and 485 over the Conservatives) in 2002, but the country was now greatly interested in the forthcoming invasion of Iraq. It was no longer a question of whether it would happen, but when. Politicians generally felt that it should happen, but the electorate was less bullish. The by election campaign was launched by Tessa Jowell, now the secretary of state for culture, media and sport, who inspected the refurbished Talacre Sports Hall with the Labour candidate, Paul Thomson. She was met by protestors waving "Don't Attack Iraq" placards.

The by election was held on 20 February 2003, five days after the (depending on whose figures you prefer) one million strong march for peace through London. Labour lost. The successful LibDem candidate was Jill Fraser, a local mother who worked in a Turkish owned fish and chip shop on Queen's Crescent. On a 25% turnout Dickie had won in 2002 with 852 votes. This time, on a 23% turnout, the Labour candidate had polled 484 votes to Mrs Fraser's 746. "LibDem poll landslide leaves Labour stunned" read the headline in the New Journal. It was an important result. It marked the turning point in Labour's fortunes. From here on, it was all downhill. Jane Roberts now faced sharing her ward with the enemy, not because her leadership had done anything to provoke a 20% swing against Labour, but because Tony Blair had signalled his intention to commit British troops to George Bush's invasion of Iraq. "Iraq was virtually on everyone's lips on the doorstep", said Jane Roberts. The LibDems, and everyone else for that matter, encouraged people to use their vote as a protest against a government policy with which not even the Labour voters were happy. "As we knocked on doors in the area", said Mrs Fraser, "it was the first thing they asked about".[34]

The New Journal sent a questionnaire to all fifty four councillors the following month to learn their attitudes towards the coming invasion of Iraq. The answers are of interest in that they showed how the local parties stood with the state of the evidence as it then was. Labour members either wanted no war under any circumstances (concerned about the repercussions on our local communities, said Sue Vincent) or

---

34 The Haverstock result showed the shape of things to come: seven months later, on 18 September 2003, the LibDems took Brent East from Labour in a parliamentary by election with a 28% swing.

only if the action was UN approved. The LibDems were only prepared to support an invasion provided the UN gave the go ahead, and the Conservatives were split as to whether an invasion was necessary, but saw the UN as irrelevant.

Steve Bundred's successor as chief executive was Moira Gibb, CBE, a fifty three year old Scotswoman who had been the successful director of housing and social services at Kensington & Chelsea. "I am the link between you and the council staff", she told Jane Roberts as she accepted a £140,000 salary. "I'm not here to impose my own vision". Impressively, she had achieved at K&C that which Camden's director of housing had failed to do: "win overwhelming support from the council tenants for the bid to become an ALMO", where the pill was sweetened by allowing the tenants to elect over half the management board running K&C's housing stock.

Camden's own proposal for setting up an Arms Length Management Organisation (ALMO) to manage the council's housing stock proved to be the council's biggest challenge in 2003. It followed another government drive to get councils to modernise by adopting one of three options: transferring all housing stock to a housing association, raising funds by a private finance initiative to pay for repairs, or else transferring their housing stock to an ALMO so that councillors would no longer be involved in what were essentially managerial rather than political decisions. The only realistic option of the three was that of an ALMO. The effect of the new arrangements would be that the council would sub contract its housing department to an ALMO (which would allow tenant representation on its board), leaving the tenants with the same rights as before but allowing the council to spend less time on housing. This would in turn take housing out of the direct democratic process, which would affect the workload of councillors, most of whose constituency work concerns housing complaints. [35]

In order to bring about this change, the government wielded a great carrot. It would, it said, release funding to spend on housing repairs if the council transferred its stock. The government was already

297

---

35 The government announcement was curiously similar to that (disastrous though it seemed at the time) proposal by Archie Norman at the Harrogate housing conference in 2000, a proposal that threatened revolution if the Tories had tried to implement it. New Labour was confident that they could get away with what the Tories would never be able to do: bring about the end of council housing.

considering Camden's application for £283m for repair funding, and Camden could expect to get all or most of this sum if it transferred its stock. If it did not transfer, it would receive none of the money it had asked for.

The only rub, and it need never have been anything other than a small one, was that there had to be consultation before the event. Consultation was Camden's bugbear, and brought with it the horrors of past failed traffic schemes and library closures. There were many ways in which a consultation could take place: Barnet, for example, simply carried out a sample telephone poll. But Camden, still haunted by the ghosts of the St Pancras United Tenants, needed to take care not to aggravate opposition to the ALMO. Tenants' meetings needed careful handling, and the necessary level of care was missing. In one such meeting, Charlie Hedges was badgered by the tenants into making the rash promise that there would be a full ballot of all council tenants. It turned out to be a severe and expensive misjudgement.

For decades, St Pancras militancy had lain dormant beneath Camden's political surface, posing as no more than an historical curiosity. But the magic phrase, "housing privatisation", was all that was needed to rouse the monster from its sleep and send it roaring round the estates. It appeared suddenly, organised and determined, in the form of Camden Defend Council Housing (DCH), a body that for all intents and purposes was based on the Peckwater Estate in Kentish Town and run by Alan Walter. Walter was well known at the council as a tenants' representative, trades unionist and vocal member of the Socialist Workers Party (or at election time, the London Socialist Alliance). To Walter and his friends, housing not run by the council as an immediate landlord was simply not council housing. "If the money is available for ALMOs, why not for direct investment in council housing with no strings attached? What is the justification for spending money on setting up new companies (massive consultants fees, legal costs and higher senior management salaries) when this could be spent on repairs and improvements instead?" There was no answer to this, said Walter, because the Blair government was "committed to privatisation", and intended to privatise council housing. A campaign was launched to pressure the council to pressure the government.

The housing department saw Walter and DCH as an irritating irrelevance. The government had made a decision and the Peckwater Estate Trots were not going to change things. So confident was the council in this view that in August 2003, three months before the ballot was to take place, the formation of a "shadow" ALMO board was

298

announced. The shadow board was to include tenants and councillors to "make sure the tenants have a strong voice on the future shape of the proposed ALMO". Elections were then called for the shadow board, of one tenant from each of the five housing districts. Holborn housing district elected one of the DCH people, Albert Beale, who had canvassed votes with a promise to sabotage the board. He did his best to keep his pledge.

To Charlie Hedges, the position was simple: an ALMO was the only way to "unblock" government cash. The cash was necessary, said his director, Neil Litherland, to carry out "internal work for the first time in a generation". The New Journal interviewed Keith Hill, the housing minister, on a visit to Camden in September and asked him what would happen if the tenants voted "No" to an ALMO. Hill, instead of saying bluntly that in such an event Camden would get no money, instead gave the Delphic answer that Camden would have to come up with "a further proposal". MINISTER MUDDIES THE WATERS, hooted the New Journal's ensuing front page headline. It was a gift to the DCH campaigners. "The government wants to sound tough, but has no coherent argument as to why the council can't do the repairs themselves" said Alan Walter. "The door is not closed! Ministers are Wobbling!"[36]

Suddenly the council was on the back foot, but there was no wobbling in the housing department. When the minister used the phrase "a further proposal", explained Charlie Hedges, he meant PFI or stock transfer. "The ALMO is the only option which means that council homes continue to be owned by the council". A "Yes" vote would release £283m of government cash for housing repairs; a "No" vote would get Camden precisely nothing. It was a fight that the housing department felt it could not lose: £500,000 was pumped into the project. Events were held to get tenants to inspect the future by visiting gleaming, newly refurbished show flats to illustrate what an ALMO would bring, and pamphlets were issued to all council tenants showing them the happy benefits of voting "Yes"[37]. Frank Dobson announced that he was against ALMOs. The campaign, he said, was "blackmail".

299

---

36 Alan Walter "the Robin Hood of council housing" (as the New Journal described him) died in 2009 aged 51.

37 The ALMO was "the best choice", "We believe it offers you a better future," and "if the vote is 'No' and the ALMO doesn't happen, we won't get the extra public money to do up your kitchens and bathrooms. If the vote is 'Yes' and the ALMO does happen, tenants will get the new kitchens and bathrooms, and everyone will get all the other improvements as well."

Politically, the Labour group were in turmoil. Much of Camden's housing was in a poor state and needed repairs. The chances of all Camden's homes reaching the government's decent homes standard by 2010 in accordance with government policy were, to put it mildly, remote. Camden did not have the money. The choice was either not carrying out the repairs and losing support for being a poor landlord, or else setting up an ALMO, even if it meant alienating some Labour-voting council tenants in the short term, but getting the repairs done.

In December 2003, two supporters of DCH, Albert Beale and Lesley Carty, challenged the council in the High Court. There was no fair and balanced debate, they claimed, because public money was being used to extol the benefits of an ALMO. Also, the ballot was biased and unlawful because the question favoured the ALMO by using the words "improve" and "council owned".[38] The High Court dismissed the challenge which finally served only to delay the announcement of the ballot until January.

The result of the ballot was a disaster. Despite the council's hype, the turnout was only 30%, but of those who did vote, 77% voted to reject the ALMO. Camden would have to go back to the government and plead for the "Fourth Option", direct funding with no strings attached. "I do not hold out much hope", said Charlie Hedges. He was right. Keith Hill made the observation that "the turnout was appallingly low". The decision had been taken by only one tenant in five. Camden should go back and ask the other four out of five. In any event, the result was the fault of "a combination of superannuated communists and not much younger Trotskyists", and that the whole opposition had been got together by the New Journal. The New Journal then organised a 5,000 strong petition (signed by Dobson but pointedly not by Glenda Jackson). The paper's news editor, Dan Carrier, travelled to the September 2004 Brighton Labour Party conference to present the petition to the minister. Keith Hill promised to see if there were "any broader flexibilities in local government funding". He could not find any.

The hand of the new chief executive fell heavily on Jane Held, the director of social services. Jane Held had made, said Moira Gibb, a

---

38 The ballot read: "Camden Council proposes to set up a Council owned Arms Length Management Organisation (ALMO) to manage and improve its housing. Do you agree with this proposal: Yes/No?"

number of poor management decisions, notably in halting releases from hospital in early December and in telling members that the cost of implementing the recommendations of the Victoria Climbié enquiry would be £4.2m, a grossly inflated figure which had not been checked. Just before Christmas 2003, Jane Held "was forced to resign".[39]

However there was fall out in that Jane Held had formed a friendship with Penny Abraham, the executive member for social services, who thought highly of her. Miss Held's departure was very much against the wishes of Penny Abraham who wrote an intemperate email to her colleagues on the executive. The sacking (let us call it that) was "immensely destructive", the staff are "reeling and bewildered" and she felt "revulsion". "You can expect me to be a disengaged executive member from now on. Having the head torn off the department I have worked so hard for has drained me of all goodwill". She went on to say that she would stand down from the executive in May. It was a curious situation: she was not going to take responsibility for what would happen in the department, she was not going to support the executive in their decisions, but she was going sit sulkily at the table safeguarding her additional £13,000 a year allowance until the end of her term in May. Her stance exposed a great flaw in the constitution: she had been elected to the executive by the Labour group and could not be sacked without a motion being placed before the Labour group for a highly public bout of tears and bloodletting. [40]

301

In the middle of the irritation of the ALMO ballot and Penny Abraham's foot stamping, the sun shone. While the High Court was considering the challenge, before the ballot results were announced, Jane Roberts, having led the council for three and a half years, was made a Dame of the British Empire in the 2004 New Year's Honours List. The citation was for services to local government. "I don't know who nominated

39   Jane Held's departure came as something of a surprise all round. When Steve Bundred gave his last briefing to the opposition in January, he pointed out how fragile an authority such as Camden is, and how dependent it is on the competency of a handful of its senior officers. He singled out two for special mention: "If Dennis Skinner or Jane Held left tomorrow, I don't know what we'd do. There is simply no one internally to replace them". Skinner, the son of the MP of the same name, left shortly after Bundred to join him at the IDeA.

40   It was a difficult time. With Penny Abraham in mind, Jane Roberts said as she stood down from the leadership in 2005: "In order for the leader/cabinet model to work as effectively as possible, the leader should be able to decide who is in the executive".

me", she said, "but I have admirers in the mysterious basements of Whitehall".[41] The honour, she graciously added, "recognises the important work of many councillors and officers over the years, particularly of my predecessor as leader, Richard Arthur".

As if to celebrate the honour and the status it conveyed, Dame Jane visited Bangladesh in May 2004. She was accompanied by the Mayor, Nasim Ali, Councillor Fazlul Chowdhury, the young "community leader" Abdul Hai, and the deputy lieutenant of Camden, Charles Winstanley (hailed by the Bengali press agency as "the Queen's Representative"). As there are 25,000 Bangladeshis living in Camden, and as Camden is a major donor to Bangladeshi projects in the borough, they were received by the prime minister of Bangladesh, and visited Sylhet in the north east of the country from where Camden's Bengali population originate. The delegation drew widespread press coverage in Bangladesh through the *Bangladesh Observer* and the *Dhaka Daily Star* (a paper "Committed to the People's Right to Know") but not in the Camden papers. There was no council press release because Dame Jane had decided (wholly unconvincingly) that she was visiting in a personal capacity, together with a few others including the mayor and the deputy lieutenant who were all also on personal visits, simultaneously. It seemed that at last she had begun to gather that her activities were counterproductive. She needed to tell the Bengalis how supportive she was of them, but now hesitated to tell the wider electorate of that support.[42]

302

The 2002 elections (that had left Labour with 34% of the vote, but 65% of the seats) brought about a change of attitude in the opposition. The two opposition parties got between them 57% of the vote, but only 35% of the seats. There was no complaint about the system, but there was a growing dislike of the exclusive nature of the administration. The old committee system had provided an outlet for the opposition. Now opposition members were wholly sidelined. To a guest to the

---

41   Outside those mysterious basements, no other explanation for the honour has since been given.

42   The Bangladeshi government press agency (BSS) issued a bulletin on the group's visit to the prime minister, Begum Khaleda Zia. Councillor Ali lauded her role "in consolidating democracy and development" in Bangladesh. "The country", he was reported as saying, "has achieved progress in different sectors in last few years" (sic). In response, Khaleda Zia urged "non resident Bangladeshis to protect the country's history, culture and achievements abroad as right information about the country can enhance its image abroad" (sic).

council, they were invisible. [43] When used by Jane Roberts, the word "inclusive" referred only to Bengalis who could be induced to vote Labour through the party's hold on the purse strings. In every other respect the council was hostilely exclusive. Camden was Labour and nothing else. When, in May 2004, the opposition parties argued that an opposition member should be made mayor, the Labour Party was aggressively dismissive. Only a Labour councillor could represent a Labour council. Now that the committee system had been abolished, the sense of exclusion was heightened.[44]

The council's new constitution incorporated an executive and a scrutiny commission. Participation in decisions affecting the council was restricted to those two bodies, and to the licensing and development control subcommittees. The majority of councillors, excluded from real decisions, were nevertheless offered places on scrutiny panels. There were sixteen new councillors, none of whom had experienced the old committee system and all of whom were anxious to sit on a scrutiny panel as the next best thing. There were now plenty of fresh young volunteers whenever a new panel was formed, however useless its purpose. They had joined to get involved and the panels, however weak, were the only game in town. It was just bad luck that the town was no longer offering chess, just noughts and crosses.

303

The chairman of the Overview and Scrutiny Commission (OSC), Janet Guthrie, invited ideas for new scrutiny panels, cleared them with the Labour group and the executive, and had them discussed and approved by the OSC. The one criterion was that the council was not to be criticised, and the one way in which that could be avoided was to set up panels that did not look at areas for which the council is responsible. Safe topics became hard to come by. By 2004, the OSC was scraping the barrel of its collective imagination. Suggestions dried up from the opposition. Panels were set up on road safety, employment opportunities for refugees, suicide prevention, HIV funding and post office closures. A panel was even formed to look into private rented accommodation,

---

43   Not that I ever lost any sleep over it, but it is a curious fact that for the six years that I was leader of the opposition, I was never once invited into the mayor's parlour. Guests were jealously guarded. It was all a far cry from the 1960s and the appointment of opposition aldermen, or a mayor from the minority party, or (for instance) the mixed party line up on the queen's visit to open Swiss Cottage library. .

44   In the final four years, the Labour Party made a couple of unhappy choices for mayor, and in 2005 had great difficulty in finding anyone to volunteer to fill the post. Like the spoilt child who licks all the buns to prevent anyone else having any, they chose Barbara Hughes for the third time.

but not into the council's own housing department. By the time a panel was set up on alcohol abuse the Conservatives had lost all interest and did not nominate anyone to sit on it.[45] The system proved massively more expensive than the old committees and produced nothing of value. The reports generated by the scrutiny panels are all now forgotten. Some may be found on the Camden website, while others lie quietly discolouring in the council's archives.

The one exception to the no-criticism-of-the-council rule was the scrutiny panel set up on parking enforcement. The Conservatives had been demanding a panel since 2003 but, as it would provide much scope for criticism of the council, the panel was postponed on the spurious ground that the parking contracts were coming up for tender. In October 2004, the Tories set up their own enquiry along lines that parodied the council's own panels. They took evidence from witnesses and drew publicity, especially when they called a former parking attendant who gave details of the inducements offered to issue more tickets, often in questionable circumstances.

When the Scrutiny Commission did finally set up its own scrutiny panel on the subject, it was arranged so that its recommendations would not be released until after the new five year parking contracts had been signed in 2005. It needed careful handling, needed to be supportive of the current parking regime, and was chaired by Maggie Cosin. The facts were simple enough. Parking controls are necessary and those living in controlled parking zones were overwhelmingly content that there were parking controls, but this was an area where public resentment was great.

There was a political angle as it was argued that Camden has increased its revenue from parking enforcement by stealth. Parking gave the council an annual surplus of £18m over the years without it ever having been part of a political campaign. In 2005 the council took in almost £50m from parking enforcement, more than half its total income from council tax. The suggestion that the council was targeting car owners in the borough to raise revenue followed. The parking contracts included targets for the numbers of cars to be ticketed, clamped and

---

45 This last panel was so dire that it is not even listed with the others on Camden's website. It marked the end of the road for its chairman, Charlie Hedges. He had once been a big mover within the Labour group: deputy leader, leadership contender, and chairman of the housing committee, but had lost favour after the ALMO mess. Returned to the backbenches, he fell foul of Labour's "at–least–one–woman–per–ward" rule and was deselected in Kilburn. Sportingly, he agreed instead to stand in the 2006 elections in West Hampstead where he had no chance of success. Such are the rewards of loyalty in politics.

towed away. To hit the targets the contractors were forced to clamp and tow away cars for low priority offences. Parking attendants issued tickets that should not have been issued. In 2003/4 Camden issued 446,212 penalty charge notices, the second highest number issued by any London borough[46]. Of those, some 17% were later cancelled when challenged. This represented almost 80,000 occasions in a year when drivers had felt obliged to write in to get the council to overturn a parking attendant's decision (and does not include the correspondence concerning tickets which the council upheld). The way things were done was unpopular, and perhaps of greater importance than the stark facts of the parking surplus. No one liked the enforcers, and it was impossible not to notice that the attendants themselves were for the most part African immigrants (as opposed to British Blacks). They were not allowed to exercise discretion for fear that they would be susceptible to inducements to cancel tickets. All appeals had to go to the town hall.[47] The council was encouraging racism, said Alex Henney, by employing such people and putting them in the invidious position that the parking contract demanded.[48]

It was an issue that would not go away. Just as Camden laboured under the burden of Defend Council Housing when it moved towards an ALMO, it also laboured under the presence of the London Motorist Action Group (LMAG) founded by Alex Henney (with the actor Tom Conti[49] as its front man). With his campaigner's gift for writing, and an unflagging persistence in his vociferous attacks on the council's parking policies, Henney was key to the campaign. He had once been a great thorn in the side of the council in the 1970s, and had worked hard to expose its inefficiency and waste. He now worked hard to campaign against the council's parking revenue, which he referred to as "tax farming". LMAG were of great annoyance to the environment

305

---

46   Only Westminster issued more, but Camden's figure was over 150,000 more than had been issued by the third borough, Kensington & Chelsea who led the pack of the other Inner London authorities.

47   Barry (Dame Edna) Humphries, an occasional West Hampstead resident, referred to them in his diary in the *Spectator* as "vindictive black bastards" on the grounds that both the adjectives and the noun were accurate.

48   The best line on this came from the parking manager who, on appearing before the scrutiny panel, was asked about the necessity of employing African parking attendants. He replied hotly that Camden was committed to employing staff who represented the community it served.

49   The Hollywood heart throb now best known to a new generation as the voice of Andy Pandy.

department, and were roughly handled by John Thane, the executive member. They were, he said, "a bunch of Jagworths".[50]

The "independent" (or, rather Tory opposition) enquiry's conclusions were released in May 2005, recommending an end of clamping, that parking attendants be allowed to use their discretion before issuing tickets, and that there be reviews of the ticketing targets and the practice of towing away. The final report was written by Alex Henney.[51] Its recommendations were no less valid than those arrived at by the council's scrutiny panel some months later. Neither the panel nor the independent enquiry affected anything, both had been set up for electoral advantage by the party that formed them, both acknowledged there was widespread dissatisfaction with the system, and both made recommendations for reviews. The only material difference was that one cost a lot of money and officer time, and the other cost nothing.

As if the hopelessly wasteful (at £600,000 a year) scrutiny system was not enough, in September 2004 Camden launched a new way of keeping its councillors out of the decision making process. Dame Jane unveiled a new £60,000 project, CamdenTalks, which involved a consultative panel of 2,000 people "scientifically recruited" by MORI with reference to their age, ethnicity and sex (in contrast to the councillors who had not been scientifically recruited). The panel would be asked questions by council officers and the answers would be collated and presented as an opinion poll. The results were to be published by the council in occasional magazines that would be sent to the panel, but not to councillors (and emphatically not to opposition councillors). Dame Jane addressed the press at the invitation only launch in the town hall. Alongside her sat the celebrity fashion expert and BBC London radio presenter Robert Elms who lives in Primrose Hill. "It is important the people who run this borough know what we think", he said. The press office announced that "we are really pleased and have worked hard to ensure residents have been recruited in such a way that CamdenTalks will reflect the demographic makeup of the borough".

---

50 From the *Daily Telegraph's* Way of the World Column: J Bonington Jagworth, leader of the Motorist's Liberation Front and defender of "the inalienable right of the motorist to drive as fast as he pleases, how he pleases, and over what or whom he pleases".

51 John Thane attributed authorship to the leader of the opposition. In his formal response as the executive member responsible, he described the report as "the work of an unintelligent councillor".

306

"People will say it is a lot of money but it is felt that it will provide value for money in terms of the improvements we can make", Moira Gibb gamely explained to the *New Journal*. "We want to know what people think".

The effect of the scrutiny system was that opposition within the council became sporadic. It was no longer possible for the opposition parties to have their spokesmen or shadow executive members attend each meeting of the executive, as it would result in pretty well every opposition councillor attending each meeting of the executive. The Conservatives instead attended by rota, and the LibDems when they found an agenda point of interest. Labour back benchers could attend, but were not encouraged to do so, and so were left out of the process. The level of direct engagement by back benchers of all parties was reduced to the supposedly non political licensing and development control subcommittees, to the full council meetings and to the wholly unrewarding scrutiny commission and panels. Opposition in any meaningful sense was driven out of the council chamber. All that was left was the press and occasional bursts of leafleting.

By the time of the 2005 general election, things had got politically more interesting than they had been in 2001. The invasion and occupation of Iraq had lost the government some support, although Tony Blair was safely ahead in the polls. Locally, both Glenda Jackson and Frank Dobson had come out (albeit belatedly) against the war and were less likely to suffer in any backlash. The Labour launch in Hampstead Town Hall set the tone for the campaign. Baroness Kennedy, the master of ceremonies, praised Glenda Jackson and Frank Dobson for having "been courageous and independent minded and both of them have shown their strong opposition to the war. We have to go out and show support for the MPs who have stuck to the principles and values of the Labour Party". Glenda Jackson responded by distancing herself from the government and its "many failures". She said of her constituents: "If they don't want to vote for Tony Blair, then don't. Go out and vote for the people who need the support of the Labour Party. However much we feel about the people of Iraq, we will not help them by punishing people in Kilburn, Swiss Cottage and Holborn with another Tory government. We won't rebuild the hospitals in Baghdad by letting Michael Howard close hospitals here". Dobson described the Conservative policy on immigration and asylum as "a disgrace". The Tory party on this issue was "indistinguishable from the BNP".

307

Hampstead & Highgate was still not a Conservative target and Central Office again issued instructions to party activists to campaign in marginal constituencies (Hammersmith & Fulham where they were successful and Finchley & Golders Green where by a mere 741 votes Andrew Mennear came second). The Conservative association narrowly chose Piers Wauchope as their candidate over the financial journalist and Hampstead councillor Brian Cattell (a gifted speaker who fought the election in the unpromising waste of Leeds Central).[52] In Holborn & St Pancras the Tories selected the highly personable "wealthy blonde lesbian" Margot James who had made a fortune by founding and then selling Shire Health, a pharmaceutical PR company. She had also made something of a name for herself by letting the press know that she was a lesbian so that they could react by asking her about her position in the Conservative Party, the champion of family values. Knowing that they would not have interviewed her in the first place had she not been gay, she would then gravely respond by telling them that her sexuality was not important, but the task that faced this modern inclusive Conservative Party was to defeat this disastrous government.

The LibDems were forced to seek late replacements for their two candidates. Jonathan Simpson, who had done so well in Hampstead in 2001, had since been elected as a Camden councillor. He had also remained as their parliamentary candidate, but in December 2001 he unexpectedly stood down saying that he was busy at work. His replacement was Ed Fordham, an advisor to the LibDem leader of the London borough of Sutton and one of the new breed of professional politicians attached to LibDem run councils in jobs that need not take up too much of their time. The LibDem candidate for Holborn & St Pancras, Eleanor Key, also stood down (to move to Cheshire where she stood for the LibDems in Congleton) and was replaced by Jill Fraser, the fish and chip shop worker who had won the Haverstock ward by election in 2003.

Things livened up briefly just before the election when Jonathan Simpson, who had stood for the LibDems in 2001, announced that he had joined the Labour Party. He had been unhappy with the local LibDem party for some time, he said, especially with their stance on

---

52 It was very close: the deciding factor was that the successful candidate had as his election manager the determined Rosette Irwin, one of the association stalwarts since Finsberg's days.

crime and the economy. The timing was such that it was reported in the last issue of the local papers before the election. Simpson posed for the cameras with Glenda Jackson, Ken Livingstone and Patricia Hewitt. "The election is a straight two horse race between Labour and the Tories", he told the press. "A vote for the LibDems might let the Tories in". The LibDems, he said, were "floundering".

"It is not grown up behaviour", said Flick Rea. "It is so tiring and an irritant. It is a silly distraction which goes against the trend. I don't think he has thought it through". Still nursing less than fond memories of John Dickie, she added: "Defectors are never popular". The *New Journal* rather took her side, revealing that Simpson had eleven years before (aged twenty) left the Labour Party to join the LibDems. Their headline read: "Serial defector quits to return to Labour".

In any event, the effect was not felt. There was no sense of change in the air, and the local papers were supportive of the sitting MPs. The *New Journal* was as much for Frank Dobson as the *Ham & High* was for Glenda Jackson. In March, just before the election campaign proper kicked off, the *Ham & High* devoted a full page to Glenda Jackson written by her breathless admirer, Gerald Levy, their film critic. "In *Sunday Bloody Sunday,* playing Alex opposite Anthony Head and Peter Finch, she was very honest, very straightforward, full of goodwill and kind services, but often disappointed and often exasperated. Now 34 years later she is exactly the same..."

Nationally the 2005 election was much of a rerun of 2001. There was no real doubt as to the outcome, both nationally and in the two Camden seats. Turnout was slightly better: up to a poor 61.36% from an even worse 59%. Both the Labour and Conservative parties were hit by a certain weariness: and the Conservatives were again hit by Central Office forbidding anyone to assist in Camden. The turnout in both Camden seats was well below the national average, but in each case the Labour vote fell and the majorities reduced to levels that made Hampstead appear marginal for the first time since 1992, and Holborn for the first time in decades. Glenda Jackson's majority over the Tories (who now only narrowly led the LibDems) was under 4,000 and Frank Dobson's majority over the LibDems was under 5,000. Both the Tory and the LibDem votes went up, but in Camden as a whole on a low turnout, the chief feature of the results was that of former Labour voters turning to the LibDems. For the first time the overall LibDem vote in the two constituencies was greater than that of the Conservatives. After the count Ed Fordham finished his speech by

309

bellowing: "The Tories are finished in Camden!"[53]

The LibDem efforts (and they were great) had paid off, but what affected Camden even more were the results in the neighbouring constituencies of Islington South, Brent East and Hornsey & Wood Green. The LibDems had worked hard in each of these constituencies and had enjoyed great success. In Brent East, following an extraordinary by election in 2003 in which they overturned a 13,000 Labour majority, they held on by almost three thousand votes. In Hornsey & Wood Green they performed what had appeared impossible and turned a Labour majority of over ten thousand into a LibDem majority of two thousand. In Islington South their candidate failed to overturn the seven thousand Labour majority, but reduced it to 484, and in Islington North the untouchable Jeremy Corbyn had his majority halved. Camden now found itself squeezed between Brent East on the one side and Hornsey & Wood Green and the Islington seats on the other. For the first time ever, Camden was to be a national target for the LibDems. As if to signal the new effort, Flick Rea was replaced as the leader of the LibDem group on the council by Keith Moffitt, a translator. She had held the position for nineteen years.[54]

Before the general election, the council had been mildly embarrassed by comment on its school meals, which had been found to be somewhat less than wholesome. The New Journal had published details of correspondence between Camden and Scolarest (the caterers) which showed disquiet in the town hall at the poor standards of school food and hygiene in its preparation. The executive member for education was now Nick Smith who had once been Richard Arthur's chief supporter. He had spent five years in the wilderness following Arthur's fall and had only in 2005 been allowed back into the front row as the executive member for education. Having made his way back, he became pretty well part time, since he had taken up the position of

---

53 The campaign in Hampstead was somewhat overshadowed by Andrew Mennear's in Finchley. He made headlines by demanding that Stonewall, the gay campaigning group, should pay the £70,000 spent each year by the Corporation of London in cleansing Hampstead Heath of the detritus left following the nocturnal activities of gay men. He then went one better by accusing the Labour Party of anti-Semitism for portraying Michael Howard and Oliver Letwin (the leader of the opposition and the shadow chancellor) as flying pigs. "The only well known connection between Jews and pigs", responded Hampstead's greatest journalist, David Aaronovitch in The Guardian, "is that they have nothing to do with one another".

54 A dedicated streets and pavements man: Keith Moffitt first stood in West Hampstead in 1990 and came fifth with 243 votes. He was elected in 1994 with 839 votes.

secretary general of the European Parliamentary Labour Party. He gave firm assurances of increased funding for school meals and that things would improve as the catering contract was up for renewal.

Immediately after the election, school dinners were back on the political agenda, this time to illustrate the difficulty in maintaining the alliance between the Labour Party and the Bengalis. Halal meat had been served at fifty of the borough's schools until July 2004. Following a complaint from a mother that halal meat preparation was cruel (as it involved slitting the throat of an animal which had not been stunned), the council had agonised over what to do. Such was the sensitivity, a decision was taken to act, but to say nothing. Scolarest, the food contractors, were instructed to take halal meat off the menu except in two primary schools with overwhelmingly Muslim pupils. The squeamish mother was told that her child would no longer be served halal meat, and Muslims happily ate their school dinners ignorant of the status of the beef on their plates. This peaceful compromise did not last. Joynal Uddin of the Camden Bengali Parents and Teachers Association (CBPTA), chairman of the West Euston Partnership (WEP), and joint chairman of the Standing Committee for Muslim Communities in Camden (SCMCC), led a delegation to the executive in May 2005. "One person ringing up and complaining about halal meat seems to be more important than 25,000 Muslims living in Camden", he said.

It soon became clear that no one had been aware that there had been a decision to serve halal food until 2004, and no one knew that a decision had been taken in July 2004 not to serve halal meat. Masood Khawaja, president of the Halal Food Authority (HFA) said: "Parents should have been told what their children were eating, both Muslims when halal food was removed and white parents when it was introduced". Ihtisham Hibatullah of the Muslim Association of Britain was "alarmed that Camden council have taken such actions to exclude the rights of a minority community after it has been proven that it is possible to provide halal food to all their schools. There are a substantial number of Muslims in Camden and they should have been involved in the decision".

"We will be improving halal provision", announced Theo Blackwell, playing for time in one of the many absences of Nick Smith, "and will be proactively consulting schools and local communities over the next few months to find out how school meals can better serve the faith needs of our diverse communities". The delay allowed the council to come up with a plan which was for Nick Smith to wash his hands of the whole business. "We aim" he said, "to provide a halal meal to every child who wants one, *in agreement with their school*". The council, and the Labour Party, need not face any further risk of involvement. All decisions concerning halal were to be delegated to school governors. "Every child who wants one" would mean every child who wants one in a school with sympathetic governors .

The question of halal was left to smoulder as on the morning of 7 July 2005, London was hit by four suicide bombers, all of them young British Muslims. Two of the bombs exploded in Camden, one in the tube tunnel outside Kings Cross (26 dead), and the other on top of a bus on Tavistock Square (13 dead). The Stop the War Coalition held a rally at the Friends Meeting House at Euston on the following Saturday which was addressed by Jeremy Corbyn, George Galloway and their friends. They all condemned the bombings, but sought to explain the reasons why the bombers had acted. Azzam Tamini of the Muslim Association of Britain told the thousand strong audience that "the social causes of the atrocity was to be found in the maltreatment of Arabs in the Middle East".

A week later, a crowd gathered in Tavistock Square in a council organised memorial meeting. Dame Jane arranged it so that only she would speak. She appeared in a floral dress and was accompanied by the deputy mayor, Abdul Quadir, and a group of Bengalis who stood beside her grinning with embarrassment at the front of the civic delegation. The purpose of the event was not so much to mourn the dead, as to make the point that Camden's Muslims were not supportive of the terrorists. There must be no backlash against the Bengalis.[55] In Camden there was no known Islamic militancy among the Bengali population and they were quick to distance themselves from the bombings. Camden's own Joynal Uddin (of CBPTA, WEP and SCMCC) told the *New Journal* that "These people are terrorists, not Islamic terrorists. Islam has nothing to do with terrorism. Young Muslims are being told that Islam is behind terrorism. It is wrong. It puts the idea in their heads".

* * *

55   The mayor was not present, and no member of the opposition was invited to take part. Jane Roberts instead invited one part of the local strategic partnership, the borough commander, who attempted to add formality to the occasion by performing a military salute. He was accompanied by the Lambeth borough commander, Brian Paddick, who later stood as the London mayoral candidate for the LibDems.

312

Neither halal meat nor suicide bombers had anything to do with the feud that smouldered away within the Labour group throughout 2005. Dame Jane wanted to ensure the King's Cross development's early success. The whole project was, it seemed, being thrown into jeopardy by the long serving chairman of the development control (planning) committee, the popular, softly spoken Brian Woodrow. Argent St George, who were redeveloping the Kings Cross site to accommodate the planned Cross Channel Rail Link, submitted a planning application in 2004. At 27 hectares, it was the largest brown field development project in Europe. It dominated the workload of Peter Bishop, the director of the environment department, and promised to transform Kings Cross by the provision of swish office blocks, smart shops, new housing and the most impressive rail links anywhere in the country.

In September 2004, an article appeared in the *Architects Journal* under the heading "King's Cross future under threat". The threat referred to was Brian Woodrow. He was, read the report, hostile to the planning application and was threatening to cause trouble that would delay or even prevent work on the site. He was quoted as saying "we would probably turn down" the outline planning application, and that if the developers "choose to stick to a scheme this size, then we will have to [refuse the application and] leave it to the secretary of state to decide". He did not respond to the article, but a few weeks later, Dame Jane stepped in on behalf of Camden. Her letter to the *Architects Journal* gave the impression of having been written in anger. She twice referred to him not as Councillor or Mister Woodrow, but simply as "Woodrow", as in: "I have been assured by Woodrow that he has not reached a view on the applications".

That was not the end of it. There was much at stake and Argent needed reassurance that the committee's bias against the application would not doom it to failure before it was submitted in detail. Without referring to Woodrow, outside legal advice was sought. Camden took the view that "there was a significant risk either that he would not, or will not be seen to, act in an impartial and objective manner in dealing with these applications". If the developers had to resort to legal action to remove Woodrow "the Project would be held up for months". Brian Woodrow was formally advised by the borough solicitor, Alison Lowton, not to take any future part in the Kings Cross applications. To do so would risk bringing the council into disrepute. (She also wrote to the *Architect's Journal* referring to him simply as "Woodrow" four times.) Woodrow took his own legal advice and ("firmly") rejected that of the borough solicitor. She reported him to the Standards Board.

The developers put pressure on the council, and the council officers put pressure on the politicians. Something had to be done. Neither Camden nor the developers could risk having the development rejected and stalled by appeals. Dame Jane wanted Woodrow out, which could only be done by the Labour group as a whole. The Woodrow battle was one that Camden could not afford to lose. Even if he had done nothing wrong, it was stressed, Camden must be seen to be impartial. For the good of the council, especially with an election in sight, he should go. Woodrow resisted, and his resistance became something of a rallying point for those who were dissatisfied with the new order. The Standards Board were prevailed upon to issue an interim report, without hearing from Woodrow, and found against him ("in breach of the rules of natural justice", he said.) The interim report was leaked at the Labour Party conference at the end of September 2005. An extraordinary meeting of the Labour group was hurriedly called to replace Woodrow as chairman of the development control subcommittee. The interim report was circulated by Dame Jane before the meeting. It was a difficult time for Dermot Greene, the chief whip, but he pulled it off. The Labour group voted Woodrow out of the chair by 20 votes to 13 and replaced him with Heather Johnson.[56]

314

The October Labour group meeting saw several significant but bloodless changes in the run up to the local elections. John Mills, who had for so long and so ably overseen the council's finances, stood down, as did Nick Smith from the education portfolio. Neither was going to stand in the coming elections. Before the meeting, Dame Jane also announced she was not going to stand again. She had been there and done that, and since the invasion of Iraq the old Labour voters were not to be trusted. As the Woodrow affair showed, she faced internal opposition approaching the level that had dogged Richard Arthur before her. In September an internal London Labour Party report, *Electoral Strategy and Analysis*, set out what everyone in the party feared. Labour was under attack on three fronts

---

56   After his fate had been settled, the Standards Board found that his comments to the *Architects Journal* showed that Woodrow held a "predisposition" from which he could have been persuaded to an alternative view, which the board distinguished from holding a "predetermined view". No sanction was imposed. Feeling perhaps guilty that they had issued an interim report that gave his enemies the necessary ammunition to fire him, the Standards Board published in their glossy annual report a summary both of the case and their final findings (without mentioning the damaging interim report) as an example of the good work they do.

in Camden and faced "a meltdown". There was a real danger that she would lose her seat in Haverstock ward. It was a difficult decision and she took her time in making it. The wind was not blowing in her favour. It would take the loss of only three wards to end Labour's majority. The Conservatives, Greens and LibDems all had realistic expectations of taking seats. Nowhere seemed safe and her own seat, which she now shared with a LibDem, looked decidedly shaky. The embarrassment of failure at the polls would be overwhelming: to have been created a dame for services to local government and then at the next poll to be booted out by those who had actually experienced her services to local government was a risk she was not going to take. She took the decision to take her talents elsewhere although, at that stage, she knew not where.

The battle for succession, such as it was, was confined to inside the executive. The frontrunners were Theo Blackwell and Raj Chada. Both were relatively inexperienced having only been on the council for three and a half years, but Chada was Dame Jane's candidate. As the executive member for housing he had been less accident prone than had his predecessor, Charlie Hedges, in part because the accidents had already happened, and he got on well with the press. He was seen by backbenchers as a softer, more approachable character than Dame Jane, less hectoring, less superior. Blackwell on the other hand had been at the forefront of policy making in the Labour group. He was the successor anticipated and feared by the opposition. He had been a good deputy leader and an able press officer, and active in attacking the council's critics. But there were those on his own side who had been rubbed up the wrong way by his early ambition in his first two years on the council. There were those determined to vote for "anyone-but-Theo". The group wanted to choose not necessarily the most able candidate, but the least threatening both to them and to the opposition. Blackwell took soundings and stood back. No one wanted to give the opposition any ammunition just seven months before the elections. Chada was elected unopposed.

"I want", said Raj Chada on becoming leader, "to build on the success of Jane Roberts".[57]

315

---

57 Dame Jane has since worked with IDeA, the Local Government Association Health Commission, the Local Government Leadership Centre, on the non executive board of Ofsted, and as the director of quality and performance at the Islington Primary Care Trust. In 2007 she was appointed to chair the Councillors Commission, a body set up by the Department for Communities & Local Government "to look at how local democracy can be revitalised and made both more representative and more responsive to local people". After nine month's deliberation, the commission recommended lowering the voting age to 16.

Raj Chada: the bitter end

The three biggest and most difficult local issues that the Labour Party faced in the run up to the 2006 borough elections were parking, policing, and housing repairs. Only in the first of these did Camden have real responsibility, very little in the second, and the council's hands were tied in the last because, in the absence of an ALMO, the government was withholding the necessary funding. But none of these problems was anything against the background of plummeting Labour support nationally and the fact that, for the first time, Camden had been targeted by the LibDems. The Labour Party in Camden was left a hostage to fortune. Whereas once upon a time Labour was given the benefit of the doubt, every new complaint against the council was treated as yet more evidence of an arrogant party who had won three national elections and no longer cared. Lack of public enthusiasm for the party was matched by tiredness among Labour activists. There was a great difficulty in getting supporters and outside volunteers to help fight a campaign in which Labour was facing its biggest challenge since 1982. In eight of the twelve wards they held, Labour was facing a serious threat from the Conservatives or LibDems. "We were", admitted Dermot Greene, their chief whip, "dead on our knees".

Labour candidates for the May 2006 elections had for the most part been selected before Raj Chada's appointment. Overwhelmingly, Labour councillors stayed on to fight again. Of the big names, only Dame Jane and John Mills had announced that they were not seeking re-election[1]. Maggie

---

1   And the deselected Charlie Hedges agreed to fight a hopelessly unwinnable ward held by the LibDems.

Cosin and Roy Shaw[2], both of whom had said that they were going to stand down, were persuaded to stand again because their popularity could be a deciding factor in the election of their running mates. The twelve wards held by Labour were to be contested by 27 sitting councillors and only nine newcomers.

The Labour Party's first resolve was to get the team photo right: more women and members of visible ethnic minorities were needed on the council. There was to be at least one woman candidate standing in every three candidate ward (which was achieved in every ward except Haverstock and those wards which Labour was not going to contest in any meaningful sense). Although Labour set out with the best intentions to ensure ethnic diversity, it proved a difficult task. In 2004, Sue Vincent, then one of Camden's two deputy leaders, encouraged by Labour's success in securing the Bengali Muslim vote, let the press know that she was setting out to secure the Somali Muslim vote. "We want to see Somalis standing for election in the 2006 borough elections", she told the *New Journal*, who in turn calculated that "70% of Somalis are likely to vote Labour" and that the "large communities which have developed in Kentish Town, Gospel Oak and Kilburn could help swing ballots in closely contested council wards". It did not happen, and well over 70% of Somalis stayed at home. Instead the only ethnic minority candidates in Labour held wards were the five sitting councillors[3] and three new Bengali candidates; Nurul Islam, Abdul Hai and Syed Hoque.

In each case the selection of the three new Bengali candidates caused a stir. When the St Pancras & Somers Town ward committee met at the St Pancras Community Centre, the final shortlist of four included two of the sitting councillors, Roger Robinson and Anna Stewart (Sybil Shine having stood down). They were joined by one other councillor, Abdul Quadir, who was fleeing Highgate ward where his majority in 2002 had been 36 votes, and one new candidate, Nurul Islam who had stood as a paper candidate in Hampstead Town in the last election. Quadir had made a point of encouraging his friends in the ward to join the Labour Party, and on the night of the selection, Roger Robinson and Anna Stewart walked in to find the community

---

2   After a series of celebrations to celebrate his fifty years on St Pancras and Camden councils, Roy Shaw's health deteriorated and he stood down from the council in 2007 and died later that year.

3   The three Bengalis: Nasim Ali, Fazlul Chowdhury and Abdul Quadir, and Raj Chada and Geethika Jayathilaka, both of Indian parentage, who celebrated Chada's new status by marrying each other in December 2005.

centre packed with Labour Party card holding Bengalis. When it came to the vote, Islam and Quadir won easily. Equal bottom (eight votes each) were Anna Stewart and Roger Robinson. As, under Labour Party rules, each three member ward must have at least one woman candidate, Roger Robinson was deselected.

Utterly disillusioned, Robinson and his wife left for a fortnight in Spain. In his absence, things livened up. Not only was Roger Robinson famously the hardest working Labour councillor, he was, with Roy Shaw, one of the two sitting Camden councillors who had been elected to the first council in 1964. In his absence, the formidable Maggie Cosin began her own investigation. Labour Party rules restrict voting to members of more than six months standing. She insisted that the Greater London Regional Office carry out checks, which revealed that some of the voters were ineligible under the six month rule. Somewhat embarrassingly, the selection had to be set aside, and when the new meeting took place, Islam, Stewart and Robinson was selected and Quadir was not.

In King's Cross the party selected Abdul Hai, described variously as "a community leader" or "a youth worker". Like Nasim Ali before him, he worked with Bengali youths through organisations dependent on (if not wholly funded by) Camden council. His mission in life, he said, was to stop Bengali gangs fighting one another. He had joined Dame Jane's entourage on her state visit to Bangladesh in 2004. What was not known at his selection meeting was that he had gained a certain local notoriety as one of two young men charged with the murder of Richie Everitt. The *New Journal* revealed details of Hai's past after his selection, and invited him to write for them a piece which they (somewhat puzzlingly) described as "courageous and moving". He bitterly regretted the fact that he had been arrested and held in custody, but expressed no regrets that his friends had attacked and stabbed Richie Everitt to death. He was silent on the question of the identity of the murderers. He felt only self pity. "I will always have

319

those experiences of ten years ago. I often remember them". [4]

The third new Bengali was an elderly Bengali billed in party literature as "local granddad Syed Hoque". His selection in Haverstock ward came after Dame Jane had announced that she was standing down. A third candidate was required to stand in her place alongside Roy Shaw and Mike Katz and the local party was able to justify an all male line up because the ward would be lost without the Bengali vote. Roy Shaw was not the only one to be unimpressed with the choice: "People ask me why we couldn't get an educated or a younger Bangladeshi candidate and I tell them that it is because of all the

---

4   On 14 August 1994, ten Bengali youths rampaged through Somers Town hoping to "stab a white" to avenge the theft of some jewellery by a youth called Liam Coyle. Richie Everitt a "mild-mannered, harmless, chubby and unathletic" fifteen year old schoolboy, had nothing to do with the theft, nor had the other white teenagers attacked before the fatal stabbing. Others managed to run to safety, one with a stab wound in the back. Holding a bag in which he had a pot noodle, Richie Everitt was surrounded on Pancras Road and was killed by a single stab wound. In the ensuing police investigation, the Bengali community closed ranks. The police met "almost total silence". By the time the police had got the names of the gang members, the prime suspects had fled the country. Of those who had not fled, six were arrested for the attack ("The Drummond Street Six") of whom three were brought to trial. Abdul Hai and Badrul Miah were charged with murder. They were part of the joint enterprise that resulted in Everitt's death. The third youth, Shawkat Akhbar, was charged with violent disorder. In the fourteen months that passed between the killing and the trial, the murder was national headline news. Princess Diana paid an impromptu visit to the floral shrine at the spot that Richie Everitt died. The headline in the Sun, not inaccurately, read: 'Knifed to death for being white'. Everitt had been attacked because of his race, not because of something he had done or was suspected to have done or was expected to do. The court heard evidence from two teenaged girls who said they had been approached by Hai and Miah, out of breath. Miah was eating a pot noodle. Miah said "We just stabbed some white boy, innit Abdul?" Abdul Hai replied "Yeah". Miah then gave the girls further details of the attack. The police found splashes of Everitt's blood on Miah's trainers. Miah denied being one of the attackers. His explanation for the blood was that, while fatally wounded, Richie Everitt had run past him. Both Hai and Miah denied having the conversation with the two girls. Hai gave an alibi that was rejected by the police. Hai's counsel, Helena Kennedy, argued that the evidence against him was insufficient. Mrs Justice Steel agreed and directed the jury to return a not guilty verdict. Unusually, an account of the jury's deliberations was made public and recited before the European Commission for Human Rights. The Commission was told that, but for the judge's ruling, the jury would have found Hai guilty of murder. The jury were unhappy at being directed to acquit and asked for clarification. The judge stressed that she was making "no judgment on the truthfulness or reliability of the witnesses, but simply on the sufficiency of the evidence". Consequently, the jury never had to test the truthfulness or reliability of the evidence against Hai, and they never had to test his alibi. However, the truthfulness and reliability of those two witnesses were tested by the jury when they came to consider the case against Miah. The evidence was believed and Miah was convicted of murder and sentenced to life imprisonment. The third defendant, Akhbar, was convicted of violent disorder and got three years. Both men appealed unsuccessfully against their convictions. "We will", said a police spokesman "continue to hunt for the Everitt murder gang".

Bangladeshis in Haverstock, he is the only one who is a member of the Labour Party". [5]

The Conservative Party was in a strong position to make great inroads into the Labour majority. They were in second place in seven of the twelve wards held by Labour. In the run up to the 2002 elections a joint committee of both constituency associations, chaired by Pam Chesters, had chosen the candidates for the borough elections, but things had changed. John Walter, the chairman of the Holborn & St Pancras Association unilaterally announced that there would no longer be a joint selection and that his association would instead appoint a panel on which the leader of the opposition would sit. The Hampstead & Highgate association was left to select its own candidates.

Janice Lavery, the chairwoman of the Hampstead & Highgate association, had decided that she was to be a councillor. She lived in what was then the Conservative's most urgent target, Highgate, where the Labour majority was 36 votes, and from where the deputy mayor, Abdul Quadir, electorally the weakest of the Labour councillors, had fled to seek selection elsewhere. She had stood in Highgate in 2002, but had no intention of standing there again. Stephen Hocking was standing down in Swiss Cottage, one of the two wards where the Conservatives had over 50% of the vote. She had the association executive set up a selection panel of three people. In place of Pam Chesters, Judith Barnes was selected to chair the panel which included no councillors.

Judith Barnes's panel interviewed and selected new candidates without any input from the council group. They made a firm decision to select Janice Lavery as a candidate for Swiss Cottage, and they then scrambled around to slot any volunteer into any ward where there was a vacancy. Every target ward (Hampstead, Highgate and Gospel Oak) was either left without a full set of candidates, or else with candidates who were wholly inexperienced. It seemed as if the election was to be thrown away. There was great anger in the group, and great anger in Swiss Cottage where neither the ward association nor the sitting councillors wanted Janice Lavery.

The panel's selection needed to be approved by the association executive which Janice Lavery then tried to pack. Her support

321

---

5   Hoque had at least been around for some time, having stood as a paper candidate in Fortune Green in 1994.

was confined to those association officers she had appointed, and some Highgate people who had turned up to vote for her to stand somewhere else. The selection panel's recommendations were rejected. Mrs Lavery, after announcing that she was about to undergo chemotherapy and so needed a safe seat as she could not be expected to campaign, resigned as association chairman and stormed off. Judith Barnes, who had chaired the panel for her, flounced off in her wake. The consequence was that the Conservative group leader was left to choose all the candidates and submit the final list to the executive for approval.

Meanwhile, in the south of the borough, John Walter set up his own selection panel, again without any reference to the Conservative group on the council. He made his selections and then moved to Kensington, and refused to resign. The three wards which interested the Conservatives in the south of the borough were Bloomsbury (where the Labour majority was under a hundred), Holborn & Covent Garden (respectable second place to Labour), and Regents Park (where in 2002 the Tories had managed their highest vote in the constituency). Walter's selection panel sensibly chose Rebecca Hossack to fight Bloomsbury where she lived and where she had an established art gallery. As her running mates, they chose Rob Morritt, the Hampstead & Highgate agent, and Janice Lavery, who had stood down from chairing the Hampstead & Highgate association saying that she would be too unwell to campaign. None of the councillors was told of the selection meetings in advance, and none of them was consulted.[6] Walter had narrowly won the chairmanship of the association by a single vote a couple of years before, and had used his position to exclude everyone he felt was against him. No hand of friendship was extended to those who had opposed his appointment, even though they included the most active members of the association. Those who had backed his rival for the chairmanship, Peter Horne, were driven out. Walter's chief legacy was that through the selections he made, he alienated pretty well every single activist in the constituency, while Mrs Lavery had alienated the Conservative councillors. There was no hope of support from the north. Isolated, the rump of the constituency association resolved to concentrate only on Bloomsbury ward and to in effect

6 I was not told of the meeting before it took place, and heard the news from a friend of someone in Central Office who had heard from Brian Coleman. A few days later, Walter announced the selections by email. Fearing that he may have generated irritation, he then refused to answer his phone whenever I called him. We have not spoken since.

leave the rest of the constituency alone[7].

The Hampstead & Highgate Conservative Association was left in a desperate situation. It had no chairman and no volunteer for the job. John Samiotis, a city lawyer, reluctantly stepped in during the run up to the election. The timing was against him in that he had no time to assert authority over anyone, let alone any power to stop the agent seizing for himself, as it then seemed, a seat in Bloomsbury. The horror of the situation dawned when the agent suddenly announced that he was going on holiday at the time of the deadline for nomination papers, which he had not organised beforehand. Most were left without proposers or candidates' signatures. Samiotis was left helpless. Mike Greene took control and got the job done, albeit narrowly.[8]

There were two unrelated reasons for the growth of the LibDems in Camden in 2006. The early activism of Flick Rea and Roger Billins, and then Keith Moffitt, had gained them an important foothold that had not been seriously challenged by the other parties. There were no distinct policy targets that differed from the policies being put forward by the Conservatives and, if left to the level of activism seen in the 2002 elections, the LibDems were going nowhere fast. But the political landscape was greatly changed by the quite startling results the party achieved in the general election in neighbouring constituencies; in Brent East, Hornsey & Wood Green, and in Islington South (where they had a near miss). It was a matter of geography. Camden was suddenly a target because it was a territory that would link up with the LibDem areas to the east and the west to form a yellow crescent across north London.[9] Influenced by Ed Fordham's enthusiasm for the task, the national party issued a call to arms to all constituency associations and (most promisingly) the party's youth wing, the Liberal Democrat Youth and Students.

323

---

7   Simply because the candidates in Holborn & Covent Garden and Regent's Park wards insisted on it, two inexpensive leaflets went out in those wards. There was no other campaigning activity outside Bloomsbury.

8   For a few hours it seemed probable that for the first time in the borough's history there would not be a complete list of Conservative candidates standing in Camden. Hampstead faced the spectre of the 2002 elections in Harrow where following some slapdash agenting, the entire LibDem slate for Harrow –save only three nominations– were adjudged invalid and six of the nine sitting LibDem councillors were prevented from standing again. In the 2006 borough elections Harrow was a Tory target borough, and LibDem representation was reduced to a solitary member.

9   Or as Flick Rea would have it, "a golden triangle".

The difficulty was that there were not enough LibDem activists in Camden, and certainly not enough LibDem activists to run an effective campaign. The result of the shortage was that there was a scramble to get eligible candidates to stand. Two notable activists who had stood before and campaigned hard over the years, were Dudley Miles (who lives in Belsize) and John Lefley, their long term activist in Camden Town with Primrose Hill. Miles was rewarded by being selected to stand in Haverstock, which was considered a good LibDem bet now that Jill Fraser had seized a seat there and Dame Jane was standing down. Lefley was again selected to stand in Camden Town with Primrose Hill, confident that he could at least match the 2002 result where the LibDems took (albeit briefly) a seat from Labour. But Miles and Lefley were the exceptions in that all the other candidates in target seats were new. [10]

Ed Fordham who was leading the charge, was also hit the hardest by the lack of local activists. Now that he had made inroads into the old Hampstead & Highgate constituency, he was embedding himself as the next LibDem parliamentary candidate for the new Hampstead & Kilburn constituency. Having rented a flat in Hampstead to fight his parliamentary campaign, he was confident of taking Hampstead Town ward in the council elections. The frail Margaret Little had managed to withstand Mike Greene, and so could he. It was a brave move, but such was his confidence that he felt he had time to help out his fellow candidates in other wards. His problem was that there was no one suitable to stand with him who actually lived in the ward. He was left with Linda Chung, who lived not far away, and Jonathan Fryer, who lived in Tower Hamlets with his cat, and whose only connection with the borough was through his part time job at the School of African and Oriental Studies off Russell Square. Such was the LibDem line up against Mike Greene who in Chris Knight and Kirsty Roberts had now been provided with two able candidates both able to claim some level of local activism.

Belsize was another case, where the new activist ("I only left the Labour Party because of Iraq") Alexis Rowell burst onto the scene. New to the area but encouraged by the voting in Belsize in the general election, he began canvassing with extraordinary enthusiasm. The only candidate from within the ward he could get to stand with him was Chris

---

10 Politics can be the unfairest of games. In May 2006, Miles lost by 21 votes and Lefley by 64. It is a curious statistic that in Camden every LibDem elected in 2006 was either a sitting councillor or else had never before stood for the council.

Basson who (something known at the time to his close neighbours and to the sitting councillors) was mentally fragile and wholly unsuited for the task he was agreeing to take on.[11]

Top of the agenda for the parties was the whole matter of crime and policing. The council was not directly responsible for policing, but there was much that it could do in support. Labour had tried out every new initiative on crime in Camden. They had campaigned for and heralded every new increase in police numbers (although their part locally in achieving the increases was negligible), they had employed their own "street wardens" to supplement the police, they had invested heavily in CCTV cameras, they had championed a policy of issuing anti-social behaviour orders (ASBOs) to the extent that civil liberties groups complained, they had explored issuing penalty notices to the parents of truants, they had imposed dispersal areas, and had turned the borough into a controlled drinking zone. The Labour Party in Camden could not be faulted for trying.

But in the months before the election, even these achievements seemed fragile. The CCTV installations, on which so many had placed so much faith in the fight against street crime, were found to be used for raising traffic fines for the environment department. The *Evening Standard* made much of the great profits being made in prosecuting drivers for entering a box junction on High Holborn and executing illegal u-turns on Southampton Row. A CCTV camera on Hampstead High Street raised some £150,000 in four months by allowing motorists to be fined when filmed taking an illegal right hand turn from Perrins Lane. "We worked really hard to get these cameras", said Mike Greene. "We used the no right turn from Perrins Lane as an excuse to get the CCTV we needed. But instead of using it for community safety, Camden seems to be milking it for all it is worth". [12]

The Metropolitan Police then announced that they were at last going to sell Hampstead Police Station which, behind its imposing facade,

325

---

11 Elected in 2006, Basson resigned from the council in 2009 claiming that he was going "to clear his name" against allegations he anticipated in the local papers (but which were never specified by him or by them).

12 At the same time, on Albert Street, a driving instructor was issued with a parking ticket when a CCTV camera picked up his car stationary alongside a yellow line. It transpired that at the time of being filmed, his car had stalled and he was explaining to a learner how the clutch worked.

was run down and unfit for purpose. The police did not want it in any event as foot patrols are better dropped off than made to radiate from a static location. "Police stations are a concept from which we have moved on", said Richard Sumray, now of the Metropolitan Police Authority. The opposition parties started petitions and promised council funds to keep it open. Labour, they claimed, was abandoning Hampstead.

The council's joint plans with the Primary Care Trust to establish a needle exchange for drug users in a disused public lavatory underneath Centre Point on Oxford Street met with local opposition. It excited the Tories in Bloomsbury, their single target seat in the south of the borough, who managed to get Conservative councillors from Westminster to fight their corner for them. Never mind that Camden was the only borough not to have a fixed needle exchange (it had a van), the exchange ought to be in or next to some NHS centre where drug users go in any event, rather than risk attracting them into the St Giles Circus development area. "Tens of millions of pounds are being invested in redeveloping St Giles High Street in the near future", said Jim Murray of the Bloomsbury Association. "This proposal is an affront to everyone who has tried to help improve community safety in the area".

Worst of all, the police issued several statements to say that the Metropolitan Police Authority had ordered that Camden should have variously twenty or thirty or even sixty officers reassigned to boroughs where there were shortages. Into all this stepped Charles Clarke, the harassed home secretary, for an evening walkabout in Inverness Street and Camden High Street to see how Camden's successful anti crime strategy was working. He was accompanied by Jake Sumner, the new executive member for community safety. The idea was to point out that Camden's use of ASBOs reflected well against the way that LibDem run Islington handled these matters. Sumner was able to demonstrate the lack of drug dealers on Inverness Street, who had melted away before the unprecedented numbers of police officers, PCSOs and Camden's own red jacketed street wardens who had been turned out for the home secretary. He suffered two ambushes before he even got off Inverness Street. The first of these was by the leader of the opposition and Jonny Bucknell, who invited Clarke to walk the few yards to Camden Lock where the displaced drug dealers were happily plying their trade in full view of the heavy, slow moving traffic. The second ambush was arranged by the New Journal in the person of Abdirahman Osman, a Somali refugee, who wanted to know why his son, an 18 year old "good, hard working", mosque going, engineering student, had been stabbed to death while he was waiting at a bus stop opposite the tube station on Camden High Street the week before.[13] The twin ambushes made the newspapers, the Labour Party's message of how well the fight against crime is progressing did not.

All this was on top of the *New Journal* reader's usual diet of stabbings, street robberies and pitched gang battles. When at the Labour Party launch, Raj Chada announced his party's determination to stamp out drug dealing in Camden within two years, it all seemed rather unlikely. Why has this pledge not come, people asked, two years ago rather than immediately before an election?[14]

In the north of the borough, parking had become a serious issue, and to many the decisive issue. Parking enforcement had made the council deeply unpopular. The executive member for the environment department, the combative John Thane, was targeted by the equally combative Alex Henney, the London Motorists Action Group campaigner who carried out his own "Get rid of Thane" campaign. He printed at his own expense and distributed leaflets in Highgate that were highly critical (some might say abusive). He urged voters to vote for anyone except Labour, naming both Thane and Maggie Cosin, who chaired the tame scrutiny panel on parking, as being particularly responsible for the council's parking policies. Pressed as Labour was by both the Tories and the Greens, Henney's intervention hit a raw nerve and was followed by threats to report him to the police or the Electoral Commission.[15] The difficulty for Labour was that the council needed the revenue from parking, and John Thane's treatment of those who had other ideas was unforgiving and did much to encourage opposition.

327

---

13   Charles Clarke could not have known but it soon transpired that the unfortunate youth, Mahir "Smiley" Osman, far from being the "well behaved boy caught in the crossfire of a feud he had nothing to do with" as the *New Journal* reported at the time, was in fact a knife toting, drug dealing "gangsta" from the "Centric Boys". He died in a knife fight with rival drug dealers from Wood Green's "NLS Gang" (the "North London Somalis").

14   In any event, Raj Chada was not the man to make this pledge. A promise from a local criminal defence solicitor (honourable though that profession is) to wipe out local crime lacks conviction: not unlike a tobacconist fronting a no smoking campaign, or a jam doughnut manufacturer endorsing Weightwatchers.

15   The leaflets may have had only a minor effect as the main beneficiaries of Labour's defeat in Highgate were the Greens, whose voters were the least likely to heed a call from the London Motorists Action Group.

"There's no need" said Roy Shaw "to be so bloody aggressive the whole time".[16] The establishment of a parking scrutiny panel made no difference. Its sole purpose proved to be to justify the actions and policies of the parking department, which was not to consider its limited recommendations until after the election.[17]

As the campaign got under way Labour was able to secure visits from several cabinet ministers, including David Miliband, the local government minister, who had a certain attraction because he had been educated at Haverstock School. Rather than rely on what in the circumstances were the safer choices of either or both of the local MPs, the Labour Party chose Miliband to pose for the cameras on their manifesto launch at Talacre Sports Centre. The press asked him about the £283m needed for housing repairs. "Discussions are continuing with Camden to make sure we can find a way forward", he said, cheerfully. "The other parties can say what they are against but they are not saying what they are for". Actually, they were. They were united with the Labour group in their calls for the fourth option, the difference being that it was a Labour government that was withholding the money.

Three weeks before the poll, Tony Blair visited the recently renovated Cromer Street Estate. A delighted Raj Chada seized the opportunity that neither Frank Dobson nor Glenda Jackson would risk, and posed for photographs alongside the prime minister. "I think Labour have done an excellent job here", said Blair, "and I certainly think they should be re-elected". Sadly for Labour, his recommendations no longer carried much weight. He also had nothing to say on the £283m.[18] This followed on from the Labour election launch where Chada had allowed himself to be photographed with Alastair Campbell for the *New Journal*. "I was vehemently opposed to the war in Iraq", said Chada, distancing himself from Campbell who lives in Gospel Oak. "but in the council elections, people should vote on local matters".

328

16   Shaw described Thane as being "holed up in his bunker, shooting to the end".

17   In the years following the 2006 election, revenue from parking increased dramatically yet the opposition to it (Alex Henney and LMAG excepted) stalled. How had Mike Greene (Thane's successor) managed to get away with it when Thane had not? "Basically," said Mike Greene, "Thane smirked".

18   Blair's popularity had greatly sunk since the general election. The mood was such that photographs of the Blair meeting were used by the Tories against Chada in their election literature in Gospel Oak.

The photographs were a gift to the opposition. "I am amazed they did it", said Andrew Marshall the Conservatives' deputy leader. "It demonstrates that the Labour group is associated with the Blair culture of spin".

The Tories had no such pull. Conservative Central Office had decided early on not to assist Camden at all. Everyone in London was to concentrate on the target boroughs (principally Croydon, Harrow and Hammersmith & Fulham) and throughout the campaign, Camden's activists and candidates were bombarded with emails from Central Office telling them to campaign elsewhere. The shadow cabinet was issued with instructions not to campaign outside the target boroughs.[19]

The LibDem election campaign began with the leader of the Liberal Democrat Party, Ming Campbell, posing for the photographers with local activists outside a tower block on the Chalcots estate. He visited their Belsize candidate, Chris Basson, in the twentieth storey flat he shares with his mother, and was told that the windows did not keep out the rain. Campbell blamed it on lack of finance. There was no one there to tell him of the lengthy public finance initiative negotiations the council had been conducting for funding repairs to the Chalcots estate. "Money has been held back because people didn't vote the way the government wanted", he said. "There is not much democratic about that. The government has essentially fined the people of Camden £283 million".

The Conservative message was that a vote for anyone other than the Conservatives would risk keeping Labour in power, especially as the LibDems refused to rule out a coalition with Labour. The central LibDem message was that a vote for anyone other than the LibDem candidates would risk keeping Labour in power. Labour countered with a series of leaflets with a cartoon of the leader of the opposition sharing a bed with Keith Moffitt: vote LibDem and you get the Tories.[20] As the campaign got under way it appeared that the LibDem policy issues were indistinguishable from those of the Conservatives. Like that of the Conservatives, their campaign was essentially anti-Labour, heavy on complaint and light on solutions. It seemed even that they were running

329

---

19 The only senior Conservative politician to defy the ban was Alan Duncan, then the shadow President of the Board of Trade, who paid a brief visit to South End Green to pose for a photograph with the Tories' most photogenic candidates, Lulu Mitchell, Kirsty Roberts and Chris Philp.

20 The leaflet prompted much sniggering, principally because one of them is gay.

a carbon copy campaign: waiting to see what the Conservatives were saying, and then repeating the same but louder.[21]

The one campaign that the LibDems made their own was that of the Kentish Town Baths, an impressive Victorian red brick building on Prince of Wales Road that had for generations provided the area with hot baths and a swimming pool. Age had taken its toll. The building was crumbling and the boilers kept breaking down. "Frankly", said Peter Bishop, the director of the Culture and Environment Department, "the Kentish Town Baths are squalid. They have come to the end of their life and they are in need of refurbishment". Unfortunately for Labour, the question of redevelopment was handled with remarkable political insensitivity, with no eye on the coming borough elections. Dame Jane wanted the baths refurbishment to be part of the Labour manifesto, but Phil Turner, the executive member responsible, had other ideas. Plans were unveiled to build a swimming pool alongside the Talacre Sports Centre, four hundred metres away, on land which the council had already sold off for housing. The options were either to build a temporary swimming pool alongside Talacre and reopen the Baths after refurbishment, or else to build a permanent swimming pool alongside Talacre, and close and sell Kentish Town Baths once the Talacre pool was operational. Either way it was going to cost a lot of money, between £17m and £29m, said the council.

This was a gift to the LibDems. They pledged to save the Baths. The December 2005 council meeting was presented with a 3,000 signature petition demanding refurbishment for the Baths. It was not a matter of money, Ian Dungavell, of the Victorian Society, told the council. Getting rid of the Baths would "rupture a link with the past". Phil Turner reaffirmed the council's commitment to provide publicly funded swimming in Kentish Town, pointed out the inevitable expense of refurbishing a Grade II listed building, and said that the decision was yet to be taken following a full public consultation. Feeling the heat, the Labour Party put out copies of its occasional newsletter, *Labour Rose*, claiming that the £30m refurbishment costs would force up council tax. The borough had, said Jill Fraser for the LibDems, plenty of money in its reserves that could be used for this purpose. Dame Jane, who lives in

330

---

21 After the election, Keith Moffitt was asked what differences there were in the Conservative and the LibDem policy objectives. His reply was; "Well, I didn't want Piers Wauchope to be leader of the council".

Kentish Town, complained that the baths had been "hijacked" as a political issue by the LibDems. It is a political issue, said Jill Fraser, because the council is delaying the decision on the baths because they cannot risk announcing their closure before the election.

In the new year, Tessa Jowell, the Culture Secretary, also a Kentish Town resident, told the *New Journal* that the council should face up to "the Olympic challenge" of refurbishing the Baths. The pressure built, especially as the two wards most immediately affected, Haverstock and Kentish Town, were under growing pressure from the LibDems. Voting in those two wards could well determine whether Camden remained under Labour control. In February the Labour leadership decided to douse the flames. The Baths could be refurbished for as little as £12m by sacrificing a learner pool and selling off some land behind the building. Having thought hard, and having come up with an imaginative new plan, and (unlike any other party) having carefully costed the project to keep within the council budget, Labour could now pledge to save the baths. The announcement was described as "a win-win" situation by Mike Katz, the Labour candidate in Haverstock. "I'd like to think that there will be cross party support for the proposals".[22]

The following morning, a dozen LibDem councillors and council candidates arranged a photo opportunity for the press on the steps of the Baths. They stood behind a poster which read ANOTHER LABOUR FLIP-FLOP while those with their hands free waved flip flops for the cameras. "We deplore how long it has taken for the council to listen to local voices" Philip Thompson, their young Kentish Town candidate, told the *New Journal*. "This is a cave in, a climb down", said Keith Moffitt. "This is an example of the council flip flopping".

331

Of the other parties, the Greens were greatly encouraged by their strong showing in 2002. They made great efforts in both Highgate and Kentish Town which were contested by both their 2005 parliamentary candidates, Adrian Oliver and the highly photogenic Sîan Berry (although in a surprising cross over each stood in a ward in the constituency the other had contested). The Greens were such an unknown phenomenon that the main parties were baffled by their appeal. It was difficult to

---

22   BT subscribers were sent a 60 second pre-recorded message by the Labour Party: "Hello. This is Raj Chada, leader of Labour Camden. I'm calling to tell you the latest news about Kentish Town Baths... I am pleased to tell you that Labour Camden guaranteed the continued use of the baths today, for the years to come...."

anticipate who would vote for them or why, especially when pitched against a council that had such a green agenda, and which was (especially in Highgate) under attack for the severity its parking regime showed towards motorists. Like the LibDems they had (in Camden terms) the glamour of being a new soft left alternative to Labour.

Easier to understand was the party of the hard left, Respect. East London based and almost wholly reliant on Muslim votes, the party was now fighting its first borough elections. Mukul Hira, an articulate young man who works in his family's grocers on Chalton Street, stood in St Pancras & Somers Town as Repect's only candidate in Camden. He was seen as a great threat. The Labour Party found itself vying with Hira to show that they were just as committed as he was to defending the Muslim community from attack or insult. A meeting held in Somers Town in February ("No to War, No to Islamophobia") was prompted by the approach of the third anniversary of the invasion of Iraq and the more recent publication of twelve cartoon images of Mohammed in a Danish newspaper. Those at the meeting issued a statement which was sent to the New Journal by way of a letter. "We stand in total opposition to the racism and Islamophobia that is infecting so much of British politics today. The publication of anti-Islamic cartoons is racist....We pledge to stand by the Muslim community". It was signed first by Mukul Hira; then by Abdul Quadir in his capacity as deputy mayor; Nurul Islam, Labour's new Somers Town candidate; and Roger Robinson who, after his selection fiasco, was taking no chances.

As the election approached, the New Journal was caught up in the general realisation that the elections could see the end of a Labour run council. For years the paper had been hostile to both Richard Arthur and Jane Roberts, and had given support to the LibDems as the means of punishing New Labour for not being old Labour. Now, when it seemed that Labour really was in danger, as if spurred into action by a bad conscience for its years of goading Dame Jane, the New Journal leapt to the party's defence. The paper kept its readers on a weekly diet of articles written in support of the Labour Party.[23] When the end

23 The only contribution asked for from a Conservative candidate was that written by the academic Jesse Norman (the son of Torquil Norman, then the chairman of the Roundhouse Trust, a "multi millionaire toy magnate and philanthropist" of whom the New Journal approves). Jesse Norman, the author of After Euclid: visual reasoning and the epistemology of diagrams, was standing as a paper candidate in Camden Town with Primrose Hill. He produced a witty piece criticising the Blair government's illiberality in which he was able to cite in one sentence Gillray, Hazlitt and Hogarth.

was in sight, the *New Journal* could no longer contain itself. The front page of the its pre election issue was dominated by a photograph of a smiling Raj Chada posing with primary school children in Gospel Oak. It smacked of desperation. "Young Labour leader in plea for time to do the job" read the caption. 'GIVE ME A CHANCE' howled the headline.

Raj Chada's last act as leader was to sign off, with the powers the executive had delegated to him, the £5m for the Local Area Agreement (LAA) for commissioning "a range of targeted services to ensure that Camden's Local Strategic Partnership meets the agreed Aims and Outcomes Framework of the Local Area Agreement". Every pound of the funds made available by the government, all £5,192,977 of it, the officers reported with some satisfaction, had now been allocated by the six Strategic Commissioning Panels. All that was needed was for Councillor Chada to approve the distribution. It was quietly symbolic of the way that the council had changed over the forty years of its existence. There was no agonising over the grants as in the bad old days, no press release, no fuss. The competing claims for funding had been considered by council officers who then made the decisions. All that was required was the leader's signature at the end of a list drawn up by the assistant director for community development and regeneration.[24] In the late afternoon of Monday 24 April 2006, a time designed to suit the council officers, Camden's last Labour leader put his pen back in his pocket, and resigned himself to the final ten days of the election campaign.

333

Campaigning in his own ward was an unhappy experience for Raj Chada. Gospel Oak was considered in the 2002 elections to be a safe Labour seat when, for the first time in twenty years, there was the

---

24 Without any debate at member level, funding was approved to eighty projects in all of Camden's strategic, diverse and worthy funding areas subject to LAA funding, including £50,000 for the Young People's Local Area Board (to ensure young people are engaged in decision making); £40,000 for the Terrence Higgins Trust for a sexual health outreach coordinator; £80,000 to Hopscotch Asian Women's Centre and Communities in Training and Employment (CITE) to get black and minority ethnic women into work; £30,000 for the Bengali Women's Inclusion Project and £41,000 to the African & Caribbean Elders (ACE) for research and development; £50,000 for "addressing" Somali youth crime, and £50,000 for securing the "engagement" of the Somali community; £50,000 for women entrepreneurs, £57,000 for Camden Women's Aid and £10,000 for the Sex Workers Action Group (SWAG); £142,983 for Camden's community safety team to get a communications officer to improve information exchange and facilitate communication, together with £182,808 for "partnership analysis" for the same purpose; and £163,000 to the Primary Care Trust to stop people smoking.

beginning of a Conservative challenge. It came from Lulu Mitchell who lives on the Gospel Oak estate and who came only 250 votes behind John Mills. This was enough encouragement for the Conservatives who kept up a steady flow of leaflets about once every six months until the campaigning restarted. As the election neared, the Conservative leaflets became more frequent and the messages became less complex. They were A5 handbills carrying a photo on the front and a simple message on the other side. The theme was the four words "Vote Neighbour, not Labour".[25] The only point being made was that the three Conservative candidates, Lulu Mitchell, Chris Philp and Keith Sedgwick, lived in the ward, two of them actually on the Gospel Oak estate itself, whereas none of the sitting Labour councillors did. There was no other meaning intended, nor was any other interpretation anticipated. The simple idea was for people to ask the simple question: "Why can't one of us be a councillor?"

Raj Chada and the Labour Party generally took the words to mean something quite different. It was a reference to his own background, Chada told the *Camden New Journal*. The leaflets were referring to the fact that he has Indian parents. The words *neighbour* and *Labour* in one sentence meant only one thing to Labour party apparatchiks[26]. By the end of the campaign he was telling everyone who would listen that the Tory campaign was "racist and despicable". They had "crossed the line on immigration". Even the BBC phoned him, he said, and asked him about this, "but I wouldn't give them a quote because I didn't want to encourage the BNP". For the first time, he said, people were talking of voting BNP (although there were no BNP candidates in Camden). Someone, he could not say who, had said to someone else who he could not identify, that they were going to vote Conservative "to get the Black". This was all, he felt, a consequence of the Conservative campaign.

Raj Chada was right in one respect: there was resentment, but that resentment had not been generated by any leaflet put out by the Conservatives, or by any comment made by any of the Tory candidates

---

25 © Keith Sedgwick who, to weaken Chada's assertion of a racist plot yet further, is also (in Home Office terms) a member of a visible ethnic minority being of Seychellois parentage.

26 During the 1963 municipal elections in Smethwick, the Labour MP Gordon Walker said he had overheard children chanting: "If you want a nigger for a neighbour, vote Labour!" Labour Party mythology has since elevated the phrase to the false status of a campaign slogan used by Peter Griffiths, the Conservative candidate, who in the following year took the Smethwick seat from Walker in the 1964 general election.

or activists. It had been for the most part generated by the Labour Party.

It is a simple point to make, but an important one: New Labour had become increasingly middle class. There were no manual workers on the Labour benches, no tradesmen, and the union members that they had were union employees. There was no longer a place for a railways worker like Charlie Ratchford even on the backbenches. The last three Labour leaders had been a banker, a child psychiatrist and a solicitor. They empathized with the people who lived on housing estates, but they did not live on the estates. Labour's insistence, repeated again and again, that "the council must reflect the community it represents" did not apply to the working class, the "ordinary people" so often referred to by Labour politicians twenty or thirty years ago. It was applied with the crudity of a customer choosing paint from a colour chart. Because there are many non-whites in Camden, it was important to elect more people from the visible ethnic minorities. No similar efforts were made for the white working class who had for so long been the core Labour vote. Their representatives were instead squeezed out leaving them to be represented by outsiders.[27] The feeling on the estate was that Labour had lost touch with its old voters. Linked to this was the sense that Labour was doing more and more for its new constituency of immigrants. No longer championing the old working class, Labour was the champion of the new comers. There was no youth club for local children on the Gospel Oak estate, but there was a centre for the Somalis.

The Labour Party's main campaign leaflet in Gospel Oak, expensively produced on glossy full colour A3, reinforced the point. It included endorsements of the Labour campaign by five "ordinary people". The first of these was Glenda Jackson, who lives in south London. The next three were council tenants with foreign names (African, Bengali and Italian), and the last, the only true English voter in Gospel Oak that could be found to endorse the Labour candidates was the historian Professor Sir Roderick Floud who lives in a £1½m house on Savernake Road and who was quoted as saying that Camden's schools are doing well. It is tempting for political anoraks to read too much into this, and maybe only a few people did, but it cried out to be interpreted by ordinary working class people

335

---

27 At the first Camden election in 1964 the candidates had to state their occupations which on the Labour benches included plumber, paint sprayer, electrician, butcher, toolmaker and (the leader of the council) railway clerk. In Chada's time, Camden's only overtly working class Labour councillor, Charlie Hedges, who delivered meat for a living, was deselected in Kilburn under the one-woman-per-ward rule. He was replaced by Aileen Hammond, "a transport economist".

(including those of all races who have actually embraced mainstream culture) that the Labour Party was no longer interested in them.

On top of that, Labour had simply taken its hand off the throttle. It had taken its core vote for granted. Housing expenditure had been lavished on the south of the borough while council housing repairs in wards such as Gospel Oak and Haverstock had been deferred. Funding was too little and too late. On the estates of Gospel Oak and Haverstock, Labour faced candidates such as Lulu Mitchell and Jill Fraser, both of whom, a decade or two ago, would have been seen as natural Labour voters.

The LibDem campaign was ambitious. They were fighting (as opposed to simply standing in) ten wards which if successful would give them over half the seats on the council. The more experienced campaigners thought it unlikely that they would be successful in all their objectives and that the best they could hope for was a share in the control of the council through an alliance with the Conservatives. The directing hand behind the campaign was Ed Fordham, and he was interested only in the council as a way of positioning himself for the new parliamentary seat of Hampstead & Kilburn. For this reason, not a single LibDem leaflet was put out in the two wards (Highgate and Gospel Oak) about to be detached from the Hampstead & Highgate constituency and moved to Holborn & St Pancras. The LibDem campaign, where it was felt, appeared to the other parties relentless. The sheer number of canvassers and deliverers, and the great number of activists (and candidates) of student age able to devote time and energy to the campaign simply could not be matched in all but a few of those ten wards they were contesting in earnest.

The only clashes between the Conservatives and the LibDems were in the adjoining wards of Belsize and Hampstead Town. Hampstead Town, which in 2002 had returned two Conservatives and one Liberal, proved to be the most intense campaign in the election. Belsize, where the LibDems had come a poor third in 2002 was handled rather differently by the Conservatives. The collapse of the constituency association had left the leader of the opposition with the stark choice of either targeting Gospel Oak, or campaigning in Belsize. In each case there would be little outside help, and the other sitting councillors in Belsize were unable to run the campaign alone.[28] The indications were that the Tory vote in

---

28 Sheila Gunn, now a lecturer in journalism at the City University, was too occupied at work to run a campaign, and Jonny Bucknell, although the hardest working of all Camden councillors and the most popular councillor in the ward, was simply no campaigner.

Belsize was undiminished, and if the Conservatives were to gain ground on the council, the risk had to be taken. Belsize would, with the aid of a few leaflets, be left to look after itself.[29]

The Greens concentrated their efforts in Highgate and Kentish Town with a campaign of door knocking. Dame Jane played her part by defending the council's proposals for a supermarket plastic bag tax. The *Guardian* diary noted that John Thane, the executive member responsible, was passed over "for the key task of defending the council's outstanding record on reusables". "From such seemingly slight and inconsequential scraps of evidence, reader, do we conclude that Labour is bricking it".

For the first time since the Blair government won in 1997, people seemed to be interested in local politics. Council gimmicks to get people to vote had not been needed. There were some low key adverts placed by the council, but nothing as apparent as the earlier, failed campaigns. There were no photos of More Fire Crew inviting young voters to *Oi Vote*. It was the desperate competition that brought people out. Most voted, the best way they could, to get rid of Labour, and that brought out the Labour supporters as well. Complacency had fed apathy, and complacency had left the borough.

337

The result of the May 2006 borough election was 20 LibDems, 18 Labour and 14 Conservatives and 2 Greens.[30] It was a massive triumph for the LibDems. They had jumped from being the smallest party on the council to being the biggest. Their net gain was ten seats from Labour and two from the Conservatives. For the Labour Party it was a disaster. On the evening of the poll, Gospel Oak was the last result to be declared (apart from Bloomsbury which went off for a recount the following day). Raj Chada was given notice that he had lost his seat as well as the council. There was no Charlie Ratchford bravado or handshake. Unwilling to witness the triumph of his enemies, Chada

---

29 In the event, it was a fateful decision for the Conservatives as the Belsize result was the difference between the LibDems and the Tories having 17 seats each (to Labour's 18) and, as happened, the LibDems getting 20 seats to the Conservatives' 14.

30 To put the 2006 result in a London context: the LibDem vote in London remained the same (20.3%) as in 2002, which was the lowest LibDem result for five elections. The Labour vote in London was at its lowest ever at 27.6%, and the Conservative vote was up for the fourth election running at 35.1%. The Green Party share of the vote across London (4.6%) was the highest ever achieved by a minor party. In 2002, the turnout in London had fallen below 33%, but in 2006 had risen to 38.2%.

took the opportunity to slip sulkily out of the building before the results were announced. Such was the undignified end to thirty five years of Labour Party rule in Camden.

The turnout was impressive. It was up by a third on the last election. In 2002 only 28½% of the electorate had voted. In 2006 the turnout leapt up to 37.56%. Even the Labour vote, in real numbers, had increased in every ward (except in Belsize where the Labour vote collapsed to the benefit of the LibDems). Overall they had got some two thousand more votes than in 2002, but everywhere the Labour share of the vote was down.[31] They still polled more than any other party, but it was not enough. In Gospel Oak in 2002 Raj Chada had easily won with 846 votes. In 2006 his vote went up by 44% to 1220 votes, and he came fifth. The Labour Party wrongly calculated that by holding their vote they would hold onto their seats, but their share of the vote went down from 33% to 28%. In Belsize, the only Conservative loss, the Tories fell into the same trap by assuming that they were safe so long as their vote held. The Tory vote not only held in Belsize, it increased by 20%. But they lost.

338

Wherever the Labour Party had identified a weakness, and prepared for the onslaught, they did well. The quality and expense of the glossy literature put out by the Labour Party in the wards they were defending was the best ever seen in a local election: all colour sheets of high quality A3, professionally taken photographs of friendly candidates smiling from behind red Labour Party clipboards. Of the four wards perceived by Labour before the election as being the most vulnerable, they only lost Highgate outright, and that was in part to an unpredictable Green vote that made it a three way marginal. They had in their key wards harnessed the Bengali vote and made strenuous efforts

---

31   In 2002 Jane Roberts topped the poll in Haverstock with 882 votes. In 2006 in Haverstock the lowest vote for a winning candidate was 1106, and the first six candidates all polled more than a thousand votes. In 2002, thirty two councillors (all Labour) had been elected with fewer than a thousand votes each, whereas in 2006 only six councillors were elected with fewer than a thousand votes. In 2002 Mike Greene got the highest vote in the borough with 1316 votes; in 2006, sixteen other councillors beat his record, although he again got the highest vote of 1842. Still of course nowhere near the 1971 result when James Buckland topped the poll in Camden ward for Labour with 2971 votes, in a borough election in which 38 of the 62 councillors polled more than 2000 votes.

to get their Bengali pledges to vote by post.[32] Against the odds, so it seemed, Labour held onto a seat in Camden Town with Primrose Hill, and fought off a strong challenge in Haverstock, avoiding the most highly expected LibDem gain by keeping their two seats.[33] They did the same against the Conservative challenge in Bloomsbury, dropping only one seat (and that by only two votes). But Labour was no longer equipped to fight on many fronts. They did worse where they were not expecting the onslaught –they had not rated the LibDem threat in Cantelowes, Kentish Town and Kilburn until it was too late, and they had underestimated the Conservative threat in Gospel Oak.

It was also a disappointing result for the Conservatives. They won against the LibDems in Hampstead (the only ward in which the LibDems lost a seat) taking all three seats, but lost to them in Belsize where one of their losing candidates was the group leader. They beat Labour in Gospel Oak, but in both Highgate and Bloomsbury their efforts left them with only one of their three candidates elected (in each case alphabetically their lead candidate).

The Greens, having come so close in Highgate in 2002, managed to get elected their first two councillors in 2006, taking votes from Labour and from young electors targeted by Dame Jane, the young. They also came close in Kentish Town where Sîan Berry got over a thousand votes, more than doubling the Green vote from 2002 and beating one of the sitting Labour councillors, and came within two hundred votes of

339

---

32 The frightening reality for Labour concerns the number of councillors who owe their positions to the Bengali vote, which may prove a fickle friend now that grant funding is no longer in the hands of a Labour council. The care expended by Labour on nurturing the Bengali vote was an important reason for non-Bengalis to vote for other parties. The Labour group has had to weigh up the advantage and the cost of Bengali patronage. They did so in May 2009 by choosing as their leader Nasim Ali, a decision that can only be explained by his appeal to Bengali voters. In doing so, they (again) rejected the challenge of their most experienced member, Julian Fulbrook. "We have gone against the traditional approach to leadership", explained Theo Blackwell. "We have gone insurgent!" After the 2006 elections, there were ten councillors from ethnic minorities (six Labour, two Conservative, one Green and one LibDem), and eight gay men (six LibDems, one Labour and one Tory).

33 Haverstock was an interesting result. Jill Fraser won by three hundred votes over Syed Hoque who had harnessed the Bengali vote. Roy Shaw got something of a fright and won by only 21 votes, much irritated by Hoque's inability to tell his Bengali postal voters to vote for all three Labour candidates. Following Roy Shaw's resignation from the council, the LibDems won the Haverstock by-election in July 2007. Feeling somewhat isolated, as the only Labour councillor left in Haverstock, Syed Hoque demonstrated the fragility of Labour's investment in the Bengali vote. In 2009, he joined the LibDems. He no longer liked, he said, his Labour colleagues and he disapproved of the government's support of Israel's invasion of Gaza and its policy in Iraq.

winning a seat.[34] Mukul Hira, the Respect candidate, got a respectable vote of 781 in St Pancras & Somers Town which, although some 400 behind Anna Stewart, was still seen as significant because his vote was thought to come overwhelmingly from Bengalis who would otherwise have voted Labour.[35]

Fearful perhaps of any organised public opposition such as every other Camden administration had had to put up with, Keith Moffitt, now the leader of the party with the most seats on the council, offered the Labour and Conservative groups a power sharing deal whereby everyone would be in power and there would be no one on the outside to criticise them (unless one could count on the two new wholly inexperienced Green Party councillors in Highgate to be the official opposition). All bickering could take place behind closed doors. Unsurprisingly, the new Labour group leader, Anna Stewart, declined the offer, and the Conservatives refused to be in any administration that included Labour members. Andrew Marshall, now the leader of the Conservative group, entered into negotiations with Moffitt to agree a four year deal in which the executive positions on the council would be shared between the two parties, while the council would have a LibDem leader (Keith Moffitt) and a Conservative deputy leader (Andrew Marshall)[36]. For the first time since 1971, Labour councillors were sitting on the opposition benches.

---

34 Sîan Berry stood as the Green Party candidate in the 2008 London mayoral election.

35 In 2008 Mukul Hira defected to the LibDems who, in Omar Faruque Ansari, then had a Bengali councillor of their own. The move underscored the delicacy of Labour's Bengali block vote. Not to worry, said Nasim Ali hopefully: "The Bengali communities in the south have always been supportive of Labour because they know what we have done for them".

36 Marshall did rather well on this: of the executive posts the Conservatives took environment, adult social care & health, education, and community development, as well as the chairmanship of development control. The negotiations had, said Moira Gibb, become "a rout".

STATE OF THE PARTIES
1964 – 2006

	CON	LAB	LD	GRE	TOTAL
1964	26 (+2)	34 (+8)	–	–	**60 (+10)**
1968	42 (+5)	18 (+5)	–	–	**60 (+10)**
1971	11 (+5)	49 (+5)	–	–	**60 (+10)**
1974	12	48 (+10)	–	–	**60 (+10)**
1978	26	33	–	–	**59**
1982	26	33	–	–	**59**
1986	13	44	2	–	**59**
1990	15	42	2	–	**59**
1994	7	47	5	–	**59**
1998	10	43	6	–	**59**
2002	11	35	8	–	**54**
2006	14	20	18	2	**54**

(Aldermen in brackets)

BOROUGH ELECTION RESULTS
1964 – 2006

7 MAY 1964

ADELAIDE

Madeleine du Mont	CON	2152
Richard Butterfield	CON	2134
Julian Tobin	CON	2131
Howard Sugden	CON	2123
William Page	LAB	1399
Margaret Maxwell	LAB	1398
Michael Read	LAB	1384
Thomas Sargant	LAB	1329
Richard Michael Norton	LIB	375
Graham Knight	LIB	364
Nigel Seymer	LIB	362
Barbara Bridger	LIB	349
Ernest Woods	COMM	152

BELSIZE

Norman Oatway	CON	2045
Stanley Duncan	CON	2028
Alexandrina Burnett	CON	2015
Leslie Room	CON	2009
Lyndal Evans	LAB	1651
Sheila Oakes	LAB	1649
Bernard Taylor	LAB	1616
Arthur Soutter	LAB	1585
Margaret Darvall	LIB	585
Percy Brian Anderson	LIB	575
Doris Watson	LIB	564
Timothy Webb	COMM	146

BLOOMSBURY

Harold Gould	CON	1390
William Ridd	CON	1386
Sidney Jaque	CON	1383
Gyuri Wagner	LAB	1118
Frank Dobson	LAB	1110
Irene Wagner	LAB	1097

CAMDEN

Tom Barker	LAB	2279
James Buckland	LAB	2267
Peggy Duff	LAB	2203
Peter Jonas	LAB	2154
Beatrice Bundock	CON	799
Frederick Hayward	CON	738
Elizabeth Love	CON	736
Amy Kinder	CON	721
Joyce Arram	LIB	252
Jock Nicolson	COMM	238
Jessie Fleming	LIB	233
Anne Roberts	LIB	198
Dorothy Willett	LIB	198
Margaret Rockall	COMM	151

CHALK FARM

Hilda Chandler	LAB	1082
Joseph Richardson	LAB	1055
Anthony Boosey	CON	775
Patricia Hayward	CON	771
Walter Rees	COMM	108

EUSTON

Millie Miller	LAB	738
Peter Best	LAB	730
Edward Bowman	CON	677
Horace Shooter	CON	649

GOSPEL OAK

Alexander Sullivan	LAB	1257
Charles Tate	LAB	1212
Anthony Dey	CON	560
Denis Friis	CON	557
Kenneth Herbert	COMM	130

GRAFTON

Charles Ratchford	LAB	2777

Albert "Jock" Stallard	LAB	2685
Roy Shaw	LAB	2671
Derick Annison	LAB	2621
Daphne Green	CON	710
Christina Brennan	CON	625
Esther Purves	CON	621
George Paulley	CON	604
Donald Cook	COMM	323
Harry Jackson	COMM	257

HAMPSTEAD CENTRAL

William Evans	CON	1596
Sidney Torrance	CON	1594
Geoffrey Finsberg	CON	1577
Nancy Silverman	LAB	928
Henry Totten	LAB	911
Philip Turner	LAB	872
Michael Watson	LIB	382
Mary Baring	LIB	380
David Sacke	LIB	374

HAMPSTEAD TOWN

Elizabeth Knight	CON	1961
Arthur Roome	CON	1955
Luigi Denza	CON	1947
Joan Hymans	LAB	1146
Thomas Mahoney	LAB	1127
Janek Langer	LAB	1121
Pamela Frankau	LIB	694
Sarah (Peggy) Khuner	LIB	668
Archibald MacDonald	LIB	656

HIGHGATE

Martin Morton	CON	2067
William Brennan	CON	2062
Roland Walker	CON	2054
Corin Hughes-Stanton	LAB	1465
Richard Andrews	LAB	1440
Ivy Tate	LAB	1380
Walter Davis	COMM	276

HOLBORN

Albert Shaw	CON	2063
Alan Greengross	CON	2060
John Barker	CON	2040
Iris Bonham	LAB	1662

Betty Grass	LAB	1642
Ruth Howe	LAB	1613
James Hamilton	LIB	188
Joan (Ursula) Morris	LIB	174
Yvonne Carey-Taylor	LIB	162

KING'S CROSS

Clifford Tucker	LAB	1876
John Diamond	LAB	1857
Arthur Graves	LAB	1810
Joyce Burgess	CON	1523
William McGowan	CON	1492
Thomas Morris	CON	1473

KILBURN

Victor Bonafont	LAB	1813
A E "Tim" Skinner	LAB	1768
Robert Humphreys	LAB	1763
Angus Macdonald	CON	653
Pamela King	CON	644
Winifred Peard	CON	633
Nigel Barnes	LIB	171
Gwendoline Martin	LIB	165
Ronald Sampson	LIB	164
Estella McEntire	COMM	71

PRIORY

Leila Campbell	LAB	2147
Jack Cooper	LAB	2116
John St. John	LAB	2098
Enid Wistrich	LAB	2011
Irene Ellis	CON	1557
Anthony Pickford	CON	1557
Joan Durnsford	CON	1553
Charles Power	CON	1545
Arthur Stitt	LIB	322
Mary De la Mahotiere	LIB	319
David Harris	LIB	319
Bonamy Bradby	LIB	301
Frederick Hill	COMM	159

REGENT'S PARK

Richard Collins	LAB	2299
James Greenwood	LAB	2298
Grace Lee	LAB	2260
Harold Bright	CON	1319

344

Keith Chalkley	CON	1316
Margaret Saville	CON	1300
Colin Boatman	COMM	189

BY ELECTIONS
1964-68

ST JOHN'S

Roger Robinson	LAB	1601
Gillian Macfarlane	LAB	1554
Richard Rowe	LAB	1538
George Hathway	CON	605
Betty Gall	CON	592
Ann Smith	CON	590
Peter Richards	COMM	188

ST PANCRAS

William Oakshott	LAB	2113
L P "Paddy" O'Connor	LAB	2111
Sidney Munn	LAB	2081
Samuel Fisher	LAB	2076
John Glendinning	CON	495
Eileen Wright	CON	476
Henry Salter	CON	475
Josephine Robins	CON	473
Thomas Linehan	IND LAB	291
Margaret Munro	IND LAB	224
Malcolm Davies	IND	184
John Mandeville	IND	154

WEST END

Victor Lyon	CON	1686
Lindsay Cullen	CON	1684
Susan Ayliff	CON	1651
Grace Stevenson	LAB	1536
Michael Cendrowicz	LAB	1494
Ernest Wistrich	LAB	1482
Robert Druiff	LIB	372
Felix Craft	LIB	372
Eric Abrahams	LIB	351
Terrance Thomas	COMM	125

GOSPEL OAK
1 Dec 1966
(Resignation of Alexander Sullivan LAB)

Hamish McGibbon	LAB	746
Denis Friis	CON	728
Fred Cook	LIB	99
Ken Herbert	COMM	71

ST JOHN'S
1 Dec 1966
(Resignation of Richard Rowe LAB)

Corin Hughes Stanton	LAB	711
David Theophilus	CON	433
Joyce Arram	LIB	73
Winston Pinder	COMM	53

ST PANCRAS
1 Dec 1966
(Death of Sidney Munn LAB)

Wendy Mantle	LAB	977
Kenneth Avery	CON	392
Dave Guppy	COMM	52

CHALK FARM
14 Dec 1967
(Resignation of Hilda Chandler LAB)

Peter Moloney	CON	823
Ed Rhodes	LAB	688
Guy Rayne-Savage	LIB	149

9 MAY 1968

ADELAIDE

Julian Tobin	CON	2470
Brenda Degerdon	CON	2434
Madeleine Dumont	CON	2426
Frederick Tuckman	CON	2400
Janet Whitaker	LAB	1120
Sheila Oakes	LAB	1035
Thomas Burrows	LAB	990

345

APPENDIX II

Mark Bass	LAB	976
Bernard Cohen	LIB	391
Douglas Close	LIB	357
Jonathan Flatman	LIB	337
Philip Hemelryk	LIB	334
Jack Glaster	COMM	197

BELSIZE

Kenneth Evans	CON	2355
Irene Burnett	CON	2346
Norman Oatway	CON	2345
Julian Harrison	CON	2328
Edwin Lichtenstein	LAB	1330
Joseph Hughes	LAB	1322
William Kellock	LAB	1308
Arthur Soutter	LAB	1279
Tristram Adams	LIB	488
Margaret Darvall	LIB	472
Angela Whitelegge	LIB	448
Gerald Dowden	LIB	445

BLOOMSBURY

Harold Gould	CON	1440
Sidney Jaque	CON	1440
Colin Jaque	CON	1439
David Carlton	LAB	530
Keith Morrell	LAB	522
Eileen O'Connor	LAB	522

CAMDEN

James Buckland	LAB	1616
Philip Hughes	LAB	1613
Ivor Walker	LAB	1550
Leslie Langford	LAB	1518
Peter Plouviez	CON	1513
Anthony Mayer	CON	1434
Olive Staples	CON	1417
Monia Rynderman	CON	1404
Jock Nicolson	COMM	266
Frederick Britt	Ind	155

CHALK FARM

Peter Moloney	CON	1109
George Radford	CON	1019
Edwin Rhodes	LAB	818
John Sell	LAB	748
Guy Rayne-Savage	LIB	207

EUSTON

Nigel Burton	CON	660
Horace Shooter	CON	638
Christopher Kiddy	LAB	539
Richard Madeley	LAB	530
Roger Brooke	LIB	147

GOSPEL OAK

Malcolm Heath	CON	888
Charles Tate	LAB	861
John Keohane	LAB	837
James Surrey	CON	820
Alfred Cook	LIB	199

GRAFTON

Charles Ratchford	LAB	1574
Joseph Richardson	LAB	1483
Roy Shaw	LAB	1462
Albert ("Jock") Stallard	LAB	1411
Brian Somerville	CON	1200
Michael Gromm	CON	1192
Miss Muriel Hanscomb	CON	1189
Mrs Elizabeth Ray	CON	1169
Victor Heath	COMM	200

HAMPSTEAD CENTRAL

Geoffrey Finsberg	CON	1965
Sidney Torrance	CON	1937
Cdr Ronald King	CON	1909
Peter Stephenson	LAB	764
Barry Peskin	LAB	740
James Hill	LAB	724
Kenneth Carter	LIB	344
Alison Snow	LIB	343
Jillian Vasey	LIB	328

HAMPSTEAD TOWN

Elizabeth Knight	CON	2191
Arthur Roome	CON	2162
Peter Smith	CON	2119
Anthony Clarke	LAB	987
Jennifer Keohane	LAB	958
Phyllis Hymans	LAB	946
Arcibald MacDonald	LIB	587
George Willett	LIB	532
Sarah Khuner	LIB	491
Betty Tate	COMM	200

BOROUGH ELECTION RESULTS
1964 – 2006

HIGHGATE

The Hon Peter Brooke	CON	2185
Roland Walker	CON	2165
Denis Friis	CON	2119
Peter Jonas	LAB	1275
John Palmer	LAB	1274
Florence Freeman	LAB	1272
Joyce Arram	LIB	216
Richard Franklin	LIB	207
Winston Pinder	COMM	174

HOLBORN

Kenneth Avery	CON	2096
John Barker	CON	2094
Alan Greengross	CON	2071
Patricia Carlton	LAB	728
Betty Grass	LAB	706
Margaret Davis	LAB	705

KILBURN

Robert Humphreys	LAB	1420
Albert "Tim" Skinner	LAB	1388
Edwin "Johnny" Johnson	LAB	1373
Kenneth Graham	CON	1245
Harriet Greenaway	CON	1238
James Lemkin	CON	1210
Colin Brown	LIB	166
Bickram Bhose	LIB	158
Dawson France	LIB	147
Stella McEntire	COMM	103

KING'S CROSS

John "Jack" Glendinning	CON	1689
Ian Clarke	CON	1680
Thomas Morris	CON	1672
Beverley Rowe	LAB	1106
John Diamond	LAB	1096
Louis Bondy	LAB	1083

PRIORY

Irene Ellis	CON	2005
Phillippa Raymond-Cox	CON	2003
Ronald Raymond-Cox	CON	1994
Peter Hilton	CON	1972
Jack Cooper	LAB	1838
Leila Campbell	LAB	1827

John St. John	LAB	1774
Enid Wistrich	LAB	1689
David Quirke	LIB	417
Kenneth Whittle	LIB	411
Robert Pellegrinetti	LIB	405
Peter Rowntree	LIB	391
Mrs Barbara Champion	COMM	228

REGENT'S PARK

Ernest Lee	CON	1696
Dorothy Day	CON	1681
Christopher Turner	CON	1670
Richard Collins	LAB	1523
James Greenwood	LAB	1489
John Mills	LAB	1433
Raymond Shenton	Nat Lib Front	231
Aileen Boatman	COMM	176

ST JOHN'S

Roger Robinson	LAB	1367
Corin Hughes-Stanton	LAB	1248
Ruth Howe	LAB	1217
Anthony Blackburn	CON	1038
Martin Piper	CON	999
Richard Smith	CON	983

ST PANCRAS

L P "Paddy" O'Connor	LAB	1327
Sir Samuel Fisher	LAB	1318
Peter Best	LAB	1304
William Oakshott	LAB	1293
Anthony Crofts	CON	764
Angus McWillson	CON	752
Robert Medcraft	CON	747
Malcolm S Deacon	CON	743
Mrs Jean Morgan	LIB	180
Ray Benad	LIB	169
David Guppy	COMM	119

WEST END

Victor Lyon	CON	1939
Miss Susan Ayliff	CON	1935
Miss C Stewart-Munro	CON	1897
Philip Turner	LAB	957
Michael Cendrowicz	LAB	955
Grace Stevenson	LAB	948

347

Nigel Barnes	LIB	286
Dorothy Willett	LIB	266
Hans Khuner	LIB	232

BY ELECTIONS 1968 – 1971

KILBURN
5 Dec 1968
(Death of Jonny Johnson LAB)

David Offenbach	LAB	1047
Harriet Greenaway	CON	834
Kenneth Whittle	LIB	145

HIGHGATE
4 Dec 1969
(Resignation of Peter Brooke CON)

Harriet Greenaway	CON	1426
John Needham	LAB	1027
Jock Nicolson	COMM	81

HOLBORN
12 March 1970
(Resignation of Alan Greengross CON)

Betty Grass	LAB	946
Anthony Mayer	CON	781

13 May 1971

ADELAIDE

Julian Tobin	CON AM*	2090
Brenda Hennessey	CON AM	2087
Madeleine Du Mont	CON	2068
Huntly Spence	CON	2031
Nicholas Bosanquet	LAB	1981
Mark Bass	LAB	1950
Nora Henry	LAB	1931
Barry Phillips	LAB	1917
Phillip Hemelryk	LIB	427
Gillian Latimer	LIB	244
Sheila Williams	LIB	241
Norman Latimer	LIB	226

*"Conservative Anti-Motorway"

BELSIZE

Jill Gibson	LAB	2225
John Lipetz	LAB	2132
Bernard Taylor	LAB	2130
Irving Kuczynski	LAB	2128
Norman Oatway	CON	1955
Irene Burnett	CON	1943
Julian Harrison	CON	1923
Peter Hilton	CON	1885
Margaret Darvall	LIB	352
Mary De La Mahotiere	LIB	313
Graham Bevan	COMM	292
John Swain	LIB	282
John Davies	Ass Ind	92
Anthony Cunnew	Ass Ind	74
Mary Davies	Ass Ind	60

BLOOMSBURY

Jennifer Horne	LAB	1383
Richard Arthur	LAB	1377
Florence Parnell	LAB	1345
Ian Galbraith	CON	1105
Colin Jaque	CON	1077
Horace Shooter	CON	1069

CAMDEN

James Buckland	LAB	2971
Ivor Walker	LAB	2913
George Trevelyan	LAB	2909
Philip Turner	LAB	2864
Leslie Langford	CON	970
Michael Flynn	CON	959
Philp Brandt	CON	942
G P Sutherland	CON	919
Ann Sedley	CON	362

CHALK FARM

Peter Jonas	LAB	1171
Derek Jarman	LAB	1154
George Radford	CON	884
Robert Targett	CON	800

GOSPEL OAK

John Keohane	LAB	1137
Brian Loughran	LAB	1112

348

Kenneth Graham	CON	475	Francis Rochford	LAB	2204
John Macdonald	CON	471	Martin Guiness	CON	882
Ken Herbert	COMM	90	Anthony Wright	CON	870
			Ian Tomisson	CON	868

GRAFTON

			John Gibbs	LIB	131
Millie Miller	LAB	2923	Colin Brown	LIB	122
John Needham	LAB	2900	Violet Green	LIB	119
Roy Shaw	LAB	2830	Stella McEntire	COMM	82
Barry Peskin	LAB	2830			
George Paulley	CON	628	**KING'S CROSS**		
Mary Quilliam	CON	611	Lyndal Evans	LAB	2080
Anthony Boosey	CON	599	Joseph Jacobs	LAB	2057
Malcolm Heath	CON	595	Michael Cendrowicz	LAB	2034
Vic Heath	COMM	287	David Offenbach	LAB	2032
			Ian Clarke	CON	1494

HAMPSTEAD TOWN

			Jack Glendinning	CON	1481
James Lemkin	CON	2073	Edith Martin	CON	1466
Archie MacDonald	CON	2071	Joy Burgess	CON	1436
Harriet Greenaway	CON	2064			
Arthur Roome	CON	1996	**PRIORY**		
Alix Maxwell	LAB	1574	Anthony Clarke	LAB	2170
Roger Robinson	LAB	1537	Glyn Thomas	LAB	2085
Edwin Rhodes	LAB	1511	Enid Wistrich	LAB	2067
Keith Atkins	LAB	1501	Irene Ellis	CON	1019
David Sacker	LAB	360	Ronald Raymond-Cox	CON	1016
Bonamy Bradby	LAB	337	Brian Hutchins	CON	1007
Betty Tate	COMM	258	Keith Ebbutt	COMM	131

HIGHGATE

REGENT'S PARK

Roland Walker	CON	1735	Richard Collins	LAB	2766
John Carrier	LAB	1724	L P ("Paddy") O'Connor	LAB	2688
Christopher Fenwick	CON	1715	John Mills	LAB	2667
Denis Friis	CON	1711	John Thane	LAB	2605
Jeanne Cox	LAB	1703	Ernest Lee	CON	1311
Bernard Miller	LAB	1656	Peter Briggs	CON	1309
Jean Davis	COMM	262	Roger Gale	CON	1298
			Marcelle Simpson	CON	1294

HOLBORN

Clive Robinson	LAB	1559	**ST JOHN'S**		
Frank Dobson	LAB	1554	Corin Hughes-Stanton	LAB	1761
John Barker	CON	949	John Palmer	LAB	1743
Kenneth Avery	CON	923	Geoffrey Bindman	LAB	1695
			Alan Smith	CON	583
KILBURN			Peter Bennett	CON	575
Albert ("Tim") Skinner	LAB	2263	Joan Couzens	CON	560
Robert Humphreys	LAB	2241			

349

ST PANCRAS

Brian Duggan	LAB	2357
Peter Best	LAB	2342
William Oakshott	LAB	2312
Eric Bland	CON	310
Carol Favell	CON	272
Malcolm Watts	CON	266

SWISS COTTAGE

Tessa Jowell	LAB	2026
John Eidinow	LAB	2018
Arthur Soutter	LAB	1974
Ernest Wistrich	LAB & Co-op	1893
Cdr Ronald King	CON	1804
Phillippa Raymond-Cox	CON	1792
Christine Stewart-Munro	CON	1787
Sidney Torrance	CON	1780
Kay Peacock	LIB	317
Ray Benad	LIB	298

WEST END

Geoffrey Finsberg	CON	1941
Brian Arnold	LAB	1914
Joan Hymans	LAB & Co-op	1888
Derek Pollard	LAB	1880
Edwin Lichtenstein	LAB	1878
Susan Ayliff	CON	1852
Christopher Turner	CON	1841
Gwyneth Williams	CON	1833

BY ELECTIONS 1971-1974

SWISS COTTAGE
2 March 1972

(Resignation of John Eidenow LAB)

Neil McIntosh	LAB	1576
Ron King	CON	1481
Ray Benad	LIB	267

GOSPEL OAK
15 June 1972

(Death of John Keohane LAB)

Edwin Rhodes	LAB	920
Denis Friis	CON	381
Ken Herbert	COMM	45
David English	NF	39

GRAFTON
7 June 1973

(Resignation of John Needham LAB)

Christopher Gardiner	LAB	1413
George Radford	CON	415
Sidney Rawle Community Action		140
Vic Heath	COMM	72

2 MAY 1974

ADELAIDE

Julian Tobin	CON	2134
Madeleine Du Mont	CON	2101
Huntly Spence	CON	2080
Donald Degerdon	CON	2073
John Palmer	LAB	1911
Stephen Mullin	LAB	1908
Allan Mathias	LAB	1906
Miles Seaman	LAB	1865
Margot Aptaker	LIB	417
John Raine	LIB	412
Geoffrey McKeenan	LIB	394
Phillip Hemelryk	LIB	385

BELSIZE

Richard Arthur	LAB	2010
David Mills	LAB	1951
Richard Ford	LAB	1915
Bernard Taylor	LAB	1898
Julian Harrison	CON	1847
Arthur Roome	CON	1815
Timothy Coghlan	CON	1801
Peter Grosz	CON	1773
Margaret Darvall	LIB	539
Richard Franklin	LIB	465
Hubert Bevan	COMM	264

BLOOMSBURY

John Guy	LAB	1164
William Evans	LAB	1154

350

John Thane	LAB	1139	Alexandra Lawrie	LIB	178
Mark Batchelor	CON	892	Peter Dee	LIB	152
Colin Jaque	CON	853	Victor Heath	LIB	143
Horace Shooter	CON	839	Phillip Blackwell	LIB	133

CAMDEN

HAMPSTEAD TOWN

Nicholas Bosanquet	LAB	1892	Archibald MacDonald	CON	1980
James Buckland	LAB	1859	Alan Greengross	CON	1956
Philip Turner	LAB	1761	Gwyneth Williams	CON	1924
Ivor Walker	LAB	1728	John Ratzer	CON	1902
David Coleman	CON	612	John Darlington	LAB	1141
Anthony Boosey	CON	609	Lord George Archibald	LAB	1137
Ian King	CON	592	James Parish	LAB	1132
George Paulley	CON	558	John Rigby	LAB	1087
Mary Taylor	LIB	288	Sarah Khuner	LIB	557
Alan Mather	LIB	284	Nicholas Salmon	LIB	548
June Mather	LIB	276	Marion Friedman	LIB	523
Daphne Morgan	LIB	271	Raymond Benad	LIB	494
Stephen Sedley	COMM	215	Betty Tate	COMM	152
Marjorie Mayo	COMM	203	Andrew Urquhart	SLAG	73
			Charles Carey	SLAG	57

CHALK FARM

			Robert Fysh	SLAG	53
Jonathan Sofer	LAB	1013			
Derek Jarman	LAB	1010	**HIGHGATE**		
Peter Brooke	CON	642	John Carrier	LAB	1607
Phillippa Raymond-Cox	CON	631	Mrs J D Cox	LAB	1462
Eric Watson	LIB	182	A J Crouch	LAB	1380
Peter Knowles	LIB	177	Martin Morton	CON	1369
			Christopher Fenwick	CON	1319

GOSPEL OAK

			Roland Walker	CON	1306
Tessa Jowell	LAB	1072	Clive Coates	LIB	423
Brian Loughran	LAB	1033	Alfred Cook	LIB	395
Denis Friis	CON	376	Peter Richards	COMM	210
Robert Targett	CON	347			
Henry Martin	COMM	75	**HOLBORN**		
			Frank Dobson	LAB	1375

GRAFTON

			Derek Godfrey	LAB	1323
Christopher Gardiner	LAB	2112	Ralph Stone	CON	550
Roy Shaw	LAB	2015	Peter Bruinvels	CON	546
Neil McIntosh	LAB	1995	Peter Davison	LIB	218
John Lipetz	LAB	1920	Mairi Turner	LIB	176
George Radford	CON	483			
Joanna Radford	CON	446			
Sally Mustoe	CON	442	**KILBURN**		
Brenda Friis	CON	440	Albert ("Tim") Skinner	LAB	1432
Sidney Rawle	NCA	320	Francis Rochford	LAB	1423

Robert Humphreys	LAB	1384
Peter Briggs	CON	664
George Maxwell	CON	652
Ronald Rees	CON	638
John Standish	LIB	252
Dennis Darnes	LIB	229
Gillian Little	LIB	217

KING'S CROSS

David Offenbach	LAB	1745
David Windsor	LAB	1730
Margaret Robertson	LAB	1721
Lyndal Evans	LAB	1698
John Glendinning	CON	1193
Graham Hirschfield	CON	1110
Kenneth Avery	CON	1108
Kenneth Graham	CON	1089
John Bishop	LIB	431
Anthony Connell	LIB	405
Raymond Marks	LIB	363
Margaret MacLaren	LIB	360

PRIORY

Anthony Clarke	LAB	1846
Derek Pollard	LAB	1604
Glyn Thomas	LAB	1451
Frederick Kingsley	CON	806
Colin Mackay	CON	752
Anthony van der Elst	CON	707
Iain Scarlet	LIB	385
Alan Thomas	COMM	225
Ronald Champion	COMM	115

REGENT'S PARK

Richard Collins	LAB	2053
Anthony Bethell	LAB	1986
L P "Paddy" O'Connor	LAB	1975
John Mills	LAB	1974
Clare Mansel	CON	1085
Malcolm Watts	CON	1054
John Blundell	CON	1052
Michael Flynn	CON	1038

ST JOHN'S

Roger Robinson	LAB	1488
Corin Hughes-Stanton	LAB	1473
Sarah ("Sally") Peltier	LAB	1438

John Livingston	CON	379
Dennis Murfitt	CON	376
Christina Brennan	CON	368
Florence Elliot	LIB	167
Christopher Evans	LIB	165
Micheline Sartoretti	LIB	133

ST PANCRAS

Brian Duggan	LAB	1865
Florence Parnell	LAB	1739
John Toomey	LAB	1729
Jaqueline Wilson	CON	306
Ian Clarke	CON	305
Christopher Turner	CON	294

SWISS COTTAGE

Ron King	CON	1636
Ronald Raymond-Cox	CON	1625
Anthony Kerpel	CON	1616
Brian Stoner	CON	1559
William Budd	LAB	1535
Walter Burgess	LAB	1533
Arthur Soutter	LAB	1508
Gurmukh Singh	LAB	1465
Kenneth Carter	LIB	412
Robert Pellegrinetti	LIB	369

WEST END

David Blake	LAB	1858
Samuel Waldman	LAB	1842
Robert Hefferman	LAB	1784
Joan Hymans	LAB	1777
Ian Tomisson	CON	1762
John Steel	CON	1759
Peter Clemerson	CON	1725
James Turner	CON	1723
Kathleen Peacock	LIB	447
Claudina Eastwall-Naijna	Ind	86

BY ELECTIONS 1974-1978

BELSIZE
25 March 1976
(Resignation of Richard Arthur LAB)

Martin Morton	CON	2196
David Walker	LAB	1455
Mary De La Mahotiere	LIB	251

GOSPEL OAK
25 March 1976
(Resignation of Brian Loughran LAB)

Richard Turner	LAB	841
Peter Barber	CON	570
Kenneth Herbert	COMM	69
June Mather	LIB	62
Louis Koolman-Darnley	NF	49
Brian Manning	IND	4

HAMPSTEAD TOWN
15 July 1976
(Resignation of Archie MacDonald CON)

Stephen Rowlinson	CON	1743
James Parish	LAB	548
Nigel Barnes	LIB	376

HOLBORN
27 Jan 1977
(Resignation of Frank Dobson LAB)

Kenneth Avery	CON	885
David Walker	LAB	802

ST PANCRAS
27 Jan 1977
(Resignation of John Toomey LAB)

Thomas Devine	LAB	1118
Laurence Atlas	CON	514

SWISS COTTAGE
20 OCT 1977
(Resignation Ronald Raymond-Cox CON)

Michael Brahams	CON	1682
Anna Bowman	LAB	1081
Andrew Bridgwater	LIB	189
Gwendoline Evans	NF	68

4 MAY 1978

ADELAIDE

Julian Tobin	CON	1825
Donald Degerdon	CON	1793
Graham Hirschfield	CON	1749

Peter Gresham	LAB	1223
Nova Gresham	LAB	1208
Nirmal Roy	LAB	1133
Jaqueline Kelly	LIB	224
Nicholas Collins	LIB	204
Kwamina Sackey	LIB	169

BELSIZE

Anthony Beaton	CON	1712
Anthony Kerpel	CON	1667
Michael Brahams	CON	1641
Roy Mathias	LAB	981
Arthur Soutter	LAB	979
Verghese Varkki	LAB	924
Anne Box	LIB	306
Hilary Hawkins	LIB	275

BLOOMSBURY

Martin McNeill	LAB	1494
David Harris	CON	1399
John Thane	LAB	1385
Glyn Thomas	LAB	1373
Christopher Radmore	CON	1355
David Stone	CON	1310

BRUNSWICK

Kenneth Avery	CON	1131
André Potier	CON	1017
Ricardo de Freitas	LAB	1015
David Offenbach	LAB	966

CAMDEN

Anne Robertson	LAB	852
Ivor Walker	LAB	775
David Coleman	CON	496
Ronald Sears	CON	440
John Philpot	NF	59
Esther Sizer	NF	54

CASTLEHAVEN

John Tysoe	LAB	1,000
John Lipetz	LAB	996
Thomas Crawford	CON	439
Denis Friis	CON	406
Gordon Callow	NF	76
Malcolm Keith	NF	66

353

CAVERSHAM

Nicholas Boanquet	LAB	1289
Philip Turner	LAB	1120
Lilian O'Callaghan	CON	721
Morag Valentine	CON	718
Michael Harkins	NF	117
Bernard Robinson	NF	108
Elizabeth Harrison	COMM	100

CHALK FARM

Jonathan Sofer	LAB	1336
Derek Jarman	LAB	1223
Anthony Blackburn	CON	1089
Peter White	CON	1013

FITZJOHNS

Ronald King	CON	994
John Athisayam	CON	920
John St John	LAB	485
Peter David	LAB	477
Olive Paynton	LIB	193

FORTUNE GREEN

Richard Almond	CON	1055
John Steel	CON	1010
Haydn Gott	LAB	852
Robert Hale	LAB	788
Clive Agran	LIB	203
Bryan Karet	LIB	180
Paul Kavanagh	NF	37
Carol Warren	NF	31

FROGNAL

Alan Greengross	CON	1363
Julian Harrison	CON	1319
Alan Yates	LAB	481
Richard Wigley	LAB	453
Brian Sugden	LIB	258

GOSPEL OAK

Ronald Hefferman	LAB	1125
Tessa Jowell	LAB	1059
Peter Barber	CON	546
Anthony Earl-Williams	CON	523
Kenneth Herbert	COMM	102

GRAFTON

Christopher Gardiner	LAB	1058
Roy Shaw	LAB	1049
David Roberts	CON	455
John Martin	CON	454
Linda Evans	NF	71
Ian Tomkins	NF	56
Granville Jones	WRP	37

HAMPSTEAD TOWN

Ian Tomisson	CON	1251
Gwyneth Williams	CON	1234
Philip Greenall	LAB	647
David Bookless	LAB	628
Nigel Barnes	LIB	297
Anthony Diamond	SLA	61

HIGHGATE

Martin Morton	CON	2026
Roger James	CON	1981
Derek Spencer	CON	1966
Walter Burgess	LAB	1809
David Webster	LAB	1787
Albert Crouch	LAB	1774
Margaret Lee	COMM	194

HOLBORN

Derek Godfrey	LAB	1234
Julian Fulbrook	LAB	1224
Edith Martin	CON	1080
Brian Rathbone	CON	1080

KILBURN

Patrick Driscoll	LAB	1242
Neil Fletcher	LAB	1214
Kenneth Livingstone	LAB	1198
Peter Bolton	CON	999
Ann McMullen	CON	983
Ronald Rees	CON	980
Francis Rochford	Ind LAB	496
Albert ("Tim") Skinner	Ind LAB	442
Richard Waddington	LIB	155
John Billouin	LIB	141
Catherine Wilson	LIB	128

KING'S CROSS

Anthony Craig	LAB	840
Roderick Cordara	LAB	812
John Glendinning	CON	777

Aileen Griffin	CON	758
Patricia Langton	COMM	48
Margaret Obank	WRP	40

PRIORY

William Budd	LAB	1211
Anna Bowman	LAB	1184
Iain Horsburgh	CON	903
Richard Smith	CON	902
Patrick Cooney	LIB	91
Alastair Seaton	LIB	80
Alan Thomas	COMM	51

REGENT'S PARK

John Mills	LAB	1714
Florence Parnell	LAB	1699
Andrew Bethell	LAB	1685
Laurence Atlas	CON	1551
Ian Pasley-Tyler	CON	1522
Catherine Mallison	CON	1510
Sydney Daly	NF	145
Gwendoline Evans	NF	129
Martin Moloney	NF	127

ST JOHN'S

Sally Peltier	LAB	1187
Maureen Robinson	LAB	1170
Paul Brandt	CON	546
Roland Walker	CON	536

ST PANCRAS

Michael Morrissey	LAB	1024
Joan Hymans	LAB	1005
Anthony Cheverton	CON	386
Catherine O'Sullivan	CON	362
John Haines	NF	79
John Warren	NF	61
Jeffrey Sawtell	COMM	39

SOMERS TOWN

Brian Duggan	LAB	1095
Thomas Devine	LAB	1093
Jaqueline Austin	CON	443
Noel Moncaster	CON	399
Andrew Cordier	NF	73
Andrew Kimber	NF	59

SOUTH END

Anthony Kemp	CON	1107
Anthony Robinson	CON	1081
Michael Boye-Anawomah	LAB	1007
John Chanin	LAB	969
Robert Pellegrinetti	LIB	215
Hubert Bevan	COMM	98

SWISS COTTAGE

David Osborne	CON	1648
Michael Flynn	CON	1633
Brian Stoner	CON	1602
Christopher Heginbotham	LAB	1353
Enyd Norman	LAB	1326
Denis Macshane	LAB	1274
Andrew Bridgwater	LIB	297
Jillian Newbrook	LIB	292
Janet Heller	LIB	291

WEST END

Neil Bourhill	CON	953
Kevin Gould	LAB	938
Cathleen Mainds	CON	911
Sandra Wynn	LAB	896
Ida Linfield	LIB	215
Martin Biermann	LIB	209

BY ELECTIONS
1978 – 1982

ADELAIDE
3 May 1979
(Death of Donald Degerdon CON)

Ian Pasley-Tyler	CON	2298
Michael Kirk	LAB	1635
Andrew Bridgwater	LIB	596

SWISS COTTAGE
3 May 1979
(Resignation of Brian Stoner CON)

Ronald Rees	CON	2282
Enyd Norman	LAB	1885
Roger Billins	LIB	719

355

BELSIZE
17 April 1980

(Resignation of Anthony Beaton CON)

Cathleen Mainds	CON	1235
Allen Mathias	LAB	785
Andrew Bridgwater	LIB	288

FORTUNE GREEN
17 April 1980

(Resignation of Richard Almond CON)

Richard Rowson	CON	743
Christine Chapman	LAB	632
Felicity Rea	LIB	514

ST PANCRAS
17 April 1980

(Resignation of Michael Morrissey LAB)

Jennifer Willmot	LAB	826
Anthony Earl-Williams	CON	321

GRAFTON
30 OCT 1980

(Resignation of Christopher Gardiner LAB)

William Birtles	LAB	976
Michael Farrer	CON	328

CHALK FARM
27 Nov 1980

(Resignation of Jonathan Sofer LAB)

Hugh Bayley	LAB	914
Anthony Blackburn	CON	854
Sieska Cowdrey	LIB	121

KING'S CROSS
7 May 1981

(Resignation of Roderick Cordara LAB)

Barbara Hughes	LAB	813
Derek Lowe	CON	573
Thomas Hibbert	LIB	320

WEST END
7 May 1981

(Resignation of Kevin Gould LAB)

Sandra Wynn	LAB	917
Michael Farrer	CON	729
Ida Linfield	LIB	678

6 MAY 1982

ADELAIDE

Julian Tobin	CON	1503
Michael Brahams	CON	1500
Ian Pasley-Tyler	CON	1495
David Lewis	LAB	824
Hilary Lowe	LAB	822
Jennifer Pitkin	LAB	803
Diane Bailey	SDPLIB	583
Alan Evans	SDPLIB	552
Nicholas Collins	LIBSDP	551

BELSIZE

Tony Kerpel	CON	1411
Huntly Spence	CON	1381
Gerald Swyer	CON	1335
Margaret Little	SDPLIB	761
Robert Heyland	SDPLIB	751
Clive Agran	LIBSDP	730
Alan Griffiths	LAB	703
Anthea Muir	LAB	678
Roy Mathias	LAB	670
Lesley Sargent	Ecology	102
Steven Margolis	Ecology	85

BLOOMSBURY

William Trite	CON	1086
Andrew Gordon-Saker	CON	1085
Brian Rathbone	CON	1062
Martin McNeill	LAB	994
Anne Robertson	LAB	969
Michael Broughton	LAB	967
Peter Symonds	SDPLIB	613
Geoffrey Sell	LIBSDP	601
Dennis Strojwas	LIBSDP	587

BRUNSWICK

Peter Skolar	CON	940
Kenneth Avery	CON	935
Antony Craig	LAB	638
Ian Swain	LAB	580
John Pinfold	SDPLIB	457
Ruth Schmidt	SDPLIB	402

356

CAMDEN

Marion Chester	LAB	879
Gregory Thomson	LAB	853
Martin Parker	SDPLIB	477
Keith Roberts	LIBSDP	477
Alan Fleming	CON	369
John Malamah-Thomas	CON	292

CASTLEHAVEN

Graham Good	LAB	1014
Jennifer Willmot	LAB	960
David Aarons	SDPLIB	385
Liam Cowdrey	LIBSDP	374
Christopher Fenwick	CON	261
William Mills	CON	252
Brian Lake	Ind	163

CAVERSHAM

Julie Fitzgerald	LAB	1187
John Wakeham	LAB	1146
Nicholas Bosanquet	SDPLIB	750
Benjamin Stoneham	SDPLIB	649
Thomas Crawford	CON	410
Timothy Miller	CON	369

CHALK FARM

Hugh Bayley	LAB	996
Teresa Ryan	LAB	967
Lindsay Granshaw	SDPLIB	714
Sieska Cowdrey	LIBSDP	711
Peter White	CON	647
Sinclair Webster	CON	632

FITZJOHN'S

Ronald King	CON	883
Cathleen Mainds	CON	839
George Sandersley	SDPLIB	522
Olive Paynton	LIBSDP	499
June Ward	LAB	322
David Bookless	LAB	315

FORTUNE GREEN

Ian Tomisson	CON	778
David Neil-Smith	CON	756
Felicity Rea	LIBSDP	649
Esmond Hitchcock	LIBSDP	604
Virginia Berridge	LAB	562
Kathryn O'Neill	LAB	502

FROGNAL

Alan Greengross	CON	1170
Gwyneth Williams	CON	1124
William Laing	SDPLIB	603
Richard Waddington	LIBSDP	594
Stella Greenall	LAB	346
Marie Kosloff	LAB	330

GOSPEL OAK

Ronald Hefferman	LAB	1167
Tessa Jowell	LAB	1095
Philip Fitzpatrick	SDPLIB	543
Margaret Jackson-Roberts	SDPLIB	538
Clifford Edwards	CON	389
Paul Brandt	CON	363
Sasthi Chakravarti	SLAG	76
David James	Ind	62

GRAFTON

Roy Shaw	LAB	1040
William Birtles	LAB	1011
John Butterworth	SDPLIB	452
Harry Harding	SDPLIB	440
David Friday	CON	268
Roger James	CON	262

HAMPSTEAD TOWN

Julian Harrison	CON	992
Anthony Robinson	CON	962
David Birkett	SDPLIB	676
Brian Sugden	LIBSDP	627
Eric Mitchell	LAB	463
James Murphy	LAB	445

HIGHGATE

Anthony Blackburn	CON	1504
Martin Morton	CON	1473
Barbara Beck	LAB	1463
Beresford Wilkinson	LAB	1418
Donald Harkness	LAB	1393
Lilian O'Callaghan	CON	1377
Catherine Walton	SDPLIB	1151
John Coss	SDPLIB	1143
Rex Winsbury	SDPLIB	1049

357

HOLBORN

Julian Fulbrook	LAB	1070
Michael Kirk	LAB	1008
Barry Greenway	CON	631
Gillian Kinder	CON	596
James Morris	SDPLIB	397
Roger Karn	LIBSDP	391
John Mason	IND LAB	141

KILBURN

Katherine Allen	LAB	1517
Angela Birtill	LAB	1409
Alan Woods	LAB	1394
Steve Allman	LIBSDP	829
Roger Billins	LIBSDP	809
Nicola-Jane Taylor	SDPLIB	722
Frederick Copeman	CON	597
Alan Mackay	CON	583
Stephen Massey	CON	567

KING'S CROSS

Barbara Hughes	LAB	812
Anthony Dykes	LAB	802
Anthony Kemp	CON	532
Stephen Robin	CON	526
Thomas Hibbert	LIBSDP	411
Derek Lowe	SDPLIB	356

PRIORY

Anna Bowman	LAB	1537
Neil Fletcher	LAB	1409
Michael Flynn	CON	849
Veronica Perrin	CON	804
Jean Austin	SDPLIB	504
Roderick Atkin	SDPLIB	485

REGENT'S PARK

John Mills	LAB	1223
Robert Latham	LAB	1195
Andrew Bethell	LAB	1194
Judith Barnes	CON	1061
Betty Wilson	CON	1046
Noel Moncaster	CON	1034
Christopher Ely	SDPLIB	651
Michael Storey	SDPLIB	650
William Sutherland	SDPLIB	617

ST JOHN'S

Mary Cane	LAB	1106
Richard Sumray	LAB	1016
John Haugh	LIBSDP	502
Jane Schopflin	SDPLIB	482
John Wylde	CON	278
Richard Zemlo	CON	226

ST PANCRAS

Sandra Plummer	LAB	893
Philip Turner	LAB	854
Brian Duggan	SDPLIB	361
Malcolm Gilroy-Stevenson	LIBSDP	290
Anthony Earl-Williams	CON	273
Martin Markus	CON	244

SOMERS TOWN

Thomas Devine	LAB	1208
Graham Shurety	LAB	1003
Elizabeth Blundell	SDPLIB	344
Helen Brooks	LIBSDP	315
Anthony Cheverton	CON	313
David Harris	CON	294

SOUTH END

Michael Farrer	CON	927
Stephen Moon	CON	899
Margaret Cosin	LAB	842
Nirmal Roy	LAB	802
Jane Atkinson	SDPLIB	540
Guy Newton	LIBSDP	506

SWISS COTTAGE

Derek Spencer	CON	1352
David Stone	CON	1322
Harry Whitcut	CON	1291
Jacqueline Peacock	LAB	1102
Ralph Cowly	LAB	1086
Harry McCall	LAB	1058
Andrew Bridgwater	LIBSDP	742
Paul Burall	LIBSDP	714
Richard Ford	SDPLIB	711
Geoffrey Syer	Ecology	91
John Comden	Ecology	82

WEST END

Sandra Wynn	LAB	860

358

Gillian Green	LAB	838
Robert Graham	CON	817
John Seldon	CON	776
Ida Linfield	LIBSDP	554
Peter Hatton	LIBSDP	541

BY ELECTIONS 1982-1986

SWISS COTTAGE
21 July 1983
(Resignation of Derek Spencer CON)

Robert Graham	CON	1168
Jacqueline Peacock	LAB	994
Andrew Bridgwater	LIBSDP	457

CHALK FARM
23 Feb 1984
(Resignation of Teresa Ryan LAB)

Richard Stein	LAB	1121
William Jones	LIBSDP	646
Martine Kushner	CON	507

REGENT'S PARK
(Resignation of John Mills LAB)Stephen

Bevington	LAB	1218
Kenneth Workman	SDPLIB	1042
Judith Barnes	CON	858

8 MAY 1986

ADELAIDE

Julian Tobin	CON	1217
Stephen Moon	CON	1158
Ian Pasley-Tyler	CON	1155
Brian Bell	LAB	939
Bryan Blatch	LAB	929
Anna Wernher	LAB	797
Vera Miles	SDPLIB	487
Aubrey Sandman	SDPLIB	421
Erich Wagner	LIBSDP	400

BELSIZE

Colin Glover	CON	1055

Huntly Spence	CON	1039
Judith Barnes	CON	1005
Margaret McPhee	LAB	888
Malcolm Bull	LAB	875
Ramen Bhattacharyya	LAB	841
David Davies	LIBSDP	818
Pauline Marriott	SDPLIB	788
Dudley Miles	SDPLIB	756
Philippa Draper	GRE	236

BLOOMSBURY

Michael Kirk	LAB	1307
Nicola Kutapan	LAB	1302
William Budd	LAB	1263
William Trite	CON	1158
Martine Moon	CON	1069
Mark Whitfield	CON	1033
James Morris	SDPLIB	447
Geoffrey Sell	LIBSDP	413
Felicity Watkin	LIBSDP	387

BRUNSWICK

Peter Skolar	CON	757
Karen Newbury	LAB	675
Kenneth Avery	CON	672
John White	LAB	652
Douglas Medhurst	LIBSDP	383
Kevin Cahill	LIBSDP	367

CAMDEN

Sheila Field	LAB	1258
Satnam Gill	LAB	1173
Jonathan Owen	SDPLIB	765
David Simmons	SDPLIB	753
Doris Davis	CON	269
Toby Corder	CON	253

CASTLEHAVEN

Graham Good	LAB	1485
Jasper (Jerry) Williams	LAB	1238
Jennifer Horne	SDPLIB	274
Keith Roberts	SDPLIB	262
Shirley Soskin	CON	221
Carl Teper	CON	187

APPENDIX II

CAVERSHAM

Gareth Smyth	LAB	1458
Mary Cane	LAB	1441
Mark Hapgood	CON	348
Mark Stuart-Smith	CON	315
Jennifer Kavanagh	LIBSDP	312
Richard Thompson	SDPLIB	265
Stephen McConnell	Humanist	84

CHALK FARM

Julie Fitzgerald	LAB	1124
Janet Pope	LAB	1048
Anthony Kemp	CON	584
Anthony Blackburn	CON	582
David Casey	LIBSDP	431
Stephen White	SDPLIB	391
Elizabeth Noyes	GRE	129

FITZJOHNS

Ronald King	CON	735
Cathleen Mainds	CON	697
Ian Swain	LAB	451
Sambhu Banik	LAB	445
David Radford	LIBSDP	332
John Howson	SDPLIB	324

FORTUNE GREEN

Felicity Rea	LIBSDP	677
Roger Billins	LIBSDP	627
Paul Crossman	CON	578
Catherine Joseph	LAB	577
Ian Tomisson	CON	567
Eric Kaill	LAB	551

FROGNAL

Alan Greengross	CON	930
Gwyneth Williams	CON	905
Amber Dobson	LAB	479
David Richter	LAB	446
Nicola-Jane Taylor	SDPLIB	401
Hilary Billins	LIBSDP	383

GOSPEL OAK

Rose Head	LAB	1455
Graham Shurety	LAB	1429
John Livingston	CON	410
Peter Somerville	CON	372

David Birkett	SDPLIB	283
Patricia Gros	LIBSDP	279

GRAFTON

Roy Shaw	LAB	1313
Patrick Denny	LAB	1190
Catherine Dillnott-Cooper	CON	245
Jane Atkinson	SDPLIB	228
Peter Golds	CON	223
Mary Gillie	SDPLIB	212

HAMPSTEAD TOWN

Jacqueline Jones	CON	788
Selina Gee	CON	787
David Brierley	LIBSDP	695
David Aarons	SDPLIB	672
David Bookless	LAB	564
Heather Kenmure	LAB	517

HIGHGATE

Barbara Beck	LAB	1966
Margaret Cosin	LAB	1844
John Wakeham	LAB	1739
Martin Morton	CON	1185
Lesley Fields	CON	1129
Peter Horne	CON	1109
James McKinley	SDPLIB	901
Jane Schopflin	SDPLIB	896
Margaret Jackson-Roberts	SDPLIB	890

HOLBORN

Benjamin Griffith	LAB	1013
Kenneth Hulme	LAB	951
Ralf (Alf) Barrett	Ind	548
Peter Smaill	CON	533
Piers Wauchope	CON	458
Trevor Davis	SDPLIB	271
Robert Forrest	LIBSDP	210

KILBURN

Angela Birtill	LAB	1925
Katherine Allen	LAB	1866
Alan Woods	LAB	1788
William Smith	CON	578
Alexandra Lawrie	CON	565
Jonathan Shapland	CON	558
Jeremy Allen	LIBSDP	518

BOROUGH ELECTION RESULTS
1964 – 2006

Steve Allman	LIBSDP	515
Heather Thompson	LIBSDP	432

KING'S CROSS

Barbara Hughes	LAB	1113
Anthony Dykes	LAB	1094
George Glossop	CON	402
James Turner	CON	382
Thomas Hibbert	LIBSDP	282

PRIORY

Jacqueline Peacock	LAB	1621
Philip Turner	LAB	1600
Andrew Lavy	CON	648
Marilyn Halbertsham	CON	600

REGENT'S PARK

Robert Latham	LAB	1554
David Horan	LAB	1489
Gillian Green	LAB	1442
William Jones	LIBSDP	1293
Lee Barr	SDPLIB	1257
Kenneth Rolph	SDPLIB	1197
Stephen Robin	CON	658
Noel Moncaster	CON	635
Peter Slade	CON	617
Terence Hargrave	Ind	326

ST JOHN'S

Hilary Lowe	LAB	1469
Richard Sumray	LAB	1462
Heather Hullah	SDPLIB	311
Soren Agerholm	LIBSDP	295
George Emsden	CON	271
Sinclair Webster	CON	254

ST PANCRAS

Stephen Bevington	LAB	978
Sandra Plummer	LAB	917
Esther Bateman	CON	241
June Moncaster	CON	241
John Davidson	SDPLIB	212
Catherine Meehan	LIBSDP	197

SOMERS TOWN

Thomas Devine	LAB	1195

Alfred Saunders	LAB	1064
Betty Wilson	LIBSDP	288
Elizabeth Blundell	SDPLIB	278
David Harris	CON	214
Blanche Mundlak	CON	212
Keith Armstrong	Ind Lab	178

SOUTH END

Paul Orrett	LAB	1115
Nirmal Roy	LAB	1064
Inge Reed	CON	635
Michael Farrer	CON	633
Jennifer Hall	SDPLIB	347
Sandra Lawman	SDPLIB	342
Fiona Johnson	GRE	212

SWISS COTTAGE

Gloria Lazenby	LAB	1326
Alan Rippington	LAB	1307
Adrian Van States	LAB	1155
Robert Graham	CON	1140
Davis Stone	CON	1136
Roberta Robson	CON	1103
Ian Bond	LIBSDP	637
Roderick Atkin	SDPLIB	613
Clive Pembridge	SDPLIB	569
Janet Crawford	GRE	280

WEST END

Kevin McDonnell	LAB	1089
Julia Devote	LAB	1087
Michael Flynn	CON	557
Harry Whitcut	CON	513
Peter Hatton	LIBSDP	446
Brian Sugden	LIBSDP	430

BY ELECTIONS 1986-1990

SOMERS TOWN
7 MAY 1987

(Death of Thomas Devine LAB)

Caroline Holding	LAB	1073
Betty Wilson	LIBSDP	681
Blanche Mundlak	CON	401

361

ADELAIDE
23 JULY 1987
(Resignation of Stephen Moon CON)

Robert Graham	CON	1007
Sada Deshmukh	LAB	521
Dudley Miles	SDPLIB	235

ST PANCRAS
5 MAY 1988
(Resignation of Stephen Bevington LAB)

Mary Helsdon	LAB	789
Andrew Broadhurst	CON	319
Stephen White	LD	293

HAMPSTEAD TOWN
26 JAN 1989
(Resignation of Selina Gee CON)

Rita Pomfret	CON	533
David Brierley	LD	373
Myra "Bubbles" Polya	LAB	239
Charles Rowlatt	SDP	74

3 MAY 1990

ADELAIDE

Julian Tobin	CON	1153
Robert Graham	CON	1151
Ian Pasley-Tyler	CON	1088
Brian Bell	LAB	987
David Bookless	LAB	885
Rose Head	LAB	876
Janine Sachs	GRE	269
Vera Miles	LD	222
Frances Tully	LD	215
Frances Tattershall	LD	206
Vicki Weissman	CAMC	86

BELSIZE

Judith Barnes	CON	1159
Cathleen Mainds	CON	1124
Huntly Spence	CON	1109
Judith Pattison	LAB	971
Michael Rice	LAB	952
Deborah Sacks	LAB	928
Conchita Vasey	GRE	393
Anne Box	LD	329

Pauline Marriott	LD	324
Ardon Lyon	LD	310

BLOOMSBURY

Peter Brayshaw	LAB	1356
John Toomey	LAB	1210
Sada Deshmukh	LAB	1177
Mark Haley	CON	751
Andrew Lownie	CON	736
Robert Ricketts	CON	719
Joanna Dickens	GRE	574
Mary Gillie	LD	269
Patricia Smith	LD	243
Brian Lake	CAMC	163
Sital Maan	CAMC	141
Robert Norman	CAMC	133

BRUNSWICK

Ernest James	LAB	851
Paul Stinchcombe	LAB	789
Peter Skolar	CON	690
Kenneth Avery	CON	681
Patricia Hooker	GRE	298
Roy Seger	LD	206

CAMDEN

Sheila Field	LAB	1046
Barbara Hughes	LAB	951
Marc Leggett	LD	634
Gavin Collins	LD	621
Toby Fiennes	GRE	379
John Davidson	CON	327
Lester May	CON	283
June Swan	CAMC	144
Hazel Saunders	CAMC	114

CASTLEHAVEN

Jane Roberts	LAB	1073
Jasper (Jerry) Williams	LAB	1002
Doris Davis	CON	235
Shirley Soskin	CON	211
Marc Lewis	GRE	207
Keith Roberts	LD	133
Trevor Long	CAMC	130
Cyra Croft	CAMC	127
Jennifer Horne-Roberts	LD	126

CAVERSHAM

Anthony Dykes	LAB	1167
Bernard Kissen	LAB	1101
Sylvia Currie	CON	427
Anthony Kemp	CON	414
Joseph Young	GRE	346
Margaret Clarke	CAMC	242
George Jamieson	CAMC	203
Soren Agerholm	LD	162

CHALK FARM

Julie Fitzgerald	LAB	988
Harriet Garland	LAB	954
Anthony Blackburn	CON	558
Michael Farrer	CON	520
Francis Atkinson	GRE	353
Joan Nimmo-Smith	LD	195
Brian Haines	CAMC	170

FITZJOHN'S

Ronald King	CON	758
Andrew Marshall	CON	713
Deborah Townsend	LAB	429
Gareth Smyth	LAB	356
Anthony Mills	GRE	189
Olive Paynton	LD	156
Henry Usher	LD	131

FORTUNE GREEN

Felicity Rea	LD	899
Jane Schopflin	LD	642
Alan Rippington	LAB	597
Sambhu Banik	LAB	579
Antoine Clarke	CON	484
Julia Densem	CON	447
Francis Butler	GRE	194

GOSPEL OAK

Winifred Parson	LAB	1345
John Mills	LAB	1269
Giselle Harrison	CON	467
Maura Lyons	CON	448
Lynda Dagley	GRE	358

GRAFTON

Roy Shaw	LAB	1198
Terence Comerford	LAB	1023

Valerie Armstrong	GRE	386
Kevin Flanagan	CAMC	357
Anthony Cheverton	CON	294
Philip Seely	CON	270
Andrew Murray	COMM	58

HAMPSTEAD TOWN

Maureen Braun	CON	643
Rita Pomfret	CON	620
David Brierley	LD	619
John Dickie	LD	549
John Saynor	LAB	432
Anna Wernher	LAB	397
John Penney	GRE	219

HIGHGATE

Margaret Cosin	LAB	1785
Richard Arthur	LAB	1780
John Wakeham	LAB	1598
Cynthia Silk	CON	1084
John Steinberg	CON	1010
Michael Stilwell	CON	992
Peter Forrest	GRE	502
Jennifer Jones	GRE	460
Stephen Molesworth	LD	329
Mark Withers	LD	268
Gertrude Sington	LD	265
Mary Hodgson-Bennett	CAMC	239
Olive Gatenby	CAMC	226
Jennifer Page	CAMC	223
Laurence Williams	TEN	77

HOLBORN

Julian Fulbrook	LAB	1119
Brian Woodrow	LAB	953
Richard Bull	CON	463
Bernard Sharpe	CON	404
Patricia Gros	CREP	386
Bruno Imerini	CREP	383
Robert Hopkins	GRE	244

KILBURN

Graham Good	LAB	1730
Charles Hedges	LAB	1602
Ramen Bhattacharyya	LAB	1509
Gwendoline Evans	GRE	489

363

Marian Harrison	CON	482
Jonathan Shapland	CON	455
David Soskin	CON	433
Jeremy Allen	LD	325
Heather Thompson	LD	297
Clive Agran	LD	240

KING'S CROSS

Gloria Lazenby	LAB	1079
John White	LAB	969
George Glossop	CON	438
John Wilson	CON	405
John Simpson	GRE	263
Casper Wrede	LD	158
Cathal McGirr	CAMC	141

PRIORY

Jacqueline Peacock	LAB	1260
Philip Turner	LAB	1133
Rose Irwin	CON	591
Timothy Evans	CON	587
Stephen Games	GRE	330
Margaret Knight	LD	254
Joseph McEnery	LD	172

REGENT'S PARK

James Turner	LAB	1594
William Budd	LAB	1566
David Horan	LAB	1545
Pamela Anwar	CON	912
Noel Moncaster	CON	897
Paul Morland	CON	879
Lauren Soertsz	GRE	317
Dudley Miles	LD	245
Margaret Jackson-Roberts	LD	237
Robert Vernon-Jackson	LD	215

ST JOHN'S

Simon McDonald	LAB	1213
Caroline Mills	LAB	1159
Leon Pein	GRE	377
John Hall	CON	298
Roland Walker	CON	224
Ian Kelleher	CAMC	179
Lindsay Northover	LD	136
Robert Nimmo-Smith	LD	102

ST PANCRAS

Mary Helsdon	LAB	865
Graham Shurety	LAB	745
Terence Hargrave	CAMC	255
Mark Hapgood	CON	238
Margarett McDermott	CAMC	205
Blanche Mundlak	CON	204
Margaret Nuttgens	GRE	147
Stephen White	LD	105

SOMERS TOWN

Alfred Saunders	LAB	1140
Robert Austin	LAB	1103
John Daley	CAMC	417
David Harris	CON	337
Sharon Keizner	CON	269
Paul Wolf-Light	GRE	188
Josephine Navarro Slater	GRE	187

SOUTH END

Myra (Bubbles) Polya	LAB	929
Nirmal Roy	LAB	905
Mark Bennett	CON	632
Jeremy Duke-Cohan	CON	591
Elizabeth de Pauley	GRE	277
Heather Formaini	GRE	251
Anthony Steele	LD	168
Peter Buonacorsi-How	LD	165

SWISS COTTAGE

Vaughan Emsley	CON	1159
Anne Morris	CON	1153
Peter Horne	CON	1120
Barbara Beck	LAB	1108
Terence Flanagan	LAB	1069
Sandra Plummer	LAB	1018
Caroline Counihan	GRE	449
Nicholas Catephores	GRE	381
Margaret Fuelling	LD	273
Diana Self	LD	250
Gillian Wagner	LD	234
Alan Rogers	CAMC	176

WEST END

Julia Devote	LAB	937
Kevin MacDonnell	LAB	931
Neil Bourhill	CON	495

364

Richard Bevan	CON	482
Keith Moffitt	LD	243
Catherine Gregory	GRE	211
Erich Wagner	LD	191
Graham Bacon	CAMC	91

BY ELECTIONS
1990 -1994

SOMERS TOWN
7 May 1992
(Death of Alfred Saunders LAB)

Robert Churchill	LAB	991
Blanche Mundlak	CON	271
Arthur Peeling CAMDEN CHARTER		227
Anthony Verduyn	LD	140
Colin Cuddehay	IND	52

SWISS COTTAGE
7 May 1992
(Resignation of Vaughan Emsley CON)

Peter Skolar	CON	1278
Nicholas Prior	LAB	940
Diana Self	LD	222
Stephen Games	GRE	91

HIGHGATE
15 Oct 1992
(Resignation of John Wakeham LAB)

Deborak Sacks	LAB	994
Cynthia Silk	CON	848
Henry Potts	LD	328

WEST END
15 OCT 1992
(Resignation of Julia Devote LAB)

David Lines	LAB	544
Keith Moffitt	LD	448
Dawn Somper	CON	326

ST JOHN'S
17 DEC 1992
(Resignation of Simon McDonald LAB)

Fiona Brocklesby	LAB	534
Sylvia Currie	CON	128

ST PANCRAS
22 April 1993
(Resignation of Mary Helsdon LAB)

Simon Fletcher	LAB	606
Ellen Luby CAMDEN CHARTER		244
Blanche Mundlak	CON	146
Jack Gilbert	LD	128

5 MAY 1994

ADELAIDE

Peter Day	LAB	996
Julian Tobin	CON	987
Peter Bourne	LAB	976
Robert Ashley	CON	947
Robert Graham	CON	926
Iain Meek	LAB	922
Vera Miles	LD	308
Candida Goulden	LD	302
Madhvi Chanrai	LD	272
Elizabeth de Pauley	GRE	178

BELSIZE

Judith Barnes	CON	920
Judith Pattison	LAB	884
Joy Silver	CON	859
Huntly Spence	CON	840
Peter Singer	LAB	804
John Saynor	LAB	797
Pauline Marriott	LD	544
Diana Brown	LD	511
James Iddon-Bowen	LD	481
Kamal Al Moosa	GRE	262

BLOOMSBURY

Deirdre Krymer	LAB	1281
Shelley Burke	LAB	1256
Nirmal Roy	LAB	1173
Mark Haley	CON	611
David Whittaker	CON	594
Piers Wauchope	CON	556
Penelope Jones	LD	499
Andrew Hoddinott	LD	421
Timothy Pitt-Payne	LD	421
Joan Savage CAMDEN CHARTER		156

365

APPENDIX II

BRUNSWICK

Ernest James	LAB	801
Brian Weekes	LAB	793
Kenneth Avery	CON	429
Michael Stilwell	CON	409
Frances Tully	LD	292
Gerard Wall	LD	273

CAMDEN

Patricia Nightingale	LAB	1304
Dermot Greene	LAB	1245
Marion Fleming	LD	395
Marc Leggett	LD	278
June Swan CAMDEN CHARTER		264
Paul Short	CON	223
Laudicia Antoine-Perez	CON	205

CASTLEHAVEN

Jane Roberts	LAB	1056
Jasper (Jerry) Williams	LAB	951
Margaret Finer	LD	271
Kate Gordon	GRE	235
William Mitchell	CON	212
Andrew Scarfe	CON	192

CAVERSHAM

Bernard Kissen	LAB	1230
Anne Swain	LAB	1196
Soren Agerholm	LD	329
John Davidson	CON	318
Sylvia Currie	CON	297
Thomas Green	GRE	280

CHALK FARM

Harriet Garland	LAB	847
William Budd	LAB	763
Jonathan Bucknell	Ind	426
Anthony Blackburn	CON	421
Michael Farrer	CON	340
Frances Tattersfield	LD	275
Ardon Lyon	LD	242

FITZJOHN'S

Ronald King	CON	552
Cathleen Mainds	CON	467
David Bookless	LAB	391

Jonathan Black	LAB	366
Ronald Finlay	LD	233
Olive Paynton	LD	215
Christopher Knight	Ind	139
Charles Harris	GRE	116

FORTUNE GREEN

Felicity (Flick) Rea	LD	1030
Jane Schopflin	LD	866
Geoffrey Berridge	LAB	523
Syed Hoque	LAB	443
Paul Crossman	CON	280
Nicholas Jones	CON	235
Lynn Lovell	GRE	83

FROGNAL

Pamela Chesters	CON	770
Dawn Somper	CON	658
Dianne Hayter	LAB	390
Regan Scott	LAB	358
Barbara How	LD	281
Nigel Barnes	LD	270
Helen Marcus	Ind	240
Sebastian Secker Walker	GRE	143

GOSPEL OAK

Robert Hall	LAB	1078
John Mills	LAB	838
Iris Coney	CON	313
Margaret Jackson-Roberts	LD	289
Michael Ost	CON	273
Frances de Freitas	LD	255
Sheila Oakes	GRE	190

GRAFTON

Roy Shaw	LAB	1147
Terence Comerford	LAB	1100
Elizabeth Hill	LD	227
Doreen Bartlett	CON	221
Anne Elliott	LD	218
Ross Campbell	CON	202

HAMPSTEAD TOWN

Margaret Little	LD	1005
John Dickie	LD	969
Helen Sinclair	CON	471

Maureen Braun	CON	466	David Charlesworth	LD	300
Janet Guthrie	LAB	336			
Simon Fitzpatrick	LAB	323	**PRIORY**		
Katharina Wolpe	GRE	97	Philip Turner	LAB	1168
			Barry Peskin	LAB	1144
HIGHGATE			Rose Irwin	CON	364
Margaret Cosin	LAB	1805	Dorin Peter	CON	360
Richard Arthur	LAB	1795	Adelaide Kernick	LD	250
Deborah Sacks	LAB	1731	Rita Landeryou	LD	211
Cynthia Silk	CON	890			
Martyn Fisher	CON	833	**REGENT'S PARK**		
Tanya Warburg	CON	801	David Horan	LAB	1464
Walter Eyres	LD	525	James Turner	LAB	1458
Stephen Molesworth	LD	520	Richard Olszewski	LAB	1328
Henry Potts	LD	484	Paul Gray	CON	624
			David Walters	CON	619
HOLBORN			John Wilkin	CON	546
Julian Fulbrook	LAB	1116	Jack Gilbert	LD	385
Brian Woodrow	LAB	1017	Jennifer Kavanagh	LD	359
George Glossop	CON	303	Ellen Luby CAMDEN CHARTER		346
Bruno Imerini	Ind	301	Pamela Lutgen	LD	317
Andrew Lownie	CON	273	Dorothy Forsyth	GRE	240
Kevin Jones	LD	212			
Caroline Deys	LD	202	**ST JOHN'S**		
Maxwell Logan	GRE	167	Penelope Abraham	LAB	1175
Clive Treliving	GRE	110	John Thane	LAB	1076
			Vivienne Collins	LD	284
KILBURN			Alastair Loraine	LD	240
Heather Johnson	LAB	1581	Andrew Wade	GRE	211
Charles Hedges	LAB	1478	Roland Walker	CON	177
Timothy Walker	LAB	1450	Anthony Kemp	CON	172
Anthony Goodman	CON	394			
Marian Harrison	CON	356	**ST PANCRAS**		
Heather Thompson	LD	349	Gloria Lazenby	LAB	859
David Mackover	CON	337	Mahmud Hasan	LAB	810
Jeremy Allen	LD	313	Ian Smith	LD	192
Matthew Pollitt	GRE	301	Harriet Goldenberg	LD	187
Lawrence Morris	Ind	296	Mark Hapgood	CON	148
Sally Twite	LD	292	Blanche Mundlak	CON	147
Sandra Copeland	Ind	142	Nigel Armstrong	GRE	131
KING'S CROSS			**SOMERS TOWN**		
Angus Walker	LAB	1180	Nathalie Lieven	LAB	1197
John White	LAB	1109	Sybil Shine	LAB	1164
Grace Gorer	CON	333	Arthur Peeling CAMDEN CHARTER		275
Norma Simon	CON	314	Elizabeth Blundell	LD	240

David Harris	CON	219
Mark Finney	CON	203
Carole Ricketts	CON	200

SOUTH END

Gerry Harrison	LAB	992
Sadashivrao Deshmukh	LAB	882
John Iredale	CON	464
David Sinclair	CON	455
Dudley Miles	LD	272
Peter Buonacorsi-How	LD	249
Jennifer Page	HC	172
Celia Busby	GRE	159
Marguerite Hazell	GRE	148

SWISS COTTAGE

Raymond Adamson	LAB	1076
John Macdonald	LAB	1070
Patrick Weir	LAB	1015
Anne Morris	CON	926
Peter Horne	CON	869
Peter Skolar	CON	865
Elizabeth Burney-Jones	LD	420
Nicholas Collins	LD	418
Diana Self	LD	374
Debra Green	GRE	232

WEST END

David Lines	LAB	933
Keith Moffitt	LD	839
Nicholas Prior	LAB	799
Erich Wagner	LD	739
Sam Mackover	CON	235
Neil Bourhill	CON	233
Judith Locke	GRE	138

BY ELECTIONS 1994 – 1998

ADELAIDE
23 Feb 1995
(Resignation of Peter Day LAB)

Peter Singer	LAB	854
Robert Graham	CON	649
Dudley Miles	LD	157

BLOOMSBURY
4 May 1995
(Resignation of Shelley Burke LAB)

Patricia Callaghan	LAB	1271
David Whittaker	CON	339
Gerrard Wall	LD	258

7 MAY 1998

ADELAIDE

Julian Tobin	CON	960
Andrew Marshall	CON	929
Piers Wauchope	CON	868
Sada Deshmukh	LAB	796
Harriet Garland	LAB	768
Deborah Sacks	LAB	746
Mark Finney	LD	384
Pamela Collis	LD	383
Madhvi Natt	LD	308

BELSIZE

Huntly Spence	CON	731
Aileen Hammond	LAB	711
Ewan Cameron	CON	706
Jonathan Bucknell	CON	705
David Taggart	LAB	650
Jake Sumner	LAB	624
Pauline Marroitt	LD	587
Dudlet Miles	LD	522
Ronald Watts	LD	455
Phyllis Ayres	GRE	290

BLOOMSBURY

Patricia Callaghan	LAB	1050
Nirmal Roy	LAB	908
Jake Turnbull	LAB	777
Barbara Douglass	CON	626
Mark Haley	CON	538
Ian Nottingham	CON	472
Tristan Ward	LD	468
Philip Moser	LD	455
Gerard Wall	LD	410
Niki Kortvelyessy	GRE	280

BRUNSWICK

Brian Weekes	LAB	653

Edward Cousins	LAB	601
Kenneth Avery	CON	443
Philip Norman	CON	376
Penelope Jones	LD	286
Robert Whitley	GRE	258
Stanley Parker	Socialist Party	58

CAMDEN

Patricia Nightingale	LAB	929
Dermot Greene	LAB	844
Helena Djurkovic	LD	323
Simieon Litman	LD	261
Douglas Earl	GRE	236
Sylvia Currie	CON	213
Iris Coney	CON	189

CASTLEHAVEN

Jane Roberts	LAB	677
Deirdre Krymer	LAB	569
Kate Gordon	GRE	208
Natasha Dunn	LD	204
Emma Chapman	CON	158
Joan Stally	CON	140
Darren Ziff	LD	128
Jane Owen	Right to Party	72

CHALK FARM

Bill Budd	LAB	615
John White	LAB	599
Charles Marquand	LD	419
Rupert Redesdale	LD	395
William Mitchell	CON	385
David Walters	CON	338

FITZJOHNS

Martin Davies	CON	590
Andrew Mennear	CON	536
Peter Dunn	LAB	393
Deborah Townsend	LAB	390
Martin Wright	LD	245
Ricarda O'Driscoll	LD	240
Dorothy Forsyth	GRE	96

FORTUNE GREEN

Felicity (Flick) Rea	LD	975
Jane Schoplin	LD	829
Fred Broughton	LAB	375
Roy Lockett	LAB	372
Carrie Ruxton	CON	226
Michael Pritchett	CON	224

FROGNAL

Pamela Chesters	CON	687
Dawn Somper	CON	640
Anne Robertson	LAB	311
Helen Seaford	LAB	279
Barbara How	LD	272
Nigel Barnes	LD	253
Charles Harris	GRE	136

GOSPEL OAK

John Mills	LAB	760
Judith Pattison	LAB	719
Margaret Jackson-Roberts	LD	336
Jeffrey Poulter	LD	281
Marian Harrison	CON	221
Henry Whitaker	CON	180
Debra Green	GRE	153

GRAFTON

Roy Shaw	LAB	705
John Dickie	LAB	660
Margaret Finer	LD	221
Anne Elliott	LD	191
Doreen Bartlett	CON	187
Sheila Oakes	GRE	170
Belinda Shapps	CON	148

HAMPSTEAD TOWN

Marget Little	LD	1082
Sidney Malin	LD	912
Roderick Anderson	CON	368
Michael Base	CON	354
Mark Leonard	LAB	301
Rudolph Champagne	LAB	259

HIGHGATE

Maggie Cosin	LAB	1275
Richard Arthur	LAB	1252
John Thane	LAB	1141
Judith Barnes	CON	930
Roger Freeman	CON	869

Cynthia Silk	CON	825
Heather MacAuley	LD	666
Richard Waddington	LD	594
Paul Gannon	GRE	471
Peter Mair	LD	457

HOLBORN

Julian Fulbrook	LAB	948
Brian Woodrow	LAB	838
William Glossop	CON	328
Pamela Lutgen	LD	264
Barbara Turner	LD	264
Shailesh Vara	CON	250

KILBURN

Heather Johnson	LAB	1181
Charles Hedges	LAB	1007
Timothy Walker	LAB	957
Robert Graham	CON	435
Jane Stanton Humphreys	CON	395
Jonathan Morgan	CON	386
Helen Mayer	GRE	362
Lawrence Morris	IND	267
David Glover	LD	233
Jeremy Allen	LD	206
Erich Wagner	LD	133

KING'S CROSS

Barbara Hughes	LAB	833
Nicholas Smith	LAB	766
James Atkin	CON	269
Rosemary Gandy	LD	240
Eleanor Freedman	LD	232
Robert Ricketts	CON	211

PRIORY

John Rolfe	LAB	823
Philip Turner	LAB	809
Martyn Fisher	CON	276
Rosette Irwin	CON	243
Rex Warwick	LD	226
Joan Hervey	LD	138

REGENT'S PARK

| James Turner | LAB | 1125 |
| Barbara Ward | LAB | 983 |

Richard Olszewski	LAB	947
Paul Cray	CON	540
Anthony Kemp	CON	468
Jeremy Bradshaw	CON	354
Arden Lyon	LD	354
David Berry	LD	350
Alan Patterson	IND	287
Benjamin Newbrook	LD	285

SOUTH END

Gerry Harrison	LAB	999
Janet Guthrie	LAB	919
Jonathan Pardoe	CON	490
Dominic Schofield	CON	431
Peter Buonacorsi-How	LD	348
Andrew Wade	LD	346

ST JOHN'S

Penelope Abraham	LAB	990
David Horan	LAB	977
Diana Brown	LD	406
Stephen Molesworth	LD	351
Michael Farrer	CON	183
Roland Walker	CON	146

ST PANCRAS

Gloria Lazenby	LAB	686
Roger Robinson	LAB	576
Fiona Palmer	LD	254
Ian Myers	LD	236
Laura Hoskins	CON	173
Blanche Mundlak	CON	162

SOMERS TOWN

Sybil Shine	LAB	815
Ernest James	LAB	743
David Harris	CON	226
Caroline Ford	LD	225
Joseph Sleigh	CON	163
Andrew Spring	GRE	154

SWISS COTTAGE

Mary Ryan	LAB	887
Bob Hall	LAB	834
Stephen Hocking	CON	756
Honora Morrissey	CON	754
Peter Horne	CON	732

Bernard Moss	LAB	710
John Macdonald	IND LAB	600
Nicholas Collins	LD	439
Sally Twite	LD	378
Herbert Newbrook	LD	365
Catherine Gregory	GRE	284

WEST END

Keith Moffitt	LD	972
Heather Thompson	LD	811
David Lines	LAB	705
Geoff Berridge	LAB	642
Neil Bourhill	CON	156
Elaine Mackover	CON	131
Mehdi Akhavan Farshtchi	Ind	62
Antoine Clarke	Ind	41

BY ELECTIONS 1998 – 2002

SWISS COTTAGE
22 April 1999

(Resignation of Mary Ryan LAB)

Honora Morrissey	CON	705
Deborah Sacks	LAB	557
Rex Warrick	LD	158
John Macdonald	Ind	126
Douglas Earl	GRE	59
Mehdi Farshtchi	Ind	45

ADELAIDE
3 Feb 2000

(Death of Julian Tobin CON)

Peter Horne	CON	655
Theodore Blackwell	LAB	250
Pamela Collis	LD	176
Douglas Earl	GRE	46

BLOOMSBURY
28 Sept 2000

(Resignation of Jake Turnbull LAB)

Peter Brayshaw	LAB	495
Patsy Prince	CON	476
Edward Simmons	LD	82
Kate Gordon	GRE	65

FROGNAL
25 Jan 2001

(Resignation of Pamela Chesters CON)

Michael Greene	CON	537
Marie Bardsley	LAB	198
Martin Wright	LD	98
Ceinwen Jones	GRE	23
Antoine Clarke	Ind	16

3 MAY 2002

BELSIZE

Jonathan Bucknell	CON	1041
Sheila Gunn	CON	1016
Piers Wauchope	CON	1005
Aileen Hammond	LAB	770
Sada Deshmukh	LAB	716
Patricia Nightingale	LAB	691
Pauline Marriott	LD	469
Ardon Lyon	LD	429
Dudley Miles	LD	423
Phyllis Eyres	GRE	274
Jack Price	GRE	236
Maeve Tornero	GRE	219

BLOOMSBURY

Penelope Abraham	LAB	771
Fazlul Chowdhury	LAB	756
Peter Brayshaw	LAB	736
Adam Lester	CON	642
Rohit Grover	CON	636
Peter Horne	CON	634
Adam Edwards	LD	335
Philip Moser	LD	295
John Ward	LD	285
Lucy Thomas	GRE	262
Saly Zlotowitz	GRE	145
Marcus Petz	GRE	137
Janet Maiden	Soc All	125

CAMDEN TOWN with PRIMROSE HILL

Patricia Callaghan	LAB	1040
Harriet Garland	LAB	986
Justin Barnard	LD	813
Jake Sumner	LAB	782
John Lefley	LD	653

371

Gloria Lazenby	IND	603
Toby Wickenden	LD	591
William Mitchell	CON	570
Peter Grosvenor	CON	560
Paul Barton	CON	541
Danielle Rappaport	GRE	385
Juliana Venter	GRE	227
Beryl Lankester	GRE	220
Elsa Dos Santos	Christian Peoples	34

CANTELOWES

Dermot Greene	LAB	861
Gerald Harrison	LAB	850
Judith Pattison	LAB	779
Soren Agerholm	LD	404
Gerald Wall	LD	377
Gaie Owen	GRE	348
Rachel Zatz	GRE	337
Rob Whitley	GRE	329
Simeon Litman	LD	303
Marcus Lloyd-Davy	CON	248
Sylvia Currie	CON	247
Oliver Milne	CON	237

FORTUNE GREEN

Felicity (Flick) Rea	LD	1295
Jane Schopflin	LD	1121
Jonathan Simpson	LD	1111
Michael Katz	LAB	483
Geoffrey Kingscote	LAB	414
Miles Seaman	LAB	409
Richard W Arthur	CON	336
Esther Baroudy	CON	323
Jean Hornbuckle	CON	314
David Sunderland	GRE	221
Susan Craig	GRE	199
Stephen Dawe	GRE	132

FROGNAL and FITZJOHNS

Martin Davies	CON	1141
Dawn Somper	CON	1119
Andrew Mennear	CON	1114
Deborah Townsend	LAB	384
Susan Garden	LD	362
Alfred Lawrie	LAB	344

Francis McGrath	LAB	336
Dominic Curran	LD	333
Charles Keidan	LD	286
Lynn Lovell	GRE	155
Stuart Houghton	GRE	153
Charles Harris	GRE	143

GOSPEL OAK

Janet Guthrie	LAB	880
Rajesh Chada	LAB	846
John Mills	LAB	791
Lindsey ("Lulu") Mitchell	CON	560
Richard Millett	CON	506
Carole Ricketts	CON	459
Margaret Jackson-Roberts	LD	430
Peter Mair	LD	347
Jeffrey Poulter	LD	336
Jane Walby	GRE	311
Howard Edmunds	GRE	296
Lesley Robb	GRE	264
Humberto Heliotrope	Christian Peoples	50

HAMPSTEAD TOWN

Michael Greene	CON	1316
Margaret Little	LD	1106
Brian Cattell	CON	1089
Katharine Steel	CON	1064
Louise Malin	LD	974
Martin Wright	LD	800
Neil Crundwell	LAB	430
Harunur Rashid	LAB	372
Brian Gascoigne	GRE	349
Nurul Islam	LAB	345
Frances Mortimer	GRE	321
Dorothy Forsyth	GRE	316

HAVERSTOCK

Jane Roberts	LAB	882
Roy Shaw	LAB	856
John Dickie	LAB	852
Margaret Finer	LD	422
Rita Marshall	CON	367
Alec Gordon	LD	364
Pamela Lutgen	LD	359

Anthony Kemp	CON	355
Joan Stally	CON	351
Sarah Gillam	GRE	319
Iola Kenworthy	GRE	277
Edward Milford	GRE	201
Angela Ozor	Christian Peoples	34

HIGHGATE

Margaret Cosin	LAB	972
John Thane	LAB	861
Abdul Quadir	LAB	849
Roger Freeman	CON	813
Sîan Berry	GRE	811
Simon Baker	CON	790
Janice Lavery	CON	775
Adrian Oliver	GRE	768
Mark Smith	GRE	715
Alison Wheeler	LD	384
Richard Waddington	LD	376
Henry Potts	LD	332
Sean Thompson	Soc All	219

HOLBORN and COVENT GARDEN

Julian Fulbrook	LAB	950
Sue Vincent	LAB	908
Brian Woodrow	LAB	884
Patsy Prince	CON	449
Dominic Valder	CON	411
Robert Ricketts	CON	389
Eleanor Key	LD	331
Alastair Loraine	LD	305
Nicholas Duckett	GRE	255
Seanine Joyce	GRE	253
Herbert Newbrook	LD	251
Hugo Charlton	GRE	205

KENTISH TOWN

Lucy Anderson	LAB	961
David Horan	LAB	868
Deirdre Krymer	LAB	797
Jill Fraser	LD	676
Alice Brown	LD	658
Nathaniel Green	LD	543
Sue Charlesworth	GRE	415

Alan Walter	Socialist Alliance		376
Kate Gordon		GRE	348
Graeme Durham		GRE	342
Doreen Bartlett		CON	224
Anthony Blackburn		CON	222
Alan Coleman-Harvey		CON	177
Celia Heliotrope		Christ'n Peoples	42

KILBURN

Charles Hedges	LAB	806
John Rolfe	LAB	797
Philip Turner	LAB	770
Robert Graham	CON	343
Rosette Irwin	CON	301
Paul Mawdsley	CON	289
Jeremy Allen	LD	285
Sally Twite	LD	254
Daviyani Kothari	LD	226
Helen Mayer	GRE	215
John Collins	GRE	205
David Reed	IND	174
Debra Green	GRE	171
Maria McCarten	Christ'n Peoples	73

KING'S CROSS

Barbara Hughes	LAB	855
Geethika Jayatilaka	LAB	730
Nicholas Smith	LAB	710
Barbara Douglass	CON	353
Charles Costa	CON	344
Mark Haley	CON	318
Diana Brown	LD	310
Nicholas Tucker	LD	243
Erich Wagner	LD	216
Richard Thomas	GRE	169
Audrey Poppy	GRE	157
Lucia Nella	GRE	149
Elsa Pontes-Betee	Christ'n Peoples	46

REGENT'S PARK

Nasim Ali	LAB	1165
Theodore Blackwell	LAB	1095
Heather Johnson	LAB	1076

Abdul Salam	CON	685
Sara Haydon	CON	656
John Walter	CON	626
Amanda Clare	GRE	584
Paul Hale	GRE	549
Debbie Dixon	GRE	466
Penelope Jones	LD	352
Philip Wainewright	LD	261
Rupert Redesdale	LD	259

St PANCRAS and
SOMERS TOWN

Roger Robinson	LAB	960
Sybil Shine	LAB	902
Anna Stewart	LAB	865
Elizabeth Hanna	LD	379
Fiona Palmer	LD	353
Ian Myers	LD	349
Simon Gray	CON	263
Damian Keegan	CON	259
James White	CON	249
Una Sapietis	GRE	219
Pol O'Ceallaigh	Socialist Alliance	211
Andrew Spring	GRE	124
Judith Stubbings	GRE	116

SWISS COTTAGE

Stephen Hocking	CON	1175
Andrew Marshall	CON	1106
Don Williams	CON	1090
Geoffrey Berridge	LAB	500
David Taggart	LAB	484
Abdul Careem	LAB	467
Nicholas Collins	LD	419
Rosalyn Harper	LD	416
Honora Morrissey	LD	391
Lucy Wills	GRE	265
Katherina Wolpe	GRE	174
Wolfgang Heiny	GRE	148
Magnus Nielsen	UKIP	36

WEST HAMPSTEAD

Keith Moffitt	LD	1133
John Bryant	LD	1028
Heather Thompson	LD	1016
Marie Bardsley	LAB	567

Michael Broughton	LAB	507
Mari Williams	LAB	469
Joanna Galloway	CON	268
Simon Cliff	CON	267
Samantha Baber	GRE	256
John Samiotis	CON	240
Michael Hewitt-Hicks	GRE	173
Lawrie Scovell	GRE	163

BY ELECTIONS 2002 – 2006

CAMDEN TOWN with
PRIMROSE HILL
20 June 2002
(Resignation of Justin Barnard LD)

Jake Sumner	LAB	652
John Lefley	LD	594
Gloria Lazenby	Ind	516
Peter Horne	CON	392
Lucy Wills	GRE	98

HAVERSTOCK
20 Feb 2003
(Resignation of John Dickie LAB)

Jill Fraser	LD	746
Paul Thomson	LAB	484
Peter Horne	CON	318
Sarah Gillam	GRE	112
Sydney Platt	Soc Alliance	84

4 MAY 2006

BELSIZE

Alexis Rowell	LD	1358
Christopher Basson	LD	1349
Arthur Graves	LD	1268
Jonathan Bucknell	CON	1233
Piers Wauchope	CON	1205
Sheila Gunn	CON	1187
Sada Deshmukh	LAB	471
Matthew McGregor	LAB	462
Jenny Westaway	LAB	410
Jane Ellis	GRE	278

374

Anya Courts	GRE	260
Adam Spanier	GRE	207

BLOOMSBURY

Penelope Abraham	LAB	1004
Fazlul Chowdhury	LAB	928
Rebbecca Hossack	CON	898
Peter Brayshaw	LAB	896
Robert Morritt	CON	835
Janice Lavery	CON	819
Linus Rees	GRE	353
Caroline Deys	LD	344
Shahrar Ali	GRE	329
Steven Deller	LD	323
George Graham	GRE	284
Philip Moser	LD	282
Andrew Halsey		53

CAMDEN TOWN with PRIMROSE HILL

Christopher Naylor	LD	1367
Patricia Callaghan	LAB	1357
Elizabeth Campbell	LD	1357
John Lefley	LD	1293
Jake Sumner	LAB	1186
Abdul Quadir	LAB	1152
William Mitchell	CON	527
Jesse Norman	CON	501
Peter Horne	CON	497
Nicola Chatham	GRE	414
Vincent Thurgood	GRE	356
Hilary Wendt	GRE	313

CANTELOWES

Paul Braithwaite	LD	1193
Benjamin Rawlings	LD	1129
Frederic Carver	LD	1101
John Doolan	LAB	923
Dermot Greene	LAB	891
Hilary Lowe	LAB	884
Elizabeth Wilson	GRE	497
Francesca Bury	GRE	440
Rachel Zatz	GRE	380
Judith Barnes	CON	372
Richard Dollimore	CON	334
Carole Ricketts	CON	305

FORTUNE GREEN

Felicity (Flick) Rea	LD	1446
Jane Schopflin	LD	1187
Russell Eagling	LD	1132
Heather Downham	CON	667
Jean Hornbuckle	CON	608
Miles Seaman	LAB	580
Peter Denison-Pender	CON	576
Howard Dawber	LAB	545
Mohamoud Nur	LAB	402
Billy Murray	GRE	354
Lucia Nella	GRE	305
Benjamin Fox-Smith	GRE	291

FROGNAL & FITZJOHNS

Martin Davies	CON	1603
Dawn Somper	CON	1513
Andrew Mennear	CON	1500
Diane Litman	LD	453
Alan Templeton	LD	394
Thomas Gardiner	LAB	364
Peter Sanderson	LAB	353
Erich Wagner	LD	342
Charles Harris	GRE	331
Luca Salice	LAB	316
Edward Ross	GRE	296
Tatton Spiller	GRE	267

GOSPEL OAK

Lindsey ("Lulu") Mitchell	CON	1378
Christopher Philp	CON	1333
Keith Sedgwick	CON	1297
Sally Gimson	LAB	1225
Raj Chada	LAB	1220
Janet Guthrie	LAB	1150
Margaret Jackson-Roberts	LD	519
Laura Noel	LD	461
Josephine Karen	GRE	428
Jane Walby	GRE	411
Herbert Newbrook	LD	373
Richard Thomas	GRE	337

HAMPSTEAD TOWN

Michael Greene	CON	1842
Kirsty Roberts	CON	1641
Christopher Knight	CON	1605

375

Edward Fordham	LD	1293	Philip Nelson	CON	731
Linda Chung	LD	1204	Elizabeth Hanna	LD	489
Jonathan Fryer	LD	980	Benedict Protheroe	GRE	449
Hugh Gracey	LAB	446	Stanley Grossman	LD	417
Myra Carr	LAB	418	Grace Hodgkinson-Barrett	GRE	364
Paul Tomlinson	LAB	384	Simieon Litman	LD	347
Brian Gascoigne	GRE	328	Stuart Houghton	GRE	319
Charlotte Collins	GRE	287			
Una Sapietis	GRE	214			
Brian Kettell	Ind	52			

KENTISH TOWN

Philip Thompson	LD	1421
Omar Faruque Ansari	LD	1268
Lucy Anderson	LAB	1213
Ralph Scott	LD	1198
David Horan	LAB	1087
Sîan Berry	GRE	1057
Deirdre Krymer	LAB	1042
Edward Chatham	GRE	772
Alexander Goodman	GRE	760
Matthew Murphy	CON	308
Doreen Bartlett	CON	306
Graham Porter	CON	271

HAVERSTOCK

Jill Fraser	LD	1417
Syed Hoque	LAB	1118
Roy Shaw	LAB	1106
Dudley Miles	LD	1085
Simon Horvat-Marcovic	LD	1058
Michael Katz	LAB	1034
Joan Stally	CON	362
Sue Charlesworth	GRE	351
Robert Bahns	GRE	347
Timothy Frost	CON	338
Ross McGregor	CON	337
Edward Milford	GRE	244

KILBURN

David Abrahams	LD	1122
Janet Grauberg	LD	1084
James King	LD	1071
Aileen Hammond	LAB	1008
John Rolfe	LAB	1005
Philip Turner	LAB	985
Andrew Cossar	CON	393
Carlo Banchero	CON	382
Sam Gyimah	CON	336
John Collins	GRE	224
Sophia Mustoe	GRE	214
Miriam Elkan	GRE	188

HIGHGATE

Maya de Souza	GRE	1336
Paul Barton	CON	1221
Adrian Oliver	GRE	1210
Quentin Tyler	GRE	1159
Gary Bernardout	CON	1129
Richard Merrin	CON	1121
Maggie Cosin	LAB	1016
George Queen	LAB	922
John Thane	LAB	873
Henry Potts	LD	406
Laura Watkins	LD	356
Philip Wainewright	LD	325

KING'S CROSS

Abdul Hai	LAB	1071
Jonathan Simpson	LAB	956
Geethika Jayatilaka	LAB	946
Trevor Harris	LD	662
Huw Prior	LD	627
David Simmons	LD	600
Barbara Douglass	CON	483
Paul Christian	CON	476
Jamieson Hunkin	CON	424
Joy Wood	GRE	375

**HOLBORN &
COVENT GARDEN**

Susan Vincent	LAB	1085
Julian Fulbrook	LAB	1079
Brian Woodrow	LAB	988
Alison Frost	CON	810
Timothy Barnes	CON	758

Kate Gordon	GRE	360
Neil Endicott	GRE	355
Alem-Seged Abay	Ind	182

REGENT'S PARK

Nasim Ali	LAB	1329
Theodore Blackwell	LAB	1204
Heather Johnson	LAB	1172
Michele Potel	CON	814
James Morris	CON	804
John Iredale	CON	792
Natalie Bennett	GRE	616
Anne Brown	LD	586
Stephen Plowden	GRE	463
Joel Derbyshire	GRE	434
Lawrence Nicholson	LD	424
Richard Waddington	LD	330

ST PANCRAS &
SOMERS TOWN

Roger Robinson	LAB	1399
Nurul Islam	LAB	1264
Anna Stewart	LAB	1212
Nuruzzaman Hira	Respect	781
Mary Campbell	GRE	517
Rohit Grover	CON	440
Margaret Finer	LD	433
Robert Ricketts	CON	429
Abdul Salam	CON	422
Richard Eden	GRE	369
Charles Marquand	LD	332
Margaret Waddington	LD	317
Matthew Hodgkinson-Barrett	GRE	213
Robert Austin	Ind	181

SWISS COTTAGE

Andrew Marshall	CON	1292
Roger Freeman	CON	1272
Donovan Williams	CON	1243
Katharine Bligh	LAB	659
Selman Ansari	LAB	638
Jillian Newbrook	LD	543
Charles Keal	LAB	522
Elizabeth Charvet	GRE	435
Harriet Sloane	LD	405
Sally Twite	LD	400
Lucy Wills	GRE	355

Alan Wheatley	GRE	255
Magnus Nielson	UKIP	63
Alphonse Komesha	Christian Peoples	25

WEST HAMPSTEAD

Keith Moffitt	LD	1189
John Bryant	LD	1107
Duncan Greenland	LD	974
Virginia Berridge	LAB	672
Geoffrey Kingscote	LAB	598
Charles Hedges	LAB	545
Elaine Mackover	CON	544
John Samiotis	CON	478
Marcus Watzlaff	CON	451
Lucy Thomas	GRE	309
Debra Green	GRE	300
Kari-Lourdes Dewar	GRE	275

PARLIAMENTARY ELECTION RESULTS 1964 - 2006

15 October 1964

HAMPSTEAD

Henry Brooke
CON   19,888   43.3%

Jack Cooper
LAB   18,053   39.3

Rene Soskin
LIB   8,019   17.5

HOLBORN &
ST PANCRAS SOUTH

Lena Jeger
LAB   15,873   54.3%

Geoffrey Johnson Smith
CON   13,117   44.9

Ali Mohammad Abbas
Ind   226   0.8

ST PANCRAS NORTH

Kenneth Robinson
LAB   20,516   61.0%

Kenneth Warren
CON   11,954   35.6

Jock Nicolson
COMM   1,140   3.4

31 March 1966

HAMPSTEAD

Ben Whitaker
LAB   22,963   46.8%

Henry Brooke
CON   20,710   42.2

Rene Soskin
LIB   5,182   10.6

Harry Baldwin
Socialist Party   211   0.4

HOLBORN &
ST PANCRAS SOUTH

Lena Jeger
LAB   16,128   59.5%

Lord Julian Byng
CON   10,982   40.5

ST PANCRAS NORTH

Kenneth Robinson
LAB   20951   64.2%

Christopher Moorhouse
CON   10440   32.0

Jock Nicolson
COMM   1253   3.8

18 June 1970

HAMPSTEAD

Geoffrey Finsberg
CON   21264   46.6

Ben Whitaker
LAB   20790   45.6

John Calmann
LIB   3550   7.8

HOLBORN &
ST PANCRAS SOUTH

Lena Jeger
LAB   12448   55.1

APPENDIX III

Lord Julian Byng
CON 10125 44.9

ST PANCRAS NORTH

Jock Stallard
LAB 16497 59.3%
James Moorhouse
CON 10648 38.3
Gordon McLennan
COMM 670 2.4

28 February 1974

HAMPSTEAD

Geoffrey Finsberg
CON 19536 43.3%
Anthony Clarke
LAB 17297 38.3
Ron Longland
LIB 8323 18.4

HOLBORN &
ST PANCRAS SOUTH

Lena Jeger
LAB 12414 49.1%
Robert Parsons
CON 8223 32.5
Tom Hibbert
LIB 4632 18.3

ST PANCRAS NORTH

Jock Stallard
LAB 14761 52.8%
John Major
CON 7926 28.3
Paul Medlicott
LIB 4825 17.3
Gordon McLennan
COMM 466 1.7

10 October 1974

HAMPSTEAD

Geoffrey Finsberg
CON 18139 44.9%
Anthony Clarke
LAB 16414 40.6
Ron Longland
LIB 5566 13.8
Maureen Maguire
Irish Civil Rights 146 0.4
Ralph Critchfield
Socialist Party 118 0.3
Chandra Rao
Ind 31 0.1

HOLBORN &
ST PANCRAS SOUTH

Lena Jeger
LAB 11790 55.9%
Robert Parsons
CON 6349 30.1
Michael Lee
LIB 2938 13.9

ST PANCRAS NORTH

Jock Stallard
LAB 14155 58.5%
John Major
CON 6602 27.3
Paul Medlicott
LIB 3428 14.1

3 May 1979

HAMPSTEAD

Geoffrey Finsberg
CON 20410 47.3
Ken Livingstone
LAB 16729 38.8
David Radford

PARLIAMENTARY ELECTION RESULTS
1964 - 2006

LIB	5753	13.3
Jean White		
NF	255	0.6

HOLBORN &
ST PANCRAS SOUTH

Frank Dobson		
LAB	12026	49.3
Robert Key		
CON	9703	39.8
Tom Hibbert		
LIB	2190	9.0
Francis Theobald		
NF	334	1.4
Peter Farrell		
WRP	134	0.6

ST PANCRAS NORTH

Jock Stallard		
LAB	14556	54.2
Peter Kirwan		
CON	9110	33.9
Malcolm Valentine		
LIB	2654	9.9
Stephen Andrews		
NF	360	1.3
Granville Jones		
WRP	159	0.6

9 June 1983

HAMPSTEAD & HIGHGATE

Geoffrey Finsberg		
CON	18,366	41.2%
John McDonnell		
LAB	14,996	33.7
Anne Sofer		
SDP	11,030	24.8
John Stevenson		
Ind Poet	156	0.3

HOLBORN & ST PANCRAS

Frank Dobson		
LAB	20,486	47.5
Tony Kerpel		
CON	13,227	30.7
William Jones		
LIB	9,242	21.4
Richard Price		
WRP	155	0.4

11 June 1987

HAMPSTEAD & HIGHGATE

Sir Geoffrey Finsberg		
CON	19,236	42.5%
Philip Turner		
LAB	17,015	37.6
Anne Sofer		
SDP	8,744	19.3
George Weiss		
Capt Rainbow	137	0.3
Susan Ellis		
Humanist	134	0.3

HOLBORN & ST PANCRAS

Frank Dobson		
LAB	22,966	50.6%
Peter Luff		
CON	14,113	31.1
Simon McGrath		
LIB	7,994	17.6
Mick Gavan		
Red Flag	300	0.7

9 April 1992

HAMPSTEAD & HIGHGATE

Glenda Jackson		
LAB	19,193	47.5%
Oliver Letwin		
CON	17,753	41.8

Dr David Wrede		
LD	4,765	11.2
Stephen Games		
GRE	594	1.4
Dr Richard Prosser		
Natural Law	86	0.2
Anna Hall		
Rainbow	44	0.1
Charles Wilson		
Rainbow	44	0.1
Captain Rizz		
Rizz Party	33	0.1

HOLBORN & ST PANCRAS

Frank Dobson		
LAB	22,243	54.8%
Andrew McHallam		
CON	11,419	28.1
Jenny Horne-Roberts		
LD	5,476	13.5
Paul Wolf-Light		
GRE	959	2.4
Mark Hersey		
Natural Law	212	0.5
Richard Headicar		
Socialist Party	175	0.4
Nigel Lewis		
Workers ag'st Racism	133	0.3

1997

HAMPSTEAD & HIGHGATE

Glenda Jackson		
LAB	25,275	57.4%
Elizabeth Gibson		
CON	11.991	27.2
Bridget Fox		
LD	5,481	12.5
Monima Siddique		
Referendum	667	1.5
Jonathan Leslie		

Natural Law	147	0.3
Ronnie Carroll		
Rainbow	141	0.3
Patsy Prince		
UKIP	123	0.3
Robert Harris		
Humanist	105	0.3
Captain Rizz		
Rizz Party	101	0.2

HOLBORN & ST PANCRAS

Frank Dobson		
LAB	24,707	65.0%
Julian Smith		
CON	6,804	17.9
Justine McGuinness		
LD	4,750	12.5
Julia Carr		
Referendum Party	790	2.1
Timothy Bedding		
Natural Law	191	0.5
Stephen Smith		
Justice Party	173	0.5
Brigid Conway		
WRP	171	0.4
Martin Rosenthal		
Rainbow	157	0.4
Peter Rice-Evans		
European Unity	140	0.4
Bruno Quintavalle		
Pro Life	114	0.3

2001

HAMPSTEAD & HIGHGATE

Glenda Jackson		
LAB	16,601	46.9%
Andrew Mennear		
CON	8,765	24.6
Jonathan Simpson		
LD	7,273	20.5

Andrew Cornwell
GRE	1,654	4.7

Helen Cooper
Socialist Alliance	559	1.6

Brian McDermott
UKIP	316	0.9

Sister Xnunoftheabove
Ind	144	0.4

Mary Teale
Pro Life	92	0.3

Amos Klein
Ind	43	0.1

HOLBORN & ST PANCRAS

Frank Dobson
LAB	16,770	53.9%

Nat Green
LD	5,595	18.0

Roseanne Serelli
CON	5,258	16.9

Rob Whitley
GRE	1,875	6.0

Candy Udwin
Socialist Alliance	971	3.1

Joti Brar
Socialist Labour	359	1.1

Marcus Nielsen
UKIP	301	1.0

UKIP	275	0.7

George Weiss
Rainbow	91	0.2

HOLBORN & ST PANCRAS

Frank Dobson
LAB	14,857	43.2%

Jill Fraser
LD	10,070	29.3

Margot James
CON	6,482	18.9

Adrian Oliver
GRE	2,798	8.2

George Weiss
Rainbow	152	0.4

2005

HAMPSTEAD & HIGHGATE

Glenda Jackson
LAB	14,615	38.3%

Piers Wauchope
CON	10,886	28.5

Edward Fordham
LD	10,293	27.0

Sîan Berry
GRE	2,013	5.3

Marcus Nielsen

GREATER LONDON COUNCIL ELECTION RESULTS 1964 - 1981

[Note: Camden returned three GLC councillors in a single borough wide constituency until 1970 after which one councillor was returned in each of the three parliamentary constituencies.]

CAMDEN [three seats]

1964

Leila Campbell			
LAB	38,198	50.3%	
Louis Bondy			
LAB	38,191		
EJ Dennington			
LAB	37,364		
FEH Bennett			
CON	30,096	38.6	
Lena Townsend			
CON	28,723		
Clare Mansel			
CON	28,588		
Archibald MacDonald			
LIB	4,839	6.0	
Joyce Arram			
LIB	4,614		
MS Watson			
LIB	4,087		
Jock Nicolson			
COMM	2,895	3.8	
BW Haines			
Ind	1016	1.3	

1967

Richard Butterfield		
CON	32,375	47.8%
Lena Townsend		
CON	32,216	
Clare Mansel		
CON	31,587	
Luke "Paddy" O'Connor		
LAB	28,504	41.6
Leila Campbell		
LAB	27,923	
Louis Bondy		
LAB	27,284	
George Willett		
LIB	4,911	6.6
Glenys Bevan		
LIB	4,269	
Alfred Cook		
LIB	4,187	
Jock Nicolson		
COMM	2,133	3.2
William Buchanan		
SPGB	907	0.8
Edmund Grant		
SPGB	419	
Thomas Giles		
SPGB	411	

1970

L.P. "Paddy" O'Connor		
LAB	26,265	46.4%
Richard Collins		
LAB	26,140	

Alec Kazantzis
LAB 25,731
James Lemkin
CON 24,416 43.3
Lena Townsend
CON 24,346
Clare Mansel
CON 24,047
John Calmann
LIB 2,565 4.2
Kathleen Peacock
LIB 2,252
Raymond Benad
LIB 2,208
Gordon McLennan
COMM 1,692 3.2
Robert Peacock
Homes Before Roads 1,311 2.1
William Walker
Homes Before Roads 1,249
Keith Jacks
Homes Before Roads 1,037
Leslie Cox
SPGB 391 0.6
Meirion Davies
SPGB 323
Edmund Grant
SPGB 299
Florence Elliott
Union Movement 195 0.4

1973

HAMPSTEAD
Enid Wistrich
LAB 12,268 48.0%
Ian Clarke
CON 9,823 38.4
Raymond Benad
LIB 2,824 11.0
Roy Champion

COMM 466 1.8
Leslie Cox
SPGB 191 0.8

HOLBORN &
ST PANCRAS SOUTH
Alec Kazantzis
LAB 7,437 60.6%
David Weeks
CON 3,520 28.7
Alick Elithorn
LIB 1,085 8.8
Doreen Davies
SPGB 99 0.8
Noel Fierz
Ind 72 0.6
Philip Goulstone
Ind 60 0.5

ST PANCRAS NORTH
Rose Hacker
LAB 9,915 67.7%
Nicholas Bennett
CON 4,226 28.9
Vic Heath
COMM 497 3.4

1977
HAMPSTEAD
Alan Greengross
CON 15,352 54.0%
Enid Wistrich
LAB 10,000 35.2
Richard Waddington
LIB 1,915 6.7
Gordon Callow
NF 425 1.5
Alan Thomas
COMM 399 1.4
David Farrer

AGLC	199	0.7		NF	372	2.9
Leslie Cox				Helen Bunney		
SPGB	143	0.5		Ind	200	1.6

HOLBORN &
ST PANCRAS SOUTH

Richard Collins		
LAB	7,099	45.2%
Christopher Radmore		
CON	6.977	44.4
Grant Knowles		
LIB	776	4.9
John Lilburne-Philpot		
NF	698	4.5
Patricia Deutz		
SPGB	156	1.0

ST PANCRAS NORTH

Anne Sofer		
LAB	7,902	49.0%
Michael Frost		
CON	6,461	40.0
June Mather		
LIB	803	5.0
Linda Evans		
NF	599	3.7
Vic Heath		
COMM	371	2.3

BY ELECTION
HOLBORN &
ST PANCRAS SOUTH

8 March 1979 (Death of Richard Collins)

Charles Rossi		
LAB	5,946	46.5%
Christopher Radmore		
CON	5,833	45.6
Tom Hibbert		
LIB	437	3.4
Francis Theobald		

1981

HAMPSTEAD

Alan Greengross		
CON	12,367	44.7%
Anna Bowman		
LAB	10,446	37.8
Roger Billins		
LIB	4,095	14.8
Iain Huddleston		
Ecology	677	2.4
Anthony Mockler		
Save London Action Group	73	0.3

HOLBORN &
ST PANCRAS SOUTH

Charles Rossi		
LAB	7,796	52.8%
Richard Bull		
CON	5,051	34.2
Roger Karn		
LIB	1,694	11.5
Paul Kavanagh		
NFCM	218	1.5

ST PANCRAS NORTH

Anne Sofer		
LAB	9,935	59.1
Ian Pasley-Tyler		
CON	5,202	31.0
Dennis Strojwas		
LIB	1,506	9.0
Cornelius Murphy		
WRP	148	0.9

APPENDIX IV

BY ELECTION
ST PANCRAS NORTH

29 October 1981
(Resignation of Anne Sofer)

Anne Sofer		
SDP	6,919	43.6
Mildred Gordon		
LAB	6,181	38.9
Ian Pasley-Tyler		
CON	2,684	16.9
John West		
GLCA	92	0.6

INNER LONDON EDUCATION AUTHORITY ELECTION 1986

[Note: Before the abolition of the GLC, the ILEA was made up of GLC councillors and one nominee from each of the Inner London borough councils. The only direct election to the ILEA took place on 8 May 1986 with two members being returned for each of the Inner London parliamentary constituencies.]

HAMPSTEAD & HIGHGATE

John Brynner
LAB   12,177   41.8%
Myra Polya
LAB   11,848
Doreen Miller
CON   9,621   33.3
David Soskin
CON   9,527
Anne Sofer
SDP   7,795   24.9
Felicity Taylor
LIB   6,530

HOLBORN & ST PANCRAS

Neil Fletcher
LAB   16,958   58.5%
Elizabeth Monck
LAB   16,627
Lady Olga Maitland
CON   6,634   22.5
Peter Skolar
CON   6,267
Liz Blundell
SDP   5,757   19.0
Paul Sample
LIB   5,176

APPENDIX VI

ALDERMEN 1964-1974

[Note: the office of alderman was abolished in 1978.]

1964-1968 Ruth Howe   (LAB)
               Michael Cendrowicz   (LAB)
               Ivy Tate   (LAB)
               Lena Townsend   (CON
               Edward Bowman   (CON)

1964-1971 Frank Bennett   (LAB)
               Lyndal Evans   (LAB)
               James MacGibbon   (LAB)
(*Replaced by* Millie Miller *in 1968*)
               George King   (LAB)
(*Replaced by* Cliff Tucker *in 1968*)
               Ernest Wistrich   (LAB)

1968-1974 Edward Bowman   (CON)
(*Replaced by* Clare Mansel *in 1971*)
               Luigi Denza   (CON)
               Kenneth Furness   (CON)
(*Replaced by* Alan Greengross *in 1970*)
               Elaine Kellett   (CON)
               Martin Morton   (CON)

1971-1978 Leila Campbell   (LAB)
               Sir Samuel Fisher   (LAB)
               Ruth Howe   (LAB)
               Roger Jowell   (LAB)
               Albert "Jock" Stallard   (LAB)

1974-1978 William Oakshott   (LAB)
(*Replaced by* Wally Burgess *in 1975*)
               William Budd   (LAB)
               George Trevelyan   (LAB)
               Arthur Soutter   (LAB)
               Gurmukh Singh   (LAB)

Chairman of the Council

1964-65	Councillor Samuel Fisher

Mayors

1965-66	Councillor Samuel Fisher
1966-67	Councillor (Paddy) L.P. O'Connor
1967-68	Alderman Mrs Millie Miller
1968-69	Councillor Norman Oatway
1969-70	Dame Florence Cayford
1970-71	Councillor Harold Gould
1971-72	Councillor (Tim) A.E. Skinner
1972-73	Councillor Brian Duggan
1973-74	Councillor Richard Collins
1974-75	Councillor Florence Elizabeth Parnell
1975-76	Councillor Bernard Taylor
1976-77	Alderman Arthur Soutter
1977-78	Councillor Robert Humphreys
1978-79	Councillor (Bill) W.G. Budd
1979-80	Councillor Sally Peltier
1980-81	Councillor Ronald Hefferman
1981-82	Councillor Maureen Robinson
1982-83	Councillor Tom Devine
1983-84	Councillor Ronald Hefferman
1984-85	Councillor Barbara Hughes
1985-86	Councillor Julian Fulbrook
1986-87	Councillor Mary Cane
1987-88	Councillor Jerry Williams
1988-89	Councillor (Bill) W.G. Budd

1989-90	Councillor Barbara Hughes
1990-91	Councillor Nirmal Roy
1991-92	Councillor James Turner
1992-93	Councillor Winifred Parsons
1993-94	Councillor Ramen Bhattacharyya
1994-95	Councillor (Bill) W.G. Budd
1995-96	Councillor Sadashavirao Deshmukh
1996-97	Councillor Gloria Lazenby
1997-98	Councillor Ray Adamson
1998-99	Councillor (Bob) R.E. Hall
1999-00	Councillor Roy Shaw, O.B.E.
2000-01	Councillor Heather Johnson
2001-02	Councillor Roger Robinson, O.B.E
2002-03	Councillor Judith Pattison
2003-04	Councillor Nasim Ali
2004-05	Councillor Harriet Garland
2005-06	Councillor Barbara Hughes, M.B.E.

APPENDIX VIII

LEADERS OF THE COUNCIL
1964-2006

1964-68	Charles Ratchford	(LAB)
1968-70	Geoffrey Finsberg	(CON)
1970-71	Martin Morton	(CON)
1971-73	Millie Miller	(LAB)
1973-75	Frank Dobson	(LAB)
1975-82	Roy Shaw	(LAB)
1982-86	Phil Turner	(LAB)
1986-90	Tony Dykes	(LAB)
1990-93	Julie Fitzgerald	(LAB)
1993-2000	Richard Arthur	(LAB)
2000-05	Jane Roberts	(LAB)
2005-06	Raj Chada	(LAB)

LEADERS OF THE OPPOSITION
1964-2006

1964-66	Leslie Room	(CON)
1966-68	Geoffrey Finsberg	(CON)
1968-69	Charlie Ratchford	(LAB)
1969-71	Millie Miller	(LAB)
1971-74	Martin Morton	(CON)
1974-79	Alan Greengross	(CON)
1979-81	Julian Tobin	(CON)
1981-85	Tony Kerpel	(CON)
1985-87	Stephen Moon	(CON)
1987-90	Peter Skolar	(CON)
1990-98	Judith Barnes	(CON)
1998-2000	Pamela Chesters	(CON)
2000-06	Piers Wauchope	(CON)

INDEX OF PERSONS

(Camden councillors in bold type)

399

INDEX

401

INDEX

INDEX

INDEX

407

409